Okmulgee Creek Nation Oc[...]

Know all men by these presen[ts] [...]
representa[tives] of the Creek Orphans, referred
to in the treaty of 1832, we hereby employ
W. O. Tuggle Esq. & empower him to prosecute
the Creek Orphan claim before Congress &
the Departments at Washington City, to collect
or adjust the same, & for said purpose we
constitute & appoint him our legal representative & the attorney, & agent of the said Creek
Orphans with whom we have a written contract.
& we agree to forward to said W. O. Tuggle Esq
said written contract with said Creek Orphans
& all other papers regarding said Claim, which
may facilitate the collection of the same &
to aid him in all proper ways in the prosecution of the Claim, & should it be deemed best to
obtain another contract signed by the Orphans
& their heirs, then we agree to get up & have said
paper signed by said Orphans & their heirs &
forward the said Contract to said W. O. Tuggle Esq.
& we most respectfully Commend him to the
authorities at Washington, to the President
the heads of Departments & to the Congress
of the United States & ask their favorable
consideration of said Claim.
As compensation for his services we hereby
agree to pay said W. O. Tuggle Esq. 10 ten

SHEM
HAM &
JAPHETH

What a strange medley of people, are here in the Indian Terty, Caucasians, Mongolians or Indians, Africans & several new breeds manufactured by judicious crossing! If there is any virtue in mixing blood here's a fine opportunity to try the xperiment— Co-partnership between Shem, Ham, & Japhet, with the possibility that Shem & Ham will finally have a rich store of xperience while sagacious Japhet will take care of the finances of the firm—

SHEM HAM & JAPHETH

THE PAPERS OF W. O. TUGGLE
Comprising His
Indian Diary
Sketches & Observations
Myths &
Washington Journal
in the Territory &
at the Capital, 1879-1882

Edited by Eugene Current-Garcia
with Dorothy B. Hatfield

University of Georgia Press

Library of Congress Catalog Card Number: 68–55755
International Standard Book Number: 0–8203–0306–2

The University of Georgia Press, Athens 30601

Printed in the United States of America
by Heritage Printers, Inc.
Charlotte, N.C.

To Elizabeth Williamson Bethea

CONTENTS

ACKNOWLEDGMENTS

In the preparation of this book we have received aid and encouragement from many sources which we are happy to acknowledge. To Auburn University we owe a debt of gratitude for grant-in-aid funds which provided for research and photographic reproduction of materials, as well as a small subsidy for the cost of publishing the volume. We are likewise indebted to Mrs. Elizabeth Williamson Bethea, a granddaughter of Tuggle's and custodian of his manuscripts, who granted us access to the original materials and permission to have them reproduced for publication. Without her gracious assistance through correspondence, interviews, and introduction to other members of the Tuggle family, including Mrs. Sara Tuggle Douglass and Mrs. Steffan Thomas, our project could not have been successfully completed. We therefore gratefully dedicate the book to Mrs. Bethea.

We gratefully acknowledge also the unstinting assistance and encouragement given us by the following friends and colleagues: Professor Celia B. Taylor of Columbus College; Miss Dorothy Brown, daughter of the late Samuel W. Brown, Jr., chief of the Yuchi Tribe; Mrs. Virginia C. Lee, associate librarian of Columbus College; Professor Walton R. Patrick, chairman of the Department of English at Auburn University; and the late Professor Edd Winfield Parks of the University of Georgia. Many others—too numerous to mention individually for fear of overlooking some—have expressed interest in the progress of our book and offered valuable suggestions for its organization and form.

E.C-G.
D.B.H.

INTRODUCTION

I love such investigations, because they may lead, someday, to a better knowledge of the first peopling of this continent. . . . Will not our children, when they grow up, wonder at our stupid unconcern for antiquity?[1]

ℬY A HAPPY CHAIN of circumstances culminating in April 1960, the author of these words has been rescued from oblivion. William Orrie Tuggle, native Georgian, friend and advisor of prominent statesmen, may have done more than any other southerner of his time to preserve for future use the records of antiquity in his region; yet, ironically, his name is virtually unknown today, except among specialists in the fields of anthropology and folklore,[2] while the value of his remarkable collection of Creek Indian folk tales and other writings, once used and admired by such contemporaries as Joel Chandler Harris, John R. Swanton, and James Mooney, has long since been forgotten.[3] That such an important figure

[1] W. O. Tuggle, "Scrap Album," Atlanta, Georgia: Private collection in the possession of Mrs. Sara Tuggle Douglass, last surviving daughter of W. O. Tuggle.

[2] No mention of Tuggle appears in the usual biographical compendia such as *DAB, Heitman Historical Register and Dictionary of United States Army, National Cyclopedia of American Biography*, or Gatschet, *Migration Legend* (BAE MSS 566, Smithsonian Institute, Washington, D. C.).

[3] Reference to use of Tuggle's MSS by Harris, Mooney, and Swanton is given below (See Appendix B). Among the others were Jeremiah Curtin, J.N.B. Hewitt, and James C. Pilling, each of whom issued subsequent publications, and all of whom were actively associated with the Bureau of American Ethnology under the administration of John W. Powell, first director of the bureau. For further details see Dorothy B. Hatfield, "The W. O. Tuggle Manuscript of Creek Indian Folk Tales—Its History and Significance" (master's thesis, Auburn University, 1960), p. 4, n. 3.

as Tuggle should have remained so long neglected by southern literary historians is due in part to the disappearance of his original manuscript collection. The purpose of this volume is to establish the basis for recognition and further study—now that the bulk of Tuggle's work is available. We believe that Tuggle's writings comprise one of the most significant sources of Indian lore open to students of primitive culture in the South.

TUGGLE'S CAREER AND WRITINGS

ACCORDING to the Tuggle family Bible, William Orrie Tuggle was born in Henry County near McDonough, Georgia, on September 25, 1841. Orphaned in childhood, he was reared by foster parents and educated at Brownwood Institute and Mercer University, where he interrupted his studies to enlist in the LaGrange Light Guard at the outbreak of the Civil War. Later, while serving with Morgan's Raiders, Tuggle was twice captured by the enemy and, under hazardous circumstances, twice successfully escaped imprisonment in the North which he later described vividly in an account entitled "Recollection of an Escape from a Northern Prison Camp by an Unreconstructed Rebel."[4] After his war service Tuggle completed his law studies and was admitted to the bar in 1865; he then married Miss Antoinette Cox, established his permanent residence at LaGrange, Georgia, and became in time the father of eight children,[5] one of whom still survives.

As a lawyer Tuggle quickly gained success and political prominence during the Reconstruction period. He was chosen to represent Troup County in the Constitutional Convention of 1877; and two years later, having meanwhile published an important work on taxation which drew favorable notice from John Sherman, United States secretary of the treasury,[6] he was appointed legal agent to represent the Creek Nation in negotiating a sizable claim against the federal government. Tuggle's suc-

---

[4] Handwritten copies of the first three chapters of the manuscript are in the private collection owned by Sara Tuggle Douglass.

[5] Margaret Antoinette Cox was the first child of Albert Ewing Cox and Juliet Warren Alford (Tuggle family Bible). Names of Tuggle's deceased children are listed in Hatfield, pp. 12–13, together with some vivid personal recollections of her childhood and family life given to the writer by the surviving child, Mrs. Sara Tuggle Douglass, in an interview on April 28, 1960.

[6] W. O. Tuggle, Direct Taxes Compilation, 46th Congress, 1st Session, Senate Executive Document, No. 24, May 14, 1879. Favorable commentary on the value of this work, signed by both John Sherman and A. H. Stephens, is quoted in Hatfield, pp. 15–16.

cessful defense of this claim for $72,000 was hailed as "a brilliant achievement [which] erased from the Treasury an enormous tax debt that hung over nearly every Southern State . . . [and] demonstrated the wisdom of the governor in securing his services. Not only Georgia, but the whole South, owes him a deed of gratitude. He has accomplished what our combined representatives in Congress failed to effect."[7]

Tuggle's role as agent for the Muscogees thus brought him into close contact not only with state and federal authorities, but also with the chiefs of the Creek Nation. Following his appointment in October 1879 he spent much of the next three years in the Indian Territory (located in the present state of Oklahoma), where he earned the respect and confidence of such prominent Indian leaders as Samuel W. Brown, Sr., chief of the Uchees [Yuchis] and Pleasant Porter, chief Indian delegate to Washington, as well as the encouragement and cooperation given him by educational and religious leaders in the Territory, such as G. W. Grayson and Mr. and Mrs. W. S. Robertson.[8] Tuggle's successful prosecution of the Creek claim, however, was but one facet of his activity on the behalf of the Indians. During his stay in the Territory he kept a detailed journal and diary, wrote articles for the Georgia newspapers and for the *Christian Index*, and collected an extensive number of Indian fables and tales, baby songs, and medicine songs, as well as a series of observations on tribal customs, which he recorded with meticulous care. It is not surprising, therefore, that Tuggle was later characterized as "an unusually rapid worker, both with his mind and his pen."[9]

After leaving the Territory in December 1881, Tuggle returned to Washington, carrying on there simultaneously his governmental duties and his efforts to organize and publish his cultural findings about the Creek Indians. An entry in his diary, dated December 13, 1881, for example, reveals the following information:

[7] Tuggle, "Scrap Album." "In Oct. 1879 the Muscogee nation passed an act making me their agt. & also agt. of The Creek Orphan claim under the treaty of 1832" (Washington Journal, January 21, 1880). As such agent Tuggle was duly commissioned by Ward Coachman, principal chief.

[8] Samuel W. Brown, Sr., chief of the Yuchi town and district judge, was born June 1843. He served in the House of Warriors and the House of Kings; in 1882 he became treasurer of the Nation. Pleasant Porter, the most distinguished member of the Creek tribe, was born September 26, 1840, about twelve miles from the present site of Clarksville. George Washington Grayson was born in 1843 near Eufaula, Oklahoma, the son of James Grayson and Jennie Wynn, a half-breed Creek Indian. The Robertsons were characterized by Tuggle as "the leading spirits of Broken Arrow Camp Ground." For fuller details on the significance of these individuals and their relationships with Tuggle, see Charles Evans, ed., *The Chronicles of Oklahoma*, Oklahoma Historical Society, xxvi (Autumn 1948), 349–53 and 287–99, passim.

[9] Tuggle, "Scrap Album."

Got copy Creek Orphan bill and gave to Mr. Deering to introduce in house.

Same in Ga. bill—for Buchanan.

Creek Orphan bill was refd by Senate Comtee Indian Affairs to Sen. Slater. . . .

Been writing out my Indian myths & stories, so as to leave with Maj. Powell, when I go home for holidays.[10]

Diary entries at this time show further that Tuggle was keeping up his contacts with his Indian friends, Pleasant Porter and Ward Coachman, who came as delegates to Washington from the Creek Nation and who, during offhour visits to his hotel, were supplying Tuggle with additional data on Indian idioms and legends.[11] While in Washington he tried repeatedly to interest commercial publishers in his Indian writings, complaining on one occasion that he feared his "baby" might "die *aborning!*"[12]

With more than passing interest Powell did examine the manuscript, and he made specific suggestions about the rearrangement of Tuggle's collection, advising him to set in order first the Indian tales, next the sketches, and finally the Black Beaver story.[13] Tuggle recorded this as sound advice which he planned to follow, but ill health and the pressure of other affairs rendered these plans abortive, since no further references to his Indian writings appear in his diary. In 1883 Tuggle was reappointed to another two-year term as lawyer for the Creek Nation, but on July 9 of that year he wrote Powell that he was too ill to return to Washington to pursue all his interests. The following March, hoping to restore his health in a more salubrious climate, he moved to Thomasville, Georgia, where he died on February 3, 1885 at the age of forty-three.

Besides a record of vigorous participation in many public affairs, Tuggle left behind as his richest legacy an invaluable collection of Creek Indian myths and folk tales, gathered at first hand, which represent the traditional stories handed down by word of mouth in the tribes for generations. Included among this varied source material are not only the important animal myths, the creation myth, and the tribal baby songs and medicine songs sacred to the tribes, but also Tuggle's carefully de-

[10] Washington Journal, Chapter IV.

[11] Ibid., December 9, 1881.

[12] Ibid., December 12, 1881.

[13] The Black Beaver story was the biography of Chief Black Beaver of the Delawares. It was evidently written by Major I. G. Vore, who gave it to Tuggle in manuscript form. See Appendix A.

tailed observations of tribal customs, with specific notations of the time and place where they were gathered. The importance of his collection was immediately recognized, among others by Joel Chandler Harris, who predicted in 1883 that "Mr. Tuggle's Collections of Creek legends will probably be published under the auspices of the Smithsonian Institution, and it will serve a note-worthy contribution to the literature of American folklore." [14]

TUGGLE'S THREE-FOLD LEGACY:
Diaries, Sketches, and Myths

THE RATIONALE for the present volume is based on the assumption that Tuggle's most significant contribution can best be seen in three related forms: his Indian diaries and Washington journals, his "observations" or sketches of life in the Indian Territory, and his collection of Indian myths. These three forms are here presented in that order, reproduced verbatim, so far as this may be possible in transferring handwritten work to type, in order that Tuggle's methods of notation and composition as well as his developing attitudes toward his role as a recorder of the social scene may be chronologically observed. Inevitably such an arrangement involves a certain amount of duplication, since stories that Tuggle picked up and hastily jotted down in his diaries while traveling through the Territory reappear occasionally (usually in slightly altered form) in his observations and then again in his finished myths. But whatever annoyance such repetition may inflict on the reader is compensated for in the overall portrait that emerges—the portrait of an active, meticulous mind and of an eager, warm personality. For one sees in Tuggle's diaries, especially, not only his efforts to record as many of the essential data concerning Indian life as he can capture on the run; he catches also in these often hurried, cryptic notes and reminders many interesting glimpses of characters, scenes, and human relationships that are both self-revelatory and objectively realistic.

To approach Tuggle's writings, however, in a form as nearly identical to their originals as possible poses a dilemma for both the reader and the editors. The advantage of seeing what he wrote exactly as he wrote it is that of gaining a close-up view of the way his mind worked. Whatever his oddities or limitations regarding such matters as spelling, punctuation,

[14] Introduction, *Nights with Uncle Remus* (New York: Houghton Mifflin, 1883), p. xxx.

abbreviation, etc.—these are among the individual personal characteristics that add human warmth to his expression, and no editor would willingly sacrifice them for the sake of grammatical decorum, clarity, and coherence. But, since Tuggle obviously wrote his diaries for his own use and not for publication, these entries in particular present various problems in interpretation and readability, which may be briefly set forth here.

As indicated in Appendix A, this edition has been made possible through the use of photostatic copies of the original manuscripts owned by Mrs. Elizabeth W. Bethea. For the most part the notebooks themselves are in fairly good condition, the paper and the writing on it, although occasionally obscured by stains, are in the main clear and distinguishable, although several leaves are missing, damaged at the edges, or otherwise imperfect so as to make problematical the exact reproduction of some words crowded along the margins. Wherever such ambiguities or uncertainties occur, they have been clarified so far as possible either in bracketed insertions or notes. Moreover within the pages of the notebooks Tuggle's writing varies considerably, depending on the haste with which he was composing at the moment. Most of his pages contain slightly fewer than 100 words, but some closely-written ones may run to as many as 150 words; and since the diaries present an abundance of abbreviations, a noticeable inconsistency in punctuation, and here and there obvious omissions of words, there is on the whole, perhaps, both more material per page and greater difficulty in interpreting it than these facts and figures would seem to suggest.

In preparing a printed edition of these private manuscript materials, which in the main were not intended for publication, we have tried to achieve an equable compromise between the extremes of rendering on the one hand an exact but unreadable photographic reproduction of the original texts and of editing or "normalizing" them on the other to the point where they might become almost unrecognizable literary versions. Either extreme involves obvious hazards, and the attempt to reconcile them must take into account the various classes of readers to whom the edition is being offered. In keeping with the established first principle of editorial practice that every detail is important and exact transcription therefore imperative, we have tried to present a reliable text reproduced as Tuggle wrote it—that is, essentially untouched in order to preserve both the form of his diary and journal writing and its significant eccentricities and idiomatic flavor. Still, since this edition is intended to interest both specialists in folklore and history as well as the general reader, a minimum amount of scholarly apparatus and editorial rearrangement of the original text has been undertaken to make it readable without excessive strain.

The peculiarities of Tuggle's style and handwriting, for example, would very likely baffle most readers. His handwriting varies all the way from near-illegibility to careful precision of old-fashioned Spencerian penmanship; while the numerous abbreviations and other shortcuts he employed often require a scrupulous attention to the text. Unrelated initial letters in his abbreviations, for example, often resemble several different alphabets, so that "M's," "U's," "T's," and "N's" become virtually indistinguishable from one another. As a result the many proper names scattered through his pages are not always precisely identifiable. Less difficult but still momentarily puzzling are many of Tuggle's spellings, many of his single short words and hyphenated word combinations being cut short through the omission of initial and terminal vowels and sometimes even internal vowels and consonants. Thus, he consistently spells the prefix "ex" without the "e"—"xcept," "xamine," "x-Congressman," etc.—and he sometimes omits final "e" in words like "delegate" and "nominate." Similarly Tuggle drastically shortens many other common words such as "agent," "committee," "territory," and "received" by omitting two, three, or even more consecutive letters between beginnings and endings; hence, "agt," "comtcc," "tcrty," and "recd." These spelling peculiarities, however, along with Tuggle's consistent practice of placing the dollar sign after rather than before the figure (for example, 40$) and his almost invariable substitution of the ampersand for the common conjunction, are less likely to confuse the average reader than would some of his innovations in punctuation.

Tuggle seldom uses periods, for instance, when his sentences or paragraphs come to an end at the right hand margin of his page, and the same thing holds true for his use of closing quotation marks and parentheses. In his haste to put down the essential data, whether in the form of a completed statement, a quoted one, or an afterthought, he apparently did not always bother to indicate precisely where one or another of these statements ended and a succeeding one began, since in his own mind he could perhaps trust to memory to provide appropriate stops and connections in the flow of his prose as well as to fill out sentences which appear only in fragmentary form. For the reader, however, the pleasure of following Tuggle's ideas would be impeded, without some editorial insertion of punctuation marks, though in general this has been kept to a minimum, except for terminal punctuation.

For the most part our editorial alterations and intrusions, silent or otherwise, have had to do with terminal punctuation and paragraphing. Except for Tuggle's Indian Diary, we have substituted the period wherever his use of the dash indicated the end of a sentence, and we have supplied periods, quotation marks, and closing parentheses where these are called for but inadvertently omitted in the text. In the diary we have kept intact his use of the dash to indicate fragments. We have also kept unchanged his varied spellings and abbreviations (for example, his consistent use of the ampersand and "&c" for "etc."), explaining these in brackets only where questionable reading may be involved or emendation called for. We have silently modernized Tuggle's practice of writing the long "s," which usually appears in words ending with a doubled consonant; and since he often ignored normal paragraphing in many of his diary or journal entries, we have provided it to avoid interruption in its continuity. Tuggle's internal punctuation we have generally kept as he inserted it, including passages which he crossed out, except when he rewrote or restated them. For the sake of clarity we have also occasionally supplied missing apostrophes for possessives and dropped ditto marks, inserting the intended material.

In order to preserve the original flavor as well as the intention of Tuggle's writing, we have therefore kept intact wherever possible not only his abbreviations but also his eccentricities and inconsistencies in grammar, diction, spelling, and punctuation. But whenever his numerous omissions of punctuation marks—occasionally of entire words—would be likely to confuse the reader, we have tried to clarify Tuggle's meaning by inserting appropriate punctuation marks needed to preserve without ambiguity the full meaning originally intended. Since our primary aim has been to secure a readable page rather than a page garnished with editorial symbols, we have used the notation [sic] as sparingly as possible in calling attention to numerous irregularities. And we have resorted to other editorial interpolations only where needed to clarify the meaning of the text when words are lost or illegible in whole or in part. Thus, doubtful readings of the text due to blurred or faded handwriting are rendered in brackets followed by a question mark (for example, "the [equality?] and tranquility of the citizens . . ."); these are shown in contradistinction to other editorial interpolations which appear without the question mark and which are sometimes descriptive as well as interpretive (for example, [blank], [journal ends here], [obliterated], etc.). Otherwise Tuggle's text is reproduced verbatim with no further editorial comment than that given in explanatory chapter notes. The reader should therefore assume that all misspelled words, inconsistencies in the spelling of proper names (for example, Stephens and Stevens), dropped apostrophes, and the like are the understandable result of Tuggle's haste in writing.

Ironically Tuggle's style as originally composed on the run in spurts and fragments is often more flavorful than it becomes later when he revised some of the same material for publication. For in his revisions he often omitted colorful expressions and quick turns of phrase which had occurred to him on the spur of the moment and substituted others which, though more dignified and "literary," lack the saltiness of the diction they replaced. This is another reason why, in preparing an edition for the general reader as well as for the specialist, we have tried to avoid excessive regularizing of the text and to keep unimpaired as much of the original flavor and eccentricity of Tuggle's style as possible.

TUGGLE AS INTERPRETER AND RECORDER OF INDIAN LIFE

THE PROBLEMS of rendering Tuggle's work as he left it and of interpreting it as he might have wished go beyond the question of merely deciphering his personal hieroglyphics. Tuggle possessed such a curious, attentive mind that wherever he went he tried to record immediately and as accurately as he could whatever new or unexpected data he encountered concerning the shape or texture or physical appearance of things. Thus while in the Territory he often tried to render graphically the appearance of Indian structures, utensils, vehicles, weapons, and home furnishings, as well as the layout for certain of their games, ceremonials, and governmental or judicial rituals. These rough sketches, scattered through his journals, add much in the way of visual impression to his verbal descriptions of them; yet it would be difficult, perhaps futile, to attempt reproducing these crude drawings in a printed text. Things of this sort, particularly Tuggle's references to the curiosa of Indian life, habits, and personalities, as well as his occasional *sotto voce* asides to himself revealing his reactions to them, add color and vitality to his work, however much they may complicate the editor's attempt to clarify the obscure and explain the significant among the many contacts and events presented in Tuggle's diaries.

For the casual reader willing to accompany Tuggle on his first trip westward by rail through Missouri and Kansas and thence southward, by wagon or on horseback, into and through the Oklahoma Territory in the summer of 1879, perhaps the first and most lasting impression gained is that of the variety of interesting items that excited his curiosity, the many contrasts he recorded between the phenomena of that virgin country and those of his settled native Georgia. The fertility of the soil; the abundance of crops and livestock; the low cost of food and farm labor and transportation; the wild beauty of the rolling prairies, lakes, and sunsets; the strange dishes offered him by his Indian hosts, their contents and manner of preparation; the character, speech, and appearance of the hosts themselves—every detail takes on added meaning through his observant eyes, and none is too trivial to yield its measure of significance. Thus he notes (in terms of percentages) not only the astonishing prevalence of miscegenation and premarital sexual relationships among the Creeks, Cherokees, and Choctaws, but also their casual mode of dress, which often reveals almost as much as it conceals. And, swiftly passing on to other matters, in another moment he tells of their schools and court sessions, their election procedures, their religious practices and sacred vessels, and their severe methods of punishment for crimes and misdemeanors.

However sketchily presented, each of these details in itself often constitutes an item of interest, if only because of its remoteness from ordinary concerns of civilized life today. But in the aggregate there is an added flavor in Tuggle's record which is due largely to his fascination with people—his interest in what they say and do and look like. At the Belchers' house, for example, he notes not only the expected facts about household arrangements, but also the amusing account of little Ben's midnight summons to his father to witness a cat fight in the dead of winter, recorded in the child's own breathless speech. Similarly he remembers to express precisely the pun on "curiosities" with which old Colonel Logan reprimanded his two equestrian daughters for getting themselves wet while crossing a stream; and to capture the wistfulness in Sam Brown's reference to his illegitimate child, "got by accident"; and to describe succinctly the contrast between Dr. Martin's shabby garments and his superlative preaching technique. Briefly but pointedly he describes Brown himself in the act of telling of the origins of the Yuchis in Pennsylvania, as well as Hepsy Leeder, sister of the famous Indian chief, Osceola. In fact Tuggle's thumbnail sketches of every prominent Indian he met and talked with—McIntosh, Porter, Coachman, Buckner, and others—show repeatedly both the warmth of his own personality and his capacity for noting individual traits that make his human subjects come to life. The latter skill, moreover, when applied to a more complex problem, enables him to re-create memorably, yet within the sparse framework of two or three pages, such an elaborate ritual as the Yuchis' ball game or their medicine festival called the Busk, which requires of the reader a fairly strong stomach.

In these and many other events which Tuggle took time to record—often under rather discomforting circumstances—his sense of humor also emerges again and again to enliven his account of the quaint customs, at-

titudes, and superstitions he encountered. Thus the Indians' firm belief
in a spirit realm is rendered doubly entertaining through Madison
Brown's vivid recollection of his grandfather's ghost in the kitchen, and
Dan Childress's tale of an abortive funeral sermon transforms that solemn
ritual into a comic performance. Religious practices, in fact, furnish much
of the humor that Tuggle discovered to be a basic ingredient of Indian
life; and his anecdotal method of recording it reminds one of the old
southwest frontier yarnspinners. McIntosh's account of Brother Broadenax's sore finger, its excruciating pain intensified by the clasp of an ardent
devotee is a case in point. So too are Brother Broch's account of Schmiker,
the Dutch backslider; Buckner's gallant reception of the veiled colored
lady; and the anonymous preacher who prostituted his wife.

Concerning this last experience, the irony in Tuggle's quiet aside—"O
tempora. O mores"—reveals also the fundamentally serious side of his
nature. For he was no mere jokester, eager to capitalize on the follies and
weaknesses of another race. On the contrary his reactions to specific facts
and developments that crossed his path show a deepening concern for the
welfare of Indian society and thus help to explain why the Creek and
Yuchi leaders trusted him to take care of their interests. In a mood of
thoughtful prophecy he wrote on September 11:

> What a strange medley of people, are here in the Indian Terty, Caucasians,
> Mongolians or Indians, Africans & several new breeds manufactured by
> judicious crossing! If there is any virtue in mixing blood here's a fine op-
> portunity to try the xperiment—Copartnership between Shem, Ham, &
> Japhet with the probabilty that Shem & Ham will finally have a rich store
> of xperience while sagacious Japhet will take care of the finances of the
> firm—

Here the yoking together of images drawn from Genesis and the modern
world of burgeoning capitalism clearly reflects the concern Tuggle felt
for the future prospects of a proud race long since doomed to a subordi-
nate role in America. And this concern comes to the fore again and again,
sometimes in an extended passage of reflective prose, more often in a
mere parenthetical aside which might be easily overlooked by the hasty
reader. It is revealed in his colloquy with Pleasant Porter concerning the
progress of education; in his efforts to codify effective marriage laws for
the tribes; in his investigation of their appalling health conditions and
primitive medical practices; his interest in their slow population growth,
due largely to the ravages of disease; his curiosity about their mode of
burial, their alleged practice of cannibalism, and their severe punish-
ments for adultery; and in his vigorous probing of their burial mounds

near the mouth of the Grand River. Finally Tuggle's painstaking efforts to record Indian phrases phonetically and to translate them accurately are further evidence of his scholarly interest in their vanishing culture. But, as he brings the reader to the end of his mission in 1879, it is clear that his was not merely a scholar's desire to salvage the vestiges of a bygone era; for the deepest impression that he makes is that of his genuinely humanitarian concern for the welfare of the living tribes: "I told them of my favorable impression & hoped the U. S. would let them alone & leave their land secured to them & their children forever—"

TUGGLE'S DIARIES AND JOURNALS OF 1880-1882

WHILE Tuggle's 1879 diary provides many interesting glimpses of his personality, his other two journals are perhaps an even richer source of information, chiefly because they reveal not only his contacts with Indian leaders, but also his impressions of and reactions to many of the leading political figures of the time and to their activities, both public and private, on a national level. Since the bulk of these journal entries records Tuggle's sojourn in Washington and focuses upon his efforts in pressing for congressional action on the Creek Orphan Claim, one finds in them many other facets of his mind and character not so prominently displayed in his hastily composed jottings in the Territory. In the first place these journals are more carefully and deliberately written and accordingly clearer and fuller. Secondly they disclose a perceptive, analytical mind, reflecting judiciously, on the basis of firsthand contact, upon many of the leading political events and issues of the day, as well as upon the prominent individuals involved in them. Thirdly, and most significantly, they complete the self-portrait of Tuggle himself, ambitious to succeed, to make a name for himself both as Indian agent and writer; delighted with his role as an "insider" on the Washington political scene, yet warmly human also in the confession of his private agonies and doubts touching upon his responsibilities as a father, husband, and friend.

The problem of presenting Tuggle's two later journals consecutively, however, is complicated by two factors: the longer of the two, containing only references to his activities in Washington, covers a two-year span from January 1880 to January 1882, part of which time he had also spent on a second visit to the Territory; while the shorter one, labeled "Memo while in Indian Terty 1881 and Journal of 1882," devotes little more than a fourth of its contents to territorial matters and then switches abruptly to a further record of his Washington activities from the beginning to the end of 1882. In effect this second document is therefore mainly a continuation of Tuggle's Washington Journal of 1880–1882, although the opening references in it indicate that the little notebook was purchased in "Eufaula, M.N. Indian Terty" on September 3, 1881, and that Tuggle originally intended to use it primarily as a means of recording Indian myths related to him at first hand by his hosts.

In all the shorter "Memo . . . and Journal of 1882" consists of fifty-two lined sheets or leaves enclosed in a leather cover, each sheet having two pages measuring roughly 5 1/2 by 8 1/2 inches; and the handwriting is clear and even, carefully proportioned within one-inch margins on every page. But only the first fourteen sheets contain the four fables which Tuggle says were related to him by Jim Henry as they were riding at Dr. Buckner's place. Thereafter he recorded several other myths picked up during conversations with his Indian friends in Washington, and beginning on sheet 18 he reverted to a straight journal record of his progress and associations there for the remainder of the year. Since these matters were of primary concern to him, the complete texts of Tuggle's two later journals are here set forth so as to allow for a continuous record of his mission in Washington from January 1880 to December 1882.

In its original manuscript form, Tuggle's longer journal of 1880–1882 likewise consists of a small leather-bound notebook containing 120 lined leaves or pages, each measuring about 7 by 5 inches.[15] Except for two imperfect leaves (numbers 38 and 84—see Appendix A), the manuscript is in fair condition and the writing is reasonably clear, though not so consistently legible as that of the shorter journal or "Memo." Since Tuggle wrote on both sides of his paper, the earlier journal contains 240 handwritten pages, or slightly more than twice as much material as in the later one. Taken together, the two manuscript notebooks yield less than one hundred pages of printed text dealing with his activities in Washington, but so compact and economical is Tuggle's style that these small volumes offer a remarkably succinct yet comprehensive view of a three-year span at the seat of national power.

As in his Indian Diary Tuggle of course recorded here chiefly those matters which touched his own personal experience—his aims, hopes, frustrations, and occasional delights and satisfactions. The point of view is predominantly his own, modified by his own preferences, biases, and limitations. Yet such is his capacity for detached observation and calm

[15] See William E. Fuller, Jr., "William Orrie Tuggle: Journal of 1880–1882" (master's thesis, Auburn University, 1964).

self-analysis that even in the recording of his most private thoughts one senses the presence of an honest, well-balanced, perceptive intelligence fully in control of things, so that his observations on other individuals or on matters lying outside his immediate personal interests inspire confidence in both his integrity and judgment. As is true of his Indian Diary, nearly every separate item he saw fit to record in his Washington journals will yield some morsel of interest to even the desultory reader; whereas the more attentive student of American history may find in the totality of his entries an even more significant pattern of references throwing new light on issues, events, and figures which attracted attention in the early 1880s.

If categorized, this pattern of references would include first of all Tuggle's numerous reflections on political movements and the key men involved in them; secondly, his record of meetings and personal interviews with some of these prominent individuals; thirdly, his thought-provoking disclosures of attitudes and feelings, often deep-seated and poignant, concerning his own private affairs, legal, social, and domestic. These categories would necessarily overlap, since matters of public concern and the men involved in them were often closely tied in with Tuggle's private interests, especially concerning his vigorous efforts in pressing for favorable congressional legislation on behalf of his Indian clients. Nevertheless both the public and private affairs of the day take on a quality of immediacy by being mingled and reflected through the mirror of Tuggle's mind, so that unlike the tidy, selective hindsight of the historian, his day-to-day unfolding of events gives a sense of dramatic urgency to the theme of the individual seeking order and self-advancement amid the chaos and confusion of a bygone era.

Thus the greenback question, long since buried and forgotten in the past, comes momentarily to life because it is still being argued on the Senate floor as Tuggle records his reactions to it. Similarly the "Star Route" mail scandals and the proposed Brazilian subsidy, hinting of corruption in high places, become matters of front-page gossip like their counterparts of our own time, as do the fraudulence and delay in the handling of Indian affairs, touching Tuggle personally, of course, in a tender spot. But various other events, likewise of lively interest nearly a century ago though no longer remembered, remind us of their analogues in today's news as we consider them through Tuggle's eyes: the agitation over the proposed Isthmian canal, the political maneuvering for the presidential election of 1880, Garfield's assassination and the Guiteau trial, party politicking and infighting in the scramble for power, arguments concerning the role of the vice president and the problem of presidential succession, and, most interesting of all, perhaps, as a reaction to Albion Tourgee's *A Fool's Errand*, Tuggle's prophetic comments on the political implications of the race problem in the future party relationships between North and South:

> It is rich to hear the deep toned sigh of the North over the blunder of negro suffrage. Instead of weakening the power of the whites of the South it strengthened them & now the great question with the North is, how can we remedy our mistake? . . .
>
> Fortunately for the South, one phase of the disease will be a mania for educating the negro, on the idea that whenever he becomes an intelligent voter he will cease to be a Democratic voter!
>
> In any event the South can afford to try the experiment. Let the negro be educated & yet the Southern whites can hold their own against the world —or if not, they deserve to go down. (February 1, 1881)

In these and many similar reflections on events of the day Tuggle's journal links the past and the present with fine, if inadvertent, irony. But fascinating as are all the issues resurrected from the past, the men themselves who figured prominently in the Washington waltz, and upon whom Tuggle had to dance attendance to secure his own claims, are even more interesting. For Tuggle brings many of them to life, if only in a glimpse at times, as he captures them in postures, attitudes, and utterances unrecognized in conventional history texts. General William T. Sherman, the scourge of Georgia, weeping like a girl at a third-rate melodrama; Senator Gordon foolishly resigning his Senate seat to follow the lure of a plush railroad job promised him by Henry W. Grady, a "fickle bright fellow"; Rutherford Hayes being roundly condemned as a liar by ex-Senator Mitchell of Oregon; Wade Hampton, nettled and slightly tipsy, burning to reply to an oblique slur cast upon his party loyalty at a dinner given by Alexander Stephens; Senator Hill's contemptuous dismissal of Senator Bruce, as being "only fit for a head waiter in a hotel [because] he knows no more of the constitution than a jaybird does of music"; Stephens' delightful reminiscence of his youthful encounter with the aged Dolly Madison—in these and many another bright vignette Tuggle, with Boswellian flair, captured the individualizing traits of his acquaintances. Large and small, foolish and wise, as reflected through his impressions of them, these were the men steering the ship of state—or at least striving to grasp the tiller. Thanks to the steadiness of his vision and the forthrightness of his judgments, we see many of them live again in their strengths and weaknesses.

Next to Tuggle himself, the most engaging figure seen in these pages, and the most fully rounded, is that of Alexander Stephens, the aging ex-

vice president of the Confederacy. Still mentally alert at seventy despite a
fragile body, Stephens clearly stood as mentor and rallying point for his
Georgia colleagues during these crucial years, dispensing wisdom and
sound advice concerning their efforts to restore the Democratic party in
the South, particularly Georgia's, to a position of leadership in the nation's affairs. Such, at any rate, is the portrait of him that emerges at
Tuggle's hands. His strength of character, despite age and ill health, is
suggested first by his refusal to betray a confidence touching an alleged
slander; and thereafter vigorous expressiveness, even from a sick bed, is
repeatedly manifested through the opinions which Tuggle obviously took
delight in quoting verbatim: for example, his blunt dismissal of one politician as "no account, not worth a damn!"; his thoughtful defense of
ex-President Grant; his approval of Tourgee's A Fool's Errand as "a true
picture" of the South during Reconstruction; his heartfelt grief over the
death of his Negro estate manager, Harry Stephens ("I never knew a more
trustworthy man, black or white. His loss to me is irreparable."); his
shrewd analysis of the nation's paramount political issues in 1882 and
of the dim prospects for reforming and strengthening the Democratic
party; and his forthright recommendation of Tuggle himself in a letter to
the United States attorney general. One can easily see from this letter
alone why Tuggle revered the elderly Georgia statesman, though even
without this personal interest he had many other opportunities to test the
old man's mental acumen and moral fiber, as well as his wit and sound
judgment regarding persons, events, and ideas. Thus it is not surprising
that Tuggle worked hard and skillfully to help win for Stephens the
governorship of Georgia as a fitting last reward for a great political career.

If Tuggle's associates are colorfully drawn, it is after all his own self-
portrait that emerges most appealingly in these pages, possibly because
so many of its lights and shadows are rendered unconsciously, with little
if any thought of their ultimate effect upon a reading public. In noting
the hushed-up scandal surrounding Senator Hill's amorous adventures,
Tuggle does of course write as though expecting "posterity" to be informed of it; but even here it seems obvious from his prudent removal of
an incriminating portion of his record that he did not plan to be the in-
former, whereas his comment that "such is Washington life behind the
scenes in Mch. 1880" shows that he was chiefly interested in discovering
for himself the vagaries of human behavior on even the highest social
levels.

Tuggle's graphic little exposures of human frailty in fact disclose repeatedly a combination on his part of high-minded moral rectitude and
Christian charity. He is distressed, but not outraged, to find that the

lawmakers of his own day compare unfavorably in scholarship and fo-
rensic ability with their predecessors of the 1840s. He is annoyed, but also
amused, by the rudeness of one senator, the two-facedness of another, and
the chicanery and pretentiousness of many others. He is appalled by,
yet reconciled to, the utter follies that even the most promising and influential legislators will commit for the love of money. Still, though he
sympathizes feelingly over the thwarted ambitions and wounded vanities
of his friends, as in the case of both Stephens and Hill, he does not over-
look the presence of these human weaknesses in them. (Stephens, he
suspected, coveted the nomination for vice president on a ticket with
Grant in 1880; while Hill, he saw, despaired of rising above the Senate.)
Nor could he stretch his charity to the point of suffering fools gladly
when they persisted in exposing their follies through ignorance or osten-
tatious display. In all his contacts, with friend and foe alike, Tuggle
measured the individual against a high but not unattainable standard of
human excellence; and in noting the degree or manner whereby some individuals fell below it, he also revealed unobtrusively the ideals to which
he himself aspired.

The standard Tuggle applied in evaluating his contemporaries was
neither a provincial nor an expedient one: it reflected rather his continuing interest in intellectual cultivation, as shown in his absorption and
comparison of books and ideas, especially those governing human conduct. Shortly after establishing his large family in Washington, he found
time for reading widely contrasting accounts of Napoleon, Voltaire's
life of Charles xii of Sweden, and Metternich's memoirs; and presently,
along with the many legal tomes to be searched for precedents supporting
his claims cases, he was delving deeper into Francis Lieber's *Political
Ethics*, Montesquieu's *Spirit of Laws*, and Cicero's *De Republica*. From
the standpoint of such classic utterances as these upon the subject of
government, Tuggle could readily assay the collective worth of the Congress of 1880; and it is not surprising that he found ample evidence among
its members to support Napoleon's disillusioned view that all men are controlled by self-interest. Yet, whatever their personal shortcomings, Tuggle
could appreciate and was fascinated by the fact that these men, like their
ancient counterparts, struggled daily with the ideas of government: hence
his delight in discovering that the thought of Cicero and Plato was still
relevant to current problems.

Literature of various sorts contributed to Tuggle's mental development: for a lawyer his catholicity of taste was surprisingly broad. He read
with interest Justin McCarthy's *History of Our Own Times*, as well as
Goethe's *Wilhelm Meister*, which he disapproved of on moral grounds

despite its "many fine sayings," and Charlotte Brontë's *Jane Eyre*, which
he found too absorbing a pleasure to skip a line of. On the other hand
Meredith, Thackeray, and Kinglake he sampled hastily, "mostly skipping," and turned to more solid food such as the *American Almanac For
1880* and Carlyle's *Frederick the Great*, which proved stimulating indeed.
(Tuggle noted incidentally that congressmen generally, especially southerners, read little other than newspapers and correspondence, and thus
lost opportunities through lack of time to become as literate and well informed as members of Parliament.) So too did he read Henry George's
Progress and Poverty, though Tuggle shrewdly judged it "a fraud," in-
capable of bringing about the millennium even if its doctrines could
prevail.

Still other books that engaged his attention, chiefly by way of expanding his knowledge of Indian legends, included those of Schoolcraft, Mc-
Intosh, Brinton, and "Tales of Indians by Barbara Somebody, all to see
if my Creek fables were in print, and found nothing like them." But he
also took pleasure in reading aloud to his sick wife the popular Auerbach's
novels of Germany, scarcely resisting the temptation "to stop, & copy a
few sentences for memorizing," as well as delving into studies of antiquity
such as Coulanger's *The Ancient City* and Laveleye's *Primitive Property*.
Tuggle's reaction to all his wide reading was consistently critical and in-
cisive: he judged books as he judged men, not by their titles or reputation,
but by the quality of truth they had to offer him. And the measure of his
own character can be taken from his favorable judgment of the biography
of William Wirt: namely, that a man's private writings provide "the most
faithful portrait of the man. Few can stand the test—"

TUGGLE AS A PIONEER FOLKLORIST:
The Yuchi Myths

IN MOST RESPECTS Tuggle himself stands the test quite well.
As seen on page after page of his journals, his patient and persistent labors
to secure his Indian claims bespeak a capacity for hard work that is closely
allied with his urge toward self-improvement and his gift for cultivating
profitable social relationships without compromising his dignity and
integrity. Though often balked by congressional delays due to inertia
as well as to countervailing pressures and prejudices, he never gave in to
these obstacles but kept striving to overcome or circumvent them until
his cases were won. There is thus a fair measure of dramatic interest—as

well as an illuminating study of self-reliance—to be found simply in following the progress of his Creek Orphans bill and his other cases from the beginning of 1880 to the end of 1882.

What Tuggle might have achieved as one of America's major pioneer folklorists can be seen first of all in the care with which he gathered and recorded significant details concerning the life and customs of the Yuchis; secondly, in the craftsmanship he displayed in attempting to transform this raw material—the ceremonials he observed and the myths he took down from word of mouth dictation—into a permanent body of indigenous literature. Even in its fragmentary, unfinished state, the "book" of myths, sketches, and observations he planned to publish reveals an astonishing grasp of literary technique, as illustrated for example in his account of the Green Corn Dance or Busk. For the performance of this important ceremonial special seating arrangements were followed and rigid protocol observed. Only on this occasion were the sacred vessels displayed, as Tuggle himself discovered when, in 1879, he asked to see them but was politely rebuffed with the explanation that they were only taken up at Busk. Fortunately for today's student of Indian lore, however, Tuggle did succeed in obtaining the story of the Busk, writing it down as told to him by an aged Yuchi named "Gen'l Cooper" and interpreted by the chief, Sam Brown.[16] Since the Bureau of Ethnology at the Smithsonian made no copy of this story, nor indeed of any of Tuggle's other "observations," these items are perhaps among the most valuable pieces in the Tuggle collection, despite their fragmentary nature.[17]

Though clearly lacking the stylistic polish of a professional writer's finished work, Tuggle's expository narrative technique in the Green Corn Dance or Busk reveals more than a negligible ability to select, organize, and set forth dramatically the significant details on which effective characterization, action, and humorous appeal are based. He knew how to gather the requisite materials, how to ask questions, how to pick and choose among the responses he got, how to combine and develop them in a fluid pattern and a succinct style. Had he lived long enough to rework his materials and to sharpen his effects, it seems safe to assume therefore that his book of observations on Yuchi customs would long ago have been published and recognized as a major pioneering effort in the field of cultural anthropology.

[16] In response to the question "Could you identify a 'General Cooper' of the 1880's?" Miss Brown said, "Yes, he was a respected Yuchi of olden times who occupied a high place in the Yuchi tribe." (Personal interview by conference telephone call to Miss Dorothy Brown, Mathis, Texas, on July 11, 1960.)

[17] The bureau made no copies of any of the material included in this subdivision of the Bethea collection.

That this is not merely overenthusiastic praise may be readily confirmed by the small amount of Tuggle's writings—the incomplete collection of myths—that was copied and preserved by others, largely without adequate acknowledgment of his original efforts. For Tuggle was among the earliest of nineteenth-century white Americans to recognize the value of Indian myths in his area and to strive to record them faithfully as told to him in all their pristine freshness, proving thereby that the Indians were indeed custodians of a lively imagination, constantly fed from an ample heritage of Indian lore. The truth of his judgment that these myths were both rare and of genuine literary significance worthy of careful scholarly attention has been reflected in the large body of Indian folklore compiled by specialists in recent decades.

It is a truism that the customs and traditions of the American Indians were generally ignored, if not actually scorned, by the majority of white settlers, who coveted their lands but despised their way of life. Thus, had it not been for the pioneering work of Tuggle and a few others like him, the richness of their culture might not have been as accurately preserved as it has been. For as Stith Thompson, the great modern folklorist, assures us,

> it was not until the last quarter of the nineteenth century that we began to receive faithful recordings of American Indian tales. With the development of the Bureau of American Ethnology and the influence of such scientists as J. W. Powell there began to appear an increasing number of first-rate collections, some of them accompanied by the original text.[18]

Beyond question Tuggle's manuscript was one of those "faithful recordings" accompanied by the original text. Like his earlier counterpart in the Indian service, Henry Rowe Schoolcraft, Tuggle combined his mission as agent for the Muscogee Nation with that of collecting their tales. He did not, of course, attempt to classify, analyze, or catalogue these tales in the manner of modern professional folklorists, who are likewise concerned with the problem of origins and the question of whether any given story reflects the influence of other races and cultures on that of the Indians. Tuggle was concerned primarily with the tale itself and the teller thereof. Yet it is fortunate that he gathered his materials from the mouths of living southeastern tribesmen, since the culture of these people in particular—the Yuchis, Creeks, Muscogees, and Cherokees— has been the least fully explored. According to Thompson,

[18] Stith Thompson, *The Folktale* (Chicago: Holt, 1951), p. 298.

perhaps least well studied of all our native tribes are those which originally occupied the Southern States east of the Mississippi. Most of them were moved at an early time into the Indian Territory, and the best modern studies have had to be made in Oklahoma, far from their original home. But such tribes as the Cherokee, the Yuchi, and the Choctaw still have interesting traditions.[19]

It is therefore highly significant that Tuggle was on intimate terms with prominent members of one of these "least studied" tribes and that he visited in the home of Sam Brown, Sr., chief of the Yuchis, where he obtained the Creation Myth of the Yuchi with Brown himself serving as interpreter.[20] The importance of this personal contact becomes doubly significant when it is recognized that the Yuchis, according to a living descendant of Chief Brown, never kept written records and that consequently their legends and myths, though often deserving a prior claim to authenticity, were wrongly attributed to other neighboring tribes. As Dorothy Brown, the chief's granddaughter, puts it: "In the words of an Old Yuchi, and similar words of my father [Sam Brown, Jr.], 'The Yuchis have done all these things but the Creeks made their name lead, because the Yuchis were a backward people.' In other words, the Yuchis have always known the truth, but made no effort to offset the misinformation because they knew that right would prevail, no matter how long it takes."[21]

To most readers, except perhaps folklorists and well-informed members of a tribe, race, or ethnic group, the ultimate origin of any given myth may seem, at best, a mildly academic question. For there are countless variations in the myths of all primitive peoples, the tracing of which to their original sources is a job for specialists in the fields of ethnology and folklore. Particularly with respect to the beginning of things, for example, it is well known that of the great number of creation myths gathered and classified in the past, many of those belonging to the various Indian tribes present fascinating differences, even though they may be fragmentary and incomplete. As Thompson says on this point,

> The teachings of American Indian mythology concerning the Creator and the establishment of the universe, particularly of the earth, are, for

[19] Ibid., p. 310.

[20] For an explanation of the importance of the Creation Myth, see ibid., pp. 310–12.

[21] Letter to Dorothy B. Hatfield from Dorothy Brown, granddaughter of Chief Samuel Brown, Sr., dated April 7, 1960, Mathis, Texas.

the great majority of the tribes, fragmentary and meager and such explanations are often entirely lacking. But when we come to the beginning of mankind, of the establishment of his relationships with the world, nearly every people contributes a store of interesting tales.[22]

In view of these observations by a world-renowned expert, the unique importance of Tuggle's version of the Yuchi Creation Myth falls more clearly into focus, since it is one of very few that offers a nearly complete account of these elemental matters. Most tribal myths seek to explain how the land came into being, how the mountains were made, how light originated, and how to account for the change from light to darkness. The Yuchi Creation Myth disposes of all these primary concerns, especially the last-named, since this explains their conception of their own origin—they are "children of the sun." Their Creation Myth in fact offers a twofold light-making explanation: the star made the first light, which was not bright enough; when more light was called for the moon contributed its share, but it was still too dark; whereupon the sun said, "You are my children, I am your mother, I will make it light for you." Moreover, as to the origin of this proud tribe, the sun passing over the earth dropped blood to the ground, and the union of the blood and earth produced the first people, the children of the sun—the Yuchis.

Similarly creation myths generally explain how fire and medicine were obtained, besides accounting for the presence of animals on the earth and for their relationships with human beings. The Yuchi myth covers these matters also, explaining not only how fire originated and the "Great Medicine" was found (an explanation which, incidentally, accounts for the Yuchi's reverence for the cedar tree), but also how a "second family" was chosen, each member of which had engraved on his door a picture of the sun. Whether this last cryptic avowal was intended merely to emphasize the propagation of their race or to authorize the use of symbols, such as a coat of arms, for signifying their ancestry can only be conjectured. Yet, in either case, it is enlightening to find that twentieth-century Yuchis firmly believe themselves to be the original inhabitants of the southeastern United States and confidently assert that in time this proud claim will be unequivocally established.[23] Whatever the merits of

[22] *The Folktale*, p. 312.

[23] Quite forcibly Dorothy Brown stated her belief "that the Yuchis were living in the S. E. long before the Muskogees came in. The Muskogees are Muskogees, and still are, although they are known by the Gov't. as Creeks. The original group of people, living on the creeks in Georgia, S. C., Florida, were Yuchis, but the English, being ignorant of the language, or identity, called these people Creek Indians because they lived on the vast network of creeks in Ga., etc. There is actually no such thing as a Creek Indian, anymore than there is a Creek whiteman. It is just that ridiculous,

this claim, as avowed by Chief Sam Brown's granddaughter, it must be of further interest to citizens of Georgia to learn that additional support for it has evolved out of the recent discovery of the Metcalf Stone and the theories put forth by prominent archaeologists as a result of this discovery. Upon examining this ancient artifact, a slab of Georgia sandstone engraved with primitive hieroglyphics, Cyrus H. Gordon, chairman of the Department of Mediterranean Studies at Brandeis University, expressed the belief that the Yuchis may well be descendants of the ancient Minoans, whose civilization flourished on the island of Crete about 1500 B.C.—more than three thousand years before Columbus landed on American shores.[24]

Whether such a theory can ever be incontrovertibly proved remains to be seen. In any event it offers a fascinating prospect to contemplate and can only enhance the reputation of Tuggle's pioneer work as a recorder of Yuchi myths, the bulk of which are reproduced in this volume.

As set forth in Appendix A, the extant materials written by Tuggle include, in addition to his diaries and journals, his "Manuscript," consisting of some 350 pages, a substantial part of which was copied at the Smithsonian in 1887. Inasmuch as nearly verbatim copies of all this latter material are available either in Swanton's *Myths and Tales of the Southeastern Indians* or in the BAE MSS 566, the major portion of these myths is reproduced in Appendix B, so that attention may be focused chiefly on Tuggle's diaries and sketches, which have not been previously printed in any form. Because of their special significance, however, both "The Tar Person" and the "Creation Myth" deserve more than passing notice.

As told by Joel Chandler Harris, "The Wonderful Tar Baby Story" is justly famed the world over. The basic story was reprinted by James Mooney as "The Rabbit and the Tar Wolf," and still later Swanton included it among his collection of Indian myths under the simple title of "The Tar Baby." But it is highly significant that Tuggle's version antedated all these others, for having been recorded by him in 1881, it quite possibly fathered them all as well. Moreover, of particular importance to folklorists is the fact that Tuggle specifically named the source of his version of the story.

however, I firmly believe the people ORIGINALLY referred to as Creek Indians, by the first traders, were in fact Yuchis." Letter cited above in n. 21.

[24] The Metcalf Stone was unearthed at Fort Benning by Manfred Metcalf in September 1966. A cast of the stone was sent to Gordon by Joseph Mahan, curator of the Columbus Museum, and Gordon later came to Columbus to examine the original. Details of his meeting with Mr. Mahan and his theory concerning the Stone's significance may be found in a recent news release, "Archaeologist Says Yuchi Indian Descends from Ancient Culture," *Columbus Ledger*, August 14, 1968, pp. 1–2.

Similarly the importance of the "Creation Myth" is noted by Swanton, who speaks of the rarity of such myths as this in folklore. In referring to those included in his collection, he asserts that the only story in it "which might be called a creation myth is one in the Tuggle series (Creek 90) shown by the native words which it contains to be from the Yuchi." [25] Swanton adds, further, that he knows of but one Creek origin myth, obtained by Dr. Speck from the Taskigi Creeks,[26] who had been in such close contact with the Yuchis that "it was questionable whether the story was not originally from the latter [Yuchi] tribe." [27] Tuggle's manuscript leaves no doubt that his is the Creation Myth of the Yuchi and that it was obtained at first hand from Chief Samuel W. Brown, Sr., whom Tuggle found to be "an accommodating interpreter." [28] As early as 1881, this original myth had also been written by Tuggle as a finished narrative, comparable in makeup to the Genesis story of the Bible, with dramatis personae, a narrating "voice," and dialogue. Before July 9, 1882, it had been submitted to J. W. Powell; by 1887 it had been copied at the Bureau of Ethnology; and by 1893 an account of it was published by Gatschet, with no mention of Tuggle's name whatever. Finally it appeared in Mooney's *Cherokee Myths*, squeezed down to a single paragraph précis.[29] As Tuggle himself might have wryly observed, such is the transience of human aspiration.

THE BALANCE SHEET:
Tuggle as Man and Writer

EVEN THOUGH Tuggle did not live to see the fruits of his earnest efforts as a recorder of Indian lore, and was indeed all but for-

[25] *Myths and Tales of the Southeastern Indians* (Washington, D.C., 1929), p. 268.

[26] The reference is to Frank G. Speck, who published *The Creek Indians of Taskigi Towns* in 1907. (*The Memoirs: American Anthropological Association*, Vol. II, part 2, Lancaster, Pennsylvania.) In 1909 he also published *Ethnology of the Yuchi Indians*. It can be readily seen that Tuggle's acquisition of this creation myth in 1881 antedates Speck's by many years.

[27] Introduction, p. 1.

[28] According to Dorothy Brown, owner and custodian of Chief Samuel W. Brown Sr.'s and Chief Samuel W. Brown Jr.'s extant papers (Mathis, Texas), it was part of the custom to call in the old Yuchi Indians, as the oldest were custodians of the lore, and this respect was shown them by Chief Brown, who did the interpreting.

[29] Page 421. Mooney quotes the passage from Gatschet and cites it as "Gatschet, Some Mystic Stories of the Yuchi Indian, in *American Anthropologist*, VI, p. 281, July, 1893."

gotten despite his assiduous attempts to have his work published, the fragmentary writings he left behind are more than sufficient to restore to his name the reputation he doubtless would have won had he lived to complete them. And even though he would almost certainly have refrained from publishing the private thoughts and opinions lodged in his diaries and journals—at least in the form in which they have, luckily, come down to us—yet these, paradoxically, round out and enrich the portrait of this man in a way that no formal biography or purely scholarly collection of myths could possibly duplicate. For it seems obvious that the solid core of Tuggle's character is most clearly revealed in the intimate and doubtless unintended self-analyses that flash out suddenly from time to time as matters of private personal concern jostle for attention in his thoughts and demand expression. At one point, for example, after noting with justifiable pride that four Indian tribes and several railroad companies have engaged his legal services, he itemizes the prospective income to be expected from these professional labors, yet wonders realistically how many of his "ships will come home." Eventually, as most of these efforts do succeed, he notes with a certain relish that some Georgia congressmen greet him more cordially now than formerly because "success softens mens hearts, if not their heads—& money adds to a mans opinions."

Yet success had obviously neither softened his own head nor inflated his ego at this juncture, for in the same passage he recognizes the pain suffered by meritorious strugglers less fortunate than himself and proceeds to list several of the manifold blessings received which mean more to him than fame or money—namely the restoration of his wife's health and the religious well-being of his son. And in a climactic burst of almost mystical adoration rarely associated with a legal temperament, he humbly prays "for strength to stand prosperity and to use wisely" the gifts that God has entrusted to his stewardship.

Added together, these and other facets of Tuggle's character visible in his journals disclose an attractive, responsible, fine young southerner—a loyal party member, parent, husband, and friend, as well as a genuinely devout, God-fearing man—whose earnest striving in a difficult postwar period for the cultural and spiritual betterment of his time and place deserves at least a measure of the recognition he sought but never achieved in his lifetime. Whatever his limitations as a writer, Tuggle the man was exemplary, and the annals of folklore have been enriched through his dedicated and self-sacrificing labors.

I
THE INDIAN DIARY

Disk of burnished gold rising over a sea of green velvet—
Sunrise in Cherokee Nation— Contrast striking, the
cultivated fields of Ind. Ill. Mo. & Kansas, the thriving
towns, & the rolling prairies in native wildness & beauty.
The white & the red civilization—the guest & his host.
400 yrs ago they owned the continent now Indn Terty—
The ewe lamb now being observed by the commercial
neighbor—
When is it to be sacrificed?

EITHER OF W. O. TUGGLE'S RECORDS of his experience
in the Territory or in Washington, D.C., could properly be called diary
or journal, diaries or journals. We have therefore used the words more
or less interchangeably throughout the collection. It should be said that
the Indian Diary was kept in a diary-sized notebook and that it is less
formal and detailed in presentation than the Washington Journal, which
was maintained in ledger-sized notebooks. The Indian Diary was written
mainly as a sourcebook for the manuscript which Tuggle did not live to
complete—a work principally devoted to Indian culture and lore, the
most important parts of which are presented in Chapters II and III. The
Washington Journal, in contrast, tends more in the direction of memoir
and, on occasion, of commonplace book. It is more autobiographical in
focus but at the same time more public, since Tuggle's role is generally
limited to observing the political scene at the nation's capital against the
background of his own experience and aspiration. As a document this
journal was obviously maintained less because its author wanted it for

literary purposes—that is, a lode to mine for publishable narratives and
scenes—than as an account of public figures and events which its writer
found significant. To some extent Tuggle also must have relied on the
Washington Journal as a datebook so that he would have a record of his
complicated business as lobbyist for an involved series of claims against
the federal government.

Both the Indian Diary and the Washington Journal are presented *in
extenso*, with the exception of two entries in the earlier record—one which
is largely obliterated (it precedes the entry about Osceola's sister, Hepsy
Leeder) and the other which is developed more fully and accurately in
"Wild Indians at Muscogee Fair" in Chapter II. This list of Indians who
attended the fair appears as the second entry of the Indian Diary under
the date September 28, 1879. There is of course some repetition between
the Indian Diary and the sketches and observations presented in the next
chapter. The editors have presented the material in this way so that the
reader can see how Tuggle developed his material in something like the
form that he ultimately hoped to achieve. The entries in the diary are of
varying interest and value, but we have decided to publish it virtually in
full for its autobiographical as well as its historical and anthropological
importance. Had more of the sketches and observations been finished and
publishable, we should have included only representative parts of the
diary.

What invests the Indian Diary with continuity aside from the voice
and personality of its author are the recurrent patterns of emphasis—the
detailed descriptions of various people whom Tuggle encountered, the
careful concern with the folkways of the settlers—red, white, and black,
the insistence on factual data for everything from the price of wheat to
the number of acres in a particular holding, the probing and sympathetic
attention of the observer.

Even though the Indian Diary begins in medias res with the words
"his client's case!," it does not appear that any of the initial pages of this
notebook have been lost since the first page is complete, and the remaining 147 sheets of the diary seem to cover the author's stay in the Territory
during the late summer and early fall of 1879. This notebook still presents
many editorial problems since it was obviously intended as no more than
a personal record, not a finished piece of writing.

Writing with evident haste, Tuggle often punctuated his sentences
with dashes throughout, and he began new entries at the lefthand margin
rather than indenting them. These mannerisms as well as his usual eccentricities of spelling, abbreviation, and the like make it difficult for the
editor to establish a text which reproduces the original in a form close to

the diary. The design of the present edition does in fact accomplish this to a remarkable degree. The tapered rule has been employed to indicate Tuggle's habit of separating one finished item from the next, and the individual entries begin flush against the lefthand margin but are paragraphed within. Tuggle's terminal dashes have been kept as have his occasional number signs (#). In general editorial emendation has been held to an absolute minimum, and with few exceptions emendations are indicated by brackets. Here as elsewhere editorial regularization chiefly involves paragraphing and terminal punctuation.

Although the author wrote on the run, it is evident that he took some pains to set off direct discourse he wished to preserve intact, to underline words he wanted to emphasize, and to spell precisely the names of individuals he encountered (despite some inconsistencies in proper names). Another sign of his urge for precision and order may be seen in the various little sketches he drew beside his descriptions of strange natural objects, utensils, and structures, such as rocks, pots, cradles, goalposts, and buildings. All of which is to say that Tuggle's skill as an observer and recorder of the life he witnessed and experienced was considerable.

his client's case!

———————

Have been reading "Sully's Memoirs" lately & am impressed with Sully's worldly wisdom & cannot see that human ingenuity & diplomacy have been much improved since his day. Human nature presents about the same problems in every generation—
Fort Scott, Kansas. Aug 30, 1879.
People here tell me that corn has been engaged at 12½ to 15ct pr. bushel for fall delivery.

Impressions of rich Kansas lands, crops, prices

One man told me he had bought 1000 bushels at 12½; another had engaged 5000 at 15ct delivered in his crib—
Farm laborers get 13$ p. mth & board—
Along the R.R. from Kansas City to Ft Scott the farms look well—corn being cut & shocked. They were cutting the wild grass & shocking in large ricks, 20 ft high by 50 long & 20 wide—
Easy living—buy a mowing machine & drive a double team over the prairie, & make up hay crop—

Best country I've seen yet, Southern Kansas— Have just come across Tenn. Ky. Ind. Ill. Mo. Kansas. Kansas. Ft Scott—

    50 bushel pr acre corn at 15ct= $7.50.

[Tr]oup Co Ga 10 bushels worth same.

Cattle worth 2½ to 3ct for steers— They call cows— *butchers meat*—only steers are beef cattle, & average 1000 *lbs*—cows 7 to 800.

Land along R.R. worth 12, 15 to 20$ pr acre— Mostly cultivated—

Hogs, fresh meat 2¼ to 2.75 in winter—

Coal $1.20 pr ton retail 20ct pr bushel—

Immense coal fields near Ft Scott—

Little boy at R.R. Junction was playing with a qt cup of water & a two legged "Jimson" weed—a syphon— Had found it out himself—I suppose—

Had to wait at Ft Scott from 3 PM till 11 PM for train from St. Louis— Lost a day by going via Kansas City. Ft. Scott a thriving city of 5 to 7000—built mostly since the war—

Midwestern cattle and innovative farming methods superior to Georgia's

Cattle are all improved breeds—mostly large variety of Durhams— Hogs Berkshires— Dogs fine—bulls—& red setters—

People used latest improved plows—sulky—& *ride* nearly all together plowing, planting, cultivating & harvesting— Work reduced to play—

    Why not in Ga?

America's future wealth: people, products, industry

With a dense population the country of Miss. Valley will be grandest on earth— In one more century America will have 100 millions—

Russian colony in South Kansas twist & press hay & use it for fuel— Corn has been so used when winters were cold & market for coal distant—

Georgias hope is in cotton— Spin it into thread & cheapest forms of cloth—& eventually make fine cloth— Corn & meat can be bought cheaper along Ga R.R.s than it can be raised— In a few sections this may not be true, but certainly in most parts of Ga— "Exodusters" have been distributed to Southern Kansas & other points—a few remain near Kansas City—

Expenses—

Atlanta to St Louis	$22.75
Eating & sleeping &c	5.00
St Louis to Kansas City	4.50
Kansas City (Hotel)&c	3.00
Linen coat	1.75
Kansas City to Ft Scott	3.75
Ft Scott to Eufaula	9.35
(Eating Aug 30)	1.00
	$51.10
Same back?	51.10
	$102.20

Transportation and lodging costs in 1879

Fare from Kansas City to St Louis 276 miles now 50 cts!
(3) Three R.R.s fighting.

Round trip tickets from Kansas City to Denver, Cheyenne, Omaha & back to Kansas City 42$. Brokers sell same at $38.00.
If I have time I will take this trip when I return from Indn Terty

Same weeds along R.R.s as grow in Ga—Rag weed, Jamestown weed, the purple flower weed (Iron), & also a wild sunflower, especially in Mo. & Kansas—

Aug 31st
Met Sam Marthler Creek Indian on train. Hunter & fisher— Poisoned water with buckeye roots in bag— fish buffalo &c came to surface & he shot them with arrows—400 last week— Going this week again—
Sunday Aug 31 79
At Ft Scott Junction 7 hours waiting— John Smith the bounty Jumper. Jumped it 13 times & recd $1350.00 each time. In Cincinnati, Peoria, & New York— Had a Chum, would enlist & unless ordered at once to camp, would go to another office & enlist. Take the oath & the bounty & go again. New names—new cos-

Bounty jumping: profitable mode of draft-dodging

tumes—more whiskers, then none. Red hair, long
hair, short hair— Was hunted by detectives all over
north to California, back to NY, then to England,
Germany & France— Was finally caught in Jany 1865
at Pittsburg Pa, tried & sentenced to be shot, & the
surrender saved him—

Was badly wounded at Shiloh & was discharged—

*Contrasts in
culture and
civilization*

Disk of burnished gold rising over a sea of green
velvet— Sunrise in Cherokee Nation— Contrast striking, the cultivated fields of Ind. Ill. Mo & Kansas, the
thriving towns, & the rolling prairies in native wildness & beauty.

The white & the red civilization—the guest & his host.
400 years ago they owned the *continent* now Indn
Terty— The ewe lamb now being observed by the
commercial neighbor— When is it to be *sacrificed?*

*Indian as white
man's sacrificial
lamb*

Has not the Indian the right to decline white civilization?

What chance would he have in the joint stock
concern?

What influence could he exert? To protect himself
even?

Sam E Marthler promises me a bow and arrow & to
notify me of his next fishing frolic or hunt—

Went hunting last week & killed four deer & some
turkeys—

*Tuggle meets
Indian officials
and frontier
characters*

Met Ben Porter (brother of Pleasant Porter, Creek
delegate at Ft last *winter*) at Muscogee today.

Met Billy about 11 AM Sept 2 at Prof. Doughty
(James A.) at Tuskeegee town— Billy was a manager
at election of yesterday & thinks Coachman elected,
had majority of nearly 200 in 5 towns— Ingram at
Eufaula thought same.

Prof Doughty was barefooted when we dismounted.
I rode a bay mule name "Jim", 5 yrs old, belongs to
Bro Broch cost 140.00. Splendid traveler. In debt yet
about 300$. paying 25cts pr member pr month. Mem-
bership about 70. regular attendance about 40—

Pastor Rev. Wm McComb. aged 34, blue eyes, short hair medium size—Scotch Irish & Indian— Father white man & his mother was half Creek & half Creek with some white blood—

Billy McComb an intelligent man, somewhat educated mostly by himself & at Mission School at Tuskeegee Presbyterian—

running walk— Bro Broch rode a borrowed pony— Prof Doughty soon appeared with new purple top boots on, breeches inside—

Mrs Smith—barefooted—was Prof Doughty's housekeeper. His wife died last winter & widow Smith keeps house— Doughtys house 20 x 20 log house—ceiled inside & dabbed with mud & straw, porch in front with puncheon oakfloor—

Primitive living conditions

Doughty was mending harness—Prof—because he used to teach school. Born in Tenn—raised in Nebraska & moved here in 1872. *"Grass-hoppers."* Runs a grass mowing machine— Wiry, medium size, sandy hair, black eyes—

He was hospitable—fed our stock on old corn in wagon body.

Mrs. Smith fixed dinner. Bill of fare—biscuit, fried streak of lean & fat. Rich in sugar bowl—& coffee— "Sofkey"—corn soaked in water to soften husk, beat in *mortar*, separate husk—crack corn, boil in [lye?] all day—let it cool & put in earthern pot & keep warm. (Earthen pot, is rude jug about 10 gallons) Let it *sower* & drink water & eat the corn. Doughty had no "Sofkey". But *"Abuskey"* was handed around— Shell corn, put in iron pot & sift ashes in corn—more ashes than corn by about ⅓, put on fire & stir—*ashes to prevent burning*— When you can mash between fingers—sift ashes out— Put in mortar & tap lightly, fan light husk out—then beat fine— Add water & sugar & drink—

Indian cuisine, recipes for "Sofkey" and "Abuskey"

Nothing but "Substitute Confederate—coffee out of meal" cold—

Dinner ready said Mrs. Smith—with bead headdress & earrings & barefooted. light hair & blue eyes, 140 lbs. Her little six yr old girl had on a sack, & skirt—

I could see when the wind blew that she had on nothing else whatever—

Tuskeegee Town = voting *present* = 4 houses—3 mules—3 ponies—3 men—Mrs Smith, her girl—Indian woman & 3 children, 2 sows 10 pigs & 3 geese

---

ducks, turkeys & chickens—
Politics = 3 parties

Party politics among Indians

Muscogee Party = advancement among themselves, not too much. White man, Sympathized with South—McIntoshs, McComb—*Coachman* &c
Muscogees to rule Muscogee—Know Nothings—went South during war—

Pin Party
During war had secret societies somewhat like *"Masons."*
Used a "pin" as a badge— Sympathized with North, *Cherokees began it*—
Sam Chicota a "Pin" & candidate for chief— Obligation to stick together—&c. Had no slaves—
Loyal Party—a new third party—rather between the two & somewhat Negro—has Negro candidate. 2nd chief—

Political equality
Social equality

Amalgamation of tribes and races

Amalgamation generally, one man said. Creeks = Indians crossed with negro. ⅞ negro—
Cherokees Indian x with white
Choctaw—¼ white
Chickasaw—⅝ white
Seminoles nearly Indian
Another said (Doughty) Creeks 14000
    Say 12000
    4000 = Negroes
    (More prolific)
    8000 so-called Indians & ½ (or 4000) are mixed

with Negroes in about ½ to ⅛ proportion—& almost 4000 are mixed with whites.

Doughty & Broch both say out of 12000 Creek Indians not 100 could prove they have no mixed blood in them— They do not believe one dozen young Indians are full blood—

How many women 35 yrs old now in the Churches (Methodist Baptist & Presbyterian) are virtuous, that is, never committed adultery before or after marriage?

Not one— Doughty said no woman here learned how to be virtuous till over 30 yrs old— "Every man thinks himself equal to his superiors & superior to his equals" said Doughty.

Ponies range from 5 to 25$— Work ponies from 25 to 50$—

Prices and quality of crossbred Indian ponies

Most of the peasant stock resulted from horses bought from states & bad treatment *stunted* them. Some are Indian ponies crossed with Spanish horses— Many are pretty & well shaped—small well formed horses— Doughty has been & is cutting hay with two horse "Champion" mower— Breaks prairie with 14 inch 3 horse plow—turning-plow— Cuts at $1.25. Cuts 10 acres pr day—& the prairie *grass averages* about 1 ton per acre, & sells at 5$ per ton on R.R.—

Breaks prairie at $3 per acre

Picture—

Doughty and his household

1. Front porch of Doughty
2. Figures
    1. Broch in wooden chair leaning back both feet on 3x3 inch oak angle hewn railing—
    2. Doughty in shirt sleeves & top boots.
    3. Mrs. Smith barefooted, pipe in mouth, horsehair net with blue beads, & 3 tassels— "You bet." "You're looking for *em* aint you."
       Little girl Smith—2 white *boys*—

(Bad for bad debt. Fiddle taken for board bill)

Prof Doughty owns a fiddle, an accordian, croquet set (cost $2.20)

Ball playrs generally.
Yarn ball about size of fist—trick to catch the ball with two ball sticks & throw the ball between two sticks—
    Often hit & kill one another—
Doughty had seen 120 fighting over the ball
Broch saw 1 man killed dead, wounded 3 so that they died & hurt 50 for 1 month. Last year, 1879, Cussetas & Cowetas at Capt F. B. Severs ranche about 20 miles from Ockmulgee—

Doughtys fight of 120 near Alexanders Store 35 miles west of Eufaula in 1877—

Mrs Smith little girl. 6 yrs old—Perniza Lavona Smith—"*Granny*" nick name— One boy, Siegal Cobbler sat on churn at dinner table—
Dave McComb—18 sheep, 24 sheep 10 rams & 14 ewes—

A schoolmarm's living quarters

School-marm, Miss Christy Grayson hunted for boarding place near Tuskeegee— They put her up in a stable—at Thomas McWilliams— Not used for other animals now = however—

Indian tribes and their varied dialects

Nation = Creeks
Language of Creek Indians—
1. Seminoles talk purest Muscogee, the ancient Creek or Muscogee tongue.

Tribes
2. Alabamas
   (*Cowetas & Cussetas = old Creek*).
   Hitchitees.
   Uchees & Quasoddas.

& others speak different dialects among themselves.
All understand Creek or Muscogee but do not understand the separate dialects.
A Tuskegee does not know the dialect of the Alabamas—

Sands = (Tepothleoholo)
A Creek said to a Cherokee (Wm P Ross) "You
Cherokees are so mixed with whites we cannot tell
you from whites."

The Cherokee Ross replied: "You Creeks are
so mixed with Negroes we cannot tell you from
Negroes."

Red, white, and black

Lasso, Lariat—or Stake rope—about 40 to 60 ft— (30
to 50)—
Fellow with no corn lengthens his stake rope accordingly— A length of rope shows state of Crib.

Doughty rode a Jinny 3½ ft high— Saddle leathers
dragged the ground. Went to church—& baptizing
on said "Jinny"— "Jinny" threw Preston Doughty.

Feeding = Staking out to grass—
Mrs Smiths dress = blue stripes—striped apron of
another color with ruffle at bottom. One button on
front of her dress, at neck & no other fastening down
to waist, & at side view, when wind was blowing, the
beauties of nature were displayed to great advantage.

Mrs. Smith and the beauties of nature

Doughty says Mrs Smith "is a full blooded *Arkan-
sawer*"—
Creek Indian baby song
McComb's Sept 2. 1879. At night [Three-quarters of
page left blank.]
McComb. Sept 3. 79.
House—double log cabin—rooms 15 x 20—hall loft
arranged for two other rooms above—porch in front—

McComb's living quarters

2 back shed rooms & two beautiful stone chimneys—grey stone—

Miss Grayson's school

McComb. Doughty, riding bare back & side ways, Broch, & I, after early supper rode over to McWilliams—passed Doughtys mower— Miss Grayson school teacher there. Began yesterday had 6 scholars, today 8. Old woman 75 great grandmother of McCombs children—remembers leaving Ga & Ala— "Sofkey" in blue & white bowl with big wooden spoon brought out. I couldn't go it. Was sower & too old— "Hominy in water" rather strong—

Territorial government: structure and jurisdiction

Rode to Judge Colbert's. Met him in 1874— Judge of Eufaula District—about 25 miles square— Seems nearly full blood & talks no English— Not a lawyer. Has been a member of Council

Warriors = 100. ⎞
Kings   41 ⎬ Council
1 Chief   ⎠

Jurisdiction civil up to 100. All over 100$ goes to Supreme Court— Council misdemeanors—punished by whipping, up to murder punished by shooting. Light horse cavalry—5 to district & capt. One the shff & posse— People in Eufaula District about 4000. Court house near Colberts 12 miles west of Eufaula. 16 ft sq. Log house—whipping post a post oak tree near by— Ordinary punishment 50 lashes on bare back & can extend to 100— Law reads

50 lashes for first offense
100 lashes for 2nd offense
Death for 3rd offense

McComb knew an Indian shot for stealing a chair— Indian whipped at post 26 July for stealing two (2) stray cattle—50 lashes— Hickory withe—3 ft long. Skin broken at every lik—called here "pealing his back".

Catcher—Tiger Mt about 2 miles west of McComb's —rolling prairie broken & timber.

Well-stocked Indian farms

Hayrick at McCombs 4ft wide x 36 long. 3 forks to side with railing, side poles coming together at bot-

tom—rail between & widening to 12 ft at top 15 ft high—holding 8 tons—of prairie grass—
Green corn cooked & dried used in winter
McComb has pigs, chickens, geese, ducks, ponies & cattle— Can cut grass anywhere—in Nation or stake off as much land as he wishes.
At every Indian house I saw fat dogs— About an acre fenced in with 6 rails post oak—worm fence—
I slept on thin feather bed. Broch on single bed & McComb & wife, daughter 14, another 10, & little boy 5 slept on porch floor—

Sleeping accommodations chez McComb

Jurors paid $1 per day. Judges salary 200$ per year. Dist atty = 25$ for every conviction & 100$ salary— Atty's fees misdemeanors 10 to 25$. Murder 50 to 200$.
Looked over minutes of Colberts court. Kept about in usual State Court style. Colbert opens with prayer —customary.
—6 District Courts—Supreme ct meets once a year Okmulgee. Jurisdiction 100$ up— Criminal—5 judges —salary 5$ per day. John McIntosh Chf Justice

Typical legal fees and income

In a word their entire system is a copy of the State system—
Indians look like Chinese & Japanese—
Miserable water—milky color—wells generally dry— springs = hole sunk in ground with water in it.

Doughty had a barrel sunk in bottom of the creek, or where creek used to be—

McComb cultivates 20 acres in corn.
Average farm 10 acres—20 acres—40 acres & up to 200 acres—
Charles Smith—auditor of Nation has 200 acres in cultivation, corn. 100 acres in cotton, ¾ bale to acre

Size of average farm

An Indian's mile

Indian calls a mile as far as he can see—(common man)—

How far to Eufaula (12 miles)

"The second sight"—

Two prairies broken with timber—

So 2nd, 3rd, 4th & 5th sights

To Ockmulgee 40 miles. How far? "5 sights"

Doughty's Mrs Smith—

Doughty & Bro Broch started to Eufaula—Doughty rode a mare with young colt. The colt refused to follow & Doughty returned, took off his saddle & caught another mare "Old Nance." Mrs Smith was sorry for "Old Nance" & looking at Doughty as he put spurs & started off again said "I reckon Old Nance wishes she had a colt too"—

Doughty said, "Ill tell Dr Buckner about that".

The plucky Arkansawer replied "Who cares for old Buck—he's lost all the grease out of his joints long ago"—

Indian repartee: gallantry, sex, and innuendo

Doughty Bush & Dr Buckner bought very long tail dusters & went to camp meeting— Mrs Smith & some girls saw them

"Who's there?"

"One's old Buck, dont know others"

"Reckon they got them long coat tails so their wives could use them for themselves or cut off the coat tails for the babies"

Mrs Smith "You gals better let their coat tails alone or thell be raising yr coat tails"—

Abundant wildlife on open prairies

Game seen. Field larks—crows, hawks—

McC. tells me there are deer a few miles distant on the ridges. The bucks begin to run about 3rd Oct— one bold and careless will come at full gallop right towards you—(of course not seeing you)—

Turkeys—prairie chickens by millions— Stay on ground in summer & spring, fall & winter live on acorns &c in trees—can fly 5 miles—30 to 100 gangs.

Roosters make a drumming noise in spring—like turkeys gobbling—that is time—sounds like a bull bellowing—

Average days hunting—2 or 3 turkeys & probably a deer—

Sept 3 79
Mrs McComb & Baby song
Nocha—nocha—nocha
Nochathles, chitchkit,
Mak-ĭmks,
Nochäthles, Mächkit
Lo-cha, ho-po-kun
Ayŭnks, no-che-pus

An Indian
baby song

News of election—Dave McComb—blue eyed short, sandy hair, looks like Irishman—weighs about 150 lb— Brought to Billy McComb news that he Billy was elected a warrior for next Council—
McComb was no candidate & the first he knew of it was the following note handed to him by his brother Dave.
"Okmulgee M Sept. 1st 1879. This is to certify that Wm McComb was elected in accordance with the laws of the Muskogee Nation by the citizens of Cheharyar town to represent them in the House of Warriors National Council M.N. for the term commencing Dec 5. 1879

Election news
and certification
notice

James McHenry H K
Geo Mitchell   W
Selarho   H W—
#Billy is the Indian Cincinnati#

Warriors receive 4$ p day, & Kings same—
McComb refused to run & wrote a letter to that effect

Vote   19 for McComb (M)
1 8 for Lincoln Pin

Voting statistics for
seats in legislature

2 Thomas Tiger—19 (M)
   Jim McHenry   8 (Pin)
3 Bebiska   18
   Selarho   9
Elected to House Warriors McComb, & Bebiska
To House of Kings—Tiger

Jim McHenry,
Indian fighter

Jim McHenry is the celebrated Indian fighter in Ga &
Ala—75 yrs old— Methodist elder—20 yrs.
   "They think Im an old man but confound em let
em try me"
   Broch said old Jim said to him "The Baptists are
going to take the Creek nation. If me & Sam Chicota
was to die by Thunder, the Methodists would go to
the Devil"—
He is a Mason. Out of 2500 Creek voters—most
prominent Indians are Masons— About 50 prominent, intelligent Creeks— All politicians—

Sept 3. 1879. 2 P.M.
At Smiths 32 miles from Eufaula—

Accidental
death or murder?

Smith told of a peculiar drowning 20 miles from Okmulgee in Bennett's Creek. (South of O) boy 12, &
man—boy was drowning, man went in to rescue him,
both were drowned & buried on bank—Wednesday
27th Aug— Probably murdered.

Sacred vessels
used in annual busk

Smith has seen the two copper plates kept as sacred,
handed down by God—about 18 inches in diameter—
edges quite thin— Circular in shape— Scoured once
a year by certain boys— Saw them first 30 yrs ago &
saw them last time 3 yrs ago last July— Have been
scoured thinner—one used every year at their *busks*,
or green corn dances— Little knob on back to hold
them by— A man fasts 4 days & takes medicine before
he can carry them at the festivals. Mrs Smith thinks
these used to be 4 or 6— All different kinds. Originally
there were figures or inscriptions on them— Scoured
out—
#Pickett in his Ala history speaks of them#
Tookafabotcha town has been the custodian & is yet

—used only by that town—75 miles east of Eufaula—
& 45 miles from Okmulgee
Smith went 60 miles to vote for Coachman—
Dinner, 1st water melons, (orange)   2. Fried bacon
3. Biscuit & honey   4. Coffee—
Fat dogs everywhere

*Growing
accustomed to
Indian diet*

Stopped on road at Hentz Posey's, white man with
Indian wife—son of Presbyterian preacher. They gave
us "Abuskey". "Cold flour" very refreshing— Drink
& eat it both

---

2 cranes & some partridges seen today

Martin Smith
Okmulgee

Reached Okmulgee about sundown— Large house,
two stoves, built of small hewn stones with cupola.
3 stores & a few houses—wooden single story, & some
vacant cabins for the Warriors & Kings to occupy
with their families during Council.
Stopped at Capt Belchers—stout, fat man 5 ft 7—
weighs about 200—blue eyes—Roman nose. Born in
Tenn—moved here in 1849—Indian wife—well to do
—trader— Cutting hay now with machine, says there
are several in this vicinity— He has cut for others 175
acres. Another man Jennings has cut 236 acres—

*Visits with
Capt. Belcher,
successful farmer*

Hon John R. Moore at Belchers—very large 250—very
intelligent—has represented people at Washington—
Speaker of House of Warriors— Says Indians would
vote 100 to 1 against any changes in their government,
such as has been proposed, that is, to make a territory
& Indians to become citizens— Indians would be
cheated out of their lands—that in Ga & Ala those
Indians who preferred to remain there as citizens
under the treaty were permitted to sell their lands,
provided an officer of U. S. witnessed the deed &
certified to that effect. Even then designing men
would bribe another Indian to personate any Indian

*Indian official
argues separate
government for
continued progress*

owning good land & get a forged deed— Thinks Indians have improved more here by themselves than they would have done mingled with whites. Illustrated by comparing Indians Creeks down in Texas on "Reservations," & the Cherokees in North Carolina— Contact with whites demoralizes. Keeps them down— Here emulation for position, pride & ambition are at work & the facts demonstrate the theory that they improve faster under a separate Indian government— Schools & churches are scattered over the land— Crime is diminishing & compares favorably in this aspect with the States.

Aged refugees from Georgia and Alabama

Grand children of Paddy Carr are here—Mrs Belcher one—Judge Stedham's wife another. Moore related—McIntosh's—grandchildren of Gen'l William McIntosh killed in Ga in 1825 on acct of treaty at Indian Springs—they live among Creeks— One son—D. N. McI— John McIntosh—Judge Supreme Court & a Baptist preacher now a missionary to the Seminoles— Luke, going to college at Nashville, Tenn. Roland, & William. Chilly died several yrs ago—

Jim McHenry still living, started trouble with whites in 1835. Was in fact at Columbus. At Okmulgee yesterday. Member of House of Kings—not reelected—unpopular.

Some few old men remain who came out from Ga & Ala 1836–8 & 1827—

Tales at Belchers after supper. Coffee, biscuit, peach preserves, jelly, chicken & dumplings stewed, molasses, fried onions.

—Ben's Cat Fight—

Ben's big cat fight: a chilly joke on Dad

One night Belchers little son Ben six, woke him up—midnight, freezing cold "Oh, pa, get up, quick. Be right easy"— Capt B—jumped up thought robbers were on hand, looked for his gun. Ben in whispers "Come here & see", out on porch in night clothes— wind whistling over the snow. Ben caught hold of the Capt's shirt & pulled his xcited & xpectant parent along &c.

"What is it son?" in whisper.

"Just look right there by the chicken coop—I think theres going to be one of the biggest kind of cat fights in the world." Belcher was sold—sure enough, there were the cats caterwauling behind the coop in true Indian warwhoop style—

"But Ben its too cold out here to wait for the fight". And the capt crawled in bed laughing—

Dave Watsons fiddle—

Dave bought a fiddle for 12$. He was heard sawing away on it frequently. One day the Capt noticed him playing on a very inferior fiddle

"Dave where is yr fine fiddle"

"Sold it"

"What for?"

"$12."

"To whom"?

"To the man I bought it from—I hadnt paid him for it"

A fair exchange

Capt. "When [was] a criminal [last] xecuted in Creek country?"

"Last summer. He was shot. He murdered 'Foxtail' at his own house. Was tried, condemned & shot".

"When was anybody shot before that?"

"About 6 yrs ago—"

"He stole a fiddle worth about $2—but it was his third time & he was shot".

Old Col. Logan—& his two daughters rode down to the boat landing on the Arkansaw—to water their horses—all horseback— The girls rode in water—the old man cautioned them to be careful. They were looking at the boat passing & soon the horses walked in to a hole & the girls were in the river up to their shoulders.

The old man was mad. "What are you girls doing? You Mary. You Mary".

After they were out, dripping like drowned rats.

"Now Mary you might have drowned. Mandy

Death penalty for a convicted murderer, thief

Metaphor and pun in a parental reprimand

what on earth did you go in the river for? What did you go there for anyhow? Twouldnt made much difference if you had got drowned anyhow."

"Oh, pa, just for Curiosity."

"Yes by G—— & you got your curiosities wet too."

McHenry tells of Georgia boyhood

Capt. James McHenry, Met him. 62 yrs old—gray head & white whiskers, upper lip showed, large black eyes prominent cheek bones—½ Indian—celebrated "Jim McHenry." Known in Ga—on acct of war 1836–8— Was prominent in said war. Was a boy in Columbus Ga—interpreter at Fountain & Stewarts store. Knew Walter T. Colquitt, frequently at his store—

"The boys said Colquitt would lie all day and repent all night"—

Asked about Harris, Seaborn Jones, & others—

Muscogee Capitol just completed

Been Methodist preacher 28 yrs— Is now President of the house of Kings— Showed me through Capitol. Hunted around the hamlet ½ hour for keys— Used when Council meets & not used xcept for church S.S. & lectures [?] in vacation. Not yet completed. House 2 story with cupola, 50 x 80. Stone rough—hall—16 windows & blinds to side, porch over front door. Marble stone to left of front door, about 2 ft sq.

"Muscogee National Capitol#
Erected 1878
Building Comtee
James McHenry
John R. Brown
John McIntosh"

Up stairs 30 x 20—House of Kings, 48 members room 50 x 30 for House of Warriors 92.
Supreme Court room, 30 x 20. 5 judges—

McHenry's pride in his position

Old man very proud of his position— Showed him letter from Gov. Colquitt, told me to write to the gov. that he was "Presdt of House of Kings". I was with him nearly all day. Broch, McHenry, Dr Wright &

I went to Hotel (3 in town). Met Pleas. Porter's mother & (½ negro) his sister—
Popular full Negro style— Colored girl "Patsy" bossed the dinner— Bill of Fare—Backbone, cornbread, biscuit, coffee, syrup & apple pie—

McHenry told me that in 1874 Bishop Marvin was here in Okmulgee & told him following tale.

Marvin said, "I was about 19—was rough awkward country preacher near St. Louis. There was a conference at St Louis—& a fine turn out of fashionable people— The pastor was rather fond of style & the Presiding Elder Cables was there. They did not think I would xactly suit for the occasion, but decided to write me thinking I would decline. The P.E. said I will ask him a few moments before preaching, & he will have to decline".

"I was reading under a tree. Bro Cables approached, 'Bro Marvin we wish you to preach for us.'"

"All right—I will do so".

"I went to the pulpit & preached & was invited again that night & had an ovation".

Broch spoke up & said "Yes, Cables told me all about it"—

Dr. Marvin had on a calico coat, jeans breeches, a home made straw hat & when Cables asked him he went to the woods & soon fixed up— He wore home made yellow shoes— When Cables told the pastor that Marvin had accepted he said "Well he shall not preach"—

Cables replied "He shall. I am presiding elder & you instructed me to invite him & he shall preach"—

Marvin prayed—Cables said "Well he prays well"

At the end of 20 minutes he had the crowd shouting & when he sat down Cables was called on to preach—but he cried aloud "No, for Gods sake, Call for mourners".

They made him preach that night & he did better—

McHenry's story of Bishop Marvin's sermons at the St. Louis conference: a homespun revelation of ironic reversal

Some rich man went up to Marvin after morning sermon & said, "Is that the best you can do," alluding to his clothes.

"Yes we're all poor up my way".

"Dont you get a salary".

"O Yes 25$, but I spend that for [obliterated]".

"[Obliterated] come with me" & he clothed him in broadcloth.

Cables said "Well Marvin, you did splendidly, but mind tonight"

"O I feel better now. Im in better trim" alluding to his new clothes.

"He is a great man" said McHenry "& told me that story rig[ht] there before the cr[owd]".

The furniture, gilt eagle & big ball, just come for capitol.

Violence and lawlessness in the territory

Mail contractor killed about month ago 30 miles from here, going from *Sac* agency to Kansas. Some lawless men up there. Parker, Woods & Kelly— Robbed Caneville stores lately—

Origin of the Creek Orphan Claim

McHenry told me about the Creek orphan claim. Treaty of 1832 provided certain lands in Ala for orphans of 1832— U.S. sold the land— They claim is over 200,000$. D. N. McIntosh represented the claim, but has not been in Washington in 2 yrs & is now willing to relinquish his agency. He was to get [obliterated] One Mr. [obliterated]—a lawyer at [obliterated] City has agreed to rep[resen]t it for 10 per ct.

Gen N B. Porter, McIntosh (D N), John McIntosh, Stidham, Hodge, McHenry, Belcher, Buckner, Wright & others to sign a paper recommending nil to the orphans—

[Obliterated] was virtually [obliterated] by the treaty of 1866 and said the 100,000$ paid really came from purchase of Indian lands & hence was no payment by U. S.

[Two pages obliterated.]
Met sister of Osceola. Powell was the father of Osceola—a white man by an Indian woman. Hepsy Leeder, or "Hamarty" is her name. Was 14 when she left Ga in 1838— 55 yrs old— Black eyes, black hair tinged with gray, large good looking very pleasant face—
She is a widow—Col Sam Chicola married her sister, another sister of Osceola. Her mother was not Osceola's mother—½ sister—

Tuggle meets Hepsy Leeder, Osceola's sister, a native of Georgia

Jim McHenry introduced me to Hepsy— She had just come into Turner & Harrison's store to trade. Came [in] a Studebaker wagon drawn by two ponies —followed by a colt—
Saw her buy 3 lbs of cotton padding in rolls or sheets at 16⅔ cts per lb—(or shilling a pound as Sanger said) 3 lbs at 50 cts for a quilt—

She was born in Ga— Remembered West Point. I talked to her through Jim McHenry as interpreter. When I used words "West Point. Chattahoochee" she would smile & chuckle— She was pleased when I asked her how old she was. She did not know— Knew she was 14 in 1838—

Sept 8 79—met John Ross who was with my father in California from 1850–54. Loved him & was intimate with him

Was introduced by Judge Logan Perryman—member H. W. to the House of Warriors— The Speaker asked us to talk. Dr McIntosh told them of his school mission & I spoke of my visit, favorable impressions—&

Tuggle's introduction and address to the House of Warriors

hoped U.S. would abide treaty stipulations—&c—I saw their eyes glisten with tears as I talked—they applauded me several times— Dr. Buckner introduced me to widow Bailey—husband's brother— Dr Bailey died in New York last spring & left an estate valued by [Rivers?] at $3,000,000, it goes to the sons of the Uncle [who] went away with reportedly [?]oo,ooo$ or the approximate value— The widow's husband, another brother in N. Y. & two sisters of the testator— (4) are Indians. The old man is eccentric, a doctor, a man of letters &c. The will is contested & the widow desired my opinion about the will— [Last sentence obliterated.]

Oct 9 Wrote communication from McIntosh to Chief Ward Coachman [informing] him of certain sugge[stions.]
A handsome bright blackeyed olive complected young man of about 20 yrs—Wrote note by him to his brother to meet me this week at Muscogee—

Sept 1. 79
Election tomorrow for chief of Creeks. Sam Checotee & Coachman—candidates.

Sept 2. 1879
Left Bro Buckners about 9 AM, rode with Bro Broch— missionary of Western Assotn Ga—to Eufaula, thence to Tuskeegee. *Prm*, in voting precinct—not now used —perhaps 48 such precincts in Cherokee Nation.

*Impressive new
Tuskegee Church*

Passed Tuskeegee Church about 22 x 42—6 glass windows—*well* floored pine shingle roof—Cost about [blank.] built about 1 year ago. 120$ mechanical work. Indians did building &c.
I told him my wife's grandfather was the "War Horse of Troup" (Col Julius C. Alford). She remembered him—at least knew of him— So did McHenry—
Picture 1. Hepsy—sister of Osceola—Seminole war

2. Jim McHenry—war of 1836—
3. wor agt of Ga—
McHenry says war began April of 1836 & ended in
June 1836—

Capt Belcher to Johnny. 3 yr old— Hattie's child &
brother to Ben.
At table—after we had eaten. Indians eat at 2nd table.
  "One two", Johnny said "6, 7."
  Belcher "8, 9, 10"
  Johnny repeated "8, 9, 10"
  Belcher. "Bully"?—
  "Bully. You bet?"
  "You bet".
  Both laughed—

Belcher's bright
little boys, Ben and
Johnny: amusing
family anecdotes

Little Ben was left by Belcher on prairie 2 hours by
himself to mind the hay—
  When Belcher returned he saw Ben had been crying, "Well Ben did you get lonesome?"
  "No, I sung them meeting songs" alluding to
camp meeting he had recently attended with Capt
Belcher—
  On way home from camp meeting where they had
taken communion & afterwards shouted Ben asked
"Papa, did you see them folks drunk & hollerin
around".
  "Why no, Ben, where?"
  "Old Mister McHenry & Mr Chocota & all of
em—I saw em drink whisky out of the tumbler on
that table where that bottle was & then they all got
drunk & hollered."
  "They didnt offer me none, did they give you &
grandma any?"

Osceolas half brother William Powell lives near Okmulgee (Try to get picture of Hepsy & Wm Powell) +++

Osceola's half
brother

Bens name—Benj. Cooper Bruner, now 7 yrs old =
Dick Carr's picture

Richard Johnson
Carr

    Richard Johnson Carr. Now dead, son of Thomas
C. Carr—who was brother of Paddy Carr—named
after Col Richard M. Johnson who killed Tecumseh—
Johnson had a Choctaw academy in Ky & Dick's father
was educated there—

Sept. 5. Left Capt Belchers about 8 oclock AM.
Stopped at Okmulgee to shoe Broch's pony & did not
get off till 1½ oclock. Guest of Dr N V Wright a
blackeyed small man of remarkable intelligence—
writes for the Indian officers & wrote platforms for
both parties "Muscogee & Pins," I was informed—

First meeting with
Sam Brown, Chief
of Uchees

Left Okmulgee 1½ & rode north 20 miles to Sam
Browns— First ten miles was over prairie & the sun
was very hot & the woods very dusty—a cloud of dust
around us all the way— No rain for months & this is
the main road from Txas to Kansas for money, cattle
&c—
Sam Brown is a small wiry man—blue eyes, thin
whiskers, roman nose & does not look like an Indian—
His father was a white man & his mother a Uchee
Indian. His acct of the Uchees is that they lived in
Pennsylvania when Wm Penn made the treaty, moved
west & south, divided, fought Osages, Cherokees &
Creeks & were finally conquered by the Creeks, their
language is perfectly distinct. There are about 600
Uchees & they stay close together in upper part of
Creek County on Snake Creek & Polecat Creek not
far from train view—

White man from
Mobile, Alabama,
who knew Tuggle's
brothers

Stopped 10 miles north of Okmulgee to get water at
cabin— White man named Norman lived there. He
came from near Mobile Ala 2 yrs ago. His wife has a
little Creek blood in her & entitled him to citizenship.
He knew my brothers Thomas J & Walter C Tuggle
& knew that Capt Benj Odum shot Bro Tom while
he was trying to prevent Odum's shooting Metcalf
an unarmed man— Norman says Odum was so badly

scared that he *soiled* himself. Said my brothers were brave men & were popular— He gave 100$—for his place. 14 acres in cultivation, some fruit trees, house with two rooms, well of good water. Water at Okmulgee & at Browns very good— Wells about 20 to 30 ft deep.

Sandstone along the road yesterday. Game seen on road—partridges, plover—3 times size of Kildees & fly like them, prairie chickens, doves, fieldlarks—

I am listening to a Uchee Indian full blood talk to Brown, looks like Japanese & the language sounds like Japanese & Chinese—
    They must have descended from them & came via Behrings Straits—

Uchees look and talk like Orientals

Indian has a right to all land he encloses, or stakes off & can sell his improvements, & owns his personalty in severalty. Land held in common by tr[ibe] or nation—

Indian property rights

Slept badly—2 inch mattress covered some oak 2 inch slats & I felt like a beef steak on a griddle—rolled over & over—got up folded my overcoat & shawl & tried that but mountains & valleys remained. Lying on rails crossways must be nice.
    Waked up by a coon crawling down the post by my head & the dogs were under the bed— Pet coon "Sarah"—

Sleeping deterrents: slats, dogs, and coon

Dogs everywhere— Counted 6 at one house yesterday—

Brown superintendent of Public Schools—was appointed by Chief Coachman who suspended Bill McCombs— Salary 600$. Visits quarterly—28 schools—

1500 miles in 4 weeks on pony— This trip 4 times a year = 6000 miles on horseback. Two missions— Looks after public blacksmith shop where Indians

Brown's role as superintendent of schools: duties and perquisites

can have farm work done free—plow & wagon work
&c—not horseshoeing—
Brown a leader among the Uchees & a prominent
man generally— His wife a small blackeyed intelligent
woman—½ Creek & ½ white. Both Baptists—
Passed near Severs Ranch— Severs has 4000 cattle &
cultivates 400 acres, tis said. Has a store at Okmulgee   Rich man—white with Indian wife.

Brown has 180 cattle. Saw a fine Durham bull—red
breast & white spotted body—

Brown's domestic
facilities

Room I slept in 8 x 10 ft. Walls made out of oak
boards like weather boards—about 3 ft long & 6 inches
wide & dressed on outside— Brown had a few pine
plank which was hauled 170 miles— His house, log
cabin 20 x 20 with porch in front one end 8 x 10 cut
off for company room & shed room at back Kitchen &
dining room— Had no light "out of coal oil" said
Mrs. B—& we sat down in the dark to supper & knew
the way to our mouths.

"Phonographic Piano" a toy out of fix—presented to
Browns little boy by a teacher.

Indian marriage
codes and customs

Laws. Cherokees have a code—very good one— Creeks
have no code—no marriage laws.
Creek can marry as many wives as he wishes—
Generally the Creeks have one wife—a few have two—
heard an Indian child squall & heard the licks with
my riding whip—
    "What's the matter?"
    "He didn't stand guard".
    "What guard?"
    "She. His mother put him over something, I
reckon, & he let the dog get it".
It turned out he refused to drive the hogs out.

Brown has a wife & 4 children. A girl, he got by *acci-dent* he says, when he was a "wild young man," about 12 yrs old, lives with him— "I couldnt throw my own blood away you know— I got her by accident you know—& I'm schooling her now"#

Ball-play

40 to side—Players go in to training, & drink medi-cine—snake-button-root seed & other medicine to make them active & work the slime out— Put up two poles four feet apart 20 ft high connected at the top —another set about 100 yds distant—

For play between 2 towns. Strip naked—put breech-clouts, painted, head dress, & tiger tails.
1. Run around the poles & whoop and boast at one another—each town to a pole.
2. Meet & lay ball sticks on ground in order see if the sides are equal—each man has two ball sticks made of hickory or pecan

3. Man selected to count the number of times the ball goes between poles. One on each side— Kill the ball 20 times is usual— Man selected to throw the ball into air—called "Ball-Witch".
4. They conjure the balls while doctoring the players—

5. Players are stationed at poles & at intermediate points.

6. The ball is thrown in air & then the struggle is over the ball, each side trying to get the ball & throw to between the poles—when the ball has been carried 20 times between the poles the game is won—

7. The successful party dances around the pole & raises the war whoop & are happy.

Uchees played against a party of 72 selected from 10 towns, the best players & whipped them— Uchees never whipped at ball— Uchees played again last May—56 to a side among themselves—

Had Green-corn-dances on Snake Creek, Pole-Cat, & Big pond in July 1879— Keep them up every— "Genl-Cooper" Uchee—

Green Corn Festival or Busk: preparation and ritual

Green-corn-dance—

1. Arrange for buses &c

2. Give 7 days notice—"breaking days" (—Send 7 sticks in bundle)

Take 7 sticks tie in bundles & send a bundle of sticks to each "*fire maker*"—Medicine man—a *chaste* young man—never touched a woman—& these medicine men notify all others— There are "12 fire-makers" among Uchees—

A stick is removed for every day, on 5th day they meet.

Women make "Sofkey". 6th day kill beeves, hogs, cook them in morning & feast—sweet water, sweet beans, Sofkey, honey, potatoes.

A speaker talks at dinner before eating. The orator invites everybody to eat

7th day. Medicine man or "Forked-sticks" because they carry forked poles on that day make sacred fire by flint & spunk— Same men connect 4 sticks pointing N S & E & west—

Fire in middle—& medicine in jars are put on last side several jars holding 5 or 6 gallons

Brown showed me one in his smokehouse—
One pot contains snake button root
One pot contains red root
In one pot, with snake root—

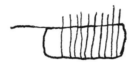

A feather with ten (10) pins, put in Snake root pot—
With this they scratch a cross on their breast— The
Medicine men blow with a cane about 2 feet long
in the medicine—

Blow cane with red string in middle— After blowing the medicine a selected man scratches on the
breast of those who have not eaten green corn before
this time— (Whole object to kill poison of the corn)
(Then Crooked Arrow Dance by men of AM) Then
they drink the medicine. Hand bowls of medicine
around—begin with the town Kings.

Tis an emetic & the amusement begins with the
puking— Some puke in public & some in private—
Begin drinking medicine at noon 7th day— Puke till
evening. Women dance terrapin shells filled with
granls— Women dance around the sacred fire &
medicine is carried off, the pots— No man is allowed
to dance with the women—

Two men sing & beat drums. Uchees now use
American drums—but usually a cast iron vessel covered at top with buckskin—

*"Blowing" and con-
suming medicine*

The Cow Dance

Then men & women dance together— Men have sticks in hands—two men & opposite them two women— What is called "The Cow Dance".

Then they take 4 ears of green corn, throw them in the sacred fire & burn them or roast them—& then the Medicine Men rub themselves with the corn, & then wash themselves—

The ceremony is over— All the men wash & go to new camp & eat green corn &c—

The Crooked
Arrow Dance

Omitted—at nine oclock in morning—or when the *Scratching* is over the men dance "The Crooked Arrow Dance".

After supper the Indians dance all night & eve, "The Stomp Dance"—

The whole ceremony is called, *"The Busk"*.

The Stomp Dance

One to be on Pole Cat Creek Sunday night, tomorrow night. A regular *"Stomp Dance"*—put off because of election for shff— They would be sleepy after dancing all night & would not turn out—

Mrs. Brown's
makeshift cradle.

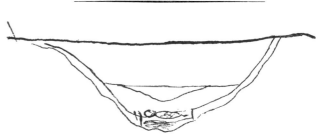

Mrs Browns cradle—two small [ropes?]—a hammock in her room—a quilt on the ropes, two sticks to keep it open—about a foot wide— She then ties a red handkerchief on the ropes just above the baby & this keeps the flies off, flopping twice to each swing—

Madison Brown's views on spirits. His father re-marked at breakfast "There was a witch in the Kitchen last night"—

*Tales of ghosts
and witches in
Brown's household*

I asked old Cooper the Uchee if he believed in ghosts. He said "Yes"—

"Did you ever see one?"

"No"

Bro Brown did you ever see one?"   "O, Yes. My wifes uncle died & was buried. I moved the body & buried it here in my yard & when the coffin was lying by the open grave I saw Danl McKillep just as I knew him, with same hat & coat, walk right along by my fence & go round the corner. I told Mrs Brown to look, but she couldnt see him".

"Madison, who was in Kitchen last night?"

"My grandfathers spirit"

"How do you know?"

"Why he comes back often just to see us & then he goes back. One day I was riding over the prairie & was thinking about a man that was dead. I kept think-ing & thinking & directly I saw him right out there. I told a boy to look & he looked & he couldn't see [h]im a bit"—

"Did you ever see another one?"

"No but I heard one. I was riding home one night on the pony & going long back there by those big rocks in the bottom I heard something make a fuss just like blowing yr nose & I saw something & I like to rode the pony to death."

"May be it was a sheep?"

"—No it was not—"

"*Gooq*"

Danl Childress acct of The Funeral Sermons at Camp Meeting—

"The Camp meeting was going on once on at Broken Arrow 5 miles off— They were preaching funerals. I don't remember how many had been preached.

Rev. W S Robinson spoke up said "Sixteen by the total count"

An Indian said 11, 2 Saturday & 9 Sunday.

Well one Indian preacher he got up & preached a funeral sermon— I know everybody about here, & I kept a listening to hear whose funeral he was preaching— After a [w]hile he picked up a paper somebody had handed him. They generally tell the last words—

Well, he looked & said "My brethren he died about" & stopped & looked again at the paper— "My brethren he died—well I dont know *when* he died"— He went on & after a while he looked at the paper again

"My brethren, our friend who died was named —————" He stopped and he couldnt find it. Another preacher got up & helped him but it couldn't be found, & he said, *"I don't know who he was,* but I'll preach his funeral anyhow"—

John McIntosh tales

Old sister "Squeeze-him-hard" and Brother Broadenax

Old Negro & the story following Judgmnt Day— & Broadenax tale—sore hand— Whitlow's grandmother

"Old Dr Broadenax was a Bapt. deacon & he was at a Camp meeting. He had a bone felon on the middle finger of his right hand & was too sick to go to the arbor. One night they got to shouting & arguing & shaking hands all around so the old Doctor thought he would try to go up to the arbor & look in. I was a wild boy & was enjoying the scene from the outer edge of the crowd— The doctor came close to me & stood there holding his right arm up with his left hand so as to keep his hand on a level with his elbow, about in the position a man assumes when he is going to shake hands. Old sister "Squeeze him-hard" came out towards us shouting & shaking hands with the brothers & sisters as she met them in the crowd. The old doctor was groaning & holding out his right hand—

The old lady saw him & shouting "Glory to God. Want to meet you in Heaven Bro Broadenax" & she seized the old man's sore hand as he held it out & gave him a squeeze & a jerk—

"O Lordy. Have mercy"—& he bowed & bent down & groaned, & the old lady thought he was shouting too & she gave him another squeeze.

"O, Jesus, O, Lord" & down he got on his knees in the grass & the old woman gave him a farewell squeeze & let him loose.

He hollered "O Lordy, Im ruined Im ruined", & broke off in a trot for his hut.

Sunday, Sept 7, 1879
Indn Trty. Broken Arrow Camp Ground 28 miles North of Okmulgee—

Reached ground about noon. They were at arbor 50 x 50—about 400 people in all—5 camps, tents & wagons, horses, ponies, & mules, tied around. Hon P. Porter saw me as I & Broch rode up, came from arbor & carried us to his tent. Dinner was soon ready—long table, plates knives & forks, &c—about 15 could be seated—& Porter fed about 50 at each meal—biscuit, beef, coffee, pies, cakes & chickens— Met Mrs Porter whom I had met at Washington last winter, also Mr D Hodge & his wife. *Broken Arrow Camp Meeting*

The meeting is under the auspices of the Presbyterian Church— Rev. Mr. Robinson, Rev Mr Elliot & Stoddard & another preacher were there, were on ground— Mrs Robinson is a highly cultivated lady— has translated several books into Creek, parts of the New Testament hymns, prepared a vocabulary based on Albert Pike's & thinks there are 10,000 words in use in Creek language, that it is arranged systematically, shows high origin, & says "it was divinely given to Indians". *Presbyterians sponsor meeting*

Religious translations for Indians

Had a conversation with her on "Spiritualism" caused by an old gentleman on the ground trying to proselyte the Indians to this vicious system, told her of Sam Brown's witch & Madisons views &c—

Not many full blood Indians on ground—more whites & half breeds. ⅘ whites & half breeds—

Heard Rev Mr. Elliot preach at 3 P.M. "Choose ye this day when ye will serve". He & the interpreter consumed only 35 minutes. The interpreter took nearly twice as long to translate as the minister to speak in English— He *paraphrased* him and explained fully—

Mrs Robinson claims that an interpreter can translate literally as rapidly as an English speaker can talk & consume no more time—

Orderly behavior at camp meeting

The order of the camp ground is unusually good & better than the average Ga. camp-meetings. Have not heard nor seen the slightest impropriety—

The boys organized a "Dog Police" to keep the dogs out of the arbor. One luckless fat dog came in the pulpit, a boy slyly approached with a long switch & cut him, he started in a run & just as he reached the edge of the arbor another larger boy hit the dog with a whip with a loud crack—a howl of agony, & yelping & howling as he struck for Okmulgee—

Out-of-doors sleeping comforts and distractions

Slept under a tree in a nice pile of prairie grass, & it was heaven as compared to Browns purgatory of night before—the oak griddle— Could hear dogs—about 100 on ground knawing bones & growling— Before day was waked by a little boy trying to pull the quilt off. He spoke to Broch. I looked up in moonshine—

"Whats yr name"? said he to Broch.

"What yours"?

"Tom Crowell".

"What did you take my quilt for"? said Tom & tugged at the quilt.

"Didn't do it Tom. This is mine. Yes it is," & away he pulled.

A female voice "You Tom. Tom come home You are at wrong place". Tom had rolled off some ten steps—

They had night service— Everything orderly— The Presbyterians do not call up mourners & simply preach & sing.

Met prominent men on ground. Perrymans, Hodges, Porters. Rev W. S. Robinson Supdt Tallahassee Presbytr Mission been here 30 yrs—

Several old Indians remembered Ga— Their hymns are translations of our old familiar songs & sung to our same old tunes— Music seems a universal language— All men can worship God together in song from all quarters of the globe— Can not talk to one another but can sing together to God— All God's children.

*Aged Indian recol-
lections of Georgia
days*

Am writing under the arbor 6½ AM. They are singing. Prayer meeting— Conducted in usual manner.

Translation of Mrs McComb's baby song
　　By Mrs. A. E. W. Robinson—Ann Eliza Worcester Robinson—daughter of Rev Sam'l Austin Worcester—condemned in Ga 1852–3. & sentenced to 4 yrs in penitentiary & served 16 months & was pardoned by Gov. W. Lumpkin. He refused to leave Cherokee County on order of Ga &c—
　　Nochathlis = it will sleep = (Nocherhlēs)
　　Ma Kunks = said it (within a week)
　　Chitchkil = Yr mother saying = Mahkit, locha
　　= turtles, hopokin = to hunt,
　　ayunk = went,
　　noche-nus = go to sleep.
　　Let it sleep, Yr mother said
　　Saying let it sleep
　　She went turtle hunting,
　　Your mother says sleep
　　sleep, sleep, go to sleep

*Mrs. Robertson's
translation of
Indian baby song*

Taylor Postoak's version—Sept. 7th, 1879—
　　Nococet o　Let it sleep
　　Mahket o　Having said
　　Cecket o　Your mother
　　Louco-tokocken　The terrapin
　　Hopoyet o　Hunting
　　Ayunke　Went
　　Noce noce　Sleep, sleep,
Sounds like this:

*Another version of
the same song*

Nocherklet o (ň) nasal o
Mahkeet o
Chicthkeet o
Loocher-tor Koachkin o
Hopoyeet o
Ayunkee
Nochee, nochee,—
Sung as the cradle or hammock swung to & fro—

Childers Ferry on Arkansas River

Sept. 8. 79
Childers Ferry Arkansas river 25 miles north of Ok-mulgee— Left camp ground, at Ferry now— This is regular road from Texas to Kansas & Mo— Many returning acct drouth— Old fellow told me Saturday that in 78, he made 298$ wheat & this year with 5 acres more he made 92—& about 2 bushels corn per acre.

Tuggle's notes on Indian myths

Write out Mrs Robinson's acct of her father in Ga. penitentiary & her mother— Also Mr R's tale on "Big Rock man"—wise Rabbit (Indian Fox) telling him he was vulnerable in ear—(Man in armor)
2. Big Terrapin—warriors on back—in sea, drowned woman— Medicine Man made trap—little frogs, little terrapins & finally Strong Medicine brought the terrapin & they burnt him.
(Ship—bad treatment & stealing Indians & subsequent situation.)
3. Snake sickness Medicine song

O Spirit of Gray Fox
Come. You hate snakes.
They've bit this man. Come & kill snakes—
So with spirits of red, black foxes &c

Superstitious belief in medicine tricks

Mr Robinson thinks many church members still believe these Medicine tricks do good, especially conjure guns now to kill deer &c—
Marriage laws needed—
Picture Porter, Hodge, Coweta-Micco—Post-Oak, Thomas Perryman (blue eyes) Mr Robinson—30 yrs

a teacher here—like *Sewards* picture. Sanger & family
—*Walter*—
#Beautiful river at Childers Ferry—now about 275
yds wide, beach of white sand on north side 100 yds
wide—
timber Cotton wood, elm, sycamore, pecan, walnut,
Chestnut oak, hickory & other oaks— Post-oak & black
jack oaks on hills— Blackjack seasoned polishes like
mahogany—

---

30 mourners up last night at church— One woman
shouted a little— Presbyterians discourage all such
emotional displays—
Organ at arbor
Arbor 36 x 48—
Indian girls taught at Mission played on organ & sang
S.S. songs—

Presbyterian emotional restraint

Blew Conchshell at hours of assembling—
Order & plenty to eat—

Mr Robinson thinks that it is best to translate school
books into Creek, that when the children learn the
characters & sounds of English they seldom attend
school long enough to understand what the words
mean. Children often read 3rd Reader & do not know
anything whatever of the meaning—that they speak
at home with their parents & family & friends who
speak Creek & that in brief the education need in
English at the Day school is almost worthless. Esti-
mating the Creeks at 11000, or 2000 families very
few families speak English, that is any member of it,
perhaps 100 families— One can ride a whole week,
outside of the towns, & not find an Indian who speaks
English—
Hon. Pleasant Porter thinks it best to teach altogether
in English— The mission schools do better work & the
pupils of Askiny & Tallahassee missions are the leading men of the Creek Nation—together with the Indians who are educated in the States.

Contrasting views on teaching in English or native language

Porter says one Indian educated in the States is equal in influence towards progress to an entire public school—(28 public schools & 2 missions)

Fairview near Arkansas river presents a very fair view indeed—a lovely valley closed in by ridges covered with timber. Davis, a Bapt. brother, has a store there & this is Fairview— Porter lives in the timber near Fairview facing the valley, his house south of valley— Land makes 60 bushels of corn & 30 bushels of wheat—

Bro. Broch's tale of John Schmicher's religious tergiversations

On the prairie, riding "Jim" who fared well at the Camp-meeting—& Bro Broch on "Johnny the Bounty Jumper" and I named his wild-tribe-notch-eared pony—

He told me several tales of his Dutch neighbors— He was an orphan, a Catholic, then "Dutch-Reformed" & recently a Baptist.

"Near Centralia Ill. there lived an old Dutchman named John Schmicher. He wore a coonskin cap & wears it yet I reckon. Schmicher several years ago gave a dinner & invited some friends & I was among them— I approached him on the subject of religion— I said to him, 'Friend Schmicher, You are a clever fellow & as you are getting old you ought to mend your ways & be a religious man & join the Church.'

Schmicher began; 'Nein mine frent, I do not think I'll ever fool wid de damn tings anymore— Vell I vas a memper of Catolic Chirch. From when I vas a little poy to ven I was a big man. De prcest he vant money from me all de time, vas taking all I could make.'

'Den I quit dat I jshoined de Luteran Church— Den I finds he vants more as de Catolic priest. Den I heart de Metodist preacher, dat he preached a free salvation to ebery pody— Den I joined de Metodist Church. Den I go to the glass meeting. De glass leader he goes around & ax ebery pody how he feel today. Ebery pody told him he feels pretty goot. Den he comes to me— Den I tell him I dont feel pretty good.

I vanted to get to Heaven ven I die, but when I try to do goot den I vas guilty of my ole mean tricks again. De glass leader he didnt say much to me but only he *grunt* all de time.'

'Vell, den he goes right ober dere to old man *Climber*. Vell, he ax old man Climber how he gits along all aready. Vell, Climber he jumps up & talks like he vas a going to heaven mit a handbasket right away— De glass leeder he popped his hands & said, "Go on budder Climber"'

'D——n Old Climber—he vipped his vife last week & I knowed it. D——n his ole soul— Vipped his own vife ober dere—'

'I dont tink I'll fool mid de d——nd tings any-more'".

A Dutchman living on the public road was asked the way & he replied. "Vell. You shust go round mit de corner of de fence, & you goes till he combs to two roads & you den takes de fork hand & ven you comes to de house vere my son John lives deres a little bob-tailed dog vill come out & say 'Boo woo.' 'Boo-woo!' You shust ax dere & dey can tell you better as I can".

A Dutchman's directions

Hon Pleasant Porter has just been elected to the House of Kings, from his town without opposition. He has been a leader for years & a delegate from the Nation to Washington. He was an officer on the Southern side during the war 1861–5, & during an xpected civil war with Terty in 1871 he was made General of the Creek forces. He is about 40 yrs old. Is over 6 ft high, black hair eyes & beard, slightly Roman nose, high cheek bones, broad brow, & alto-gether a splendid looking man & would attract atten-tion in any crowd— He is married to a Cherokee & has only one child, a little boy Willie, 7 yrs old. He lives at Fairview 28 miles north of Okmulgee near the Arkansas river in a lovely valley enclosed by timbered ridges— Intelligent & cultivated & philosophical—

Pleasant Porter's unopposed election to House of Kings

Tuggle's snapshot portraits of prominent individuals

Hon David Hodges is a medium sized, black haired man with good features, black eyes & a pleasant address. He is the National Interpreter, a delegate to Washington, & has just been elected to House of Warriors— He is a prominent man & a leader although young perhaps not over 35—

Rev W. S. Robinson is a small thin man grey hair, blue eyes, near sighted & has been spent 30 yrs here as teacher or Supdt of the Presbytr Mission— His face reminds one of the pictures of Seward. Well informed on all Indian matters, traditions, history, manner, morals & in a word is a walking dictionary on Indian affairs—

ft high, black straight hair now iron-gray, black eyes, very powerfully built, will weigh 225 lbs. Is a Methodist minister, & has been a town chief & is a leading man—
Coweta-Micco is a large magnificent Indian over 6

Thomas Perryman is a Presbyterian minister, conducted the xercises at the Camp meeting Sept 5–8— Is medium size black hair, straight nose blue eyes & a very pleasing manner—

Taylor Postoak is a stout built man about 55, round well shaped head, hazel eyes, regular features & is a man of native talent & force of character. Was ordained a Presbyter. Ruling Elder at Broken Arrow 7 Sept 1879—

A large anthill

12 miles South Okmulgee on Kansas & Texas trail— Red anthill—1 ft high, 7 ft across to outer edge, 21 ft in circumference— Gravel covered & gravel stones 3 times size of ants brought out of the house— Saw one ant carrying grasshopper head 5 times his size— They attacked me as I tore down their house & I had to

stop & fight— One bit my hand & one my ankle, felt like bee sting—

Ponies with black birds on their backs. Jackass on prairie off from ponies his ears looking like a buzzard lighting on a mules head—
Mound—10 miles south of Okmulgee, 100–125 ft? high—one side steep & other gradual slope & on crest an earth work appearance

---

Stopped at pool of water where the ten yr. old boy & man were drowned last Tuesday week.
1st Tale. shallow 2 ft water, hole in man's body, boys head crushed, Going to Texas
2nd Man's wife along, distressed, En route to Mo. water deep
3rd Boy was drowning, his father jumped in, boy caught him around waist & both drowned
    Motive at first seemed robbery & last was paternal affection— I found the poles which were used to pull the bodies out & measured the water & was satisfied it was deep enough to drown a man

Varied accounts of a recent disaster

Took dinner 19 mi. south of Okmulgee at Col Robinson's place. He gave it & 200 cattle to McKillep to marry his daughter (enciente) they say—McK. was keeping an orphan girl elsewhere at same time— No marriage law & badly needed—
    A white family was on the place. A widow Meeks, a grown son sick with chills & fever, two single & one married daughter. They came from Arkansas & Cherokee in February. Daughter married an Indian Grayson (mixed with Negro). He is now under charge of stealing they say.
    Mrs Meeks is a Baptist. Gave us a good dinner, biscuit, butter, (fresh & good) butter milk, coffee & cream, jerked beef & bacon. Would not accept pay. We read (I) & Bro Broch prayed before leaving & I thought the girls showed some feeling—

Need for marriage law in territory

Travelers take meals with families along way

They had a cooking stove, & I see many as I travel —some flowers, touchmenots & marigolds. #Saw some geraniums at Norman's above Okmulgee#

Bought 14 yds calico & left at Turner & Harrisons store for the 2 little girls who cooked dinner for us. Their mother, Mrs Norman was sick. She is a grandaughter of Wetherford the Creek chief who fought Jackson—

Preacher expelled
for impropriety

Passed a cabin 18 miles south of Okmulgee. "Who lives there?"
Bapt. Preacher, Indian, white wife little Negro in her— He was under Norther Bd. One day he told an Indian he might sleep with his wife for 2 bushel of pecans & they xpelled him from the Church— Now he charges 4 bits!
   "O tempora. O, mores"

Bro. Beekin's little boy Sumner quite sick with cholera morbus. Drank water yesterday out of pool in a dry creek & dead muscles were in it. & then eat fresh meat. Having involuntary actions while asleep at 11. oclock. AM. Sept. 10th

Miltonic sunset
at Wewoka

Reached Wewoka. Benson & Haisha's store, on Txas road—35 miles south of Okmulgee, at sundown Sept 9th 1879. Setting sun on prairie looked like globe of fire, all his beams shorn as Milton describes the "sun new risen shines through the horizontal misty air shorn of his beams"—

Commercial credit
transactions

They sell calico 12 yds to $. They pay 50 cts per 100 freight from R.R. & about $1.50 per 100 from St. Louis. Prices of goods are very reasonable—at Okmulgee & at Wewoka— Most of the trade is on a credit. Merchants advance half the value of cattle in goods & pay balance on delivery of cattle when the value is agreed on— Percentage of bad debts not large— Berkshire hogs & Durham *cattle & grade Cotswold sheep* are seen frequently. Occasionally a "razorback hog" a la Ga. breed—is seen dashing from roadside like a racehorse with a loud—"goof, goof"!

———

Sept 10. 1879—
At Wewoka Camp Ground—only a few came in yet. Arbor about 35 x 80 ft. Built with posts covered by poles & prairie grass, seats made of puncheons laid on logs—a few benches brought from the Bapt. Church right at the arbor. Church 20 x 30 & 10 ft high made of upright puncheons like a picket fence in Ga —stripped with oak boards & covered oak boards—

Wewoka Camp Ground: arbor and membership

Number of members at Wewoka Church 86— Rev. Mr. McCombs, preaches here and lives 40 miles distant, preaches also at Tuskeegee— McCombs was the last pastor—& the Church paid him nothing. Some of the members are in good circumstances. Benson & [illegible] Harjo—deacons.

Slept splendidly in a bedstead under Bro David Benson's arbor about 30 x 50. He has a wall tent bought in St. Louis. Cost $9. 10 x 12.
8 camps here now—
Joseph Harjo = in Indian
Coony—Harjo = means a
Harjo = crazy
Coony = polecat—

Met a man the other day named "Chewata-fixico", means a "Goat-without-a heart."

———

Dave McCombs flock are surpassed. He had 24 sheep, 14 ewes & 10 rams. "Goug" Childres told me he saw a flock a few days ago containing 12 sheep, 1 ewe, & 11 rams.

———

An amusing scene—
Benson's little boy *"Dr Williams"* 3 yrs old—was dressed in a shirt on night of my arrival. Next morning I heard a protracted scream & continuous crying. I looked around & there stood the manly little Indian pulling at his clothes & trying to get them off. His

Indian sartorial preference at age 3

mother had dressed him in a bran new suit of brown cloth—coat & breeches & he determined not to go back on his forefathers costume.

Fife's store and clerk's residence

Passed a store about 10 miles from Wewoka owned by Judge James Fife, one of the Judges of the Supreme Court of the Cherokee Nation. The store was about 12 x 20 & made like a stockade, upright posts, with the cracks covered with oak boards— The door was shut at 4 P.M. The clerk lived in a log cabin nearby 10 x 12 made of logs with the cracks chinked with mud & straw, & a porch of poles with oak brush on top.

Not long ago the clerks wife was accidentally killed in a strange way. Her husband left a loaded pistol at the house. She took it up to shoot at a hawk & it went off in her hands & shot her through the body— A little child ran to the store, told the clk. He went & found her mortally wounded & she died next day—

Meeting with Major Vore

Met Maj. Vore, clk for the Indian agt. He has been here long & is indispensable to the various agts & is consequently all ways kept in the office near Musco-gee— I talked with him last night & this morning & learned many facts about the Indians. He is said to be the best posted man in the Creek Nation.

He thinks the Indians have not been fairly dealt with by U. S.

Drafting a marriage law

Told Bro Buckner that Mr. Robinson wished the Assotn to pass resolutions asking the Council in Oct.

to pass a marriage law. He replied "All right I'll have you appointed on the comtee & you can draft a marriage law now & have it & a memorial ready"—

Indian Doctors.

    Dr. K. O. Cutler, a young & very intelligent physician practiced 6 yrs among Choctaws & Txans near line & has been near Wewoka about 3 mths. He related the following: "About a month ago I was called to visit a child sick with intermittent & remittent fever. It was an Indian family & an Indian doctor about 25 yrs old was there blowing medicine. He had one leaf of poison oak & some sumac leaves & crabgrass in a vessel & with a cane he was blowing in the pot of water where these leaves were. Then he took the water & instructed the mother to sprinkle the child with it. He also took a little bit of hog meat, put it on a sharp stick & while mumbling some words, he pushed the meat up on the stick towards the point little by little till it reached the end & he then took it in his hands, walked backwards with the meat in his hand & threw it over his shoulder. He told the mother of the child that it had "Hog-sickness" & that it would recover."

    "I informed the mother that all this foolishness would do no good— She was disinclined to let me administer medicine. I told her I would drink a quart of the Indian medicine, that it was of no value & harmless. She would not consent. Finally I told her to try my medicine & if it did not benefit the child in two hours I would yield to the Indian doctor. She let me administer medicine & soon informed me to go ahead. I cured the child".

    "Another case. I was passing a house, went in & I & another doctor diagnosed the cases. I said this child will die, the second child will die if not treated, the third was not so sick. An Indian doctor was blowing medicine for them. The father trusted in the Indian doctor & refused to let me even give him any medicine— The first child died, & the second & then the

Dr. Cutler's experiences: modern medicine vs. the medicine man

Three children die after medicine man treatment

father came to me. I went & examined the child & told him it was useless that the child would die that night. It did die. The Indian stuck to the Indian doctor till his children were nearly all dead— They had *whooping cough*. When I practiced among the Choctaws 6 yrs I never saw medicine *'blowed'*. But here among the full bloods it is common. The more intelligent have left it off."

Maj. Vore spoke up & said "When I first remember, this Indian treatment was practiced more generally but has moved west."

Dr. Buckner said "Bro T—suppose you had chills & fever 14 months, had tried quinine, blue moss, & everything in the world that our white doctors could suggest, would you then try the Indian doctor?"

"Well, I might".

Curative value of "Rabbit pills"

With a laugh, Bro B. said "Well, thats what I did. An old Indian over 90 yrs old came to see me after I had chills 14 mths & said he could cure me. He was very old, his toes were worn off he was so old—He said 'Rabbit pills' would cure me & what do you think, I actually swallowed 6 'Rabbit pills' "

"Did they cure you?"

"Why, no, of course not."

Well if a doctor of Divinity acts that way what can be expected of a rude unlettered Indian.

Sheep saffron

"But Dr. Cutler does sheep saffron do any good? You know its a common physic in the States among the old ladies?"

"No, none in the world. They usually give it in hot water & the water alone would do as well."

Travelling King

Prof Doughty spoke up & said "Well, I'm accustomed to hemmorhage at the nose & have bled a gallon. I fainted three different times one day. I tried every known remedy. Corded my arms, held them up & actually tied them up. One day I tried the Indian doctor. He gave me a medicine made of the 'Travelling King' a species of dogwood (or willow). It did no good that I could see"—

The Indian dogs.

Dogs have sense. They learn languages. Doughty had a little dog named Jack. "When I first came out here" said Doughty "I would say 'Jack get out' & away Jack would run— I boarded with an Indian family & they would make a noise with their lips like the noise we make when we call pigs 'tschick, tschick' & say '*Osus chay*' & all their dogs would run out of the door. Jack would look up & wag his tail. The little boys would say 'Osus-chay' & Jack wouldn't run. 'Whack' they hit Jack & away he scooted. Pretty soon when they cried out 'Osus-chay', Jack was the first dog to get out & strange to say he forgot his mother tongue for when I would say 'Get out' Jack would lie there in the corner, but let that Creek warwhoop sound '*Osus-chay*' & Jack would travel for his health".

Indian dogs' linguistic adjustment

A Bit of Romance.

This afternoon a thin old man drove up in a wagon drawn by two little bay ponies. A little boy sat beside him—

He inquired for Dr. Buckner's tent & drove to that point. Dr. B. met him & sung out "Bless my life. Here's E. L. Compere. Bro Compere how do you do" & they shook & shook & laughed for joy.

"Jump out & be at home with us."

Bro B. stepped to his tent where sister B. was fanning little Dr. Sumner.

"Wife, who do you reckon is out here? Bro Compere your old sweetheart."

"No, it is not. It is Lee Compere his brother. Now stop that, will you?"

"Bro Compere he[re']s my wife."

They met. She was not happy. She was engaged to him 20 yrs ago & Bro B cut him out & this was their first meeting since. Here she sat Mrs. Buckner with a girl 14 yrs old, one 13, & three boys 6 & 6, twins & one 3.

Such is life—

Dr. Buckner's wife meets old sweetheart

"Who is this friend Bro B"

"Why this is Bro Compere. He went 4 yrs to Mercer & graduated with Mummi. He's not so old. 19 yrs ago he was a young man. He is a "Hygienic doctor" & will not eat meat &c & I told him yrs ago he would starve himself & children to death & now see how old & thin & haggard he looks?"

"How far has he come to the Association?"

"From Sebastian County Ark. At least 150 miles."

"I am so glad he's come, dear Bro Compere. His father was a Missionary among the Creeks in 1827 & 1828. The son of a Missionary. Dear Bro Compere, I'm so delighted who could have thought it".

"Hush, Mattie. I do not wish to hear any more of this foolishness"—

"Mama, he was your old sweetheart"— & the children had their fun & the young brethren told the Indian women & sister Buckner's old sweetheart was the centre of observation that evening#

Heavy postage for "special delivery"

Wrote to Dr. W. H. McIntosh & Bro Eugene Levering, Balt. Md. about stocking the Bapt Mission House at once. Wrote out a telegram. Hired a little boy, Tom Watson to ride to Eufaula & carry the letters & another to my wife & the telegram. Agreed to pay him $3.00. He promised to get there by 12 tonight, & started about 2 o'clock. 50 miles. He hunted up his little iron grey pony & away he went on his 100 mile ride— Rather heavy postage however—

Excessive drought at Wewoka

At 6 P.M. Wednesday Sept 10, '79. No Indians came in today. Bro B. says it is very unusual & assigns the drouth as the cause. Maj Vore says "only 4 rains this year & never knew Wewoka dry before in 40 yrs".

I traveled from north of Arkansas river since Monday at 9 A.M. & only crossed 3 running streams. 1 Ark river, 2 Deep Fork, & 3 North Fork of Canadian river#

Sept 11. 79

Went to Benson's spring to bathe. It was a well about 12 ft deep— His bee gums were made of gum logs about 4 ft long & some had inch auger holes (one & two) about 10 inches from bottom. The bottoms had mud dobbed around them & planks on top also dobbed & a rock on the plank.

Some were box gums with a smaller top about 10 inches square & were suspended between two strips about 2 ft from the ground—

Benson's primitive apiary

Hickory withes are suspended from ceilings on porches &c as hooks to hang the water buckets on to "keep water cool" they say, & also to keep dogs out I reckon.

At meetings when a brother is called on to pray they say "Brother please lead us in singing & prayer"

They all rise & the brother "lines out" a song, usually a long one & while singing the last verse they all turn around in their places & at the close of the song, they all kneel & he leads in prayer. When the brother "lines out" two lines, they begin singing almost as soon as he begins "lining out", & always before he finishes giving out—

Assotn by appointment should have been organized at 10 AM Wednesday, it was postponed till evening, then till Thursday at 9 AM & now at that hour from my seat under Bro Benson's arbor I count 7 brethren at the "Large Arbor". Brethren Buckner, Vore, Jennings (White), Billy McCombs & 3 other Indians—

Sister Buckner is considerably teased about Bro Compere#

"Lining out" the hymns

Good sermon by Bro E. L. Compere "Fear not little flock, for it is yr Father's good pleasure to give you the Kingdom."

Christs flock small in the world, in country generally, in this section at Wewoka. In time of Jesus &

Bro. Compere's reassuring sermon; his background in Georgia now, but Fear not &c. He is our Father & *will*, yes will *give*, not sell us the Kingdom—

Dr. Buckner introduced Rev. E. L. Compere, said his father was a teacher in 1826 in Ga among the Creeks, & afterwards a preacher. At first Creeks opposed him & once whipped a crowd of negroes who was listening to the father of Bro Compere. One old negro still lives who remembers this whipping: Bro C. had a brother named "Tomachichi" after the Indian whom Oglethorpe carried to England with "Mary" & had a sister named "Muscogee" & had spent many years preaching & laboring for the Cherokees.

Justice McIntosh, a vigorous spiritual leader of wild Wichitas

About now Bro John McIntosh & Bro James Factor ride up. Bro McIntosh is the Chief Justice of the Supreme Court of the Muscogee Nation & a Bapt. preacher & now laboring among the Wild tribes— Wichitas & 8 other bands numbering about 1700. In answer to questions he told me he had baptized 36 in all & now had 2 churches with a membership of 51.

"These Indians" said Bro Vore "in 1840 used to ask for blacksmithshops to make hoes for the women to work with & arrows for the men to hunt with, afterwards for teachers & in 1873 they petitioned for teachers to tell them more about that Great Spirit, that they were tired of the *Sleepy* teachers (Quakers) & Bro John McIntosh was sent in accordance with their own petition".

Wichitas ask for teachers

For 17 mths while Bro A. J. Holt was there among the Wichitas, McIntosh was not there— It has been about 2 yrs since he first began to preach & was the first one to preach to them said Bro Vore.

"How far is it Bro John?"

"About 180 miles".

"When did you start?"

"Monday morning".

He rode 75 miles one day & reached Seminole Agency 15 miles from Wewoka last night & preached there at Bro James Factor['s] Church for Job 19. 25-6. "For I know my Redeemer liveth" &c. Bro John picked up his Bible & said "I preached from this text last night" & pointed to Job 19. 25–6—

He describes the country as tolerably good, the people orderly & the white men bad, & says that there is a band of robbers who are marauding, plundering & murdering, that they robbed the U.S. Paymaster of 10,000$ not long ago & murdered 2 cattle traders in Aug. *Not certain.*

Desperate lack of law and order

The section over which his work xtends is about 15 miles in length. The bands live close together for protection. Bro Vore says the following bands are included among the Indians where Bro John preaches,

Make-up of McIntosh's flock

Wichitas about 4 to 500 ⎫
Wacos   "   160 ⎬ one language
Towocconies   few   ⎭

Keachis (Caddos, Anadorkos, Janai, one language)

Pennateka band of Comanches—

[Illegible]

Rev John McIntosh is a medium sized man, fine regular features, slightly Roman nose, handsome face, hazel eyes, black curling hair sprinkled with gray, straight & graceful in movement & would be a marked man in any crowd— He is about 46 yrs old, but looks younger & has a very agreeable address & affable manner.

McIntosh's appearance and background

He is a grandson of Genl Wm McIntosh, the Creek Chief whom the Creeks murdered in 1825 because of the treaty at Indian Springs—

Took dinner Sept 11. with Bro Robert Carr, son of Tom Carr, who was brother to Paddy Carr of Ga. He is an Indian in color but has Irish features, very black stiff hair, black eyes, & stout built & of medium height— He is a deacon of Wewoka Church—

At the table were Dr. H. T. Buckner, Rev. E. L. Compere, Maj. I. G. Vore, Rev. Wm McComb, Prof Doughty, Mr. Jennings, (his bro-in-law) & Rev. P. O. Broch.

Sparse attendance   No mission of Assotn in afternoon because of small
at camp meeting   attendance. Bro Buckner xpected some wild Indians
with Bro John McIntosh, but none came. "The[y]
are coming to the Fair at Muscogee 20th Sept."

Rev Daniel Tiger—a full blood Creek preacher is
now preaching in Creek at the arbor to about 50
people—

Picturesque blacks   A few old negroes who came from Florida with Semi-
from Florida   noles are here. Two are dressed in loose sackcoats
made of blue cotton stripes, broad collars, & with
turbans on their heads—one made of an old brown
shawl & another made of a large handkerchief, yellow,
blue, red, & white stripes, & barefooted—they look
picturesque— One of them has gray, or white Burnside whiskers—the old fellow with bright colored turban & his picture could grace *Frank Leslie*'s weekly— These two gentlemen from Africa, via Fla. &
Seminole Nation are about 60 yrs old—

The territorial   What a strange medley of people, are here in the In-
melting pot and   dian Terty, Caucasians, Mongolians or Indians, Afri-
the brotherhood   cans & several new breeds manufactured by judicious
of man   crossing! If there is any virtue in mixing blood here's
a fine opportunity to try the xperiment— Copartner-
ship between Shem, Ham, & Japhet, with the possibility that Shem & Ham will finally have a rich store
of xperience while sagacious Japhet will take care of
the finances of the firm—

Bro Vore gave me his version of Rev. A. J. Holts history among the so-called wild tribes & said Holt
labored there 17 mths & baptized his own child & not
a single Indian; that he denounced Rev John McIn-
McIntosh de-   tosh because he asserted that McI. rec'd *unconverted*
nounced for   persons & baptized them & because of the character
baptizing the   of his sermons.
unconverted   "How about that Bro John?" said I.

"Well, if that book is right," pointing to his Bible, "I was right. That says 'He that believeth on the Lord Jesus shall be saved'. 'He that believeth & is baptized shall be saved' & if a man tells me he believes on Jesus I will baptize him every time"—

"Well, Philip baptized the eunuch in that profession, Bro John & you cannot go wrong in following such an xample"—

Near the tents & arbor are poles on which are thin slices of fresh beef drying in the sun— I saw them slicing the beef yesterday & today you can see the beef hanging on the poles drying—

Indian mode of burying

Bro McComb said "During the war I was up on Crane Creek & I saw something up in a tree about 15 ft from the ground. I thought it was a crows nest, & I climbed up there, but I tell you I came down in a hurry. I found a dead baby up there lying on some sticks & brush"—

"Who left it there?"

"The Osages had camped near there & I think they put the child there. It was in 1863. I have often seen children's bones in hollow trees. They would cut to the hollow, put the child in & nail boards over the hole. It was generally a young baby".

I mentioned that I had heard of bodies being buried in open log pens above the ground.

He said, "Yes, I know the Indians use to bury that way".

Infant burial practice among Osages

Antediluvian relics

Bro Buckner spoke, "I was upon the Verdigris once & saw Mastodon bones, which an Indian was using to make slip-gap for a cow pen. They were 6 inches in diameter. Some one asked an Indian what they were & he said,

'The bones of Noah's steers that he used in hauling the sills of his Ark' "—

Prehistoric remains found by missionaries

"I've seen teeth of some animal of bygone ages which weighed 7 lbs. I had one of the Jaw bones".

Bro Vore said, "Yes I remember sending some of those large bones to Fort Smith. I once heard a good story as follows. Some white men were riding with a Comanche chief out in the West among petrified stumps, tree tops, logs &c, & one of the white men asked the Indian what he thought the petrifactions were.

'Why, don't you know? They are pieces of wood left by the big flood & turned to rock' "—

Souvenirs: their value and continuing appeal

Bro John McIntosh had a cow horn at his saddle bow.

"What is that horn for Bro John, To blow yr congregation up?"

"No, just for my children. When I'm dead & gone, they can say, 'My father brought this from the plains' "—

"Well, that's the way I feel. I'm trying to get some things now for my children. Can I get Moccasins out among the Wichitas?"

"O, Yes, plenty."

McIntosh's impressive prayer in Creek

Bro Danl Tiger has finished his sermon & now Bro John McIntosh is praying in Creek. His voice & tones are very affecting. I do not understand a word he says & yet I'm moved when listening. I heard him pray at Jefferson Txas in 1873 when I was Secty of Sou. Bapt. Conventn—

I can distinguish Jesus="Chesus," & "Mt Calvary"— Many of our words they simply transfer & not translate.

Jeff Davis's kinsman?

I was introduced to one of the old turbaned darkies. His name was "Davis."

"Any kin to Jeff Davis?" I asked him.

He grinned.

"You've heard of him?"

"O, Yes," & still smiled.

"When did you come out here Bro Davis?"

Bro Vore answered for him (he had introduced me), "He came in 1838 & is about 60 yrs old"—

Bro John McIntosh showed me two specimens of gypsum, discolored & yellow—& a peculiar seed pod with the end curled over like a horn & when pulled open the horn divided & looked like two horns shaped about like a goats horns, or "*Ibex*"—

Bro Compere stated in his sermon that the country covered by his Assoctn in 1866 had 7 churches & 200 members & now the same section has 4 Assotns, 130 churches, & 6000 members. About 40,000 Baptists in Ark. Has baptized 47 in his home church (1) during 13 mths

Rapid expansion of Baptist church membership in territory

Bro Buckner said that there were 2500 Baptists among Creeks & that many were in Heaven—

Had known 10 preachers to die in 2 yrs from xposure. They would preach in a close cabin by the fire & then ride miles in night air & sometimes preach under brush arbor while snow covered the earth—

---

1. Bro John McIntosh told tales about Deacon Broadanax, white doctor, felon on middle finger of right hand, at Camp meeting when Johnson a boy at old North Fork, holding out his right hand with his left at the elbow— An old sister during the Shouting saw him & grabbed his sore hand. He pulled & groaned & prayed & she squeezed the harder. He fell to the ground & finally pulled lose & shouted "O Lordy, Have Mercy. Im ruined. I'm ruined".

Amusing Indian tales

John was then a wild young man & roared with laughter ++

2. Old negro John Grayson in Ga when stars fell. Had been helpless from rheumatism 3 yrs & when stars fell he jumped up & broke through the corn field—an old negro woman yet living says "Brudder John had been down tree yrs. The stairs fell & brudder

John, he went tru de corn & de corn stalks went 'truck
truck' & brudder John he's been a well man eber
since".

---

3. Old negro was out in yard singing. It was raining
a little. He was member of the church. The folks in
the house listened & he was singing a bad song about
what a good time he used to have in Ga when he had
two wives & was a young man, & he was happy patting
his foot & singing away when "crack" comes the
lightning & hit a tree close by him & all of a sudden
he went to sing,
　"O, how I lub Jesus,
　O, how I lub Jesus"
But they turned him out of the church anyway.

"John do the Wichitas have Medicine men now?"
"O Yes."

Indians
Indian population　　"Bro Vore how many Indians are there in U.S."
in United States　　"The last report of the Secty of Interior estimated
the Indians at about 300000 & this has been the esti-
mate for years. There [are] about 55000 Indians in the
5 civilized tribes, about 20000 more in balance of the
Indian Terty & the balance of the 300000 are scattered
in the Western part of the U.S. & a few in New York,
North Carolina & other States".
　　"Have they really decreased as compared with
other people as much as some have stated?"
　　"Well I know that up to 1838 27000 Creeks were
brought out & 5000 were here before the emigration
making 32000 & before the late war I took an accurate
census & there were only 13000 Creeks".
Indian population　　"What caused the large decrease?"
declining　　"There were many causes. Exposure, small pox
swept them off fearfully soon after they came, the
war & ordinary sickness & it is only within the last few
years that the civilized tribes have been increasing.

They have learned how to take care of themselves".

"We speak loosely of the wild tribes, who are they? Is brother John McIntosh preaching to the wild tribes?"

"Well, Brother John was sent to the Wichitas & other neighboring bands in compliance with their own request some 5 or 6 yrs ago. They are not wild Indians. They cultivate the soil, most of them wear clothing like white people, a few schools, a mission & under control of the Quakers. The Comanches, Cheyennes & Sioux might be called wild tribes with more propriety than the Wichitas".

Wild Indians cultivate soil, go to school

"Did you ever know or hear since you have been out here of Cannibalism among the Indians?"

Possible cannibalism

"Yes. I have heard of two cases. Toncaways were fighting the Wichitas & during the fight a Wichita-warrior was killed. The Toncaways took his body & roasted it in the fire, the Wichitas drove them from the field & found his body in the fire."

"But perhaps he was simply thrust in the fire for revenge & they did not intend to eat him."

"O, Yes, there is no doubt from their customs in war that they intended to eat him".

"When was that?"

"Chisolm told me of it in 1857. It occurred perhaps 10 yrs before, say 1847".

"Did you know of the other case yourself?"

"Yes. One day an Indian woman came to the store on Little river & had a bone of a mans fore arm which had been made into a corn husker or 'shucking peg'. It was taken from her & inquiry decided the fact that the man had been killed & eaten. He belonged to Pawnee Maha tribe & the Kickapoos were at war with that tribe. Killed him in a fight, cut off his arm & ate it. His arm had been cut off & this woman had one of the bones. (Another woman had his penis & testicles wrapped in a rag.)"

Savagery in war

"When was this?"

"This occurred in 1847. I was living out there at the time".

Re John McIntosh—

"Good morning Bro John. They tell me you are the Missionary to the wild tribes & I wish you to tell me about them— Are they wild Indians, the Wichitas & the other bands near them?"

The Chief Justice of the Supreme Court of the Muscogee Nation, the grandson of Genl Wm McIntosh, a Baptist preacher & Missionary 250 miles from his home, smiled & said "Wild Indians? No, they are not wild— They live in houses, they have farms, some of them 300 acres in one farm. They have mowing machines, improved cultivation, wagons, buggies & cooking stoves & had a very fine Mission under the Quakers, but it was burned two years ago & one of their best scholars was burned up in the house. They are building a very fine large Mission now. It is 90 ft on one side, 60 on another in an "L" shape— It is built of lumber hauled from the R.R. They have a telegraph line, the U.S. running from there to Fort Sill 12 miles west from where I preach, then to Fort Elliot & out on the plains".

Agricultural progress in Wichita tribe

Large mission under construction

"Do they come to hear you preach?"

"Yes. The town chief makes them dress up every Sunday & go to meeting. They are fond of dressing up & wear finer clothes than we do, some of them. I often have 300 to hear me on Sunday. I pay my interpreter $1. for every sermon he translates for me".

"What salary do you get for you, your interpreter & your horse & expenses?"

"500$. I will have to give it up. I cannot afford it. My home matters are suffering".

"I should think at $1. for your interpreter for every sermon you wouldn't get rich. Have you baptized any of the leading men?"

Witchita chief baptized

"Yes, the first man I baptized was [blank] the chief of the Wichitas. Several other leading men have been converted & I lately baptized 12 converts".

"Are they quiet & orderly & peaceable?"

"Yes sir, they are. The only trouble out there is caused by bad white men roving over the country stealing horses & robbing. You know it was out near

Ft. Sill, they robbed the U.S. paymaster & killed 2 cattle drivers not long since".

"Any buffalo out there John?"

"No. They are further west & in the plains".

"When will you return to the Wichitas?"

"About a month I reckon & maybe later. I must hold the Supreme Court & I will be detained till after Council".

The Seminoles

"Good morning Bro Factor! Tell me about Bro John Juniper & yr people. You remember at Jefferson Txas you were his interpreter."

Similar progress among Seminoles

"Yes, I remember & you were the Secty of the Convention. Well, Bro John is still preaching. I am pastor of a church & preach some at other churches."

"How many Seminoles are there now?"

"About 2600 I believe."

"They are about like the Creeks I suppose, & have schools & are improving in civilization."

"Yes, we have schools & the people are getting on very well & learning the ways of the white men."

"How many preachers do you know who are preaching among the Seminoles?"

"There are Bro John Juniper, Bro Alligator, Bro Hacock, myself, & Tewih Ke (Throw him down)".

"How many Baptists?"

"About 700".

About 2500 Creek Baptists—

Strange scene. Sept. 12, 1879. Bro John McIntosh preached from text "Ye have not chosen me but I have chosen you"—a magnetic, eloquent sermon—had his audience first in tears then smiling— Full of illustration, preaches with his hands— I could not understand a word but enjoyed the sermon— The Creeks killed his Grandfather & here he was preaching to them—

McIntosh's magnetic sermon to tribe who killed his grandfather

Osceola the Seminole chief killed the whites—& here sat John Powell—a white man raised by Lucy Powell, Osceola's sister. His parents were a Spaniard & English woman & they died when he was a baby— He lives among the Seminoles, is a Baptist, an interpreter & an xhorter.

Osceola's sister
rears white orphan

Osceola's sister raising an orphan white baby to preach & sing to the Indians the white man's religion. He loves to sing & sang one of Levi Mitchells songs— (a Creek Poet, who died in Mch 1879 & who made many beautiful songs, words & tunes—) at close of Bro John's sermon—
(Get the song.)

Powell is about 35—has blue eyes—roman nose, light curly hair, medium height, stout built, & wore today a loose striped blouse—like a sack coat, wide colar & ruffles all around the edge of entire coat. Has married a Creek woman & after her death married his present wife—a Seminole, & lives in Canadian near John Juniper.

Dramatic need
for civilized
marriage law

At suggestion of Bro. Buckner I drew a resolution about a "Marriage law"— While it was pending Bro Billy McComb made a speech & referred to fact that the Creeks had no law on the subject, that the old custom had been dropped & nothing substituted. He illustrated the old law by telling about Hoyupu's cutting off the ears of his unfaithful wife & her betrayer "Bunny"—

A Creek's revenge
on unfaithful
wife and lover

Afterwards I was introduced to Hoyupu, a full blood Creek—about 35 yrs old, long straight black hair, black eyes, roman nose, a few stray hairs on upper lip & under the chin—medium height—small hands & feet—

I asked him through Bro McC about the cutting. He laughed & answered my questions.

"You cut the ears off?"
"Yes."
"Both of them, the man & woman?"
"Yes."

"How?"

"I went where they were in a house together & I had about 30 Creeks with me & we went & cut their ears off."

"Did you have both ears taken off close to the head?"

"Yes"—

"Where is the man?"

"He lives in Creek Nation yet."

"Where is the woman?"

"She lives with the man."

"What evidence did you have?"

"The man took my wife away from me & she went & stayed with him at his house."

"What is yr English name?"

"George."

"How long had you been married, George, when this happened?"

"About a year."

"You married again?"

"Yes."

"Billy tell me about this old custom?"

Billy M C: "Well, it was our law & sacredly observed & every man called on had to go. I had a chance once to go but my heart failed me."

Tribal punishment for infidelity under old law

"The husband notifies the men & they select several strong men. They rush in, seize the man, throw him out of the house & the crowd begin beating him with sticks & beat him till he is senseless & then with a dull knife they cut, or saw the ears off— They wont use a sharp knife but will hack it. They say cutting is too good. They saw the ears off—"

"And the woman?"

"They do her same way. Sometimes they get sorry & do not beat her so badly, but the law required them to beat till senseless & then the ears were cut off. The husband had the right to say whether a part or all of the ears must be taken off."

"What was the substance of yr speech today Billy?"

"I told them about the old law & that since that was left off, we had no law whatever to protect our daughters & that a man could live with them awhile & abandon them at pleasure as is frequently done & urged them to petition the Council to pass a marriage law."

John Powell song—
Made by Levi Mitchell a Creek Poet who died in Mch 1879—
[Remainder of page left blank, indicating that Tuggle evidently intended jotting down the words of the song in this space but possibly failed to secure them.]

Camp meeting disrupted by heavy rain

Last night while McComb was preaching a sermon in Creek & had his audience well in hand a rain set in & lightning flashed— He was nearly through & quit— The crowd was left in the dark, as violent gusts blew out the candles & lamps & lanterns— Most of them ran into the Church & soon crowded that to overflow— I went to look after my papers, books & clothes left on my bed under the straw arbor. Some one had carried the bed in Benson's tent & the things were on it— I followed suit & there I remained— Slept in bed with my clothes on. Grayson a half breed but white, slept with me & Benson his wife & 3 children slept on a pallet— It rained hard & confusion reigned supreme in the Camp—

Indian land claims against federal government

Private Vore says the Orphan claim is $251,000.00, that U.S. owes M. Nation for 500,000 acres which they obtained over ½ as the contract was, that besides that U.S. owes for land now actually occupied by Seminoles as they are last of the right line—; that $100,000.00 paid under Treaty of 1866 to "Loyal Claimants" really came from proceeds of land due the Creeks; that the Wichitas have a good claim & that he is their agent or atty & also he is interested in a claim of 2 millions down in Texas, that Butler, Shank & members of Congress formed an *"Indian ring"* & made large sums &c.

Picture of I. G. Vore—
   Came from Pennsylvania when young & had been here since 1838—41 yrs— Fine figure, erect & has a Military bearing—wears short beard & large mustache, sandy hair reddish, fine forehead & splendid head, blue eyes & regular features & spare made—6 ft high—

Description of prominent officials: I. G. Vore

Picture of Rev Wm McComb—
   5 ft 10 in, weighs 160, dark curly hair, blue eyes, mustache, & goatee, straight nose & a well shaped head & reminds me somewhat of Byron's head— Has been a Baptist preacher some years. Supdt Public Instruction of Muscogee Nation & is now a member elect of House of Warriors. 35 yrs old, very strongly built, active & graceful in his gesticulation. He is a practising lawyer in Dist & Supreme Ct—

The Rev. Wm. McComb

Met present chief Hon. Ward Coachman—a very large heavily built man 6 ft high & weighs about 200 lbs—dark hazel eyes, black hair, thin whiskers & has a very pleasant address. I selected him in a crowd as the chief— He was dressed in dark gray suit of citizens clothes, a black felt hat & appeared about 50 yrs old—
   He thinks he has been selected—

Ward Coachman

Dr. H. F. Buckner preached a fine sermon at night Sept 12th on "Heaven the Christians Home"—"I go to prepare a place for you"—
   Good audience & the singing was melodious—

Fervent religious worship through-out the night

Sept 15. 1879
Tis now 6 AM & the Indians have been singing & praying all night long. As I watched them just now & heard their melodious songs, their heartfelt prayers,

saw their joyous faces, I was deeply impressed at such fervor, and patient worship, such prolonged supplications for mercy & blessings. At 5 Oclock just as day was breaking they were singing, slapping their hands for joy. Bro John McIntosh leading with his musical voice, the sisters happy & shaking hands, the white haired Indian albino was shouting. The horn was blown & as the blasts burst on the morning air & the grey dawn was breaking—the scene was touching. I found myself in tears—

The service began at 7 P.M. & ended 6 A.M.— Is not such fervor & zeal worthy of emulation?

Tuggle refused sight of buried sacred vessels

Sept 15.
Left Wewoka Camp Ground & Assotn 9 AM. The Indian town chief Harjo refused to let me see the old pieces of copper supposed to be shields & pieces of armor— They said the medicine man who had them in charge died before the last "Busk" & no one could dig them up; they had elected no "firemaker" or medicine man & if an *unholy* man should see the sacred vessels he would die ere he reached home, that the vessels were kept buried & only taken out at *"Busk"* & in the meantime no one could be permitted to see them. They have a tradition that the English gave these things to them during some war (perhaps 1812). No persuasion could overcome their objections, so I was compelled to leave my curiosity ungratified.

Col Wm Robinson & Betty McComb & a relative of Harjo—all tried in vain.

Camping out between Wewoka and Eufaula with motley crew

Sept 16.
Camped about half way between Wewoka Church & Eufaula— Could have gone further but had to xchange wagons— Pitched Bro Buckner's tent, cooked supper & had a pleasant evening around the camp fire— Dr. B, sister B, Mattie, Rebel, Helen, Boyce, & Sumner—Pres. Doughty, 2 negroes, Jackson with rings in his ears & Wilson, a very short black lazy negro— Such was our company. I drove the spring wagon

pulled by two gray ponies *"Dick & Bill"*, Bro B rode a fine bay mare, & the children took turn about on little *"Dixie"* a gray Indian pony with roached main & an ambling gait— I write in a creek bottom, sitting on a log right in the bottom of the creek—or where the creek usually runs. It is dry xcept pools here & there & from these stagnant looking mud holes we drank water last night— The want of good wholesome water is the curse of this lovely looking land—

I see & hear gray squirrels from my seat, hear the big woodcock, & the owls greeted me as I rose when the gray dawn was breaking & the stars were twinkling.

We are detained because the ponies "Dixie & Jack" cannot be found—having strayed off on the prairie during the night.

Reached Eufaula Sept 16. At Bro Buckners writing letters to Index, Kind Wds., Religious Heral, At. Constitution & private letters to Bro McIntosh about the Bapt Mission House & to my wife on Sept. 17.

Tuggle works on diary and letters

On 18th have been all day writing up my sketches.

This evening rode with Bro Buckner to North Fork of Canadian Passed Old North Fork town where I bought the little faun 5 yrs ago "Lilly Buckner". He told me how he lost his Journal from 1849 to 1859.

Loaned a blank book & wrote order to his wife to send Mr Rush, a half-witted white merchant, "the blank book in the trunk" & she sent the journal & a few days afterwards Rush told him that she had torn out & burnt up the writing— Indian towns used to trade through their Chiefs, whole towns sell their annuities in advance—

Buckner tells of losing journal

Tale of Rush & his brother. Rush died poor#

North Fork once in the present bed of the river. Land in cultivation 50 yrs in corn; weeds 15 ft high.

4 places on road to river saw corn ears hanging in trees & on poles. Sign—"Come to sell". "Yes, & they will want to buy before Spring".

Burr oak with large acorns in a burr looking shell.

White oak runners 3 ft high & filled with acorns. Hogs straddle bushes & pull down & eat acorns—

Went on island below the ford & took a bathe. Saw a bald eagle, two blue cranes, & one white crane.

Describes unusual rock formations

Peculiar rocks on island & above the ford, one a reddish brown flat rock with round spots covered with dimples on them.

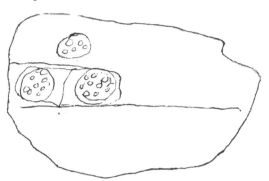

Looks like lava from Vesuvius to me. Same kidney iron ore, & same volcanic looking rocks, [illegible] stone, Sand stone &c—

Met oxcart, two spotted little steers, man & thin hatchet faced woman, & 4 or 5 little half starved children, peeping from under the wagon cover.

Bro. Buckner and the "veiled lady"

Write out Buckner's politeness to a veiled woman at Church. When he first came 1849. He wished to set an xample to some young men educated in the States. D. N. McIntosh, Bony Hawkins, Ben Marshall, National Treasr & some other bloods. The lady rode up finely dressed & riding a fine bay horse. Dr B. helped her off the horse, & took her horse & hitched it. As the lady walked off to the arbor crowded by people, she raised her veil & behold she was a *colored* lady. The boys roared & it was a standing joke for years. This woman was a concubine of old Col. Logan—

Judge Stidham's account of bribery

Sept 20th.

Took tea & stayed all night 19th at Judge G. W. Stidham, Eufaula. Married a white woman in Washington over 20 yrs ago; his first wife was a daughter of Paddy Carr. Paddy married the widow of Hawkins son in law of Genl Wm McIntosh & H. was killed in 1825 with McI. Stidham says McIntosh was bribed & recd 25000$ for his land, much more than the real value. Dr H. F. Buckner says that yrs ago he lectured in Brooklyn, N.Y., & an old man told him that he was cashier of a Ga Bank in 1825 & paid—thousand dollars to McI. to sign the treaty of 1825.

and death of
William McIntosh
in 1825

Judge Stidham says McI was not the Chief & had no authority to sign the treaty.

Stidham is 62 yrs old, tall, stout, dark hair, dark eyes, grey mustache & walks very erect. Has been a merchant all his life & is now & lives in a very large new framed house, well furnished, piano &c. Has three married daughters, all married under 18 & one about 14, whom he thinks of sending to States to school. Has one son Lee, very dark by his Carr wife, & George about 20 just finished a course of Medical lectures at Nashville. Dr. W. H. Bailey married Stidham's daughter Ella, 17 yrs old, about a year ago. She is very pretty, black restless stunning eyes, long black hair, & regular features, sings & plays well on piano, & is said by Dr. Buckner to be a good girl. Thinks she might join Baptist Church. Dr. Bailey a wild young fellow, plays on fiddle, banjo, drinks & has lately fallen heir to a fortune (180,000?) in N.Y. His uncle died. He was not at Stidham's last night. They put me in Dr. Bailey's room. It was well furnished, marble top bureau & washstand &c. Some pictures & books & a banjo. Mrs. Bailey was there. She was attending school in the States when Dr. Bailey about 26–8 insisted that he had waited long enough & they married. Tis said he neglects her since the fortune &c.

Stidham's family
and friends

Stidham is a member of present & next council & wishes to be chosen a delegate to Washington I think. We went over several of the Creek treaties together#

Sept 20.
Bro Buckner told me of an Indian woman running to him when he first came out. She was screaming & he

"Long scratch":
harsh punishment
for adultery

without knowing what was the matter raised a puncheon in his floor & let her in a cellar. Some Indians soon came up with long poles—but went off. He let her out in the evening. He afterwards learned that she had committed adultery & they wished to give her the "long scratch" whip her & cut her ears off. The "long scratch" was administered with a shark's jaw & the victim was stripped & scatched from head to heels with the teeth on the back—

"Did you ever see in yr 30 yrs sojourn, a really beautiful Indian girl, full blood?"

"No sir, not even handsome. Their work was so hard. Beating sofkey with 10 lb pestles is like black smithing. They are improving & not working their women so hard# I heard Maj Vore say he had seen women carry turns of wood—a one horse load apparently of dry wood on their backs with a band around their forehead"#

Tuggle learns of manuscript on customs, traditions

Dr. Buckner told me an old manuscript prepared by Grant Lincecum who was once Choctaw agent in Miss. Said to be a valuable collection old customs & traditions &c. Lincecum is dead— Wrote about 30 yrs ago perhaps?

See M.P. Roberts editor of Indian Journal at Muscogee, whom Bro B. thinks has possession of the manuscript—

Dr. H. F. Buckner is working at odd times on His "Reminiscences" 30 yrs among the Indians & has written up to 1853—only 4 yrs. (26 yrs left.) & up to book three, a division of a volume. Trying to embrace it in one volume. What has to be written will cover over *100 pp.*

Know of no book with Creek customs, traditions xcept "Pickets History of Ala".

Buckner's hospitality extended to all sorts

Rev John McIntosh, William McIntosh an elder half brother & his young wife been married about one month, & she had an illegitimate bastard child 2 yrs old—came to Bro Buckner late Saturday evening on way to Eufaula Church. They went on before sun down to camp at church— They saw 3 deer while coming here. Tramp came in, old blue eyed & white whiskered— Was no tramp spoke contemptuously of "these tramps who go about & wont work xcept at their trades". Remained all night— Would pick cotton, had never picked any, from Ohio & going to Texas, but not hunting work down there, some mysterious mission of course—

Sept 21.
Bright sunny Sunday morning. We are going to Eufaula Baptist Church some four miles distant today— The air is balmy & a little cool—

The Tramp asked Bro Buckner "What is my bill" & fumbled in his pocket. "Nothing". Still he insisted on giving him half a dollar in silver & Bro B. took it & said "Well I'll put it in the contribution collection at church today". He felt of it, rattled it on the porch & said "Why its pewter". The tramp was disgusted, & as he walked off said "Here's a good quarter. I've got nothing less than five dollars xcept this"—

"The old rascal is passing counterfeit money on the Indians" said Dr. B. Exit Tramp.

Tramp tries to pass bogus coins

Went with Dr. B. to Eufaula Bapt. Ch. 3 miles west of E. A log house, upright logs, chinked with mud & oakboards over the cracks & ceiled & walled inside, the walls of boards & the ceiling of pine. House 20 x 35 & will seat 175. Was full & about that number outside. Funeral day. Rev John McIntosh began ¼ after ten & talked nearly an hour & read 5 or 6 pages of last words of *Mary Whitlow*, 10 yrs old. I thought he was done, but he sang a song & took his text "I am the resurrection & the life &c" & preached an hour & a half. Then a few minutes recess & Rev Washington Cunard preached another funeral—

Nothing to eat on ground for the audience—the visitors anyway— A crowd of Indians, one old fellow

Funeral sermons at Eufaula Baptist Church

wore long black hair, a handerchief on his head, a red striped hunting shirt & over the red one he wore a green & white mantilla or rather another shirt with the sleeves loosely thrown over his shoulders. He had gold earrings—

Washington Cunard was named Perryman, but changed his name. He has a fine head & a very high forehead—kin to Ga. Perrymans, says Bro B. Old Indian preacher with a face like Tecumseh's pictures sat near me. "Was a *Mormon* preacher & I baptized him".

I was thirsty & asked "where do you get water".

"A spring ½ mile down in bottom".

I went & found a barrel sunk in the bed of a dry creek—half full of very muddy & stagnant water & from this spring the audience was watered—

Tuggle visits Asbury Mission

Sept 22, 79. Asbury Mission.

Visited. Met Prof W. N. Martin Supdt appointed by Southern M. E. Br. & they pay his salary. 70 pupils now. 80 allowed & Muscogee Nation pays 70$ board & tuition.

Daily routine, rise & have prayers at 6 AM. Breakfast, then work 1¼ in field, then School till 4 PM. with one hour intermission at noon & then field till sundown— Will make 35 bushels corn per acre this year (usually 50) & 15 bales cotton. Thinks cotton suits the land & the boys like it. Will clear 500$ this year in farm he thinks. Nation pays well—

Amazement at development of Muscogee grammar

Looked Buckner's grammar. Wonderful that a nomadic race, without literature should have a grammar language. Conjugate verbs, 10 tenses, about same moods as English, decline nouns, adjectives, prepositions & some of the adverbs & even conjunctions— Surely a civilized race made the language, & here is a mound worth xploring & surpassing the dirt mounds of the moundbuilders.

Write out Vore's views on moundbuilders, Buckners seem about like Conant's—

Mission House, 30 x 110, portico in front length of house. 3 stories high, eat, sleep & teach in same building; a little house in yard for hospital—new plank fence around the yard—grass & locust trees— House cost $10,000 & built of brick—very ugly, looks like a factory.

Sept 23, 79
Slept on mattress on floor with Dr B. last night at U.S. Agncy, 3 miles from Muscogee on "Moccasin Hill". Moccasin tracks been on a rock long time— made by Indians—big & little.
    Maj. I. G. Vore—clk—
    Col Jno Q. Tufts, Agt—
2 horse buggy 3$ pr day— Rev Leslie—black wife— pastor, 5000$ residence. Simon Brown's ferry over Arkansas beach on north side 100 yds wide & heavy timber# Bro Buckners reminiscences. "Fosters Church," Foster's house gone— "Coming back to another planet"— Tried to make acknowledgements for being in war. "Didn't steal horse & lands like Simon Brown from his mistress"—

Tallahassee Mission House 30 x 100—brick— A success—the farm pays—will return perhaps $1200.00 to Nation this year—
    Passed Big John McIntosh's, cousin of Bro John. Son of Roland McI— Big flop hat, striped coat, negro 200 lbs on a little barefoot pony guided us across the Verdigris river—very low & rough— Mr Robertson gave me a part of a petrified elephant tooth found in the Verdigris about 1 mile above Van's Lake— Went near the lake—passed Gibson station & reached Mr Norman's near the mounds about 2 PM. Went to work on the largest mound about 25 ft high—giant oak growing on edge of it, hundreds of years old—
    Norman came with *his rifle* & stopped us, *cursed*, "By God, who gave you authority to dig &c". Soon quieted him. Bro B. talked to him in cornfield, he refused to come to us— He evidently thought we were hunting for gold & wished us to *divide*. At night Bro Buckner went to a meeting 1 mile distant—a Meth-

Mound diggings halted by rifle-toting resident

odist service, not an Indian present, & Norman came up & shook his hand during the call for mourners & said "I want to meet you in heaven." At 3 P.M. with his rifle he wanted to meet him on earth & did so—with his rifle!

Mound diggings near Verdigris and Grand rivers

Mounds—near Roland McIntosh's about 6 miles from mouth of Verdigris—others at Fort Davis on Arkansas 6 miles from Muscogee. Genl Pike put his flag staff on a large mound during war— Dr Hams is digging into one now— These mounds are about ½ mile from Grand river. Dirt seems surface dirt—either was wet when they put it there or they made it wet as the mound was erected—

In digging the large lumps came out & look like dried wet dirt—

Dug about 2 hours, Sept 23 in evening, started a horizontal shaft 4 ft wide in the side about half way up the mound. Say 50 ft from edge of mound & about 15 ft high vertically. Stepped the mound & from ground to top about 100 ft & about 25 ft high— Regular potato hill, the dirt was piled as steep as it would stand & the top is about 4 to 6 feet broad & slopes evenly all around— Up to 10 AM 24th Sept I & Dr Buckner with a little volunteer aid ran the shaft about 12 ft horizontally & about 8 ft deep from highest up-

Diggings largely unsuccessful, no labor available

ward edge— Found a piece of human bone 6 inches long & a large warriors bed, perhaps arm or leg bones, also charcoal about 4 ft from outer surface. Offered a dollar pr day for hands in vain— My hands are blistered—no royal road to knowledge—not with a shovel & grubbing hoe.

Another mound low flat but large in circumference, the edge touching the large mound & several modern Indian graves on it. The neighbors say ten years ago they found a double handed jug & some little articles of pottery in one of the smaller mounds while digging a grave—

Bro Buckner is satisfied the large mound is the one he visited 20 yrs ago. No holes in it, however— The large mound is about ½ mile west of the Grand river, 7 miles east of Gibson Station, & 12 miles from the mouth of Grand river. It is surrounded by a plain, but broken prairie & timbered ridges within a half mile—

Walked with Bro Buckner to Grand river, very low but clear & beautiful. Splendid timber in bottom. Yellow cottonwood 5 ft in diameter, walnut, hackberry, sycamore &c— Burr oak but no mast this year of consequence because of the drouth— Gravel beds 100 yds wide & 1 mile long. Indications of levees, & canals, in river bottom.

Beautiful timber in river bottoms

Negroes very idle & roguish near **Gibson Station** & steal for living. At least 1000 in 10 miles of Muscogee & up Arkansas, Verdigris & Grand rivers— Great complaint, robbed the train while stopping at Gibson Station not long ago & a fight resulted, 20 shots xchanged# Think our guide was lame yesterday from the skirmish—#

Report of a train robbery and shooting skirmish

Alone at Norman's. All gone to meeting, & Dr Buckner just left for Muscogee 12½ Oclock Sept 24. Am tired & blisters on my hands digging—

Norman came from Tenn. Cleveland 7 yrs ago, his wife has Indian blood in her! Enough to get land on— Met Aunt "Susie Harris" fine looking old white lady from Cherokee Co. Ga— Has Indian blood in her & came out a few yrs ago. Invited me to visit her son Dr Harris, 7 miles from Muscogee. He is digging into a mound there near Ft Davis (named after Jeff) by Pike during War— She knew some Tuggles in Ga— The dean of women can trace family relations back to Adam! Blood will tell—

Benefits in having Indian blood

Bro Buckner told me that his father & mother separated when he was a baby, that she decided to go back to his father & she hid him out several weeks on prairie & elsewhere from her kinfolks who opposed her return— He met an old woman a few yrs ago at whose house he was hid at 7 yrs of age & had never

More light on Buckner's background

seen her afterwards & he kissed her as his first love & told his 2nd wife of it!—

E. L. Compere jilted [illegible] wife—& Bro B. thinks the Lord has punished him for it. He does not get along well with Mrs Compere it seems.

Sept 25, 1879.
My birthday, 38 by the grace of God— Thank Him for his Providence which has followed me from my cradle to this hour.

Started a shaft from the top of the mound—

Mr Norman went to the Revival last night & "professed religion"—

Diggings continued
with little success

Sank the shaft in top by 12 Oclock. 6 ft deep— 5 x 3½ size shaft— Striking soft places—as if something had been buried & decayed, the dirt is very fine, soft & greasy, with white bits here & there—one white round ball about size of an English pea was found— it broke easily—was hollow—another dark cup like formation (Tumble bug?) about size of an ordinary thimble—a little larger & brittle—full of very fine dirt—

Only one man to help me—16 yrs old—white boy—

Norman asked me to have prayer with his family— I read 8th chap Romans & prayed with them—

Sunk shaft about 11 ft deep, occasional holes & soft places & whitish pieces, very small, little decayed bones—

Sept 26, 1879. On mound before sun up—& was there about sun down— Fine temple for Sun worship— Mound 90 ft from upward slope, but 100 to 110 from where it rises above level of prairie—540 ft in circumference from 90 ft below top—& by measurement 25 ft high— Hired men not here at 7½ AM.

My man of yesterday Robert Brunnet professed religion last night. He was cursing at sun down—

Sunk the shaft about 21 or 22 feet. No discovery— Found charcoal at the lowest point. Night stopped us. About 14 ft down struck a hollow about size of a mans body, some small pieces of bone, apparently burnt, & pieces of burnt flint & muscle shell. Several smaller holes running into side of the shaft— The dirt indicated decayed animal & vegetable matter— Small round charcoals, as if a piece of arrow & pieces of flint were found—

Digging and religion didn't mix

Sept 27. At work on several smaller mounds today. Dug into a flat mound in Grand bottom little over ¼ mile west of river & just on edge of 2nd bottom. Found a beautiful wheel, then another wheel, then a broken pot, then a piece of lead ore, & then a stone-pipe all within 2½ to 3 ft from surface & on top of the mound. The mound is about 5 ft high, 30 feet from plain to top—in the woods—location, 20 miles west of Tolequah, 12 miles from mouth of Grand, ¼ mile west of Grand, & 5 miles from Creek line, & in Cherokee country— Opened a grave, grown person & buried perhaps 20 yrs ago—

Dug into a small flat mound near the other, 2½ feet high, & found a body buried perhaps 40 yrs ago & a small flint arrow head— This mound might have been heaped over the body—

J. H. Baugh
Choctaw, (RR) M K T.
Cherokee N. I. T.

Results at last: several artifacts, adult skeleton

Will sell books#

To Gibson Station—on Baughs gray mare. Willie Norman riding behind—

"What are you going to do with yr quarter?"
"Have my picture tooken at the Fair".
Prairie fire night of 27th Sept. I saw the blaze,

Spectacular prairie fire, water shortage

magnificent—about 3 mile distant— Cobb left church
in alarm—it came to his blacksmiths shop & near Capt
Jacksons— Rode through the burnt space— Burnt
Jacksons fences last year, Normans hay &c—

Freight train— No water—ate ice—melted it in
cup— Tranlee had been at Gibson Station from ten
to 3 PM without water & then found none on the
train—

Met Maj I. G. Vore & Col Tufts agent at Muscogee & went to Agency 3½ miles in Majs double
buggy pulled by 2 black ponies— Jumped prairie
chickens on road "Our chickens we are saving them"
said Col Tufts.

Sunday Sept 28. At Agency—

Whole bed to myself— At Normans slept with a
sweaty carpenter & turned my back & scratched bed
bugs all night— 7 of us slept in one room about
12 x 15!—

Saw 3 prairie fires in distance last night—from agncy
—about 12 to 15 miles off—looked like moon rising
till flames shot above horizon—

Creek-black couple minister to black congregation

Went with Bro I. G. Vore to Muscogee. Met Rev
R. A. Leslie & went to his S.S. Just starting. He distributed Bibles & testaments. All colored—about 25
present. Sang badly— Went to his residence. His wife
is coal black. She was raised in Ohio & taught school
in New Orleans & south after war 10 yrs. Leslie married her in N.O. in 1874— Her name was Nellie Coles.
He is 38—a full blooded Creek. Went to Tallahassee

Both are well-educated

Mission School, to Commercial College at St. Louis—
Was in Southern army, was captured & imprisoned at
Alton Ill. & to escape to South enlisted in Northern
army but never got South— Studied Hebrew & Greek
in N.O., taught Freedmens School in U.S. Agency
Buildings in 1878–9 to June 30, & Creek Nation gave
over 2000$ for 40 boys schooling— He is now getting
400$ salary from Northern Baptist Board as a
preacher & lately organized a Bapt. Colored Church

with 40 members & contemplates building a Church.
His low stature, black eyes & hair, regular features—
nose a little Roman or aquiline & wears Episcopal
preachers coat, buttoned to chin. Mrs L. [w]as raised
an Episcopalian. She is peculiar. Her hair is long &
somewhat like an Indians but very wavy, though she
is black— She is educated & behaves very ladylike.
Was playing on a Rosewood piano in a nice carpetted
parlor & gave me an xcellent dinner with some white
boarders. She did not sit at the table—

Met Bushyhead—Chief elect of Cherokees— Is very
stout, 5 ft 10, very black small eyes, black hair & mustache & goatee, ruddy complected, & will weigh over
200— Dressed in dark blue navy goods, & black felt
hat— I quoted Falstaff & he replied with Hamlet.
About ¾ white, I guess—
   "Loaves & fishes," he said were the essence of
Indian politics.

*Indian chief
quotes* Hamlet

Talked 20 minutes from 24th Psalm to Leslies Congregation—about 50 to 60 at 3½ P.M. & went out with
Maj Vore to Agency.

Leslie thinks English should be taught to Indians—
also that 5 civilized tribes were always ahead of the
other Indians & were Aztecs from Mexico—

Sept 28, 79. Left Agency & went to Muscogee &
roomed with Maj I. G. Vore in Mrs. Highleyman's
well furnished room— Met Comanche chief Toashaway—about 60, long iron gray hair, good face—a sky
blue eye from age— Wore a large silver medal "Millard Filmore Presdt & a bust of F." Large brass earrings 2 inches in diameter—
   Met Towackanay Dave Chief of Wichitas— Also
another burly full blood Comanche with big earrings,
black piercing eyes—

*Tuggle meets
Comanche and
Wichita chiefs*

Saw Indian women fixing the tents while the men lounged around—Comanches, & [blank.]

Comanche women *very picturesque* The women ride straddle but their saddles are like pack saddles & their feet hang down only a little ways. They wore loose sacks, shawls tied around their waists & leggins all the way up made of buckskin & they wear moccasins— They look very picturesque, their long black hair flowing, red costumes. Many of the Indians wear leggins, moccasins, pleat their hair, long tail of hair hanging down their backs— Leggins with wide dew flaps & beads— Very dirty indeed—

Indian words and *English equivalents* Ashay habeet = Milky Way
Penyteky—Comanche = 2d chief
Honey eating—Comanche. His wife = Wushah— wahweet means = striking
2 boys—Comanches 10 & 14—latter half Mexican & no larger than the 10 yr old— Dress of boys. Leggins & flap-shirt, & blanket.
Ashay habeet—wore large brass earrings—& long beads drops & chain 1 ft long—
Tosh a way = (white handled knife). Teh seh weit, wife = (Refusing to come). Chap karre weit, 2d wife / Pulling you one side. His son Ar roas.
Meah quat (going about). Me chas soo wah, his wife (Tearing it).
Mah seit (Finger nails)—Woh pe, his wife = (gambling with sticks, Jack Straws)
Kah hab be waht: Running about all night.
Dont Sleep = Yeah peet ter, his wife = Coming home after sun down. E kah weit tah (going into tent), son.
Down in Asa ha beit above Penateka, Yam pa reka.
Band = Root digger.
On nah we yah = (getting the salt).
Shar ne te ker = Dog eater.
Band. An soo tine = (to be kind).
Tah che nip took who wah (Black Star). Yaht tee = wife (crying).

Kiowas—
Bah weit = Cat
Tanar za da dah = Dangerous Eagles
Cowapah Kah = Lone wolf—
Apache
Ah cah nah weich
Ah pache—
Kiah wa
Kohk ta—
Chah ke—
E mah hah—woman
Wichita
Soo rah ah Kah
Kin chase
Towaccame Dave
Towaccame Jim
Kechai
Kah wah hun tas
Waco
Sibley.
Cadoo
He's mi showa (Big man), Cherokee Charley = Margaret wife.
Chak ah tak (Head halter)
James Edwards.
Ben o She = Ne naht wife
Kah hah teh che / captain
Te yune nah (Little Sam)
So yah te pah
Chah pah che.

Distinctive tribal appelations

Wm P Ross—Cherokee ex chief, delegate to Washington—at Fair— Met him—very pleasant educated neat old gentleman. Below medium, hazel eyes & gray hair & whiskers—⅔ white.

Ex Gov Atlen. Wright—full blood Choctaw, Presbyterian preacher— Presided over International S.S. Convention at Presbyter Church— They invited me to a seat—about 30 present— Mrs Tuttle made a good speech—had taught Modocs—150 in all—30 men—

Tuggle meets Ross and Wright at Muscogee Fair

Bogus Charley Chief of Modocs at the Fair—

Highly & Phipsy

Laura Highleyman
Helene H Phipps
"Highly & Phipsy"—these youthful misses escorted
me through the Fair—both married there at Sedalia—
Lily white, dust & bloom of youth beautifully
combined—

Terrapin scene—

Mrs. Dagnett and tax claim

Muscogee Oct 2.
Mrs Sarah D. Dagnett (Maiden name Driver, Mothers name Matilda Hicks, Baxter Sprgs Kansas—)
Claims that she did not receive returned taxes paid on
real estate in Wyandot Co Kansas about— Fail to
receive 2 payments of annuities— —Taxes are $100.00
Am = $100.00—

Toashaway and his two wives

Oct 2, 79—Fair less dusty. Had pictures taken of
Toashaway & his 2 wives, Lone Wolf & his wife, & a
woman.
Toashaway asked for my picture— Had two
taken—

Dutchman Schurz

Met Schurz—lone Dutchman, with a long head. Was
with Dr Buckner— He didnt talk much. Had been
talked a day & night by Indians—

Ben F. Bumey, Chickasaw chief

Oct. Met Ben F. Bumey, Chief of Chickasaws (G
Wm)—medium size, dark hazel eyes, black hair—
about 35 yrs old—Bro-in-law of Overton—

Bros. Bacone and Journey-Cake

[Met?] Oct 2, [illegible] of brethren who are under-
taking to start a Theo. Semy—Mormon Ch— Rogers
Secty— Ingalls Financial Agt. Bro Bacone Presdt
Cherokee College—Bro Journey-Cake, Chief of Dele-

wares present—old—fine forehead—hazel eyes, ½ white, thin & tall—iron gray hair & bushy short beard— Bapt. preacher—

Specimen Speeches to Hon Carl Schurz—Oct 1 & 2nd 1879—

Oct 3. 1879. Muscogee Fair closed— Very orderly— only one drunk negro & one drunk white man seen by me— 13 ponies were stolen during the fair—5 from Kickapoos Tuesday night near M. & 8 from Comanches & associated bands Thursday night— Will have bad effect— U.S. might spend 500$ pr an. in feeding visiting wild tribes to fine advantage— The rain today made wild Indians leave off moccasins & leggins & wear only shirts & blankets & with bare legs &c looked picturesque— The Osages have large shapely heads & sinewy legs— They spoke of bringing their race horses next year—

Closing scenes at Muscogee Fair

Got sketch of Jim Barker, the Cherokee Indian lately killed. He & his father were sent to Detroit Penintentiary by U.S.— The father died in prison— Barker claimed that he was unjustly condemned & vowed hostility to mankind. He waylaid, arrested, carried off road to Mountains *Sekrets* a witness against him—& killed him over 2 mths ago; raided in Caneville, Kansas & gutted the stores, committed various robberies & finally took 32 head of cattle in Aug. from same man in day time. The Lighthorse waylaid & shot him some 10 days ago, & he was carried to Coffeeville Kansas, his leg amputated, & he died last Saturday night—27th Sept—

Violent end of vengeful Jim Barker, Cherokee highwayman

Oct 3' 79. Dr W. H. McIntosh was on train this morning. Met him & told him Dr Buckner xpected him at Eufaula & agreed to visit & go to Okmulgee next Monday with him— He comes to look after a Bapt Mission School & has 5000$ to expend—

Okmulgee mer-
chant wealthy
through doubtful
means

Capt S. B. Severs, a large dark complected white man, weighs 220 lbs perhaps, hazel eyes, iron gray hair & beard cut close, was private Secty to Sam Checote, got away with from $17 to 40000.00 in some crooked way—is a merchant at Okmulgee, owns a ranche, & has 3 to 4000 cattle, with an income of 5 to 10000$. Married a Creek wife & thereby hangs this commercial tail.

D. W. McIntosh,
son of Gen. Wm.
McIntosh of Ga.

D. W. McIntosh—tall & very slender, 60 yrs old, hair done up behind, good regular features, straight nose, hazel eyes. Son of Gnl Wm McI. of Ga—uncle of John McI—

Has been delegate & treaty maker for yrs, was a Bapt preacher but fell from grace—was on race course yesterday & entered a horse for the race— Is unpopular now & out of office—

Tuggle's hospitable
host at fair

I. D. Highleyman of Ohio—our host at Muscogee Fair. Gave to me & Maj Vore his well furnished little one room house at his lumber yard 50 yrds east of RR. Was hospitable & generous. Tall, auburn short curly hair, hazel eyes, xpressive face & very intelligent. Wife off on a visit— Graduated at Pittsburg Com. College— His bro's wife, "Laura & Phipsey" were his guests on Wednesday last & entertained us highly—

Oct 2. The agts, Myers, brothers, Quakers, Hunt. —Tuapaw agt. Col Jno Q. Tufts, Union Agt & Maj I. G. Vore meet in my presence in Highleyman's rooms & prorated the provisions accts for wild Indians ($106.) during Fair— Toashaway & his crowd included. Vore paid over $5. Individually in the goodness of his heart—

Awe-inspiring view
at sunrise

Union Agency, Sun rise Oct 5. 79—
From this hill—the magnificent view of prairie &

mountains in the distance veiled in a robe of mist, the
bald ridges & mounds like monsters swimming in the
deep, & others like waves of the ocean, cattle here &
there, neighing of horses, cawing of crows, tinkling
bells—& then the Sun bursting in a blaze of glory
above the horizon— Who can wonder at the primitive worship of the King of Day! O God, how grand
thy creation. How incomprehensible thy power &
glory— Ephemeral man how insignicant.

Spent a delightful day with the rocks on Verdigris
river about ½ mile above Vann's Lake. Col Jno Q.
Tufts & I went in Maj Vore's buggy. Took lunch
along—started about 9 AM. Crossed Ark. at Brown's
Ferry, went via Talahassee Mission, got two Mastodons bones there & then to Big John McIntoshs &
then just above Vanns Lake & then across prairie
several miles—were lost time & again & finally returned to near Vanns Lake & behold we had been
150 yds up the Ford 2 hours before.

Short expedition
yields artifacts

We found some broken Mastodons bones above
& below the Ford—& the rocks in the bed of Verdigris
river, now xposed on account of low water, are one
mass of petrified shells of an endless variety— It is a
perfect conglomeration of sea shells & petrifaction
generally— We loaded the buggy & left about 4 P.M.
Were lost several times again, missed the Mission,
got among the Negro cabins which abound between
the Ark & Verdigris but reached the Ford & saw a
beautiful Sun set on the river— Got in the quicksand
in trying to reach the ferry boad about 100 ft out in
the river—had to drive out & have the boat go down
lower to deep water. Saw a man cross river on horseback & water was not 3 ft deep—

Am sitting on the Moccasin Track rock near Agency
Building & Dick the bird setter is sleeping at my side
on this lovely Sabbath morning Oct 5. 79—

Tuggle given Vore's "Black Beaver" manuscript

Oct 5. 79. Maj I. G. Vore presented me with the Manuscript of "Black Beaver's life & Adventures" a fine sketch written by Maj V. at BB's dictation—

Story of "d—n fool white man who wanted to hunt grizzly bear— Went. BB. bleated like a fawn, here come bears. You shoot, no you shoot &c. B. fired, & wounded, white man snapped & ran down hill, bear caught & like to have eaten him up &c— B. shot & killed bear & toted white man to camp. W. M. never wanted to hunt grizzly again—

Numerical nomenclature

Oct 6. 79. To Okmulgee with Drs McIntosh & Buckner—
Big hundred = thousand
Old thousand = Million
Grandfather thousand = Billion

Visit to House of Kings

Describe visit to House of Kings with Drs B & McI— Had been in Chief's office. I copied & had certified act 1875—authorizing Bapt Assotn to erect School houses &c, & contract of Nov 1876 between Council & Managing Board.

Meets members, makes address

Then about 11 AM we entered Council Chamber of House of Kings— Maj Jas McHenry, Presdt welcomed us. We were then introduced to all the members of the H.K. We three stood in a row. W.O.T. in middle, then Dr McI. on his left, & Dr B. on the right. Porter called names & each shook hands. Then Porter told us we could speak. Dr. McI. told of his mission. I told them of my favorable impressions & hoped the U.S. would let them alone & leave their land secured to them & their children forever—& Bro B. told how long he had preached here 31 yrs & how he still loved to preach for them & of by gone days—

Genl Porter informed us that the Presdt said they would consider any plans we might submit about our Mission work &c.

Dr N. V. Wright gave me a pair of Cheyenne moccasins & a pair of leggins presented to him by the Arrapahoe Indian who won the foot race at Muscogee Fair—

II
SKETCHES &
OBSERVATIONS

*The flood of emigration will break over all imaginary
lines, and [in] ages to come the blood of the Indian will
flow in the same veins with the blood of the white man.
... F[rom] one blood all nations came and back to one
blood all nations will eventually return. This territory is
now a hash-pot of nations and most of the nations are
represented.*

THE MATERIAL in this chapter represents a sampling of
one of the major types of writing that Tuggle hoped to publish but did
not live long enough to complete. Reduced to as nearly organized a form
as could be managed, it represents also the most coherent and valuable
part of a disparate mass of manuscript salvaged from the original Tuggle
papers—in all a total of several hundred sheets. As shown in his diaries
and journals, Tuggle intended to bring out a collection of the Indian
myths he had gathered, as well as a number of descriptive accounts of
actual Indian life to be called *Sketches and Observations,* and a biographical narrative known as the "Black Beaver Story," which he acknowledged having received in manuscript form from his friend Major
I. G. Vore. (See entry for October 5, 1879, in Chapter 1 and see also
Appendix A.) From the Smithsonian copy used by Swanton, only the
myths appeared, eventually, in published form, a stroke of fortune in
itself since very few of those in Tuggle's original manuscript have survived

intact. These are identified and discussed briefly in the headnote to Chapter III.

Next to the Indian myths themselves the most interesting writings Tuggle produced are the accounts of Indian life he observed at close range during his brief sojourn in the Territory. In some respects these are, in fact, more engaging, since even though unfinished they bear a stamp of freshness and admirably convey his own feelings of wonder and fascination over the discovery of a culture totally different from that of the settled white society of central Georgia from which he sprang. There is no way of knowing precisely how extensive these sketches and observations might eventually have become, or what sort of structural organization he might have given them; for the only clues to their makeup and to his plans for them are the occasional references in his journals to his efforts to find a publisher for them. Lacking evidence to the contrary, one can only assume that J. W. Powell, head of the Bureau of Ethnology, was justified in asserting that these writings were not sufficiently well organized to be considered publishable in the manuscript form which Tuggle offered to him.

The passage of nearly a century more, however, alters the literary value, if not the essential quality, of these writings. What is left of the original manuscript is even more fragmentary and disorganized than the material Powell read and rejected, parts of it existing in two, sometimes in three versions, which we have attempted to splice together coherently. Yet, because of their freshness and the fact that they were never published, these sketches now possess at least a historical interest which they did not have in 1881. Yet they possess more than that, for Tuggle not only explains what experience was like at a given time and place—how these people lived, ate, dressed, spoke, and acted—but he also conveys the very feeling of their activities and attitudes, their relationships, their needs, pleasures, and sufferings.

In the sketches below, representing the bulk of Tuggle's extant manuscript from this source which can be intelligently presented, we are given intimate glimpses of the territorial Indian as an individual, a family member, and a citizen in a community. We see him engaged in rituals and activities such as the Green Corn Dance and the Muscogee Fair; we share briefly in his religious observances, as well as in the horrors of a vividly recalled abduction and massacre; we endure, vicariously, his physical ills; and we savor, reluctantly, his traditional foods. Thanks to Tuggle's close observation and faithful recording, we not only know what it was like to be a member of one or another of the territorial tribes in the 1880s: we can sense how the Indian himself felt about his predicament. Thus, even in its rough, unfinished state, what is left of Tuggle's writing discloses a mind keenly aware of the distinctive features of Indian life and a creative talent for depicting them sympathetically and vividly; for in each of his sketches of contemporary scenes there is both humor and pathos, together with an abundance of richly informative factual detail.

In presenting the following sketches we have tried to follow as nearly as possible the order in which Tuggle presumably would have arranged them in the book he intended to publish. His manuscript notation begins, for example, with the heading "Chapter 1. Sam Brown, the Uchee Ghosts, Witches, Green-corn dance, or busk." The manuscript pages for this chapter and the one following it carry two sets of numbering, however, one series (35–43, 44–53) centered at the top of the page, the other (1–9, 1–10) in the upper right hand corner. But the second chapter, which begins on manuscript page 44 with the heading "Chapter 2. Indian boy's ideas of witches. Broken Arrow Camp-ground. Baby-songs," is incomplete, ending abruptly on page 53 before reaching the point where Tuggle evidently introduced his description of the baby songs. (The baby songs, which appear later in the manuscript, are too fragmentary for inclusion.) This fragment is a continuation of his account of the visit with Sam Brown, who together with his son Madison accompanied Tuggle part of the way on his trip toward the Arkansas River; and included in it is Tuggle's description of the camp meeting they encountered en route, where he met Pleasant Porter and many other Indians who had gathered there to worship under the direction of several missionaries.

By comparing Tuggle's diary notations with his more finished narrative in these sketches, one can see how he made use of original data jotted down while they were fresh in mind, how he developed and expanded specific details to achieve focus and continuity, as well as color and dramatic immediacy in occasional passages of dialogue. In his diary entry for September 5, for example, he notes that Sam Brown "is a small wiry man—blue eyes—thin whiskers roman nose & does not look like an Indian"; then he goes on for the next eight or ten pages listing numerous other specific details in no particular sequential order: Brown's occupation, his family members, the dimensions of his log cabin and of the room Tuggle slept in, the rules and arrangements of the Indian ball game and the Green Corn dance, and finally the colloquy with little Madison about the presence of witches and ghosts in the house. Interspersed among these notes Tuggle inserts also an occasional parenthetical reminder to himself to include some other specific matter in his book on Indian customs, along with several small drawings of objects like Mrs. Brown's cradle and the instruments employed in the dances and ball games.

In the finished narrative these details are brought more sharply into focus and at the same time rendered coherently through Tuggle's rearrangement of them in consecutive order. Here the effect is rhetorically fluid as Tuggle begins his chapter in medias res with his description of Brown and his house and proceeds to record their conversation on the porch, their supper in a darkened room, his early retiring in a "lilliputian bed chamber," and his startled awakening later by a pet coon climbing down his bedpost. Tuggle's breakfast conversation the next morning begins dramatically with Brown's announcement that there was "a witch in the kitchen last night"; and this in turn leads naturally into the information Brown supplied concerning the difference between Uchees and Creeks, his summary of his duties as superintendent of schools, and the extended discussion of ball play and green corn dance, which Tuggle renders in the form of a quoted narrative spoken by the "venerable Uchee," General Cooper. In similar fashion Tuggle then records his experiences with Brown and his son on their way across the river and at the camp meeting itself.

Tuggle's method of combining and expanding these details occasionally imparts a puckish literary flavor into his narrative, as for instance in his remark that the little boy who tried to snatch his blanket "like Pickwick . . . had inadvertently entered the wrong room." And yet, in the process of transforming his original impressions recorded in the diary entries, he sometimes omitted striking details which might have added even more color to his finished narrative had he seen fit to include them. Many examples of these may be seen in the miscellaneous entries recorded in the month between September 3 and October 3, 1879, during which time Tuggle undertook his extended camping trip by horse and wagon from Okmulgee, the capital, to Wewoka, Eufaula, Muscogee, and back to Okmulgee, stopping at each of these places for several days at a time to visit friends in the surrounding areas, attend church and camp meeting services, engage in amateur archaeological experiments, and witness strange sights at the annual fair. When he reordered these experiences in his sketches, Tuggle apparently planned to follow a similar chronological order; but various revisions in the pagination and chapter headings of extant manuscript material, as well as variant versions of certain portions of it, suggest that he was still seeking a final form for his book when he turned it over to Powell.

Thus what appears to be the logical order of extant sketches following the initial ones dealing with Sam Brown and the green corn dance are the two entitled "Characters Among the Indians" and "At the Indian Council," two combined under the title "Wild Indians at Muscogee

Fair," another entitled "Mormons Among the Indians," dealing mainly with the McLean story and the massacre at Mountain Meadows, and finally the two Wewoka scenes. In each of these it can be seen that Tuggle sought to dramatize the most colorful aspects of Indian life he had encountered or heard tell of, though prudently omitting or softening at the same time certain specific instances noted in the diary of gross behavior, cruelty, sexuality, and the like which he may have felt likely to offend the sensibilities of his readers.

The problem of presenting some of this material in its most appropriate form here, however, involves a calculated risk in selectivity which Tuggle himself might not have approved. For the two sketches dealing with the Muscogee Fair, for example, there are three extant fragments: these are labeled "Chapter xxv—Muscogee Fair," "Chapter xxvi—Wild Indians at the Fair," and an untitled section which is a revision of the two earlier parts. This third section is clearly an effort on Tuggle's part to combine the two chapters into a continuous whole, but the fact is that portions of the original versions are superior to the rewritten one. To preserve these and at the same time avoid needless duplication in reproducing significant material which Tuggle added in his revision, we have therefore decided to splice the two versions together as indicated in the bracketed notes, relying for the most part on what appears to have been Tuggle's original version.

Similarly, in dealing with the manuscript material for the sketch entitled "Mormons Among the Indians," we have had to piece together portions of four fragments listed as follows:

1. "Chapter viii—The Rescue" and "Chapter ix—Revenge" (pp. 107–117 in ms)
2. "Chapter x—Mormons Among Indians, McLean's Story, Apostle Pratt's death, Massacre at Mountain Meadows & its origin" (pp. 136–146 in ms)
3. "Chapter vi—The Missionary's House" (pp. 190–192 in ms)
4. "Chapter vii—"The Missionary's Tale" (pp. 193–194 in ms)

Numbers 3 and 4 and the two parts of number 1 make up the original story in rough form, while number 2 is the full-length version of it, but 2 is the better version only through the first half; the second half is much shorter than its original version, which is Chapter ix or number 1; while number 4 is a false start for the tale, which begins in a much better way in number 2. To achieve continuity while preserving at the same time the best of Tuggle's treatment of this material, we have therefore begun this sketch with the material listed in number 2, splicing into it the relevant portion of number 3 and continuing with the story of the rescue and revenge as presented in number 1. Finally the sketch is concluded with Buckner's account of the massacre as it appears also in number 1. (Here, as elsewhere in this part of the book, we have used a title as close as possible to Tuggle's original.)

Exactly what Tuggle's book might have achieved had he lived to carry out his own design by reshaping its structure and polishing its style can, of course, never be known. Since he was neither an Emerson nor a Melville, minute cancellations and revisions are perhaps not so important a consideration as they would be in establishing a text for those writers. Yet it might be said that a holograph manuscript by an unknown author like Tuggle presents unique problems which we have tried to solve in order to show how, even in their fragmentary state, Tuggle's "Sketches and Observations" offer rich insights into Indian lore.

Lack of continuity of both among and within these "observations" necessarily detracts from their interest as parts of a projected, unified account of Indian life as Tuggle saw it; and the reader can at best only surmise the quality and form it might have achieved, had he lived to see his book through the press. Nevertheless, as an example of Tuggle's craftsmanship in the management of vivid detail, his account of the Green Corn Dance or Busk offers clear proof of his ability to capture and re-create the deep tribal significance of a ceremonial which, for generations, has been traditionally kept among the most revered of Yuchi rituals.

GHOSTS, GREEN CORN DANCE, CREEKS & UCHEES

ON A ROCKY TIMBERED RIDGE, surrounded by a prairie on which grazed fine Durham cattle and a few sheep, was situated the home of Sam Brown, the Uchee Indian, superintendent of public schools and public blacksmith shops. Rather a peculiar combination, but why not sharpen agricultural as well as mental tools at national expense? A small wiry man with Roman nose & blue eyes came to the gate followed by several dogs. At one house I had counted six and was informed that more were behind the chimney. We stopped at the well and took a deep draught from the bucket, doubly appreciated on account of a long ride over a dusty trail. We sat on the little porch in front of his house and talked till dark, when his wife, a small blackeyed woman invited us into a shed room to supper, saying in an apologetic manner that the coal-oil was out. We groped in the dark room to the table, having but one lamp to guide us

& that was the lamp of xperience, which answered very well on the route to our mouths. On that question it did not cast any light, nor did it illuminate the countenances of our companions, nor local surroundings.

Being weary from a long ride I retired early to a bed in a cunning device cut off at the end of the porch, a lilliputian bed chamber, eight by ten, the walls constructed of oak boards, three feet long by six inches wide, dressed on the outside and nailed on like weather-boarding. A peculiar scratching sound like a cat clawing at the side of a house caused me to wake next morning and my eye caught sight of an object above my head moving down in my direction. Closer inspection revealed that this was a coon. He was climbing down the long bed post. Not knowing his intentions, nor whether he was wild, or civilized, I called in most soothing tones "cooney, cooney, coon-ey" in order to pacify any possible hostile emotions, but he changed his course, perhaps his mind, and crawled through a crack before he reached my devoted head. Hearing several dogs under my bed and not knowing the supply of coons on hand, I decided to rise. A little ten year old son of Sam was playing with the coon & calling it "Sarah" as I walked on the porch. He brought out a toy phonographic piano to amuse us till breakfast.

"There was a witch in the kitchen last night" said Brown as he helped our plates at breakfast. Thinking he was jesting, I asked him if he ever saw one.

"Oh, yes. I have seen a ghost."

"Where?"

"Out there in the yard," he gravely replied. "My wife had an uncle who died & was buried some distance from here, and as she was desirous of having him buried near us, I went after the body, and brought it here to my house. I dug a grave out there by the fence, & while the coffin was lying by the grave just before we lowered it, I saw him walking around my fence & turn the corner."

"Could you not have been mistaken?"

"No, sir, I was not mistaken. I was not at all frightened. I saw him as plainly as I see you now. He had on the same old hat & jeans coat I had often seen him wear."

"Was any one with you?"

"Yes."

"Did they see the ghost too?"

"No, I called to one of the men to look, but he said he saw nothing."

After breakfast I asked Brown how it was that the Uchees spoke a different language from the Creeks with whom they were incorporated.

"I have no doubt" said he "that we were once a separate people. Tradition among my tribe says that when William Penn made his treaty, the Uchees lived in that part of the country. At some later period they migrated farther south and after being weakened by repeated wars, were conquered by the Creeks."

In response to a question as to his official duties he stated that the Creeks had twenty eight public schools, kept open ten months during the year, the teachers receiving forty dollars per month, and books being furnished to the children. The instruction was imparted in English. There were also two Mission schools of a higher grade than the public schools, which were also maintained from national funds. His duties required him to visit each of these schools quarterly, and also to look after the public blacksmith shops at which agricultural implements were sharpened free of xpense to the farmer. He received a salary of six hundred dollars.

There was an old Uchee Indian, General Cooper, present and I requested Brown to get him to describe a ball play. The old man smiled and with Brown, whom I found very clever and accommodating, as interpreter he spoke as follows:

"The players go into training after being chosen and all drink medicine, made of snake root, and red root, which slimes them out and makes them active. The day is set & the ground selected. Two poles are put up at each end of the course, four feet apart and twenty feet high connected at the top by a cross piece, and at seventy five or a hundred yards distance, two other poles are set up. When the game is between rival towns it is very exciting. They meet at the ball ground, strip themselves, put on breech-clouts with fancy tails, some wearing tiger tails, others wolf, buffalo or such as they may fancy, and after painting their faces and bodies they run around the poles, each town to itself, raising the war-whoop & bantering each other for the game.

"The two sides then meet half way between the poles and lay down their ball sticks in order to see that the sides are equal, each player having two ball sticks. These are usually made of hickory, or pecan, and are about three feet long, an inch in diameter, and open at the end forming a cup, or basket about the size of the hand, and interlocking buckskin strings, for the purpose of catching the ball. Each side selects a man to kill the ball, or count the number of times the ball is thrown between the poles. Killing the ball twenty times usually wins the game. Another man called the ball-witch is chosen to throw the ball in the air. The medicine men conjure the balls while the players are in training. The players take their

places, the ball-witch throws the ball into the air, and the struggle begins, each side trying to get possession of the ball, and by any means to
throw it through the poles, & this is repeated till one side wins. Often in
the struggle over the ball blows are given and heads & backs, legs & arms
are injured & sometime death results, though not often. The successful
party raises the whoop of triumph and dances & sings around its poles."

"When was there a busk, or green corn dance among the Uchees?"

"There were green corn dances this year" continues the old Uchee,
"Up on Snake Creek, Polecat and Big Pond."

"How do your people celebrate this dance?"

"The first thing is to get up enough meat to feed everybody. Notice is
then given, generally seven days, & for this purpose a bundle of sticks is
sent to each fire-maker, or medicine-man, who must be a perfectly chaste
young man. The fire-makers notify all the others, breaking a stick for each
day. Among the Uchees, there are twelve fire-makers. On the fifth broken-
day the women make sofkey and the sixth day the cattle are killed, the
cooking is done and they have a feast, consisting of the meat, sweet
beans, potatoes, honey, & such other articles of food as they have on
hand, and drink sweetened water, & sotkey. A talker is selected & he makes
a talk. On the seventh day the medicine-men, or forked-sticks as they are
called on account of carrying forked poles, make sacred fire with a flint and
punk. They take four sticks and arrange them so as to point to the four
points of the compass, north, east, south & west. The sacred fire is put in
the centre, and medicine is placed in two pots in front of the stick which
points to the east, one pot having snake button-root, and the other red-
root & water. In the snake-root mixture they put a feather bent so as to
form an opening across which ten pins are inserted, forming a comb, or
rake. The medicine men now blow into the jars through a cane about
two feet long around the center of which are tied red-strings. After the
blowing, a man chosen for the purpose takes the feather-pin-rake and
scratches the breasts of all who have not eaten any green corn before this
time, in order to kill the poison of the new corn & prevent it from injuring
them when eaten. After the scratching follows the 'Crooked Arrow'
dance." Here the old Uchee took a stick and hobbled & trotted in a
crooked, rambling way to the music of an imaginary drum, which is often
made of an iron-pot covered with raw-hide.

"The medicine men now hand around the medicine in bowls, offering
it first to the town-kings & head-men. It makes everybody sick, and soon
they all begin to puke, some in public & some in private, some where
they sit on the ground & some running to the woods near by, and they
puke all the evening. The women then dance around the sacred fire, terra-

pin shells, filled with little rocks, being fastened to their ankles, and rattle to the music of the drums. No man is allowed to dance this dance with the women. The medicine pots are next carried away, the drums beating all the time. The Uchees now use American drums. The men and women then dance the "Corn-dance," the men, with long sticks in their hands, on one side, and opposite them the women.

"The medicine men take four ears of green corn, roast them in the sacred fire, and rub themselves with the burnt corn, and then wash themselves. All the men then wash themselves, return to camp and eat their first green corn. After supper they begin the great "Stomp-dance," which lasts all night long, and the busk, or green corn dance is over."

[While?] Sam and the venerable Uchee were describing ball play and green corn dance as practiced among the Uchees and their neighbors, Brown's wife [was?] in the little house, attending to household matters and rocking her baby in a cradle of peculiar construction. Two ropes were suspended from the rafters forming a kind of swing, a quilt being wrapped around the ropes so as to make a bed for the baby, at whose head and feet sticks were inserted between the ropes to keep them apart. Just above the baby a red silk handkerchief was tied so that two corners hung down near the baby's face, the handkerchief being folded in a triangular shape, and as the hammock swung back and forth, the handkerchief would flop, flop, and act both as a fan and as a fly brush.

The ponies were saddled, and Brown saying that he would ride over the prairie with us to the Arkansas river as he wishes to hunt for some missing cattle, we were soon on the trail, or rat[her] two trails, for generally there are two paths running parallel about as far apart as wagon tracks and between the two grass & weeds grow sometimes three fe[et] high, while the trails have cut into the soil six inches and often deeper. Browns little son, Mad, rode a bay pony by my side and sat with all the ease of an old cavalry man. The witch incident of the previous night being mentioned I asked Mad what he thought about it.

"Why I know who it was. It was my grandpap's ghost." He spoke with great earnestness. "He comes to our house a heap o' times."

"How do you know who it is?"

" 'Cause he and my pap used to drink out of a big bottle together and he just comes back."

"Does he ever talk to any of you?"

"O, no, he just comes at night when we are all fast asleep, and he looks at us through the cracks, but he don't say nothing, and when the rooster crows for day, he must go back."

"Did you ever see him, Mad?"

"No, sir, but I have seen sperits" said he, looking me squarely in the face with an air of unwavering faith.

"How was it?"

"Why one day I was ri[ding] along the prairie looking for our cows, me and another boy, and I got to thinking about a boy that was dead and I kept on just a thinking, and a thinking, and a thinking, and the first thing I knowed I just seen him right out in the grass before me."

"Did the other boy see him?"

"No, I told him to 'look a'there, look a'there', but he said he didn't see nothing."

"Well, did you ever see another one?"

"Yes, sir. You saw them big rocks way back in the bottom." I nodded assent. "Well, I was riding along there one night by myself, coming home from the store where my ma sent me, and just as I got in that deep rocky bottom I got jest as scared, and the cold shivers run up my back and I saw something among the rocks and it made a fuss like this—" and the little Uchee snuffed and sniffled and blew his nose with great violence, "just like that, and, whoopee, good grashus, I felt so curious, and I like to a rode my pony to death gittin home."

Reader, do you feel sorry for the "untutored mind" of the ten year old Indian? How much tutoring will remove these fancies? Before answering too positively it might be well enough to remember that Sir Matthew Hale, then Chief baron of the exchequer, presided at the trial of Amy Duny, and Rose Cullender, two poor old women who were charged with being witches, & that he told the jury that the Scriptures left no doubt that there was such a thing as witchcraft, and instructed them that all they had to do was, first, to consider whether the children had been really bewitched as alleged, and, secondly, whether the witchcraft was sufficiently brought home to the prisoners at the bar. The jury found them guilty & they were hanged in March 1664. Recall the scenes enacted at Salem, Massachusetts in 1692, when persons claiming the gift of "spectral sight" were sent from town to town at public expense to discover who were witches, before becoming impatient with little Mad, the Uchee.

A gaunt, hollow-eyed ferryman put us across the Arkansas. "I always puts everybody over. If they can pay, all right, and if they can't pay, all right." The river was low and muddy, a white sand beach greeted the eye on the opposite bank, while a dense forest of immense cotton-wood trees, interspersed with sycamore, pecan, walnut, burr-oak with enormous acorns, skirted the lazy stream, and presented an agreeable contrast to the vast stretches of prairie, dotted here and there with a bunch of stunted-black-jacks.

As we rode up a gentle, sandy slope covered with stunted trees, a few miles north of the river, we saw ponies staked out in the grass, a few wagons here & there, and soon, in an open space, we perceived a large arbor covered with brown prairie grass, and at a little distance, surrounding the open plot, were the white tents, and small arbors with a roof of bushes or prairie grass. Beneath the large arbor, or booth, sat a crowd of Indians listening in perfect silence to a sermon. A tall, military figure approached as we halted at a tent on the edge of the open plot. He was well-dressed in a suit of black cloth &, when he removed his white felt hat, a high brow, black eyes & hair were seen, and with a smiling face, and a grip which bespoke a smiling heart he welcomed us to Broken Arrow Camp Ground. This was General Pleasant Porter, a Creek, or Muscogee Indian, and though a young man his nation had frequently called on him to serve her at home and abroad. His title had been bestowed during a threatened civil war among his own people, and as a delegate to Washington he had discharged delicate and important trusts, pertaining to the interests of the Muscogee nation, and also had contributed to the solution of the vexed Indian problem, contending with other enemies, who were prolific in schemes for robbing the Indian of his home, so solemnly guaranteed by treaty stipulations, and striving with no less ardor to stem the flood of philanthropy which menaced the future of the red man.

He carried us to his tent, where his wife, a handsome Cherokee, greeted us with a smile, and words of generous hospitality. The discourse soon ended, and after a wild, yet melodious song, the Indians scattered to their rustic shelters. The camp meeting was held under the auspices of the Presbyterian Missionaries although all denominations were invited [& some?] participated in the duties, hospitalities and pleasures of the occasion. The fare was excellent in quality and bountiful in quantity. At Porter's table fifty persons usually ate. Biscuit and beef, chickens, coffee & cakes, pumpkins, pies and figs, offered in a variety of ways satisfied the appetite of the heartiest guest. The tables were set under a grass arbor, and neat crockery on white table cloths presented a tempting scene after the cooking stoves had performed their function. Such coffee! Equal to French drip, and not confined to any one tribe, but every Indian seems to know the art of making good coffee.

At night some slept with the tents but most of the crowd found comfortable beds under the trees, with a mattress of prairie grass and a blanket for the "we sma' hours beyant the twol," especially if a slight touch of a norther should honor the camp-meeting with a visit. During the night I felt some one pulling the cover from my bed and looking up as I waked I saw in the moonlight a boy standing over me tugging away at the blanket.

"What are doing? Let my blanket alone!"

The boy stopped & asked "What's your name?"

"What's yours?" was the reply.

"Tom Crow" he blurted out, and pulled away like his namesake in a corn field saying between jerks, "I'm going (jerk) to git (jerk) my quilt (jerk). This here (jerk) is my (jerk) quilt."

"O, no, Tom, this is my blanket," but Tom took a fresh hold and would have pulled the camp-ground off judging from his jerks & grunts, had not the air been made musical by a shrill female voice ejaculating in suggestive tones, "You Tom! You Tom!" Tom Crow stopped suddenly & looked in the direction of the voice. "You Tom. What are you doing down there. Come up here." And Tom went. In the night he had rolled from his own bed, and getting cold towards morning he began pulling at the first cover he found, but like Pickwick he had inadvertently entered the wrong room, so to speak.

Twas Sunday. The horn blew at sunrise and the Indians were summoned to prayer at the big arbor. They sang with evident enjoyment, and their prayers were earnest. When the hour set apart for a sermon by one of the missionaries arrived there was an audience of about four hundred people at the central stand, and the deacons deportment would have reflected credit on communities boasting a higher degree of civilization. Not a single feature of the wild Indian could be detected in the costumes, unless here & there an extra flash of red color struck the eye. Before the congregation settled down for the regular services there was a performance of striking peculiarity. Young lads quietly but rapidly glided between the seats, peeping here & there, under the benches & everywhere, holding in their hands whips with very short handles and very long lashes. They were the Dog-police. Every dog was found and without noise driven from beneath the arbor, but when the edge of that sacred structure was reached, alas for the poor dogs. One boy would swing his whip and skilfully touch the flank of the fat disturber of the proprieties of the camp ground, when with an incipient bark and a suppressed growl of xpectancy the dog would start to run the gauntlet of the dog police. The second boy with a wonderful twist of his right arm would welcome the canine approach with a whir, whiz, crack, and such a howl would belch forth as Cerberus himself could not excel, and limping on three legs, each dog seemed to improve the record of canine speed. The cow-whip seemed to lift the dog from the ground, & when he dropped his mind appeared in no doubt as to the best course to p[ursu]e.

The missionary preached through an interpreter, David M. Hodge, and the interpreter occupied twice as much time as did the minister. He afterwards claimed, however, that he could translate as rapidly as the English could be spoken, saying that in interpreting a sermon he always explained the meaning until he saw that the Indians understood him.

Rev. W. S. Robertson and his wife, whose maiden name was Ann Eliza Worcester, were the leading spirits of Broken Arrow camp ground. He had served as preacher & teacher over thirty years and as the presiding officer at Tallahassee Mission School had done much to elevate the Indian character. Mrs. Robertson was a lady of rare culture and in answer to a question as to how a savage, nomadic race could construct and preserve such a language as the Muscogee, or Creek language she replied, "It was divinely given. A language with conjugations of verbs almost as perfect as Latin or Greek, with declensions of nouns, adjectives and sometimes of conjunctions and adverbs, [was] not produced by savages. So far as history [revea]ls the red man, in no modern [period?] [obliterated] been capable of building up . . . [Fragment ends here.]

CHARACTERS AMONG THE INDIANS

THE NEXT MORNING as I walked into the hall there sat Captain Belcher with an Indian baby in his lap.

"One two" said the Captain. "One two, [one] two," repeated the little child. "Three four," "free four," "[fiv]e six," "five, six," "seven, eight," "seven, eight," "[nine,] ten," "nine, ten." "You bet," "You bet," a [big] laugh from the fat captain and a merry scream [fro]m the Indian pupil.

"Indian alphabet" I asked, emphasizing the last syllable.

He saw the pun and [re]plied "Not exactly. The science of chances ought to be taught the Indian for their future is a game of chance."

"The science of numbers will have much to do with it, perhaps," I suggested.

"No doubt of it. In the past, numbers settled the questions, & will settle the Indian question finally. The flood of emigration will break over all imaginary lines, and [in] ages to come the blood of the Indian will flow in the same veins with the blood of the white man. It may [take] a long time but the squaw now will solve [the Ind]ian question. F[rom] one blood all nations came and back to one blood all nations will eventually return. This territory is now a hash-pot of nations and most of the nations are represented. The Mongolian is not here, unless the Indians themselves are so descended as some of them think. They have a tradition that a big bird flew across [the] great water and brought the first Indians to this [con]tinent. A sail boat may have been that bird. [Tr]avelers say that near Behrings straits there are [pe]ople resembling the red man and some of the [an]cient Indian customs are very similar to some customs of the Chinese & native tribes of northern Asia.

"Strange in his origin, and stranger in his [set]ting, the Indian appeals to tender consideration. The right of discovery and right of conquest have pushed him to a small corner of his once proud, continental domain, but the same right had Rodenett Dhu.

"Let him take who has the power, and let him keep who can." Can we not as well say the "wrong of discovery & the wrong of conquest?"

"Volumes have been & will be written before the Indian problem will be solved. Many claim that the quickest way to extinguish th[e] title of the [Indi]an is to extinguish the Indian and that the only good Indians are the dead ones, or the fellows who stand quietly as signs before tobacco shops. Appropriately called the Red man, his history has been written in blood & you seem to think that the flowing of blood will end the chapter, the blood of once hostile nations flowing in the same veins."

"You see what is being [done]. I think it will increase with time. It is now difficult [to] find many full-blooded Indians among some of the [tri]bes."

Ben came up, a round headed seven-year [ol]d boy—eyes like two jet beads, & his hair shingled. [He] was shy and stood leaning against a post, his head [han]ging down. With a little coaxing he came up. "What's your name?" I asked.

He looked up at the Captain. "Tell him, Benjamin Cooper" said he, and Ben repeated "Benjamin Cooper."

"How old are you, Ben?"

"Seven."

"Where's your cat?"

"In the Kitchen."

"The other day" said the Captain, "I was out on the prairie mowing grass and left Ben by himself for about two hours. I told him to stay right where I left him near the machine. When I returned t[here] he was but his eyes looked red and I saw he had [been] crying. "Why Ben did you get lonesome [?"]

["Yes,"] said he "but I kept a singing meetin[g] songs, and kept on &

kept on till I saw you coming." He had been to camp meeting with me and had heard the songs. When we were riding home from the camp meeting, where they had held communion service, and there was shouting, Ben said to me, "Did you see them folks drinking whiskey out of the bottle and when they all got drunk they just [ho]llered around?"

"No, Ben. Where did you see it?"

"Why, all of 'em. I saw 'em. They had a bottle on a table and some tumblers & crackers. They didn't give me any though."

After breakfast Belcher & Moore accompanied [me] to the Capitol where the Council soon assembled. General Porter introduced me to James McHenry, the President of the House of Kings. He stood before me, a tall slender old man sixty odd years old, his hair gray, his whiskers long & white, cheek bones very prominent, and his eyes perfectly black. He is a half-breed. He figured in the Indian war in Georgia, Alabama & Florida in 1836. In response to a question regarding his connection with that war, he said: "Yes, they call me Jim McHenry. I was a boy in Columbus [Geor]gia, acting as interpreter for two traders Stewart & Fountain. I knew Walter T. Colquitt. He was a great man. The Indians could hardly reconcile his being a lawyer and a preacher at the same time. They would hear him speak in the Court House during the day and at night preach in the church, and they xpressed their idea by saying, 'Colquitt tells stories all day and repents all night.' But they knew he was a good man. I have been in [th]is office frequently. I got a little start in Stewart & Fountain's store and was running a store myself in 1835 when the troubles started. It was [c]harged that I robbed the United States mail and had the mail boy murdered, but it was not true. I was captured and kept in prison for some time in Columbus Georgia.

"Have you seen our new Capitol? Let me show it to you. I am the Chairman of the building committee. It is about eighty by fifty and two stories high. The lower rooms are for the Chief, his secretary, the treasurer, and for committees. Up stairs, one side is divided into two rooms, one for the House of Kings, of which I am the President, and the other is occupied by the Supreme Court; acros[s] the hall is a large room for the House of Warriors, and when our council is not in session, we let preachers and lecturers use it, and every Sunday it is used as a church for Sunday school and preaching."

The old man was evidently proud of the building. It was made of yellow stone, the edges dressed, while the outer surface was rough, cobblework, and with its little porticos, and modest dome, made quite a creditable appearance.

"We have not quite finished [o]ur work. We have paid out nearly fourteen thousand dollars. The lightning rods and the bell—let me [s]how you the bell," he led me down stairs & there in a box was his new bell; to be put in the dome, its use, once a year to summon legislators to assemble, and every Sabbath to invite Indian children and adults to prayer and praise, to ring out the old and ring in the new. In another vacant room Major McHenry—for that was his title, exhibited the lamps and chandeliers for the building.

Major McHenry was a methodist minister, and had been preaching for many years. He introduced me to Hepsy Ho-mar-ty, a sister of Osceola,[1] the famous warrior who died in prison at Savan[nah.] Hepsy was stout, had a pleasant face, hazel eyes, somewhat resembling the picture of her brother. She was fourteen years old when her people left Alabama. She had come to the store to trade, traveling in a northern manufactured wagon drawn by two little boy ponies, one of them followed by a very diminutive colt. Talking with her, Major McHenry acting as interpreter she said that her father was a white man named Powell, who was also the father of Osceola,[2] but their mothers were not the same; that she remembered some of the incidents [in] the war of 1836, and was now a widow. She did not know her age.

Many strange characters are found among the Indians, and in forming an estimate of the progress they have made, and are likely to make in the near future, all the influences by which they are surrounded must be considered. If only good men visited the Indians, or located temporarily or permanently among them, they would be aided in their efforts to improve and advance to a higher degree of enlightenment and civilization, but unfortunately for the Indian his home is reg[arded] as the refuge of the outcast from white civilization and society, and every avenue of approach is occupied by the designing, scheming adventurer, and frequently escaped

[1] Osceola, one of the greatest of the "Patriot Chiefs," was born about 1804 in a village near the Tallapoosa River in Alabama. His people, called Tallassees, belonged to the Creek nation of Indians, but his father was believed to have been a half-breed Scottish-Creek trader named William Powell. An intrepid leader in the Creek and Seminole Wars, Osceola was captured in Florida and imprisoned at Fort Moultrie on Sullivan's Island in Charleston, South Carolina, where he died on January 30, 1838. The poignant story of his capture, death, and subsequent decapitation is told by Josephy in "The Death of Osceola," *The Patriot Chiefs* (London, 1962), pp. 177–208. A contemporary account of Osceola, together with illustrations, may be found in George Catlin's *Letters and Notes on the Manners, Customs, and Condition of the North American Indians* (Minneapolis, 1965), II, 218–222.

[2] Catlin, writing in the 1830s, confirms the fact that Osceola was known as Powell among his fellow tribesmen (p. 219).

criminals find shelter among friendly Indians only to return demoraliza-
tion and degradation for kindness and hospitality. These evil influences
the Indians must resist and counteract, and any just calculation must include such elements of obstruction and retardation.

At an humble home I met a feeble tottering man, not old, but crippled.
He limped badly, and on his right jaw there was a deep, ugly scar. He
was feeding pigs when I saw him & evidently he did odd jobs of a light
nature in return for his food and shelter. The children called him Johnny,
the only name I heard given him. When we were alone he began to talk
in an indistinct manner, and gave the following account of himself.

"My folks were French and I was born in Paris, and was six years old
when they came over. At the beginning of the late war I enlisted in a
Zouave regiment and in the very first engagement a shell exploded in my
company and a piece hit me here on the right jaw where you see this sink.
I fell and was left in the field for dead. The first thing I remember on
coming to was that somebody was giving me some water and I was trying
with difficulty to swallow it. I was informed that the shell had killed &
wounded thirty men. I was severely wounded in the body too. When I got
well enough to walk on crutches I was discharged and returned to the city
where I enlisted.

"The war went on and as I was not subject to military duty on account
of wounds, I thought I would make a little money." He hesitated and
looked around in a half-scared way, as if he feared some one might hear
what he was saying, though no other house was in within a mile of the one
we were in, and no other person in sight. It was growing dark. He came
nearer to me and talked in a very low tone, almost a whisper, during the
remainder of his story. "Well I guess you've heard of 'Bounty Jumpers.' I
thought I'd be a Bounty Jumper. It was getting hard to get up soldiers for
the war, because so many men being killed in the battle that the boys
didn't like it. The rich men would pay out, and hire men to go in their
places. It took two to play the game I intended to play, so I got me a pal
and one day we went to an office in one of the wards where they were
enlisting soldiers, and they swore us in, paid us the bounty and told us to
report out at the camp beyond the city limits. We didn't think of re-
porting, but went right off to another office in a different ward and enlisted
again and got another bounty. We then changed our clothes, put on false
whiskers and went to a third office and were sworn in again, making three
times that same day.

"We gave most of the money to a friend to keep for us, and this time
we reported out at the camp. In a few days one of us was put on guard,

and that night about midnight we ran off. We threw our uniforms away & put on citizens clothes and broke for another State. In a short time we began our business again, and joined the army the fourth time. They paid us more bounty money, and the first chance we got we left the camp of instruction. By this time it was getting hot for us, as the officers had advertised for us & the detectives were on the look-out. We couldn't disguise the color of our eyes, our features, nor our shape, and I found it very difficult to hide my jaw. But we managed to dodge about, some times in the woods, sometimes in garrets and got pals to help us beat the officers. This cost us a sight of money though and cut down our profits mightily, but we had to shell out or they would sell us out. We kept on in business till we jumped her eight times. Then we broke for another State a thousand miles off and then we had a good time and jumped the bounty five more times, I think. I know we jumped thirteen times in all.

"I tell you it was getting hotter and hotter. Every where we went we were shadowed. We went across the whole land, hiding out and dodging, but we got so scared at last that we got on a ship and went to England. After a while we went to Germany and France & had a bully time and made the scads fly. We had to write for more money to our pal. When we got tired we came back to this country and like two fools we went down near an old stomping ground and the officers caught us up in the fourth story, in a garret.

"I tell you it was rough then. They chained us and put a sixty pound ball on our right leg, and starved us, and worked us in the chain gang till I thought we'd just die. One day I picked up my ball and broke for it, but they shot me in the right leg and it is a running sore now. They sent us to the front, three hundred and seventy of us, and made us build breast works. They picked out eight of the worst of us, and condemned us to be shot. They give us twenty days. Things looked pretty black. I thought I'd try my old officers, and they did all they could to save me. I was a pretty good sort of a soldier at first & they said so, but it wan't no use. They said I must go up. I didn't see no chance, and just give up. We had done a tolerably good business and had a jolly time spending the bounty, but we couldn't jump the bounty any more. Day after day went by till only seven more days were left, when we heard that the surrender had come and they told us we would be turned loose. When they first knocked the shackles off we couldn't walk. We were poor, and weak, and our legs were sore with the chains and my right leg was still running. I think the ball was pisened and the doctors tell me to let it run and it would kill me to let it get well and heal up. They ought to give me a pension any how."

"Why Johnny—after deserting thirteen times."

"Well, that's so—I made a right smart of money anyway. I wish I had some of it now. My pal died about two years ago, and here I am among the Indians pigging away yet."

AT THE INDIAN COUNCIL

THE COUNCIL was in session at Okmulgee the Capitol of the Muscogee Nation.

Hon James McHenry, who was prominent in the Creek War in Georgia & Alabama in 1836, was President of the House of Kings & Hon John R Moore was speaker of the House of Warriors, while Hon. Ward Coachman, the chief, occupied the Executive Chair.

Here is a picture of their new Capitol, just completed under the supervision of the building committee, James McHenry, John McIntosh, & W. F. Brown. It was constructed of stone at a cost of about 14000$ & the interior is commodiously arranged in modern style. A gilded eagle perches on the spire of the dome, while a flock of sheep peacefully slumber on the steps & in the yard of the Indian Capitol, Liberty & peace.

The Muscogee Nation adopted a Constitution in 1867, & have a form of government similar in many respects to that of the States. They have a chief elected by qualified voters every four years, & a House of Kings, & a House of Warriors corresponding to the Senate & House of Representatives in the State governments. They have a Supreme Court consisting of five judges, & six circuit courts. They have twenty eight public schools kept open ten months in the year & pay the teachers a salary of 400.00$ pr. an.

Dr William H McIntosh, Corresponding Secretary of the Home Mission Board of the Southern Baptist Convention was on a visit to the Muscogee Nation & we were invited with Dr Buckner to the House of Kings while it was in session. President James McHenry welcomed us & with the assistance of General Pleasant Porter, a member of the House of Kings, we were introduced to all the members. We stood in a row before the Presidents chair & the members filed past & shook hands with us, as General Porter called their names. The Presiding officer then informed us that they would be glad to hear anything we deemed proper to say.

Dr McIntosh told them the object of his visit, to establish a manual labor Mission School for the education of Indian boys & girls & that he was here to cooperate with the Council in said enterprise.

Dr Buckner spoke of his labor of love among the Indians for over thirty years, that he still labored prayed & hoped for the cause of Indian missions, & felt as one of them & not as a stranger needing introduction.

I referred to my travels among the Indians, my favorable impressions, & stated that the outlook was hopeful if both parties should faithfully abide by the terms & stipulations of the existing treaties between the Indians & the United States.

The President informed Dr. McIntosh that the Council would cheerfully cooperate with him & would be glad to consider any measure he might submit for the establishment of the manual labor Mission School.

The following day we were introduced to the House of Warriors by Judge Legus Perryman, a member of the House. Hon John R Moore responded to our speeches & assured us of a hearty welcome.

In the speedy passage of laws the Indian Council presents a striking contrast with the legislative assemblies in the States. One measure was introduced at ten Oclock in the morning in the House of Kings, was discussed & passed, transmitted to the House of Warriors & there concurred in, duly signed by the officials of both houses & approved by the Chief by four Oclock in the evening. True the measure had been thought over & discussed privately before its introduction.

At night the hall of the House of Warriors was occupied by some preacher, or speaker on religious, moral, or educational topics. They had preaching or speaking at the Capitol every night.

Of course, the speeches were delivered through interpreters. David M. Hodge was the National Interpreter & spoke with great ease & satisfaction.

The leading topic of conversation in Indian politics was the election for Chief. Ward Coachman, the incumbent & Sam Checote, who had been Chief for several terms were the candidates. The election was close & the friends of both parties claimed the victory. They were fortunate in having two good men for candidates & the interests of the Nation had been safely confided to both of them in the past.

Sam Checote was universally spoken of as a good man. His face indicated great amiability & his character was well established. He was tall & symmetrical, had a fine head, hazel eyes, dark hair turning gray, thin whiskers & a very pleasant xpression. He spoke no English. He has been a Methodist preacher for years & Presiding Elder of his district. It is a peculiarity of Indian politics that nearly all their public men are either preachers, or men of well known religious character. The mission schools have had an influence in this direction. A traveler may mingle freely with the Indians for months & not hear an Indian curse nor see an Indian drunk.

It is a custom at the Indian Councils for the committees to employ as clerks educated Indians, & sometimes white men living among them. Dr N. V. Wright, a physician located at Okmulgee, has acted in this capacity frequently & his office is a popular resort. He is quick, intelligent, kindhearted & very naturally is called upon often by the Indians to write letters & other documents for them.

One morning I walked from the hotel—a log house of six rooms, but very comfortable, to Dr Wright's office. There lay the doctor & General Porter asleep on the floor of the front room.

"Where's your bed doctor?"

He rubbed his eyes. "Gave it up last night to a sick woman." He stepped in the back room & brought out a bundle—a new baby! "What shall I name it?"

"Muscogee."

"All right, Muscogee it shall be." Porter walked up & sanctioned the christening.

The Indian who won the foot race at the Muscogee fair presented a pair of buckskin leggins handsomely trimmed to Dr Wright & he gave them to me.

The members & other officials attending the Council numbered about one hundred & fifty & perhaps there were that many more people at the Capitol.

How were they accommodated? There were three hotels capable of accommodating one third of the crowd, with the aid of the few private houses, & the remainder of the crowd lived in log cabins & tents. The little town looked like a camp meeting during the sessions of the council.

After adjournment in the afternoon groups of Indians would gather around the three stores, while others would play croquet for hours, the prominent officials frequently indulging in this innocent pastime with all the zeal & hilarity of children.

The meals at the hotels were at sun rise, twelve Oclock, & sun down generally.

John McIntosh, although a preacher & Chief Justice, did not permit his dignity to be troublesome, but was full of fun & the life of every crowd.

His peer in this regard was General Porter, familiarly called *Pleas* & between the two there was a happy supply of jokes, tales & anecdotes.

"John you remember the fellow who was always bragging. Well, one day we were herding the cattle & there was an unruly steer among them in the pen & the men couldn't handle him. This fellow kept on giving orders & making suggestions as to the management of the steer. Finally I said 'Why don't you go in the pen & show them how to handle him?'

"He felt ashamed to confess that he was afraid so he climbed over the fence, & said, 'Now, watch me & I'll show you how to manage that steer.' He approached the steer & hit him. The steer darted at him & knocked him clean over. He tried to get up & as soon as he was on his all fours the steer, who was behind him, made a rush, & hit him a centre lick & turned him heels over head.

"The boys howled with delight, & the fellow crawled & ran to the fence climbed to the top & said in a tone of pretended triumph, 'Well, I reckon, I satisfied that confounded steer this time.' "

"Brother John, can you not give me one more good joke on Dr Buckner before we part?"

John smiled, removed his pipe from his mouth, looked at Dr B—.

"When Dr Buckner first came he attended a big meeting. The best young men in the Nation were there. One day they were sitting near the arbor before preaching began when a lady rode up on a very fine horse. She was closely veiled & was dressed very finely. It was before the war when there was a plenty of money.

"To the astonishment of Dr Buckner none of the young men offered to assist the lady in dismounting. He determined to rebuke them quietly, & set them an example of politeness to ladies. He approached the lady while all the crowd was looking at him.

"He very politely requested the privilege of assisting her. She graciously consented, & he aided her in dismounting, took her horse & hitched him to a limb.

"Then he turned to escort her to the arbor. The lady lifted her veil & behold she was as black as a crow. It was in the days of slavery & the doctor himself owned slaves & you can imagine the roar of laughter that greeted him as he discovered his mistake."

WILD INDIANS AT MUSCOGEE FAIR

CROWDS OF WILD INDIANS made the scene strikingly picturesque. War paint, beads, & bear claws abounded, but peace prevailed.

The cavalcade which escorted Secretary Schurz to the fair grounds from the hotel, was a combination between the Knight errants of the days of chivalry & the grand parade of a circus. The wild Indian, in his holiday costume, his head shaved back to the scalp lock, his face painted in red & yellow, his beaded leggins & moccasins, his bow & quiver handsomely encased in decorated otter skins, presents no mean picture, & the clowns of the stage, & the festive knights of saw dust & the mystic crew of Comus, may well look to their laurels.

It was said that twenty nine different tribes of Indians were represented at the fair. The five civilized tribes were largely represented. [Obliterated], chief-elect [of the] Cherokees was there. He is a stout man, about five ft ten inches high, has very black eyes, black hair, & wears a mustache & beard. His complexion is ruddy. He was dressed neatly in dark blue navy goods & wore a black felt hat. His conversation was that of a man of intelligence & culture, & when I quoted Falstaff to him he replied by quoting Hamlet. Having just come out of a campaign I asked him what was the essence of Indian politics.

"Not much difference here & in the States. Loaves and fishes," was his reply. The old fight between the *Ins* & the *Outs*.

Col. William Penn Adair, delegate from the Cherokee Nation to Washington, prominent in the affairs of his people & just elected second Chief, was there, his tall form, long black hair & handsome face attracting attention in every crowd.

The Chickasaws were well represented by Governor Ben[jamin] F. Burney, and othe[r] leading citizens. Governor Burney looked quite young, was of medium size, dark hazel eyes & black hair & was well dressed.

It is needless to remark that the civilized Indians as a rule dress like citizens in the States, & at public gatherings their appearance will compare favorably with that of similar crowds in the States.

Governor Wright of the Choctaws had a large crowd of friends with him, & the Choctaw display at the fair was very interesting. Governor Wright was President of an International Sunday School Convention, which assembled at Muscogee during the fair. Rev. J. S. Murrow, Missionary for years among the Choctaws, was with them, a delegate to the Sunday School Convention. He has labored long & successfully for the elevation of the red man & is loved by the Indians as he deserves.

Most of the prominent men of the Muscogee Nation were present, notably General Pleasant Porter, Judge G. W. Stidham, Hon. D. M. Hodge, Col. D. N. McIntosh, the Perrymans, the Moores, & the Graysons.

General Schurz[3] was escorted by a committee selected from various tribes & headed by a brass band, which discoursed patriotic airs, & after encircling the grand pavilion in the fair grounds, the procession halted beneath a tall flag staff supporting the Stars & Stripes at the foot of which a platform had been erected. The Secretary was welcomed in a short, pointed address by Hon. William P. Ross of the Cherokee Nation.

[3] Carl Schurz was United States secretary of the interior from 1877 to 1881. Tuggle had called on Schurz in November 1879 with letters of recommendation from Governor Colquitt of Georgia and President Hayes. See the Washington Journal.

General Schurz spoke of his visit to the Indian country & said that his impressions were favorable & that he believed under proper treatment that the Indians would advance to a higher civilization; that the present administration was friendly to their best interests & would exert its power in protecting them from aggression & in the enforcement of treaty stipulations; that he feared that at some future time the flood tide of emigration might overflow the borders & admonished them to prepare for such a change by dividing their lands in severalty & giving to each man his share with a fee simple title, while they controlled their own affairs. He encouraged them in their efforts for a higher development & assured them of his cordial friendship.

His speech was well received & the Indians all spoke of General Schurz as their friend. He held a reception in the second story of the main fair building and evinced great kindliness of heart in patiently listening to the talks of the various Indian tribes during the day & most of the night. As specimen speeches of the Indians, the following extract is made from the Indian Journal published at Muscogee; Big Man a Caddo said: "Brothers when I left home to come here I thought I would see many of my brothers of other tribes & I do now see them & am glad. I have no education & cannot say much. But I see what education has done for my white brothers & I am willing to give my children to the teacher so they can do & speak good things, & learn to do what I have failed to do. Help us & pray for us."

Of course he spoke through an interpreter as did all the other tribes. Indeed sometimes several interpreters were employed before the words could be translated into English.

Left-Hand, a great man & chief among the Arrapahoes said: "I consider all these tribes & people brothers, and we have one great Father. We want our children to serve God & have the white man's religion & ways. I have come a long way to see my brothers & I have been paid for coming. I thank you all for wanting to do us good. Long ago we did not know these things, but by sending our children to school they will be like whites. I like what my Caddo brother has said. On Sabbath I & my people meet with our agent, & the people & learn the Book of God."

Asa habbee, whose name means *Milky Way*, a Comanche chief and for a long time a great General on the plains, a terror to the Mexicans & who fought a successful battle against Kit Carson during the late war, but who is now trying the white mans way, said, "Our brothers we come to speak to you. When I was on the plains fighting fifteen years I saw nothing good, but Col. Adair, our Cherokee brother came out to see us at Ft Cobb & gave us a good talk & we did not fling it away on the ground but kept it. He told us to stop on a piece of ground & to work corn & raise pig & cow & build house. White man had told us to do this before, but we would not listen to him, but when our Cherokee brother told us, we tried his advice & have found it true & good. I have come far to see my brothers & sisters, but now my heart is changed from what it was on the plains & I now love my brothers & sisters. God knows that my heart is true in these words. Long time when I lay down to sleep I think of all you, my brothers, & I want to see you & when I wake up I want to see you & today I am glad to see you."

General Schurz purchased a bow arrows, bow & quiver case from Asa habbee, who insisted however on reserving some arrows which belonged to his father & grandfather. His bow, quiver & accouterments received the premium as the handsomest at the fair. The case was made of otter skins beautifully decorated.

George Washington, a Caddo, said: "I am glad to meet our brothers & sisters in this house. Many white men know me & I will do all that our brothers want me to do. Our people have quit what our grandfathers told us to do & now we try to do what our friends tell us of the new way. I have a good home like you & live well."

Many of the talks to the Secretary told of the bad crops, an account of the long drouth, & that the United States government ought to help them as game was scarce.

Hour after hour did Secretary Schurz patiently listen to tribe after tribe recite their complaints with a childish faith that the government would provide for all their wants.

Rev. W. S. Robertson, aided by his wife & daughter, made a fine xhibit from the Tallahassee Manual labor Mission School. The agricultural display was not large but the big pumpkin, the big turnip & a beet about three feet long demonstrated the fertility of Indian soil & that the Indian had caught the white man's idea of a fair. The big hog was there too. Weight doubtful, but the owner, with a doxology face, insisted that his hog weighed over six hundred pounds, & was not he a friend of George Washington?

The horse race was there,—who can doubt that the noble red man is following in his white brother's way?

Beaded trinkets in profusion were xhibited by the wild tribes. Moccasins, leggins, necklaces, belts, bow & quiver cases, buckskin suits, tapestry woven by Navajos & other tribes, mink & otter skins, tanned entire, & made into tobacco pouches, greeted the eye of the spectator on every side. One curious Indian doll from the Nez Perces was xhibited. It was made in imitation of an Indian woman, with a papoose strapped to a board & slung over the head.

The Indians were delighted with the fair & they wandered around among the different collections with an evident relish of the spectacle presented.

One splendid specimen of the red man in all his native simplicity, in the costumes of his ancestors, his long hair plaited & wrapped in red flannel, his face decorated in red & yellow & his brightly colored blanket falling in graceful folds like the toga of a Roman patrician from his broad shoulders, stood among the crowd & gazed in mute admiration at a handsome silver mounted pipe made of the Minnesota red stone.

"Money, much?" he asked.

"Twenty dollars" was the reply, & for fear he did not understand, both hands were held up with outstretched fingers, then shut & then the fingers were xtended again. His eyes grew larger as he grunted. "Heap—money heap!" and gazed again at the magnificent pipe.

When wild Indians meet & do not understand the languages spoken, they can communicate by a rude sign language with the aid of pantomine. By watching their faces & hands one can guess with some accuracy at their meaning. They all understand what you mean when you offer them your right hand & say "Howdy."

They will smile, shake your hand & say, "How," & give a grunt of peace & good will— [Sketch breaks off here.]

[The following sketch calls to mind Tuggle's direct question to John McIntosh recorded in his Indian Diary: "Are they wild Indians the Wichitas and other bands near them?" And McIntosh's smiling reply: "Wild Indians? No they are not wild. They live in houses. They have farms. . . ."]

As they marched into the fair grounds the men rode first followed by the squaws & the pack ponies, which in addition to the loads on their backs dragged bundles of lodge poles about six feet long at their sides, one end of the poles trailing on the ground. On dismounting, the squaws began to pitch the tents, or lodge, which they did by fastening [t]he tops of five poles together & placing the bottom end of the poles about six feet apart so as to form a circular lodge about six feet in diameter & not over five feet high in the centre. Some were a little larger, but ordinarily this was the size. Around the poles they wrapped a blanket, a tent cloth, or any covering they owned. Some of the lodges were so small that the buck or warrior could barely coil himself up under the covering after piling his saddle, bridle and other [t]rappings within the lodge, and spreading a blanket [for] a carpet by day & a bed at night. A stick would be inserted in the ground at the door of the lodge on which to hang such articles as could not be packed within the lodge. The squaws after arranging the lodges prepared for cooking by cleaning away the prairie grass & scooping out a little shallow hole in the ground for a rude fire place. Here they built a fire of sticks & roasted their meat by hanging it on sticks near the fire, & sometimes stewing it in small camp kettles.

When beef was issued by the agents, who very generously entertained the wild Indians while they were attending the fair, the squaws would slice it very thin & hang it on poles, or as poles were scarce within the enclosure, spread it on the grass to dry. Frequently they would draw a terrapin from a sack, carry him by the tail to the fire & gently drop him among the coals. Soon "pop" would be heard, & the squaw would run to the fire, look at the delicious terrapin: as the [thick?] foam stewed from between his shells & then she would turn him over to roast on the other side in his own sweetness.[4]

As they travel over the prairie they catch these terrapins, & carry them along to camp to be roasted & eaten as a great delicacy. Why not? Not so nice as a clam bake, or raw oysters, or snails, or crabs, perhaps, and yet it might require great discrimination to decide which dish is the very nicest in the abstract.

Let us take a stroll among the wild Indians as they are encamped in the fair grounds & as they sit in the lodges & in groups before the lodge doors.

Here is Toosh-a-way, or White handled Knife, an old Comanche chief, sitting in his lodge with his two wives seated on his left. Teh sehweit (Refusing to Come) about sixty years old sitting next Toosh-away, & then by her side & to her left sat Chah-kar-se-weit ([P]ulling you to one side) his second wife, about eighteen years old. The squaws evidently love each other, & occasionally the young wife would lie down & put her head in the lap of the old wife & as a mark of affection she would *look her* head.

---

[4] Tuggle evidently rewrote this sketch, carefully elaborating, rearranging, and omitting certain details included in a second draft, which describes the process of pitching camp as follows: ". . . forming a lodge six feet in diameter and often not more than five feet high, under which the warrior would coil himself up after piling his saddle and trappings in the rear, and spreading a blanket, or robe for a carpet. While he proceeded to make an elaborate toilet, the squaw, or squaws, for many of them boasted of several better halves, scooped a hole in the ground for a fire place, built a fire of sticks, and roasted their meat before or on the fire, or stewed it in small kettles. The fresh beef, not needed for the present meal, would be sliced very thin and either hung on poles to dry in the sun, or spread on the grass. Frequently a terrapin would be pulled out of a bag, dropped alive among the glowing coals and when he 'popped', or exploded, the squaw would run to the fire, gaze at the delicious terrapin stewing in his own [red-real?] foamy sauce, bubbling from between his shells, and then gently [turning it] over to roast on the other side."

They shared the household burdens & doubtless the old squaw was rejoiced to welcome the young wife as a companion, who would help her pitch the lodge, gather the wood—work the corn patch, & aid generally in waiting on the lord of the forest.

In Tooshaway's lodge sat his son Arsoas, also Meah quat (Going about) & his wife, Me-chas-soo-wah (Tearing it).

Through Mr. William Shirley, an Irishman who has lived with the Comanches twenty five years, I asked Tooshaway which wife he loved best. He looked at them & answered, "Both." Doubtless he did love both, the old squaw was his first love & the young one was his last.

As a mark of especial favor, as he said, Tooshaway permitted me to have his picture taken by a traveling artist on the fair ground.

Behold Toosh-a-way and his two wives. [Tuggle's note to identify missing picture.]

A Comanche woman followed us to the artists tent gorgeously arrayed in a red cotton table cloth, & Tooshaway made signs indicating that she wished her picture taken. Here it is. [Missing.] It was amusing to see Tooshaway & his two wives munching ginger cakes, to which he had treated them with some money I slipped in his hand before leaving his lodge, & they had just finished their feast as they sat for their pictures. This may account for their pleasant xpression.

When the artist handed the picture to Tooshaway, he & his two wives looked at it intently & the old fellow grunted out a laugh & said "Papoosy, papoosy," evidently thinking the artist had taken a part of him & made a doll, baby or papoose out of him. The squaws chuckled with pleasure and they [ins]isted on my returning the favor by presenting my picture to them. Tooshaway wore a large silver medal presented to him by President Filmore. Let us be introduced to the other Comanches.

Here is Mah-seit (Finger nail) & his wife Wo-he, (Gambling with sticks, or Jack Straws), Kah-hab-be-waht (Running about at night &, don't sleep) & his squaw, Ye-ah-peet-ei, (Coming home after-sun-down), E-kah-weit-tah (Going in the tent), On-na-we-yah (Getting the Salt), Shar-re-te-kei, Ah-soo-tine (To be kind), Tah-che-nip-took-who-wah (Black Star) & his wife Yaht-tee (Crying).

Asa-habbeet (Milky Way) and his wife Wush-ah-wah-weet (Striking).

Asahabbeet was a grave, dignified man, over six feet & powerfully built & was handsomely dressed in black velvet leggins, a fine robe & wore large ear rings with chain & pendents a foot long.

The above Comanches belonged to several bands [of] Penetekas, or Honey eaters, the Yam-parikas, or Root-diggers and Sharseters, or Dog Eaters.

THE KIOWAS: Bah-weit-cah, Tanai-za-da-dah, Dangerous Eagle, Cowah-pah-Kah, Lone Wolf.

I succeeded in getting Lone Wolf & his wife to sit for their pictures & here they are. [Pictures again missing.]

APACHES—Ah-can-nah-weich, Kohk-ta—Chah-ke, E-wah-hah.

WICHITAS: Soo-nah-ah-kah, Kin-chose, Towaceanie Dave, Towoceonie Jim.

KEOCHI: Kah wah him-ta.

WACO: Sibley.

CADDOS: He-mi-sho-wa (Big Man), Cherokee Charley, Chah-ah-tah (Head Halter), James Edwards, Ban-o-she, Ne-naht, wife, Kah-hah-teh-che, Te-yune-nah, So-yah-te-pah, Chah-pah-che.

DELEWARE: Long Horn, Jack Harris, Little Jim Ned.

CHEYENNES: Living Bear, White Shield, Crazy Lead, P[l]enty of Horses, Man on the Cloud, Black Rock, Fox Tail, Bear Lying Down, Starving Elk, Little Bear, Long Neck, & Chief for All.

ARRAPAHOES: Yellow Bear & wife, Left Hand, Cut Finger, Sun Rise, Curly, Medicine Pipe, White Buffalo, Black Kayote, Left Hand No. 2, White Bear, White Man & wife, Bear Robe & wife, & Black Wolf.

EASTERN SHAWNEES: John Jackson, George Beaver, & Lazarus Flint.

MODOCS: Bogus Charley, (the present Chief).

SENECAS: Joseph Spear, John Winney, & Joseph White-Crow.

WYANDOTTES: Irving Long & Nicholas Cartier.

PEORIAS: James Charley, James Fry, and John Wadsworth.

TUAPPAWS: Charley Tuappaw.

OTTAWAS: Henry Clay, James Black, William Herr, John Early, Francis King, Isacc McCay, Levi Dagnett, Arel Dagnett, and Lewis Angel.

The Osages had a large delegation headed by Joseph Pah-no-pussy, who had large holes in his ears filled with rings, and wore a bear claw necklace set in otter skin.

Black Dog, Water-inky, Big Chief and other Osages were at the fair—

The wild Indians were the most attractive feature of the fair, & the visitors from Texas, Kansas, Missouri & other States found constant enjoyment in mingling with them at their lodges & talking to them through interpreters, & watching their movements generally.

One scene was very amusing. Mr. J. D. Highleyman from Ohio, who was located in Muscogee, was accompanied by his brother's wife from Sedalia, Mrs. Laura Highleyman, a bright, blackeyed, handsome matron in the full bloom of womanhood, and by Mrs. Phipps, a quiet sedate lady, who had *nerves*. They were seeing the wild Indians. The squaws were roasting terrapins about the time of their arrival & one squaw was passing the carriage in which the ladies were seated, & she was holding a terrapin by the tail. The ladies had just asked a squaw to bring a pair of moccasins to them, and said as the woman passed—with the terrapin, "Bring it here" meaning the moccasin.

The squaw started towards the ladies with the terrapin, which was alive & wriggling & kicking, & as soon as they saw her intention they began screaming, "O, don't bring it, don't come here, carry it away."

The squaw enjoyed the fun & all the Indians began laughing. She carried it nearer as she reached the carriage the ladies were in terror & shouting "O, Lordy, O Lordy, don't, don't!" The squaw was delighted & dropped the terrapin in Mrs. Phipps' lap, as she turned white as a sheet and held up her hands in dumb horror, speechless with fear—while her friends made the air vocal with operatic screams.

A mouse in a room full of ladies can create some amusement, or a bat of a summer night, but the perfection of a galvanic battery of femi[ni]ne horror is a live terrapin dropped suddenly in a nervous woman's lap.

A friend came to the rescue and threw the terrapin from her lap as there was no time for a funeral.[5] [At this point Tuggle's first version concludes with a brief summary of the fair's general significance (given below); but in reorganizing and composing his second version, he added the following commentary on the impact made by the presence of Carl Schurz at the fair.]

At a given signal a cavalcade of civilized and wild Indians escorted Secretary Schurz into the Fair Ground. It was a ra[re] sight, not only as a strange spectacle, but [as an] omen of future possibilities. The [sight was] picturesque. A brass band led the procession. The Secretary was seated in a carriage with a committee composed of leading men from the Chero-

---

[5] In his rewritten version of this episode, Tuggle evidently decided that although the terrapin incident was too good to omit, it would be more prudent to give less specific detail. But his revision, which follows, also lost much of its original vividness: "The five civilized tribes were re[presented] by their leading officials and it [was interesting] to observe them watching the movements, exam[ining] the costumes and trappings of the wild tribes [as] a curiosity second only to that of the white [men] who had come in crowds from the adjoining [and] more distant states to witness the novel spectacle of the Indian fair. Two white ladies were seated in [a] carriage intently watching some squaws as they roasted terrapins in the blazing fire. The squaws held a whispered consultation. When one of them went to a bog, dived down and brought up a wriggling terrapin, which holding by the tail she carried near the carriage on her way to the fire, but as she passed she gave a sudden jerk—and down fell the live terrapin in the lap of one of the ladies. Scream after scream rent the air, while the squaws chuckled at the fun till a civilized Indian came to the rescue of the nervous fair one, and removed the destined roast."

kees, Creeks, Choctaws, Chickasaws and Seminoles. Then came the wild
Indians in holiday costume, heads shaved to the scalp-lock, faces painted
in yellow and red, white beads and bear-claw necklaces lent a charm to
the festal array. After encircling the main pavilion the procession halted
at a platform at the base of a tall flag-staff from the top of which floated
the stars and stripes.

The cabinet officer was welcomed in a pointed address by William P.
Ross, of the Cherokee nation, whose language, appearance and delivery
bespoke a man of intelligence and culture.

The Secretary spoke of his favorable impressions of Indian progress,
and thought under proper management the Indians would advance to a
higher civilization; that while the stipulations [of] treaties guaranteed
protection from all aggr[ession], he feared that in the future the flood tide
[of emi]gration would overflow the border, and h[e] admonished them to
prepare for such an emergency by a division of their lands in severalty
while they could control their own affairs.

The civilized Indians hung their heads at this foreshadowing of their
fate. Their whole history had been full of illustrations on this subject.
Lands were ceded, others occupied only to be ceded again, divided often
in severalty to such as chose to remain among the whites soon to pass into
the possession of shrewder neighbors and when their continental domain
had dwindled into this last refuge, still this ghost of destroyed homes
haunted them and presided at their holiday festival. With an uncertain
future, with their homes threatened, how could they encourage the wild
Indian to venture on the devious path of civilization? They knew the
Secretary was their friend, and this very fact gave additional weight to the
evil prophecy.

The Secretary held a reception in the second story of the central pavilion, as all [wanted] to shake the hand of the representative of the Gr[eat]
Father. Twenty nine tribes were reported at the fair, and each one desired
to have a talk with the Great Father, the United States government.

[At this point the second version continues with the speeches of Big
Man, the Caddo, and Asa-habbeet, the Comanche chief, quoted above.
Then Tuggle concludes his second version with an illuminating analysis
of the Indian tribes' present and future prospects under the aegis of a
civilized United States government. Presented as a direct quotation from
the mouth of General Pleasant Porter himself, this analysis gives a penetrating insight into the thinking of intelligent, forward-looking Creek
leaders.]

The Choctaws maintained their reputation for intelligence and progress. Their departments in the exhibition was in some respects superior to the others and a large delegation, headed by Governo[r] Wright, contributed to the attractions and interests of the occasion. A Sunday School convention composed of delegates from schools in the Indian Territory was in session during the progress of the fair, and Governor Wright, who was a Presbyterian minister, was elected President of this Christian organization. With the Choctaws was Rev. J. S. Murrow, who has labored long and successfully for the elevation of the Indians and is justly esteemed.

The Creeks were represented by most of their leading men, among them Porter, the McIntoshes, Graysons, Moores, Perrymans, Hodge and Judge Stidham.

On the last day of the fair I met General Porter. "What do you think of the fair?" said I.

"As a civilizer it would be cheaper than war. There is no limit to the influence of a free show, and a free lunch. It might pay the United States to test the question by a few years xperiment on the Utes, Apaches, and Sioux."

"What of the Secretary's speech?" I asked.

A deep sigh. "It is a sad confession for the representative of fifty millions of civilized people to make, that a few land speculators cannot be kept from encroaching on Indian lands. We ask nothing except good faith in abiding by the treaties, but alas, a thousand treaties have been negotiated and just a thousand treaties have been violated. Our treaties guarantee the right of self-government, and when we are making reasonable progress, we are constantly annoyed and hindered by the suggestion that we should divide our lands in severalty. Individually it would be to my interest, but it would be a curse to the mass of my people. They are not ready for it. Patience must be exercised. A nation can not be civilized in a day, nor in a century. How long did it require the Anglo-saxon race to become free, civilized, enlightened?

"Then too, the Indian must develop from within. He can not be developed from without. He can be aided, but you can not put civilization on him like a suit of new clothes. The wild Indian can be best approached through the civilized Indian, and there would be few Indian wars if the government officials would ask the cooperation of the civ[il]ized Indian. But what can we do when every year our nations are put to the expense of maintaining delegations at the Federal Capital in order to watch Congress, and to protest against the violations of our treaties by grants to railway corporations. We have no objection to such railroad facilities as are needed by our country, but we claim the right to decide all questions pertaining to our property. If Congress can grant a right of way to a railroad company through our country without our consent, it can grant every foot of it.

"It is not encouraging to the wild Indian to become civilized when he knows how we are disturbed by our white friends, for I know that many of our white friends think that dividing our lands in severalty would be a great step forward. We have no paupers. What community in England, Ireland, or some portions of the States can say as much? How can the Indian be advised with so much confidence to cease to hold lands in common when the latest writers on social science are suggesting that holding re[alty] in common by granting the fee simple [for] the government is the only remedy against the evils resulting from monopoly in land tenure and over crowded population?

"See Ireland today. Is she better by reason of holding realty in severalty? Suppose land was held there in common, would there be as much suffering among the poor people? That is the question, what is best for the poorest classes, for the rich can take care of themselves under any form of land tenure. We have many difficulties to contend with in solving the so-called Indian problem—and one of the greatest results from the impatience of our friends. They would have us jump from semi-civilization into a progressive enlightenment, onward & upward. Well, too much education, too much enlightenment will only retard, not advance. We must have time to grow, assimilate—develop from within. Experience is the wisest teacher, and history does not furnish an xample of a forced civilization being permanent and real.

"The future of the Indian is involved in mystery. Three destinies are before him; fir[st,] extermination, either by war, or an over d[evelopment] called civilization; second miscegen[ation.]" [Tuggle's record of Porter's analysis breaks off here, but see his cryptic diary reference to the probable outcome of the mixing of breeds in the Territory—a "co-partnership between Shem, Ham, & Japhet." His own concern for the future welfare of the Indian tribes and his speculation as to the possibility of civilizing without submerging them are clearly implied in the questions he asked himself at the conclusion of his first narrative treatment of the fair. Noting how orderly it had been—"I saw only one man drunk—a white man. I heard only one man swear—a [c]olored man"—he wrote the following comments:]

The wild Indians enjoyed the fair & promised to come annually. The Osages watched the horse races with intense interest and said they intended to bring their race horses next year, that they came to find out all the tricks of the turf this year so as to profit by them at the next fair.

How would it do for the government to [get] up a fair for all the wild tribes every [ye]ar & give a free barbecue daily during [the] fair? As a civilizer it might be [ch]eaper than war, & there is no telling [the] influence of a free show & a free lunch.

The continental domain of the red man [of] four hundred years ago has dwindled [to] very small proportions, & if the white man desires his red brother to walk his [ro]ad could he adopt a more persuasive [ar]gument than a yearly cordial invitation [to] a family dinner out on the [pr]airie at an Indian fair once in every twelve months?

MORMONS AMONG THE INDIANS, McLEAN'S STORY

"THE INDIANS" said Dr Buckner "are entitled to great credit for not being polygamists, for in addition to their own ancient customs, the Mormons have made efforts to proselyte them, but with little success, and I know very few Indians who have more than one wife. In this respect they are ahead of their laws. I had a strange experience regarding a Mormon apostle since I have been a missionary. One day while reading in my cabin I heard the clatter of horses feet & soon there was a call at my gate. I went out and there sat a well dressed man on a magnificent horse.

" 'Your name is Buckner?'

" 'It is.'

" 'My name is McLean.'

"I invited him to dismount and come in. He had a sad face and a wild look in his eyes. When we were seated he said: 'I have come on a sad mission. Here is a bundle of letters in cipher which you must decipher for me. It is a life and death matter. Are you a Mason?'

" 'I am.'

" 'He extended his hand and with tears in his eyes silently grasped my hand. 'I know I can trust you. Will you help me?' and he gazed at me in such a way that I feared he had lost his mind. 'My dear sir, You have my sympathy in your unknown sorrow. Whatever is right I will do after learning the facts.'

" 'God knows I wish nothing but what is right, to rescue my darling little ones from a fate worse than death, to meet the accursed despoiler of my once happy home. Oh, let me meet him face to face. But I forget that you do not know my story. I lived in San Francisco. I had a wife'— his strong frame quivered with emotion, 'and two children a son and daughter. I was prosperous in my business, happy at home and dreamed not of the sad fate in store for me.'

" 'I saw in the papers an announcement that a Mormon preacher was in the city and my wife told me she believed that she would like to hear him, and accompanied by a friend she went. In a few days she went again and seemed interested. She had a strong mind, was well educated and frequently became enthusiastic on some subject which she fancied for the time. To indulge her I consented for her to attend the Mormon apostle's lectures as often as she liked, and thought very little of the matter, supposing she would derive temporary gratification from investigating the doctrines he promulgated. So you can imagine my horror on returning home one evening to find a note from my wife saying that she had been spiritually enlightened and had discovered that the Mormon apostle was her true spiritual husband, and that she had decided to forsake the ways of the Gentiles and cast in her lot with the Saints. I could not realize the awful reality till the servants informed that my wife—mine no longer, had left in a closed carriage some hours before taking the children with her. I thought till my brain seemed on fire—and I would say to myself, "It can not be true, impossible—she could not—there is some terrible mistake," and then I would read her letter, and look around my desolate room, the playthings of my children scattered on the floor, and her portrait staring at me from the wall. I rushed from the house and wandered along the street during the night.'

" 'I abandoned my business and determined to devote my life to rescuing my children, and if possible saving my lost wife. Employing detectives I pursued the fugitives to Utah only to find they had taken the alarm and disappeared. After long search I heard of them in New York. I went there again to be disappointed. I was here satisfied that my wife had gone to New Orleans with the children, and that Pratt, that was his name, Parley Parker Pratt, had taken some other course. I have reason to believe now that they intend to meet in the Indian Territory and these letters I think will throw some light on the subject.'

" 'He handed me the letters. They were directed to "Mrs. Pratt, Fort Gibson." I could not understand them. I asked McLean to describe the Mormon apostle. When he had done so, I said to him: 'Now, Mr. Mc-Lean, I can not in any way assist or connive at wrong doing, violation of legal, or moral law, and you must promise me that you will do no violent act while here.' He assured me he would not. 'I think your man is here. About three weeks ago I met such a man, who called himself "Rev. Parley Parker," and I hope we can devise a plan to rescue your children, should they be brought here.' He was in raptures. On examining the letters I found that the date and heading were composed of consonants. At the head of one letter was an explanatory note cautioning Mrs. Pratt to watch the change in the vowels as an alteration had been made since she left Salt Lake. I first endeavored to decipher the words by using certain marks for the vowels in the ordinary order, a,e,i,o,u,y, but soon found that this was wrong. I then reversed the vowels, and translated the letters easily. Pratt had been in New York. Mrs McLean had gone to New Orleans and was to join a colony of Mormon emigrants soon to start for Utah via the Indian Territory, where Pratt was to meet the train and resume possession of his fourteenth spiritual comforter, whom he addressed as his wife.

"I told McLean there was a man working on my little farm who had formerly lived among the Mormons. I sent for him and he agreed to start towards Louisiana and meet the Mormon emigrants in order to ascertain whether Mrs McLean and her two children were with them. He was to return and report as soon as practicable. McLean gave a careful description of his wife and children and the man immediately set out on his journey.

"Information was sent to the officer in command at Fort Gibson, and he sent a company of soldiers under Lieut. Little to Old North Fork town to protect us from the Mormon emigrants in the event they attempted violence. The messenger returned and reported that he had met the train and by pretending to be a Mormon, he had won their favor, and that he was satisfied that Mrs. McLean was disguised in men's apparel and was driving an ox-team, and that the children were in the wagon, the boy dressed as a girl, and the girl as a boy. The soldiers were notified and also the Masons and when the train was expected a considerable crowd had gathered near Old North Fork. McLean being mounted on his powerful horse. When the train was seen in the distance McLean could not be restrained, but charged alone towards the approaching colony. Fortunately for him his wife was driving the first wagon. As he dashed up the children recognized him and cried, 'O, mama there's papa.' [From this point on, Tuggle's first version of McLean's rescue of his children is actually more dramatic than his later one, in which he substituted generalized narrative for specific dialogue, omitting a number of the more colorful details which he had noted on the spot as Buckner told the story. The first version continues as follows:]

"McLean reached the first wagon. There was his wife, the refined, cultured woman he had loved & whom he had won as his darling bride, the mother of his children—there, seated in a rude ox-wagon disguised as a man, driving to deeper infamy, to meet the Mormon apostle.

"Two little heads peeped from the covered wagon, four little hands were xtended in joy. 'O, mama, look, there's our papa.' In spite of all disguise the precious little ones knew their father.

"Not a word he spoke. Relentless as Fate he hastened to the rescue. All depended on a moment. The Mormons in the rear would be on him in a twinkling. He snatched one child & put behind him; the second he seized & seated before him, & away he sped like the wind with his darlings.

"I saw McLean coming. I met him. 'Follow me! Quick. They are coming.' I hurried past my house, which then stood down there by the weeping willow where my wife is buried. 'Here is my ice house. Put them in.'

"He dismounted. He hugged his long lost darlings to his bosom. In he rushed, a kiss, the door was slammed, the key was turned, & they were safe.

"Mrs. McLean became frantic. She came running to the fork of the road below my house. She asked the Masons, 'Which way did he go? O, where are my children?' They deceived her and she went the wrong road.

"The soldiers came. They camped near here several days. They came not a day too soon as they reached here the day before the Mormon train arrived. Pratt had agreed to meet Mrs. McLean at Perryman's. Riley Perryman was a half-breed Creek Indian, who had been converted to Mormonism not a great while before. The Mormons had been here in the Territory & made a few converts to their faith, & among them was Riley Perryman, brother of Joe Perryman, one of our native Baptist preachers. Perryman lived about three miles from North Fork, where McLean recovered his children. Pratt, in the letter I deciphered, warned Mrs. McLean about McLean being in pursuit & told her to be cautious with the children & to meet him at Riley Perryman's.

"When she discovered that she had taken the wrong road she returned to old North Fork town & mounting a wagon tongue made a speech, in which she defended her course, & insisted that she had yielded to the strongest impulse of her nature in taking up with Pratt. I never heard that she displayed any feeling about her children after finding that she had taken the wrong road.

"The Mormons saw they could do nothing & renewed their march the next day.

"The soldiers started to Fort Gibson & met & arrested Pratt near Elk Creek. In a few hours Pratt & his 14th spiritual wife would have met.

"McLean remained with his two children at my house some days, during which time we had clothes made for them. His recital of his mental anguish at his wifes desertion, & during his long search for his children was heartrending. He said his hair turned white in a very short time after the fearful disaster.

"Pratt was carried to Van Buren Ark. was imprisoned & afterwards tried. Mrs. McLean attended the trial.

"The trial came. Pratt was acquitted on some technicality. Pratt was jubilant. McLean was in torture. His heart was the theatre of contending passions. What should he do?

"Pratt was a powerful man. He could have weighed 225 pounds, & was physically a brave man.

"McLean was not very stout as compared to Pratt, & seemed by nature quiet & gentle.

"Pratt made a speech in Van Buren, defending his course & said that he would do the same thing again if opportunity presented.

"Mrs. Pratt, or McLean, sympathized with the Mormon apostle.

"The good & evil were at war in McLeans heart.

"Pratt became alarmed. He saw that the citizens were opposed to his course. He started from Van Buren in haste & McLean hearing of his flight followed him. It had rained & Pratt's tracks could be plainly seen. He was overtaken by McLean. 'Bang' rang out the clear, awful report of a navy revolver. For life the Mormon apostle fled. Again the pistol of McLean was heard. Still the fugitive fled on wings of the wind. The third xplosion—& still he fled. Could nothing kill the Mormon Saint? Could the spirit of Joe Smith protect his faithful apostle?

"The fourth, the fifth, the sixth shots were tried in vain. The revolver was xhausted. The Mormon is flying, & the avenging husband was pursuing. Nearer & nearer. He reaches him. There they stood, face to face.

"Pratt, the Mormon, McLean—the ruined husband—the raven locks again their natural, yet unnatural hue—his soul on fire—his nature revolutionized—one passion supreme. It has urged him on days, weeks, months, years & now!

"A moment's stare. Like the lightning flash it came. Another crash. A wild scream of agony. The Mormon fell. A derringer did the work. It was concealed & no one knew that McLean had it.

"The body of the Mormon apostle was carried to Van Buren. McLean had killed him about twelve miles from Van Buren at Frog Bayou. [Tuggle lined out this last sentence.]

"Mrs. McLean wrote poetry about Pratts death. She wrote a letter to

Joe Smith, long since dead, & put the letter in Pratt's bosom to carry to Smith.

"Mrs. McLean went to Europe, it was reported and the children were sent by McLean to New Orleans to the parents of Mrs McLean.

"The man who went to meet the Mormon train was named Smith.[6] I afterwards trusted him freely. He borrowed $140.00 of me to go to keeping house, after marrying a Cherokee woman, & one night he took a canoe & went down the Canadian. I never heard from him till after the late war—in fact, during last fall, when he wrote to me & sent me a copy of 'The Life & Confessions of Jno. D. Lee, the Mormon, with a full account of the Mountain Meadows' Massacre & xecution of Lee.' Smith wrote me in his letter that we knew about the origin of the Massacre, alluding to McLean's rescuing his children & ultimate killing of Pratt, who claimed to be a Mormon Prophet.

"In September 1857, the year after McLean killed Pratt in Arkansas, a company of emigrants from Arkansas were traveling through Utah, & were massacred at Mountain Meadows, men, women & all the children, xcept 17, according to Lee's confession.[7] There were about 150 men, women & children, four hundred head of Cattle & seventy or eighty horses. The train was wealthy & carried money, jewelry, bedding, household goods & fine wearing apparel.

"Parley Parker Pratt was one of the original apostles & prophets & the Mormons vowed vengeance upon McLean & his friends. I was alarmed myself. I had done nothing wrong, but I knew the Davites obeyed the orders of their leaders. Lee confessed that he had with him at Mountain Meadows about fifty eight whites & about four or five hundred Indians, & that they shot little girls who went to the spring for water for the famishing emigrants, & that after four days of fighting by the brave emigrants, the Mormons deliberately decided on a plan of treachery. They sent in a flag of truce & promised protection, if the emigrants would give up their arms, & come out of their fortifications.

"The emigrants were starving. They acquiesced. The arms, the wound-

[6] This man may be Lot Smith, who answered Brigham Young's plea for aid in combatting federal troops following the Mountain Meadows Massacre. See note 7.

[7] The Mountain Meadows Massacre, which occurred September 11, 1857, was one of the worst atrocities in a continuing series of clashes between the Mormons and other emigrant groups beginning with the destruction of Nauvoo and the murder of Prophet Joseph Smith in 1838. Details of the massacre, directed by John D. Lee and perpetrated upon a large party of emigrants from Missouri and Arkansas, bear out Buckner's account as recorded by Tuggle. See *The American Heritage History of the Great West*, ed. Alvin M. Josephy, Jr. (New York, 1965).

ed & the children were put into wagons driven by Mormons. Then came the women marching in single file & then, a little in the rear, followed the unarmed, wounded, perishing band of despondent men.

"Lee fired & killed a woman in the forward wagon. This was the signal for the massacre. The helpless men were shot down like dogs. The screaming women were butchered, the poor little children were dragged from the wagons & their throats were cut from ear to ear. Sick women were driven from the cor[r]al & butchered & stripped. Some suffered worse than death. Rumor had it that one young wife & mother saw her husband shot down. She sprang to his side. A ruffian seized her for a hellish purpose. She put her little baby on her dead husband's breast, drew a dagger & turned like a tigress on the vile monster. He recoiled, but another villain stabbed the noble heroine in the back & she fell dead across her husband's feet, & then the fiend took the mother's dagger & pinned the baby's body, with a single stroke, to the body of its dead father, & laughed at the death struggles of the little innocent.

"Eight days after the massacre, witnesses in the trial of Lee, the Mormon, testified that they counted 127 bodies of men, women & children, that no clothing was on the bodies, that some were shot, some stabbed & some had their throats cut & that wolves and ravens had lacerated the dead bodies.

"The massacre occurred in Sept. 1857. On March 23d 1877 John D Lee, the Mormon, was xecuted at the scene of the massacre for participation in this blood-thirsty massacre.

"A monument was erected in memory of the ill-fated emigrants. The inscription on the monument of his victims could be seen. It read, 'Vengeance is mine. I will repay saith the Lord.'

"Blindfolded Lee sat on his coffin twenty feet from his xecutioners. 'Fire.' Five bullets pierced his heart. The murderer escaped punishment for twenty years, but Justice overtook him.

"Of the children who were saved, were Wm Garrett & his sister Malinda. He was ten & she six years old at the Massacre. He remained with the Indians a captive & during the campaign in which Custer was killed, Garrett was captured by the Federal soldiers. He was taken to the home of his childhood & identified. He resided near Oak Hill, in Missouri a year or two ago, has married & practices medicine in the Indian method having been a 'Medicine' man. His sister married Red Cloud the Sioux Chief & [is] the mother of three children.[8] Such is the report."

[8] If Buckner's report is correct, Malinda Garrett became the wife of one of the most intrepid Indian leaders in the history of the West.

SCENES AT WEWOKA

JOHN TOOK a few whiffs from his inseparable companion, a merry twinkle was in his eye and he began; "Down among the Seminoles where brother Factor & brother John Jumper preached, there are a good many colored people. I see some here at the camp meeting, the old fellows up there at the arbor today."

I had seen them. Two were dressed in peculiar style. They wore loose sack coats, made of blue cotton stripes, & had large turbans on their heads. One turban was made of a brown shawl twisted around the head, & the other was made out of a large handkerchief with stripes of yellow, blue, red & white. Both were barefooted. The old fellow with the bright colored turban had Burnside whiskers which were as white as was his hair, for he was indub[itab]ly very old, & when he opened his mouth to sing his teeth shone like ivory. These Negroes came from Florida with the Indians & have been the means in many cases of converting the Indians to Christianity as often the Indians would listen to a colored man preach when they would not care to attend religious services conducted by white men.

"Well," continued John, "during a revival among the Seminoles one old colored preacher was preaching about Heaven & telling them what a good place it was & he told them that one of the best things up there was good eating, & he said, 'O, Yes, my brudderin, Tank de Lord, when we gits to dat blessed place, we'll fust hab good things to eat all de time. Bes tings in de world. Glory to de Lord. Up in Heben, we will just eat dem good hog heads, & cabbages all de time.'

"One brother in the congregation got happy and began shouting, 'Bless de Lord, Glory.'

"The old preacher warmed up to his work & went on, 'O, Yes, my dear brudderin & sisterin, good eating all de time & plenty ob it. We'll have hog head & cabbage all de time & we'll eat dem hog heads till de grease pours down de sides of our moufs.'

"The old brother in the congregation was overcome, he jumped up clapped his hands & shouted out, 'Go on, my brudder in de Lord, & speak unto us some more of dem blessed *greasy* words.' "

John enjoyed the story himself & the Indians laughed heartily for they enjoy jokes & tales.

"John, I heard that John Jumper was coming with you and some of the wild tribes."

"They will come to the fair at Muscogee & put off their trip till then."

"I've heard John that some said that you baptized some of the wild Indians without sufficient proof of their conversion, how about it?"

"Well, if that book is right," taking up his Baxter Bible, "I was right. It says he that believed on the Lord Jesus shall be saved, 'He that believeth & is baptized shall be saved,' & if a man tells me he believes in Jesus, I'll baptize him everytime."

"John, I see a very long cow horn tied to your saddle, what is that for, to blow your congregation up?"

"No, just for my children. When I'm dead & gone they can say, 'My Father brought this horn from the plains.' "

Johns allusion to dying suggested a conversation on death & burial. Rev. William McComb, called by everybody "Billy" said, "During the war I was up on Cave Creek & one day while going through the woods I saw something up in a tree, about fifteen feet from the ground. I thought it was a crow's nest but it looked much too big for that. I climbed the tree to it, but I tell you I came down in a hurry. I found a dead baby up there, lying on some sticks & brush."

"How did it get there?"

"The Osages had camped near there, and I think they put the child there. That was in 1863. I have often seen children's bones in hollow trees. They cut to the hollow, put the child inside the tree & then stop up the hole some way. The bones always looked small."

I mentioned that in the old Nation in Georgia [I] had heard that bodies were often buried in open pens made of poles.

"O, Yes," said Billy, "the Indians used to bury that way. They would lay down some poles, put the body on them & then build a little pen around the body so that wolves & other animals couldn't reach the body."

Brother Daniel Tiger preached at the arbor in Creek, & brother John McIntosh prayed after the sermon. I could occasionally hear a word "Chesus," "Calvary," but the rest was foreign to my ears, yet it was touching to listen to John's plaintive, pleading tones.

I met one of the old colored men, the bright turban, & was introduced by Maj. Vore. His name was Davis. "Any kin to Jeff?" He smiled and showed his ivory cargo & said through Maj. Vore that he had heard of him. He told me he came from Florida in 1838.

Many of the civilized Indians are members of the church & evidently enjoy religious services, especially singing. They will sing by the hour & sometimes their services continue all night long.

Among the Creeks the Presbyterians have had a manual-labor-mission school for about thirty years. The Methodists have had a similar school

& great good has been accomplished in the education of the Indian children. Most of the prominent men in the Indian Territory have been educated at the mission schools, while a few have attended schools & colleges in the states.

The Indians are ahead of their laws. The Creeks have lived under a constitution since 1867, have laws on most subjects & yet they have no marriage law. A man can have one wife, or a dozen. Practically, public opinion, shaped by the missionaries & religious organizations among the Indians, controls the matter, & it is very rare to find a man with more than one wife. The Association at Wewoka adopted a memorial addressed to the Creek council urging the propriety of enacting a marriage law suitable to the conditions & circumstances of the Muscogee Nation.

The number of schools & churches, the membership of Christian organizations, the percentage of people who can read & write will compare favorably in these respects with the States. Dr. Buckner states that there are about twenty five hundred Baptists among the Creeks & that at least that number have died during his missionary labors of the last thirty one years.

The people continued to come to the Camp ground & by Saturday the scene was picturesque. Hundreds of ponies grazed near the Camp, some hobbled & some staked out, groups of Indians were about the grass-arbors & tents, beef cut into thin strips & slices hung on poles to dry in the sun & wind, a few cooking stoves & more log heaps were kept busy preparing a feast for the inner man, & no inferior feast it was. The bill of fare consisted of coffee, milk, biscuit, beef in a variety of forms, chickens, turkeys, cakes, pies, sofkey, & abuskey. I saw a barrel of sugar & a sack of coffee distributed late Saturday evening, & Shem, Ham & Japhet dwelt together in unity & found it sweet & pleasant.

The Chief of the Muscogee Nation, Ward Coachman invited me to supper at his camp. He is a heavily built man, six feet high & will weigh over two hundred pounds. His eyes are dark hazel, his hair black, & his whiskers are dark, tinged with grey & very thin & scattering. He was born at Wetumpka Alabama, & moved to the Indian Country about 1848. He wore a suit of dark grey citizens clothes, a black felt hat, & seemed about fifty-five years old. He is a man of intelligence, speaks English & has a pleasant address. He is a Baptist & attended the association as a delegate.

The last night of the camp meeting the Indians continued the religious services all night long. About dark they gathered at the big arbor, & sang until the preacher was ready, then followed a sermon & after that the all night services began. They would sing, then pray, then some one would talk, & so the exercises were protracted till daylight. During the night there was a severe rain accompanied with wind & the crowd was driven from the grass arbor, which leaked like a sifter & as many as could be packed into the little church continued to sing & pray there. The scene was very striking & impressive.

About an hour before daylight they were still singing, slapping their hands for joy, & John McIntosh stood in the pulpit, his tall, graceful form wrapped in a bright colored blanket, & his musical voice could be easily distinguished. "Chesus Ninny," John would sing out, & at the same time point upwards with his right hand. Then melodious songs, heartfelt prayers, joyous faces gave token of deep fervor & patient worship.

The morning star seemed to twinkle with a happier radiance as it looked down on these all night worshippers, still supplicating the Deity as the east was brightened with the coming Day.

"Why, John, do they worship all night long?"

"They say they used to worship the Devil all night, & now they think they ought to worship God all night."

At one of the camps I met a town chief, Harjo, & asked him if he would permit me to see certain copper, or brass plates, which were in his keeping at his own town, some twenty miles distant. Picket, in his history of Alabama, refers to these same copper relics, which are probably pieces of armor left by DeSoto's band in 1540 & the Creeks have preserved them as trophies of war. Time has rendered the relics sacred & the present keepers have a tradition that the Great Spirit handed them down from Heaven. Others say that the English people presented them to the Indians. Years ago there were inscriptions on these plates, but the annual scouring to which they are subjected has obliterated all trace of the letters. A man who saw & handled the plates several years ago described them as almost circular in shape, about eighteen inches in diameter, quite thin, slightly convex, & with a small projection in the center on the outside. Probably they were Spanish shields. There are two pieces of these dimensions & several others smaller & different in shape.

The Indians keep them buried & only dig them up at the annual festival of the green corn dance, or busk. When I asked Harjo where they were, he hesitated, but after awhile said they were buried in the town house, & that the medicine man who had them in charge had died, & consequently his town had held no busk that year, as no one was authorized to dig up the sacred vessels. His town had not yet elected a fire maker, & if an unholy man should disturb the hiding place, or should see the holy vessels he would die ere he could reach his home. Several intelligent Indians attempted to persuade Harjo, a full blood, to permit me to see the vessels, but in vain. He finally said that even were he willing, the other Indians of his town would find it out & would hate him as long as they lived & might do him an injury.

During the camp meeting it became important to send a dispatch to a distant state, & the first thing necessary was to ascertain whether any one would ride fifty miles to the railroad to carry the message.

A little half breed, Tom, agreed to go & came ready mounted on his little iron gray pony. What time he made going to the railroad was not known, but he handed me a telegraphic dispatch before 4 Oclock in the afternoon & the date of reception was marked on the telegram, "11 minutes after 10 Oclock AM." Tom had come fifty miles in less than six hours & insisted that he had not ridden his pony very hard.

The tents were struck, the wagons loaded, the ponies mounted & the Indians returned to their homes. I had the honor of driving the missionarys family in a spring wagon drawn by two little gray ponies, Dick & Bill, while Dr Buckner rode on a fine bay horse, the children took turns on Dixie, a little white pony, with roached mane, & an ambling gate. We camped one night near a dry creek & were compelled to drink stagnant water. Dixie & one of my ponies ran away during the night, having slipped their hobbles. I caught a lame mule near our camp & hitched him beside the other pony & away we went over the prairie, "skippety hop, hoppety skip," as Boyce & Helm called it. Once we turned the wagon over, while going down a steep hill, but fortunately I held the ponies, & none of us were hurt. We turned the wagon right side up & proceeded on our homeward journey.

III
MYTHS

*"If you don't speak I'll hit you." He struck the tar-person
& his foot stuck. Again he asked, "Why don't you speak?
Turn my foot loose or I'll hit you harder." The second foot
stuck as he hit him again. "I've got another foot, stronger
than these & I'll hit you still harder," & the third time he
hit the tar-person. "I've got one more foot, & I will have
to kill you, if you don't turn my foot loose." The last foot
kicked & stuck fast. The rabbit then struck with his head
& it stuck.*

PRESENTED HERE ARE SIXTEEN MYTHS—eight from
the notebook Tuggle evidently intended to use to continue his Indian
diaries of 1879 and eight from the manuscript which he worked on regu-
larly from 1879 until shortly before his death, hoping that it would be
published (see Appendix A). Since the myths are not an integral part of
the diaries containing Tuggle's experiences and the fruits of his research
in the Territory, they are brought together here. These legends are also
presented in a separate chapter as a subject and a mode which differ
markedly from the substance and form of the scenes and narratives that
make up Tuggle's sketches and observations. It goes without saying that
these examples of Indian lore have an interest and value independent of
Tuggle's journals and of his other writing which is based on those journals.
   The first four myths appear under the heading "At Dr H. F. Buckner's," and the entry is dated September 3, 1881. Tuggle begins: "While
riding with Rev James McHenry—M.E.—formerly known in Ga & Ala
in the War of 1835–8 as Jim Henry, he related to me the following Indian

fables." In order of their appearance these are "Rabbit Deceives the Other Animals" (Swanton's title for his no. 76), "How the Rabbit Won the Widow's Beautiful Daughter" (no. 70), "How the Alligator's Nose Was Broken" (no. 15), and "The Boy with the Flute & Singing Birds" (no. 9).

The next two myths were related to Tuggle by D. O. Fischer, a Choctaw Indian, on January 13, 1882, after Tuggle, Fischer, and Pleasant Porter had visited J. W. Powell of the Smithsonian Institution. They are "The Panther & the Coon" (no. 48) and "How the Terrapin's Back Came to be in Checks" (no. 35). The following day J. P. Folsom, another Choctaw (whom Tuggle described as an alumnus of Dartmouth College), told "Why the Possum Grins" (not in Swanton), and then Walker (whom Tuggle described as clerk of the Choctaw House) narrated "Why the Possum Has No Hair on His Tail" (no. 37 and no. 38 in Swanton). All four of the myths which Tuggle recorded in Washington are untitled in his notebook, and the titles have been supplied from the context, with reference to Swanton.

The remaining eight myths have been drawn from various places in Tuggle's manuscript. "The Tar Person" (no. 75) and "The Rabbit Complains to God" (no. 51) are credited by Tuggle to Cusseta-fixico, an Indian preacher whom he met at Wewoka; and they appear in an untitled chapter numbered 8. "The Big Rock Man" (no. 32) and "The Monster Turtle" (no. 31) make up a chapter numbered 14 and entitled "Indian Fables & Tales," and they are credited to William S. Robertson, the venerable minister, educator, and scholar whom Tuggle mistakenly named Robinson (see the Indian Diary entries for September 3 and 8). "The Creation of the Earth" (no. 90), "The Terrapin Gets His Back Broken" (no. 36), and "The King of the Tie-Snakes" (no. 28) appear together in an untitled section; and the last of these eight legends, the fragmentary "The Tale of the Tie-Snakes" (not in Swanton), appears elsewhere in the manuscript.

If Tuggle's diary or manuscript version of a myth is compared with its counterpart in Swanton's collection, many important changes are noticeable at once. In the partridge myth, for example, Swanton introduced changes in wording, and therefore in emphasis, in practically every line, chiefly in the direction of creating a smoother, more grammatically acceptable, or more "literary," effect.

Since the story of the rabbit and the tar baby is perhaps the best known of all these myths—due largely to the widespread popularity of Joel Chandler Harris's Brer Rabbit version—a detailed comparison between Tuggle's and Swanton's treatments of this myth may most readily illustrate both the extent and the results of Swanton's revision of the original, beginning with the title itself. For "The Tar Person" Swanton substituted "The Tar Baby" (the title which he applied also to at least five or six other variants of the same basic myth located among other southeastern tribes), but thereafter he employed Tuggle's phrase to refer to the rabbit's nemesis. He capitalized Rabbit throughout, giving the protagonist a proper as well as generic name; he substituted "I will" for "I'll," "paw" for "foot," "Let go of my foot" for "Turn my foot loose," "but the second paw" for "the second foot," "I have got" for "I've got," "if you don't let go of my feet" for "if you don't turn my feet loose," "he kicked with the last foot" for "the last foot kicked," "next morning" for "the next morning," "he pulled him away from" for "he pulled him loose," "fastened the Rabbit, saying," for "fastened the rabbit to the stake saying," "had left" for "left," "because I could not do so" for "because I couldn't do it," "into a hollow tree" for "in a hollow tree," "changed yourself so as to look" for "changed yourself to look," "then he sat" for "he sat," "splinter into" for "splinter in," etc.; and he carefully inserted stage directions, such as "said Wolf" at the beginning of the final paragraph, and replaced nouns with pronouns, as in the second line of this passage.

Clearly, the result of such alterations, repeated consistently in Swanton's version of Tuggle's other myths included here, makes for greater accuracy and polish. But at the same time something is lost in the process of striving for clarity and correctness, namely the colloquial flavor conveyed in expressions like "turn my foot loose," "his shot-bag got hitched," and "yes, I did talk about you." One cannot escape the impression that in capturing expressive native idioms, Tuggle's ear was more acute than Swanton's.

RABBIT DECEIVES THE OTHER ANIMALS

THE RABBIT HAD BEEN GUILTY of some offense and all the other animals held a council to try him, & it became evident that he would be found guilty—condemned—so he fell upon the following plan to deceive them. When the council assembled & he was brought out he said, "I have an important message to deliver to all of you. God has appeared to me & informed me that he intends to destroy the world because you animals are so wicked & unless you do better & choose me to rule over you to guide you aright, he will surely destro[y] the world & that in a short time."

They all laughed at him & sai[d] "You are such a great lia[r] that we think this is another one of your lies."

"Well, all you have to do is to wait & see."

"We are not afraid of your lies" said they.

That night after the councils separated the rabbit called to him the King of the partridges & said to him, "I have a plan by which you can save me & I can be of service to you & if you will help me [out] of this scrape I will bring it to pass that you & your subjects shall have the privilege of roving over the whole world & eating out of every field at your own pleasure."

"What can I do" asked the King of the partridges.

"This. Go & gather all the partridges together & have them tomorrow, when the council meets, south of the council ground & when you see me standing up before them, then let every partridge fly up in the air & flutter, flutter, flutter with all his power & make as great a noise as possible."

"I will do so."

"Then on the next day, carry them all to the east of the council ground & do the same, and on the third day go to the north, & on the fourth day go to the west and make each time a louder noise than on the previous day, & you shall be richly rewarded."

They separated, the rabbit remaining in jeopardy & the King of the partridges proceeding to carry out his agreement to summon his subjects to the South of the council ground.

The council met & ordered t[he] rabbit to appear before the[m.] He came smiling & happy. When asked what he had to say he spoke: "I am sorry for you. You will all be destroyed. God will not permit such wicked animals to live. Today he will send a warning in the south. If you do not heed it & turn me loose, then tomorrow, a second warning louder than the first will be heard in the east; if this does not satisfy you, on the third day you will hear a greater & more terrible thundering in the north, & if still you refuse on the fourth a terrific rumbling like an earthquake will burst on your ears from the west—and then—on the next day God will destroy the world."

They greeted his speech with jeers & cried, "Oh, what a lie, tell us another."

But hardly had they ceased when a strange noise was heard in the south, a low, rumbling sound.

"What is that?" said they.

The rabbit replied, "That is God's warning to you wicked animals for conspiring against an innocent creature like me."

Some of [them] said, "Let us turn him loose." Others said, "It is just some trick of this little rascal." So they refused to let him go.

The second day on the assembling of the council, the rabbit was brought before them for sentence to be passed on him. He came & said as before, "You wicked animals will be destroyed for persecuting me. Today another warning will come, but from the east."

As soon as he finished louder thundering noise burst on their astonished ears.

"Perhaps, he is telling the truth this time. Maybe the world will be destroyed."

"No, it is one of his tricks" said some.

"How can that be? He is here where we can see him. He cannot be making that awful noise."

But still the council decided to wait & separated for another night.

Again they met on the third day & the rabbit appeared, looking solemn & when called on, said, "You still refuse to do right. The warning will come today from the north." And as he spoke there came a terrible roar like thunder shaking the ground & making the animals tremble with fear.

"He is right. Let us turn him loose. The witnesses were false."

"No, let us await another day & if then we do not discover his trick, we will let him go."

On the fourth day the animals came looking afraid & took their seats in silence. The rabbit seemed more cheerful.

"Alas! What destruction—all the animals to be destroyed, when they could so easily avoid such punishment."

And then there came from the west such a fluttering, buzzing, humming, shaking noise, that the very air was in a tremor, the ground shook beneath their feet & the animals cried aloud, "Turn him loose, turn him loose. He is rig[ht.] The world will be destroyed. We will all be killed."

And they turned him loose & away he ran laughing as he went, till he came to his friend the King of the partridges & said, "You did well—rove over the world & eat where you will" & ever since then the partridges have wandered where they pleased through every field. Whereas before then they possessed no such privilege.

HOW THE RABBIT WON THE WIDOW'S BEAUTIFUL DAUGHTER

ONCE THERE WAS A WOMAN who lived with her daughter who was very beautiful, and who though often desired in marriage had ever refused her lovers, & who still remained single.

The rabbit lived near by—an old bachelor, & he fell in love with the widows pretty daughter but thought he stood no chance where so many more likely beaux had been rejected.

Still he determined to see what cunning could accomplish, so he made him a new blow gun & selecting his opportunity he slipped up to the house of the widow & succeeded in making a hole in the back of the chimney near the ground and in this hole he inserted his blow gun so that one end of it entered the fire place & the other end reste[d] on the outside. The first night after he finished his device he creeped up & put his ear to the blow pipe & listened to hear what the widow & her daughter were saying. He heard the old lady say, "My daughter, why do you not marry? I am getting old & you ought to marry."

"But Mother, I have met no one I like."

"You are too particular."

He waited to hear no more but ran home. The next day he returned to his blow gun & listening heard the widow tell her daughter to go down to the spring & bring some water. He ran to the spring & concealed himself in the grass.

It was not long before the beautiful maiden came to the spring & while she was dipping up the water the rabbit said in a low, deep voice—"Hoke-te, marpe hum-ke—esekart—elun, elun, elun." "The girl who remains single will die, will die, will die."

She stopped & looked in the direction of the sound, but saw no one. She was frightened but resumed her task. The rabbit ran around to the opposite [side] of the spring & again said, "Hoke-te &c. The girl who remains single will die, will die, will die."

The girl in alarm fled to the house—the rabbit following and running to his blow gun.

The girl cried out, "Oh! Mother, I heard the strangest noise down at the spring. I was dipping up water & no one was near when a voice said, "Hokte &c elun, elun, elun" and I looked & looked, but no body was there, and soon, I heard it again from the other side of the spring."

"Just what I have xpected. I have been telling you all the time that you were too particular & that you ought to marry."

The rabbit was listening at his blow gun & in the same monotonous tone said, "Hokte &c elun, elun, elun. The girl who remains single will die, will die, will die."

"That is it," cried the daughter, "the same sound at the spring."

"Oh, I hear it. I told you so. You ought to marry, & shall marry the very first man who asks for you."

"Yes, I am willing," said the girl, frightened out of her senses.

The rabbit galloped off delighted at his success and [dreamed that night of his honeymoon; lined out] the next day he sent for an old female relative. She came. He said to her, "I wish to marry the daughter of my neighbor the widow & I sent for you to ask her hand for me."

The old woman consented to serve him, and visited the house of the widow. They talked awhile, & the widow told of the strange occurrences of the day previous, adding "I have always told my daughter that girls ought to marry & I am determined she shall accept the very first offer that is made."

"That is my business here today. My relative the rabbit says he wishes to marry your beautiful daughter & authorizes me to request her hand in marriage."

She hesitated, for she did not like the rabbit's reputation, but that awful voice sounded from the ashes of the fire place "Hokte &c elun, elun, elun, elun. The girl that remains single will die, will die, will die."

"He shall have her. Take her for his bride."

So they were married & the rabbit thus won the beautiful girl.

(How he afterwards won his sister in law—the council, its order, the hunt, the fork of the road, the beds, the sister in law & the black-ants &c &c.) [In this parenthetical note Tuggle reminds himself of a related tale or tales.]

HOW THE ALLIGATOR'S NOSE WAS BROKEN

Far back in the old days all the animals determined to have a big ball play.

The four footed animals with the alligators were chosen for one side, & all the fowls & birds, including the aegle, were on the other side. All the preparations were made, the ground selected, the poles erected, the ball conjured & the game began, after dancing around the poles & whooping at each other.

The ball was thrown in the air & as it came down the alligator opened wide his mouth & caught the ball. Away he ran, waddling along through the other animals while the birds & fowls flew & fluttered around his head but were afraid to put their heads between his glittering teeth. All was dismay & the birds were in despair.

The animals cheered the alligator & his wife clapped her hands, exclaiming, "Look, everybody look! See the little striped alligator's daddy—how he catches & carries the ball. Just look at him," and she screamed till she cried.

The aegle flew on high, sailing round & round till he seemed a mere speck in the sky. Suddenly he darted down like an arrow from the clouds & struck the alligator on the nose, broke it & out fell the ball, which a bird seized and carried between the poles, & won the game.

Ever since that time alligators have had a broken nose—

THE BOY WITH THE FLUTE
& SINGING BIRDS

A WOMAN HAD AN ONLY SON, whom she cautioned against ever passing beyond the mountains, which were in sight of her home. "My son do not go beyond the mountain," she often said.

One day while hunting he reached the top of the mountain & looking in the valley below he saw a lovely city, surrounded with green meadows, lakes & forests. He was tempted to visit it & yielded. He saw strange scenes of beauty, beautiful women—& all that could please the eye.

When he returned home at night he was silent. His mother saw that something unusual had occurred. "My son, you have passed beyond the mountain."

"I have mother & saw the most beautiful visions. Oh, why can I not go back."

"Yes, that is why I warned you. Once there I knew home would never be attractive [any] more. There you must live & be ever discontented. Since it must be so, I will do all I can for you."

On the next day she made him handsome clothes, & sent him to the forests to catch all manner of singing birds. She also made him a musical instrument. When every preparation was concluded she dressed her son, put on him a wonderful headress on which the singing birds perched, & then said, "Play on your instrument."

He began to play & no sooner did the birds hear the first note than they sang their sweetest songs in accord with the melody of the instrument.

"Now, my son, go to the beautiful city beyond the mountain, & when you enter, ask for the council of the King, & as you enter the council play on yr instrument while the singing birds accompany you with the charming music of their voices."

He obeyed her suggestions. He entered the city, found the council, & as he approached the music of his instrument broke forth while the birds on his head made the air vocal with their delicious notes.

The wonderful stranger was accorded a seat of honor & all were enraptured with his music.

No honor was too great for him & every one strove to do him a kindness. Soon it was rumored that the hand of the Kings daughter was to be offered the young stranger.

One day he invited the King & the council to go with him to the river near by & on reaching the stream he quickly threw aside his costume, jumped in the water & dived under & across the river four times when all the fish floated to the surface. Vast numbers were killed with arrows & spears & a grand feast was enjoyed by the tribe.

The rabbit had heard of the wonderful stranger & envied him his conquests, especially the rumored one of the King's daughter for a bride. He followed to the stream & while all were intent on the hilarity of the feast he stole the costume, headdress, singing birds & musical instrument & ran away to the forest. When the young warrior sought his garments they could not be found.

The next day while the council were assembled in walked the rabbit, dressed exactly like the young stranger & was invited to his seat of honor. He tried to imitate the young stranger in every particular. Being asked for music he put the instrument to his mouth—but alas! only an ugly sound came. He reached up & struck the birds to make them sing, but not a note! In alarm he invited the council to go with him again to the river & enjoy another feast.

They followed him & he dived four times across, but not a fish appeared.

"It is the lying rabbit. It is the lying rabbit. Seize him. Seize him."

He was taken & tried. A decree was made that the stolen garments, musical instrument, & the singing birds should be restored to their real owner & the rabbit chased from the council ground as a rascally deceiver.

The hand of the King's daughter was bestowed on the wonderful stranger, while the singing birds flapped their wings & sang for joy.

THE PANTHER & THE COON

THE PANTHER MET A COON & was about to eat him when the coon said, "Im a little fellow, don't eat me, it wouldn't do you any good, let me fix up a way by which both of us can get plenty to eat."

The panther agreed. The coon said, "You make out you are dead, lie down & stretch out, & I'll get some old rotten wood & stuff [it] in your eyes, nose & mouth so it will look like the flies have blowed you & then I'll tell the deer about it & get a crowd of them to come & dance around you. I'll sit at your head & be at the drum & sing for them to dance by &

when a big buck comes near I'll touch you & you can jump on him & kill
him, cut his throat & both of us will get plenty to eat."

The panther consented, & lay down & stretched him self as if dead &
the coon stuffed the rotten wood in his mouth, eyes, & nose & then ran
off to call the deer.

He met an old doe & told her the news "Oh, you knew our enemy the
panther was dead. Come & see him."

But she was shy & said, "If he is dead, let him stay dead."

He then met a fawn & persuaded it to come & see the dead panther.
The fawn looked & then ran away & told a number of deer & soon a crowd
was collected. The coon got ready took his seat & proposed a dance. He
beat his drum & sang a song:

> "Ching a ching
> Ching a ching
> Ching a ching ching."

The deer danced around their enemy. When the coon saw a fine buck
come very close he touched the panther, who jumped up, seized his
victim & killed him.

HOW THE TERRAPIN'S BACK
CAME TO BE IN CHECKS

A TERRAPIN WENT HUNTING & met a woman & she accused
him of slandering her. He denied it, but when they came to a hollow tree,
he thought his chance good to escape, so he said, "Yes, I did talk about
you. Im the man" and tried to crawl in the hollow, but his shot bag caught
him & the woman beat his back to pieces. He lay there & the ants came &
eat his blood & fat. He said "I'll give you my blood & fat if you help me
get my back together."

So they helped him stick it together with tar (or resin) but his back
was always checked & he never had any blood nor fat afterwards.

WHY THE POSSUM GRINS

"DID YOU EVER HEAR why the possum grins?"

"No."

"Well the wolf was nearly starved to death & as he couldn't get anything to eat, he went to a pond & drank water. This didn't satisfy him. He went along & looking up a tree he saw the possum eating persimmons.

'How do you get up there?'

'I climb up but sometimes the simmons fall down on the ground & I pick them up.'

'I wish I had some.'

'Well, you go way off yonder & run with all your might & butt your head against the tree & shake some down.'

"The wolf did as directed, came with all his might, hit the tree & killed himself. The possum was so delighted at his death that he has never stopped laughing. He laughs & grins yet."

WHY THE POSSUM HAS NO HAIR ON HIS TAIL

"DID YOU EVER HEAR how possum's tail had no hair?"

"No."

"Well, the coon met possum & the possum said 'how did you get all these pretty rings on your tail?'

'I wrapped bark around my tail & stuck it in the fire & made the rings.'

"The possum wrapped bark on his tail, made a fire & followed the coon's directions. He stuck his tail in the fire & it burned all the hair off, & ever since the possum has had no hair on his tail."

THE TAR PERSON

A MAN MISSED PEAS from his garden & after various efforts to catch the thief, he made a tar-person & put it in the garden near the peas.

A rabbit had been coming every night for the peas & the tar-person was quickly discovered by him. Stopping near he said, "Who's that, What's your name?" and receiving no reply he hopped close to the figure and said "If you don't speak I'll hit you." He struck the tar-person and his foot stuck. Again he asked, "Why don't you speak? Turn my foot loose or I'll hit you harder." The second foot stuck as he hit him again. "I've got another foot, stronger than these, & I'll hit you still harder," & the third time he hit the tar-person. "I've got one more foot, & I will have to kill you, if you don't turn my feet loose." The last foot kicked & stuck fast. The rabbit then struck with his head & it stuck.

The next morning the man came into his garden & when the rabbit saw him, he called out, "Oh, I have caught the thief who's been taking your peas. Here he is."

"Yes, I see the thief," replied the man, "and I intend to kill him." Seizing the rabbit he pulled him loose from the tar-person and carried him to a stake near a pig pen. There he securely fastened the rabbit to the stake saying, "I will go to the house & get some boiling water to scald you."

As soon as the man left, a wolf came along and seeing the rabbit tied asked what it meant.

"Oh, this man wanted me to eat up all these pigs in the pen and because I couldn't do it he tied me here."

"I can eat them for him; let me take your place." "All right," responded the rabbit, so the wolf untied the rabbit, & took his place at the stake & was in turn tied by the rabbit, who ran away & crawled in a hollow tree. When the man returned & saw the wolf, "So," said he, "You are at your tricks & have changed yourself to look like a wolf. Well, I will scald you anyway." He poured the boiling water on the wolf who howled in pain & finally broke the string and ran off. He sat at the foot of the very tree in which the rabbit was concealed & as he licked his scalded hide, the rabbit reached down & stuck a splinter in him.

Jumping up, the wolf exclaimed, "I wish the ants would stop biting me and adding to my afflictions."

THE RABBIT COMPLAINS TO GOD

"CUSSETA-FIXICO,* did you ever hear the story of the rabbit going to God & complaining of his fate, & how he brought the rattlesnake & the swarm of gnats to his Creator?"

"Oh, yes. The snake was mad at first but the rabbit flattered him and then he crawled out of his coil & the rabbit tied his head & tail to a stick & ran off with him. And the leader of the gnats was persuaded to enter a bag & the other gnats followed, when the rabbit tied the bag & ran away with them."

"What word is used for God."

"Esar-ke-tumese, life controller, one who gives it and takes it away and controls it."

* Cusseta-Fixico is described by Tuggle as one of the "Indian-preachers at Wewoka" who was a "full blood Muskogee."

THE CREATION OF THE EARTH

IN THE BEGINNING the waters covered everything. It was said: "Who will make the land appear." Sock-chew, the Crawfish, said: "I will make the land appear."

So he went down to the bottom of the water and began to stir up the mud with his tail & hands. He then brought up the mud to a certain place and piled it up.

The owners of the land at the bottom of the water said: "Who is disturbing our land?" They watched and discovered the Crawfish. They came near him. He suddenly stirred the mud with his tail and they could see him no more.

Sock-chew continued his work. He carried the mud & piled it until at last he held up his hands in the air and so the land appeared above the water.

The land was soft.

It was said: "Who will spread out the land and make it dry & hard?" Some said: "Ah-yok, the Hawk should spread out the soft land and make it dry."

Others said "Yah-tee (the buzzard) has larger wings. He can spread out the land & make it dry & hard."

Yah-tee undertook to spread out and dry the earth. He flew above the earth & spread out his long wings over it. He sailed over the earth. He spread it out. After a long while he grew tired of holding out his wings. He began to flap them and thus he caused the hills and valleys, as the dirt was still soft.

"Who will make the light?" it was said. It was very dark.

Yōh-ah, the Star, said: "I will make the light."

It was so agreed. The Star shone forth. It was light only near him.

"Who will make more light?" it was said.

Shar-pah, the Moon, said: "I will make more light." Shar-pah made more light, but it was still dark.

T-cho, the Sun, said: "You are my children. I am your mother. I will make the light. I will shine for you."

She went to the East. Suddenly light spread over all the earth.

As she passed over the Earth a drop of blood fell from her to the ground, & from this blood & earth sprang the first people, the children of the Sun, the Uchees.

The people wished to find their medicine. A great monster serpent destroyed the people. They cut his head from his body. The next day the body and head were together. They again slew the monster. His head again grew to his body.

Then they cut off his head and placed it over a tree on the top so the body could not reach it. The next morning the tree was dead and the head was united to the body. They again severed it and put it over another tree. In the morning the tree was dead and the head and body were reunited.

So the people continued to try all the trees in the forest. At last they placed the head over Tan, the cedar tree, and in the morning the head was dead. The cedar was alive, but covered with blood, which had trickled down from the head.

Thus the Great Medicine was found.

Fire was made by boring a stick into a hard weed.

The people selected a sacred family. Each member of this family had engraved on his door a picture of the sun.

In the beginning all the animals could talk. One language was used. All were at peace.

The deer lived in a cave. A keeper watched over them. When the people were hungry, the keeper selected a deer and killed it.

Finally the deer were set free. They roved over the earth.

All animals were set free from man. Names were given to them so they could be known.

THE TERRAPIN GETS HIS BACK BROKEN

A TERRAPIN went hunting & met a woman. She accused him of having slandered him [her]. He denied it, but when they passed a hollow tree, in which he thought he could crawl, he said: "Yes, I did say it, I am the man."

He tried to crawl in the hollow but his shot-bag got hitched and he could not get in.

The woman caught him [and] beat his back into pieces.

The ants came. He said:

> "I will give you my blood,
> I will give you my fat,
> [If you will help me mend my] back."

[Swanton (no. 36, p. 41) continues: "They consented and brought him some tar with which he mended his shell, but it was always in checks, and he never afterwards had any fat, nor any blood." It should be noted that Swanton's other version of this myth (no. 35, p. 40) is altogether different from either of these.]

THE KING OF THE TIE-SNAKES

A CHIEF SENT his son on a message to another chief, and delivered to him a vessel as the emblem of his authority.

The son stopped to play with some boys, who were throwing flat stones on the surface of the water. The chief's son threw his vessel on the water, and it sank. He was frightened. He was afraid to go to the neighboring chief without the vessel, & he did not like to return home and tell his father of his loss. He jumped into the stream, & reaching the spot where the vessel sank, he dived into the water. His playmates waited a long time for him, but he did not appear. They returned & reported his death.

When he was beneath the surface of the stream, the tie-snakes seized him & bore him away to a cave & said to him: "Ascend yonder platform." He looked and saw seated on a platform the King of the tie-snakes. The platform was a mass of living tie-snakes. He approach[ed] the platform and lifted his foot to [as]cend, but the platform ascended as he l[ifted] his foot. Again he tried, with the [same] result. The third time he tried in vain. The tie-snakes said, "Ascend." He lifted his foot the fourth time & succeeded in ascending the platform & the king invited him to sit by his side. The king said to him: "See yonder feather. It is yours," pointing to a plume in the corner of the cave.

He approached the plume & extended his hand to seize it, but it eluded his grasp. Three times he made the attempt & three times it escaped. On the fourth attempt, he obtained it.

"Yonder tomahawk is yours" said the tie-snakes' King.

He went to the place where the tomahawk was sticking & reached out his hand to take it, but in vain. It lifted itself every time he raised his hand. He tried four times & on the fourth trial, it remained still and he succe[eded] in taking it.

The king said: "You [ca]n retu[rn] to your father after three days. When [he] asks where you have been reply, "I know what I know,' but in no event tell him what you know. When he needs my aid let him walk towards the east, & bow three times to the rising sun and I will be there to help him."

After three days the tie-snake[s] carried him to the same spot where he dived into the stream & lifted him to the surface of the water & placed his lost vessel in his hand.

He swam to the bank & returned to his father who was mourning over his death. His father rejoiced over his son's wonderful restoration.

He informed his father of the tie-snake King & his message of proffered aid. Not long afterwards his father was attacked by his enemies. He said to his son: "You understand [what the King of the Tie-snakes] said. Go and seek [his aid."]

The son put [the feather on his] head, took the tomahawk, [walked towards] the [ea]st and bowed three [times t]o th[e] rising sun.

The King of the tie-snakes stood before him: "What do you wish?"

"My father needs your aid."

"Go. Tell him not to fear. They will attack him, but they shall not harm him nor his people. In the morning all will be well."

The son returned to his father and delivered the message of the King of the tie-snakes.

The enemy came & attacked his town, but no one was harmed. Night came. In the morning they beheld their enemies, each held fast in the folds of a tie-snake & so all were captured & the chief made peace with all his foes.

THE TALE OF THE TIE-SNAKES

     ... THE WONDERS of the famous tie-snake were resurrected from fairy-land, and recounted to us as we passed a pool of water in a dry creek. A man and a boy had been drowned a few days ago, and the tie-snake did it. The boy went in and the tie-snake caught him, he screamed for his father, who went to his rescue, when the tie-snakes caught him too, and both sank to rise no more. Two fresh mounds on the bank of the stream told the fate of two emigrants. ...

THE BIG ROCK MAN AND
THE MONSTER TURTLE

     "MR. ROBERTSON can you tell me some Indian fables. I suppose they had Aesops and Miltons too."

"Did you ever hear about the Big Rock Man?" asked the venerable minister looking at me through his glasses.

"No sir. Tell me about him. Must be something solid about such a story," and I leaned forward to catch every word.

"The story goes that the Indians went out to war, & among their enemies they saw the 'Big Rock Man.' They shot arrow after arrow & could not wound him. They were in despair. They finally consulted the Wise Rabbit. You know the Rabbit takes the place of the Fox in Indian fables. Well, the Rabbit told them that the 'Big Rock Man' could be wounded only in one place, right down his ear. So away they went, and after a while one warrior made a lucky shot & hit the Big Rock Man in the ear and killed him."

"What was the meaning of this fable [do you suppose]?" I queried.

[I don't know] unless it was a man in [some primitive armor]. [This line is illegible. Apparently it introduced by title the myth Swanton labels "The Monster Turtle (no. 31).]

The warriors were on the war path. They wished to select a suitable battle ground. They saw a large rock as they thought & decided that they would ascend the rocky mound & fight from that place. One warrior objected & refused to go, saying that it was no rock at all, that an evil spirit blinded their eyes, & that the rocky mound was a Big Terrapin. They called him a coward & told him he was afraid to fight, & to go back to the squaws. He warned them. In vain. They climbed to the top & soon they saw their mistake. The mass began to move. They were alarmed & tried to get off. Their feet were fastened. Away it went. The sea burst in their view. It still moved on. They sang the death song as the Big Terrapin crawled deeper & deeper into the waves of the sea. The warrior returned & told of their fate. He was not believed. He told them to watch the trail & see the big tracks of the Big Terrapin. And so they did, & followed him to the sea. They then consulted the Medicine man. He made medicine, & "blowed" it. They made a great trap of logs near the sea. [The] Medicine man blew his medicine. It was [Illegible, and fragmentary from here on.]

[Swanton, pp. 37–38, supplies the following conclusion: "Soon the frogs came out of the sea. He made the medicine stronger, and, while he was blowing, the little terrapins came out of the sea. He made the medicine still stronger, and as he blew and sang a great noise was heard in the sea and out came the Big Terrapin.

They built a pen of logs, caught him, and burned him up." It will be noted that Swanton's version differs considerably from this one in wording and narrative detail.]

IV

WASHINGTON JOURNAL

Genl W T Sherman sat next to me, & I saw him
wiping his eyes several times, & was surprised
that the hero of the March to the sea could weep.
The broken hearted women who saw him burn
their homes in the dead of winter in Atlanta
Ga. would have been edified by seeing Sherman
crying at the imaginary woes of an actress.

AS DESCRIBED in the Introduction and in Appendix A, Tuggle's Washington Journal consists of two handwritten parts, the larger one contained in a leather-bound notebook of 120 pages and the smaller, totaling about thirty additional pages, filling the latter portion of a second notebook. Together, except for a hiatus of nine months, the two parts cover a three-year span from January 21, 1880, the date of Tuggle's first entry, to December 19, 1882, the date of his last entry. During his absence from Washington between February 7 and December 4, 1881, Tuggle spent some time at home in LaGrange and, later in the summer, again journeyed into the Territory before returning to the capital in December. Thus the entries covering his two sojourns in Washington, coupled with those of his Indian diaries and sketches, round out—at times delightfully—a portrait of Tuggle and his work, unselfconsciously sketched by the man himself at the height of his career.

Of all the surviving manuscript material, Tuggle's Washington Journal is the most nearly complete unit, so that a consecutive, week-to-week record of his activities unfolds in its pages. Moreover, despite his haste in composition and his use of various shortcuts which make the task of editing it both difficult and problematical, the record is carefully articulated, indicating that Tuggle intended and found the time to put down in detail the names, facts, events, ideas, and problems with which he was concerned, as well as his varied reactions to them. As a result one sees in these pages not only an active participant engaged in some of the momentous state and national affairs of the period, but also a vigorous mind seriously striving within its own natural limitations to achieve order amid potential chaos.

Numerous references in the journal, however, allude to persons, events, or documents which require fuller explanation for a reader today than Tuggle needed for his own purposes. In his opening pages, for example, he refers to the Creek Orphan Claim and shortly thereafter to a Mr. Hayt, a Mr. Schurz, a Mr. Roach, and so on. Many such references scattered throughout the journal would be meaningless without further editorial clarification, and a few are obscure to the point of defying even persistent editorial scrutiny. Amplification of those that can be explained is provided in the notes supplied for this chapter. These notes are the fruit of a close study made of Tuggle's journal by William E. Fuller, Jr. and entitled "William Orrie Tuggle: Journal of 1880–1882," an unpublished master's thesis written at Auburn University in 1964. In editing Tuggle's Washington Journal, Mr. Fuller dealt only with the longer first part mentioned above, but his introductory commentary offers a more detailed analysis of its contents and significance than can be given here.

As in the preceding chapters Tuggle's Washington Journal is reproduced here verbatim, or as nearly so as possible. His various idiosyncrasies of usage, excepting terminal punctuation, have again been kept intact and passed over without editorial comment in all cases where their meaning is sufficiently clear. Tuggle's habit of drawing a single line across his page to signal a new topic or break in thought also reappears, though less frequently; but his penchant for inserting rough line drawings disappears almost entirely, except for one sketch representing the seating arrangement at a dinner party at which he was a guest.

The journal opens abruptly beneath a heading bearing his name and city and two dates, scrawled across the first two facing pages as follows:

W. O. Tuggle   LaGrange, Georgia   Jany 1880

Jany 21, 1880.

The greenback question

Just returned from the U. S. Senate where Beck of Ky made an earnest speech against Bayards resolution to withdraw the legal quality from the greenbacks. Beck opposed it, though he regarded Bayards motive good.

The Democrats can not make any political capital out of Bayards resolution. Both parties are divided on this subject. The power of the Federal govmt under the Constitution to make anything but gold & silver a legal tender is doubted. But this is not the present issue, but rather this, is *now* the time to declare even an illegal act wrongful, is *now* the time to repeal the law making greenbacks a legal tender?

Most of the Democrats who oppose Bayards resolution think now is not the best time to repeal said law, & fear it would injure the business interests of the country, & tend to give the National Banks control of the currency.

The Creek Orphan Claim

In Oct. 1879, the Muscogee Nation passed an act making me their agt, & also agt of the Creek Orphan Claim[1] under the treaty of 1832.

I came to Washington in Nov. '79 to see Comr of Indian affairs & to get him to send to Congress in Decr an estimate for an appropriation to reimburse said orphans. Various technical objections were raised, & on this day Jany 21st 1880, my contract with the Creeks had not been approved. First, the objection

[1] The Creek Orphan Claim grew out of the treaty which the United States made with the Creeks on March 24, 1832. According to this treaty twenty sections of land were to be selected by the President for the orphan children of the Creeks. This land was to be retained or sold for their benefit. The land was sold in 1837, and the proceeds ($108,713.82) were invested in stocks. The Creek orphan fund was composed of the money received for the land, and of the interest thereon. Prior to Tuggle's appointment as Creek agent only two payments were made to the orphans, one in 1868 and one in 1870. Sums amounting to $251,055.97 were expended from the trust fund illegally. This sum constituted the claim of the Creek orphans. See Senate Reps., No. 599, 46th Cong., 2nd Sess., Vol. VI.

was that my contract did not comply with the statute because of various technicalities. The Indian Council passed a resolution in Dec 1879 authorizing their delegats to enter into a contract. On Jany 13, 1880 they did so & the papers were filed. Delay ensued & yesterday the contracts were not approved. I rewrote them & complied with all objections & filed them again today.

They told me in Decr that an estimate had been made & forwarded (Brooks). This had turned out to be untrue.

Then last week I was told it was made out again, (Bennett), & today I hear it is yet to be made. Mr. Hayt[2] is certainly unfortunate in his methods. He does not dispatch business.

I think he has been secretly opposed to me, & perhaps some friend of his desires the job of working the Orphan Claim through Congress.

At least his conduct & that of Brooks his chief clk has been peculiar & Porter[3] told me that Brooks asked him why the Creeks made any contract with anybody? Porter replied because it is impossible to collect anything from the government otherwise.

Called on Mr. Schurz[4] in Nov 1879 & handed him my contracts & a letter from A. H. Colquitt, Govr of Ga. commending me, & endorsed by Mr. Hayes:

The Washington merry-go-round

> "Col Tuggle who bears
> this note is altogether
> worthy I am satisfied
>
> R B Hayes"

Mr. Schurz smiled & said he would affirm the contracts after Mr. Hayt, Indian Comr acted on them.

Last week, or rather Monday of this week, Mr.

[2] Ezra A. Hayt, Indian Commissioner. Hayt was removed from office soon after Tuggle made this entry.

[3] Pleasant Porter, delegate of the Creek Nation to Washington, 1880, and last elected principal chief of the Creek Nation.

[4] Carl Schurz, secretary of the U.S. Department of the Interior, 1877–1881.

Hayt verbally referred me to Mr. Schurz & said if I &
Mr. S— would agree on the commissions (10 pct) he
would act at once. I called on Mr. Schurz with Porter,
but he referred me back to Mr. Hayt, & so like a
shuttle cock back I went, & being nettled by this style
of not doing it, I spoke curtly to the clks, they became
indignant, wrote "Unapproved &c" & forward the contracts to me today. Then I rewrote them & have started
anew in the mills—not of the gods, but grinding very
slowly.

One night last week I was in the room of Col.
J. H. Blount, M. C. from Ga. & now acting Chairman
of the Comtee on Apptns while Mr. Adkins is sick
& the New York Sun reporter, Gibson came in and
during the talk Gibson said that Brady, Asst P. M.
Genl & Ex Senator Dorsey were undoubtedly interested to a large extent in the contracts of the Star

The Star Route
scandals

Route Service,[5] that one batch of contracts had been
increased in pay from a comparatively reasonable sum
to an enormous amt & that in 6 days after the contracts were let, & in a word that the deficiency in this
service was caused by corruption. It is being investi-
gated. Gibson also said that Tilden was not consulted about the electoral commission[6] until Mr. Hunt
notified him that the Senate had agreed on a bill.

Gibson said that last winter while the Brazilian

[5] "Star Routes" were mail routes, on which the mails were
carried by private contract. Arkansas Senator Stephen Dorsey,
Asst. Postmaster General Brady, and various contractors, in
conspiracy with Post Office and Treasury officials, obtained,
through competitive bidding, 134 of the 2,000 routes. Then,
through supplementary agreements for various improvements
in route service, they managed to exact payments of three to
ten times the contract amounts. The improvements were often
nonexistent. In all, increases of almost $1,000,000 were ob-
tained.

[6] In the disputed Hayes-Tilden election of 1876, three
southern states presented two sets of electoral votes, one Democratic, the other Republican. The two parties finally shaped an
electoral count bill in January 1877. The bill provided for an
electoral commission of fifteen men to count the votes. On a
single deciding vote the Republican returns were accepted, and
Hayes was elected.

Mail subsidy[7] was under consideration that the Democratic paper at Washington, the Post, was paid $500.00 per week to advocate the subsidy to John Rooch[8] (as it was called) & that Stilson Hutchins, the editor & proprietor of the Post was promised 50000.$ if the bill passed.

That Wm E. Chandler Republican was lobbying for John Rooch & had promised 30 pct to the National Republican comtee, that when the Democratic comtee was approached, 30 pct was demanded for its influence for campaign purposes, & was promised.

Lobbying

30 pct of what, was not said. This may not be true, but still it resembles truth & indicates the methods of legislation.

Was invited & called last week on William Stickney & Mrs. S. 601 M St. Mrs. Stickney was Miss Kendall the daughter of Amos Kendall. They live in a fine house, & Mr. S. is Supdt & deacon of Calvary Baptist Church, which was built by Amos Kendall, Tis said at a cost of 125,000$, that it was burned & Mr. K. rebuilt it. The Stickneys have considerable influence & Mr. S. Is the Secty of the Board of Indian Commissioners, a power behind the throne, under the peace commission idea, that religious organizations should manage Indian affairs, or suggest names of Indian agts. & be morally responsible for their good behavior.

Amos Kendall's political influence

H. Persons, M. C. of Ga., & N. A. Hull M. C. of Fla. room with me or rather we have two rooms communicating.

[7] The Brazilian Mail Subsidy was a proposed subsidy in 1879 for the establishment of steamship mail service between the United States and Brazil. At this time mail from the United States to Brazil was carried via commercial sailing vessels. The Roach steamship line had just entered into a contract with Brazil and, accordingly, became the most probable beneficiary of any forthcoming subsidy. See Senate Reps., No. 386, 45th Cong., 2nd. Sess., Vol. ii, and Senate Misc. Docs., No. 72, 45th Cong., 3rd. Sess., Vol. i.

[8] John Roach was the owner of large shipyards at Chester on the Delaware River. He was the friend of William E. Chandler, a power in the Republican Party and, later, secretary of the Navy.

Persons told me yesterday of a little quarrel between Cook & Blount. It seems some paper stated that Blount had obtained an apptn for a certain man, & Cook asked Blount to deny it, as Cook claimed that he (Cook) obtained the apptn. Blount declined to do so, & hence the quarrel, which ended in a drink & all parted friends.

Political infighting

Felton is in hot water Persons says. Gordon will oppose the confirmation in the Senate of Simmons as Census Supervisor in Ga. Felton endorsed Simmons who is a Republican, & it seems that Felton wrote a rather ugly letter from a Democratic standpoint & this letter has been found by the Bohemians. Felton is riding two horses & occasionally the horses pull considerably apart. He calls himself an "Independent Democrat" & was elected by aid of Republican votes against the regular Democratic nominee.

He blows hot & cold & of course occasionally the blowing is not consistent.

My Family moved to Washington 28th Nov. 1879 & returned to Ga. early in Jany 1880, on account of the prevalence of small pox & scarlet fever. We kept house at 117, 6th N. E. on Capitol Hill, & our necessary xpenses for rent servants & provisions were about 120.00$ per mth.—self, wife, seven children & two servants. Of course this does not include clothing, car tickets, nor anything xcept rent, provisions & housekeeping.

Cost of living in Washington

The children enjoyed the Smithsonian, the Corcoran gallery, the Navy Yard &c but soon grew very homesick.

The advantages of the galleries, the national library, the observatory, & other public places, cannot be overestimated as education, but young children not over 13 do not appreciate them as much as older children, & really cannot derive such information as these facilities afford.

A quiet home in a country village, with competent teachers is better for children than a city life. So it seemed to me.

Read in Dec Napoleon at St Helena (Abbott) Charles xii of Sweden by Voltaire, glanced over some other books History of Morgan's command (Duke) & as a member of Morgan's command I was deeply interested. Deleted minor inaccuracies in engagements in which I was a participant.

Am now reading the Memoirs of Metternich, just out. Have just finished Memoirs of Madame De Rémusat & she certainly portrays Napoleon in colors dark enough to suit even an Englishman. She makes him a cold calculating despot, a heartless, selfish man, licentious, corrupt, a liar & the very embodiment of Machiavellianism—a very devil incarnate, ignorant, cruel & delighting in the unhappiness of those around him.

Quite a contrast with the picture drawn by Abbott from the sketches of Las Casas & Dr O'Meara at St Helena. A cross between the two would approximate the truth, a great man, determined to succeed regardless of the means.

Tuggle's reading: Napoleon and Metternich

Wrote sketches of my Indian xperiences & finds, also arranged Vore's[9] life & adventures of Black Beaver[10] & sent the manuscript to Harper Bros New York. It would make about 350 pages of printed matter.

The Harpers have not yet decided about publishing the sketches & seem rather inclined to decline.

Major Vore and the Indian sketches

Jany 26

Called with Genl P. Porter on Ouray, the Ute Chief, at the Fremont House. He is very stout, about 5, 8 a full round face, looks like an Esquimeau—has a pleasant smile, & talks broken English a little. His interpreter was absent & we decided to call again.

Met Chepeta, Ourays wife. She was curled up on her bed, wrapped in a blanket. She was dressed in Indian Costume, as was Ouray, xcept a hat.

[9] Major Israel G. Vore, a native of Pennsylvania, was born about 1825. Vore was a Confederate states Indian agent during the war, as well as a Confederate army officer.

[10] Black Beaver (1806–1880), a famous Delaware Indian guide and scout. See Appendix A.

Pai-Utes in
Washington

Was introduced to Sarah Wannemucca, the daughter of the Chief of the Pai-Utes. She is an intelligent woman, low in stature, looks like a Japanese woman, was dressed in white folks costume, & speaks good English, having been educated in California. She is the real leader of the Utes & is treating with the Govmt about moving her people about (4000) back to Oregon where they once lived.

Sarah was very anxious to visit New York & the cities generally & lecture about her people, but Mr Schurz was unwilling & Sarah was promised an office so Col. A. B. Meacham says, & she left last night (26th) for her home. I bought two of her photographs from her, one in Indian costume & the other in American dress.

Introduced
legislation

Introduced bill in both houses to pay Ga. $27,175.00 for Indian xpenses from 1795 to 1818.[11] Refd in HR [House of Representatives] to Comtee Indian Affairs & in Senate [to] Claims. The Creek Orphan fund bill is before Indian Comtees in both houses.

Called on Sen. Coke Ch[airman] Comtee on Indian Affairs Senate, & Porter introduced me as Agt of the Creek Orphan fund & of the M. N. [Muscogee Nation]. That was 26th & today 28th Sen. Coke referred the case to a sub-comtee Walker, of Ark., & Slater, of Oregon.

Creek Orphan
Claim stalled

Gordon told me that he had spoken to Cockrell, Ch. of Claims Comtee, about Ga. case. Called on the Comtee 12 N[oon] today—28th. Had a short talk with Sen. Cockrell, who said "Its legislative history

[11] The Georgia claim consisted of sums expended by the State of Georgia in military operations against Indians within her borders during the years 1795–1800, 1812–1814, and 1817–1818. The total amount expended was $27,174.42. See House Reps., No. 230, 46th Cong., 3rd. Sess., Vol. 1.

comes first." Spoke rather sneeringly of the age of the claim &c.

Aided the clk—Morrow—in hunting up the history & saw him make the entries.

Heard Bayard's speech yesterday. Sen. Gordon invited me on the floor of the Senate & I sat just in rear of Sen. Bayard—who came & spoke to Sen. Saulsbury just before he began. Sen. S. said "Expectation is high today."

Bayard's speech

"That's all right" said Bayard smilingly.

He read the speech. It was a splendid argument against the power of the Congress to make Treasury notes a legal tender. He is right, but the question is, *Is now the time* to repeal the bad law?

When Sen. B sat down, Sen. B. H. Hill, who had been sitting just in front of Bayard, went to him & with enthusiasm congratulated him. I saw no one else congratulate Bayard.

Mr. Hill came to where I stood in door of the cloak room talking with Gibson of N. Y. Sun & said, "If the Democratic party cannot stand on that speech, it ought not to stand at all."

28th Senate galleries crowded today to hear orations in honor of Zach Chandler.[12] Mr. Bayard was speaking when I looked in.

Feb. 2, 1880.

Persons told me that Gordon told him that he, Gordon, went to Secty Schurz to get an appointment for Howard Williams & that Schurz delayed making the apptmt, & finally Gordon said to him that he (Gordon) & Lamar had succeeded in having him, Schurz, confirmed as a cabinet officer & had not they used their influence he would not have been con-

[12] Zachariah Chandler (1813–1879), United States senator, 1857–1875, 1877–1879, and secretary of the interior during Grant's administration, 1875–1877.

firmed—Gordon acknowledged to P. that he felt sorry of mentioning this matter to Schurz & wished that he had not done so.

Williams was appointed.

J. J. Martin of Alabama appointed by Grant

J J Martin of Ala held office under Grant & Hayes 10 yrs—6 yrs as 6th Auditor & 4 yrs as P. M. at Montgomery—& he is now here asking for the office of Comr of Indian Affairs, made vacant by Hayt's sudden removal. Several Southern Democrats endorsed him as competent &c. He will hardly obtain the place as he acknowledges that when he was 6th Auditor that Boutwell, Secty of Treasury, charged him with being a confirmed inebriate.

Martin came in our room 924 E. St. NW. sat several hours & related many amusing scenes of Grants administration, illustrating his (G) pertinacity in sticking to his friends. When M. was charged with drunkenness Grant sent for him & told him he must be more careful about drinking, not to drink about his office &c.

Robert Toombs of Georgia visits Grant

He told of the first meeting of Toombs[13] & Grant after the war, when Toombs called on President Grant, & both soon felt at ease & parted with kinder feelings for one another. It is said that Lamar met Toombs & taunted him for calling on Grant.

Toombs replied, "I've heard of a certain eulogy you pronounced over Sumner's dead body—a man whom you refused to speak to when living."

Corruption in Indian affairs

Hayt Indian Comr was removed by Schurz "because he withheld important information from the Dept." Gen Fisk, of the Indian board was persecuting Hayt before a comtee & everybody is convinced that Hayt was corrupt & was making money through his office.

---

[13] Robert Toombs (1810–1885), a prominent Georgian who served in both the United States and Confederate governments. He held the rank of general in the Confederate Army, prior to becoming secretary of state under Jefferson Davis.

Col. Lane, of Hancock Co. Ga, called at our rooms (924 E. NW) Sunday, Feb. 1, & stated that he had just been to New York to arrange for the purchase of the Macon & Brunswick RR. That the company represented by Cooper of Brunswick Ga, who bid off the road in Jany last at Macon, Ga. had proven utterly worthless & insolvent, (Chainey, Vippard & Co.), that he (Lane) & Col. Hazlehurst of Macon had advanced the $10000.00 cash required by the law at date of the sale, & that he had succeeded in organizing a strong company, who would take the bid & buy the RR at the statutory price 1,125000$ & build the RR to Atlanta in the time set forth, 5 yrs. That the Govnr had been very much disturbed & this arrangement would relieve him &c.

Purchase of Macon & Brunswick railroad

Mr. Schurz's lawyer—Chf Clk Indian Affairs—Mr. Vance told me (Feb. 2) that my Creek contract was approved, that Schurz seemed inclined to disapprove it entirely as unnecessary, but that he fixed the coms *at 5 per ct.* instead of 10, as the contract set forth.

Tuggle's contract approved

Porter & Hodge[14] assure me that they will see that the Indians pay me the other 5 per ct. out of the money.

(Write a memorandum & let them sign it.)

Feb. 10, 1880.

Been reading law books, fixing up an argument for sub-committees in HR & Senate on the Creek Orphan claim & interest thereon, at least from the decision of the Dept Interior that the money was due $251,-055.97 Apl. 5, 1872. Presume I ran over 100 different volumes for precedents in the history of the U. S. as to payment of interest, Supreme Court reports, Statutes, Op. Atty Genels &c.

Tuggle's legal research

Been reading also Dr Francis Lieber "Political Ethics" & "Civil Liberty," pleasant reading on dry

[14] David M. Hodge, a prominent member of the Creek Nation, served as a member of the official Creek delegation to Washington in 1880.

topics—also "Metternich's Memoirs." Finished Madame De Rémusat's Memoirs (Vol 1), & am now reading Montesquieu's "Spirit of Laws" & Cicero's De Republica.

Plato et al.
on government

Tis astonishing to see how little real progress in *ideas* in government have been made. Aristotle, Plato, Cicero—Confucius, Mencius, suggested the different forms of government, *one, many, a few, & all.* Tis true the 19th Century reduced to practice more than former periods, but it remains to be proven whether or not our work will endure. Distrust & corruption & fraud are silently at work in 1880 & how many more strains the system can stand no one knows. The people will keep just such a government as they deserve & public opinion will adjust affairs according to an eternal fitness.

Prophetic words

Napoleon seemed to think that all men were controlled by interest. Some may not be, but most are, & in 1880 it is as true as 100 yrs ago & 100 hence it will remain true as human nature will remain the same.

Let any man select the public events known intimately & completely by himself, the secret history, the scheming, the efforts pro & con, & generally he will confess that very small things, often personal to the main actors, have contributed to shape public events.

How will it affect me? Is the question, & then may come the other question, is it best for the country, & lastly is it right per se?

The growing
bureaucratic
giant

The more I see of the real, actual workings of Congressional legislation, the more I am satisfied that some radical change is necessary in the methods of transacting public business. It averages about 2 hours to each important measure before Congress & under the present idea that Congress ought to attend to the business of 40000000 of people, the difficulty of transacting business will increase.

By restricting Congress to general laws on general

affairs & leave local laws for States—much of the business would be disposed of. It is simply impossible for Congress to deliberate on the thousands of bills annually presented & as the population increases the bills will increase.

Too many laws are passed even now & the intelligent people are utterly ignorant of the laws of the U. S. & the States.

Is it an innocent amusement? A safety valve? Escape pipe?

Gordon & Hill are again at loggerheads over Simmons apptmt as Census Supervisor. Gordon spoke severely about a statement made in his presence by Mr. A. H. Stephens to the effect that he (G) wished another Republican—Smythe—appointed instead of Simmons. Gordon asked S[tephens] for the author, & on S's declining, G. told S. that he must bear the responsibility of the slander till his informant was produced.

Alexander H. Stephens

Avery tells me today that Gordon told him that he (G) had written an apology to Stephens based on his (S's) debility, & old age.

Hill came into H.R. today & had long talks with Hammond & Persons, & also conferred with Felton. Persons tells me that Hill thought he (P) had committed an awful mistake in telegraphing to Jno I Hall, Griffin Ga asking if Johnson would appint his (Ps) friends.

"Political place hunting"

Persons bluffed H[ill] & told him to defeat Johnson & appoint a Democrat. Hill evidently thought he would terrify the *organized* by going against Johnson & get his revenge for being defeated on Simmons.

The true inwardness of political place hunting, of how to get in & how to stay in—has been very much alike since Confucius lived & wrote.

Extracts from Madam De Rémusat.

"A man's character is composed, not of what he is always, but of what he is most frequently."

"Bonaparte applied himself early & skillfully to gain the young, to whom he opened all the doors of advancement in life."

Feb. 21, 1880.　Washington, D.C.

Negotiating the sale of a railroad

The Governor (AHC[olquitt]) requested me to accompany him to New York to aid him in selling the Brunswick & Macon RR.

It had been sold, 13 Jany, but the parties objected to the phraseology of the Conveyance of the RR.

After conference with R. T Wilson, & others, the matter was arranged satisfactorily & the parties agreed, about Feb. 25–7, in Atlanta Ga, to exchange papers & perfect the lease & sale.

It was intimated that it would facilitate the transaction if Ga. parties would take stock in the purchase, so I agreed, for that purpose alone, to take a small interest.

Heard several interesting interviews between Kimball, (H I) & the Gov. claimed as the next highest bidder, that the first bidders had forfeited all rights & hence he was entitled to the RR. The Gov. decided otherwise.

Touring New York

We called on Ex Gov. Woodford at U. S. Dist. Attys room—Went through the N. Y. Herald building from cellar to garret—Gen. C. B. Fisk called on Gov. C[olquitt]. Mr. F. G. Smith—Bradbury Piano Factory Brooklyn, N. Y.—came with a carriage & carried us to his new wooden plate factory, his piano factory, N. Y. Herald, or Woodford, to Brooklyn, to his house, & to Dr Talmage's residence. We met Mrs. Talmage—a small blackeyed woman, with a brightly colored dressing gown & immense ear rings.

The Dr. was at Richmond Va. lecturing.

[I] Was employed as atty of the [blank] RR Co. from San Antonio to Laredo, to aid Gen. Barnes the Prcsdt in getting a bill passed to lend US. endorsement $15,000 p mile—160 miles Fee 2000 acres land, & 2000$ in RR stock—(Feb. 20. 1880.)

Feb. 23.

My wife came Saturday night & we took rooms at 1115 1st N.W. Attended SS. at Calvary Bapt. Church, & then went to hear Dr. Harrison at Mt. Vernon Place N. E. Ch. He preached from the text "Prove all things Hold fast to that which is good" & he spoke of Wesley's life & influence & read the original rules of Wesley's society.

The Tuggles at church

Today, Monday, I called with Persons at Willard's to see Hon G. T. Barnes, on the National Dem. Comtee now in session to call the comtee & select a time & place. They selected Cincinnati on June 22nd— which is regarded as anti Tilden.

I then met a sub-comtee of the Senate Comtee on Indian Affairs composed of Sen. J D Walker of Ark. & Sen. Slater of Oregon. They gave me an hour on the Orphan claim & I was satisfied with the result. Porter & Hodge came in after I had argued about ½ hour.

Testimony to committees for orphan claims

I then called on Wellborn of Texas, who as a sub-comtee had the Ga. case referred to him, & obtained the papers in order to have them filed in the Senate for reference to Comtee on Claims—but the Senate adjourned without transacting any business, in honor of Washington's birthday (22nd being on Sunday). Saw Sen. Hereford—who is the sub-comtee in Senate, to whom the Ga. case was referred. He was rather rude, & seemed unwilling to give me a hearing. I yielded to his ideas & shall simply send him the papers.

More committee contacts

A rude senator

Called at H. R. & wrote a note to Gov. Pound who with Mr Deering & Gen Hooker, composes the sub-comtee of H. R. on the Orphan Claim & obtained certain papers to be delivered to the Senate Comtee.

Then I dealt with 4 different comtees during 2 hours & gave my business a push.

I then returned to my room & with my wife, called

on Mr. Gordon, then Mr. Stephens, then Mrs Felton, then Mrs J R Sneed. Returned to dinner at 5 PM & then called at 7 PM on Mrs Olin Wellborn of Texas.

A full day's work

We called last night on Mrs. Hill & the Senator. Thus in 24 hours we made the rounds.

Washington's birthday parade a shabby spectacle

There was a very poor parade on Penn. Av. about 2 Oclock of 100 men in shabby uniforms—"The Washington Light Infantry" & about 10000 people thronged the Av. to witness the show. Flags were flying, the day was beautiful, but alas, Washington would hardly have enjoyed such a celebration of his birthday in the capital of 40000000 of people made free by his life.

Feb. 27, '80.

Tuggle studies Cicero on government

Finished reading Cicero De Republica, & many of the ideas are so modern that one is tempted to believe that it was not written 1800 yrs ago. Still quotations & other evidence establish the fact that such a work was written by Cicero.

It seems that all ancient philosophers of every land dreamed & wrote of the best governments & naturally divided them into those by one man, by a few men, & by many men—& as all had their advantages & disadvantages, they regarded a combination of all as, perhaps, the best possible government.

So with Confucius, Mencius, Plato, Cicero, Montesquieu. A government of law, modified to suit different nations under different circumstances.

Tuggle's developing philosophy

The real government, the ideas which govern men daily, apart of themselves, is more dependent on the public opinions of men, their real, actual belief, & desire at the time being, than on Constitutions & written laws. The will of the majority is the Constitution, it has been said, in United States, & that will of the majority is based on party sentiment, & that party sentiment is founded on public opinion. Of course, within certain limits, but *construction* of law often makes new law—in governmental, or political affairs, as well as in Judicial matters.

A few xtracts from De Republica will indicate current ideas.

Rule, for the examination of all things. The *name* of the subject in discussion being agreed upon—the *meaning* of the name shall be defined.

In no other state, save where the power of the people predominates has liberty any home.

As the law is the bond of civil society and equal rights form that of the law, by what power can a community of citizens be maintained, where their condition is not an equal one? If therefore it is not expedient to equalize fortunes; if the powers of *mind* cannot be equalized in all, certainly then an equality of *rights* ought to exist among those who are citizens of the same republic. For what is a state but a community of rights?

A nation can entrust its affairs to whom it may choose; and if it wishes to remain free, it will choose from among the best. Nor can the condition of any city be more deplorable than where the richest men pass for the best. But what can be more delightful than a state virtuously governed? What more illustrious than the man, who while he governs others is himself the slave of no bad passions? . . .

The difficulty of coming to wise determinations has transferred the rule from one king to many persons, and the error and rashness of the people from the multitude to a few. Thus between the obstinacy of *one* and the temerity of many, the better class have possessed themselves of the middle and least turbulent of all the situations; by whom if the commonwealth is well administered, the people relieved from all care and thought must necessarily be happy, enjoying their independence through the labors of those whose duty it is to preserve it to them, and who ought never to permit the people to think their interests are neglected by their rulers. As to that exact equality of rights, which is held so dear by a free people, it can not be preserved—; for the people themselves, however free and unrestrained they may be—are remark-

The relevancy of De Republica

An equality of rights

Paternalism

able for their deference to many persons, and exercise a great preference as it respects men and dignities. That which is called equality also is a most unjust thing in itself, for when the same honour is enjoyed by the high and by the low—that very equality must be unjust; and in those states which are governed by the better class it can never happen.

The unjustness of universal equality

Separately I do not approve of any of them—but should prefer to everyone of them a government constituted out of all three.

The grass roots of tyranny

It is from license, which they deem to be liberty itself that a tyrant springs up as a sapling from a root. For as the destruction of the better class arises from their overweening power, so this excess of liberty effects the slavery of the free people. . . . Out of such licentious freedom a tyrant arises.

Some leader is chosen out of the multitude in opposition to the better class. To whom that he may be freed from all apprehensions, on account of his private condition Authority is given and *continued*. Surrounded by guards as Pisistratus at Athens at length he becomes the tyrant of the very citizens who brought him forward. Who, if he is subdued by the good, as often happens, the state is regenerated, if by the bad—a faction is established—another kind of tyranny. The same state of things too frequently occurs in that goodly form of government of the better class, when the vices of the chiefs have caused them to deviate from their integrity. Thus do they snatch the government of the commonwealth from each other like a ball—tyrants from kings—chiefs of the people from tyrants and factions or tyrants from them. Nor does the same mode of government ever last a long time. These things being so the regal form of government is in my opinion much to be preferred of those three kinds. Nevertheless one which shall be well tempered and balanced out of all those three kinds of government is better than that; yet there should be always something royal and pre-eminent in a government, at the same time some power should be placed in the hands of the better

A balance between mass and aristocracy

class and other things reserved for the judgment and will of the multitude.

There is no cause for change where every one is firmly placed in his proper station, and never gives way, whatever may fall down or be displaced.

Catos manner of speaking. A facetiousness mixed with gravity—his constant desire also to improve himself and others; indeed his whole life in harmony with his maxims made him admirable in the highest degree. He was wont to say that the condition of our country was preeminent for this cause. That among other people individuals generally had respectively constituted the government by their laws and by their institutes as Minos in Crete Lycurgus in Lacedemon. But that the constitution of our republic was not the work of one, but of many, and had not been established in the life of one man but during several generations and ages.

Foundations of our government

What beginning therefore have we, of the establishment of a republic so illustrious as the origin of the building of this city by Romulus born of his father Mars?

Homer by those who take the lowest period is made to precede Lycurgus about thirty years. From which it may be gathered that Homer flourished many years before Romulus.

That saying of Cato is very certain, that the Constitution of the State is not the work of one moment or one man; for it is evident how great an accession of good and useful institutions occurred under each reign.

The Royal form of government is to be preferred to other simple forms, only so long as it preserves its proper character—which is that the safety—the equality and tranquility of the citizens are to be preserved by the justice the wisdom and the perpetual power of one man. Many things however are wanting to a people subject to a king, Liberty among the first, which is not that we may live under a just master, but under none at all.

A characteristic of monarchy

First I pointed out three kinds of government that

might be endured and to these three their very per-
nicious opposites, that no one among them was the
best, but that one moderately balanced from all three
was preferable to either of them.

That in his thoughts and actions he never deviate
from himself—so that he may call upon others to imitate him and that he may offer himself in the purity
of his mind and his life as a mirror to his fellow
citizens.

That which in song is called by musicians harmony
is concord in a state the strongest and best bond of
safety in every republic yet which without justice
cannot be preserved.

Justice the
sine qua non
of all government

We must esteem in nothing all that can be said
upon government unless we can establish not only
that it is false, that injustice is necessary, but that *this*
is most true—that without the most perfect justice no
government can prosper in any manner.

For what can be more excellent than when the
practice and habit of great affairs is joined to a perfect
knowledge of the theory of the science of them?

As you have happily defined it to me Scipio, A
people does not exist but where it is held together
by consent of law and the multitude as a mob is as
much a tyrant as if it were one man. Nothing is more
ferocious than the wild beast which assumes the name
and form of the people.

Mch 2, 1880.

Went to "National" theatre last night to hear
Miss Mary Anderson in "Evadne." She acts well
but was poorly supported, xcept "Ludovico" & the
brother.

Sherman weeps

Genl W T Sherman sat next to me, & I saw him
wiping his eyes several times, & was surprised that the
hero of the March to the sea could weep. The broken
hearted women who saw him burn their homes in the
dead of winter in Atlanta Ga. would have been edified by seeing Sherman crying at the imaginary woes
of an actress.

His criticisms on the play were occasionally good.
When his lady friend spoke of the poor King, Sher-

man said, "Well, Kings are generally made of very poor material."

One scene being peculiarly fine his friend wished an opera glass & he looked at me. I had none & borrowed of my nearest neighbor. He took it & said "My eyes are yet good at 60 yrs of age."

Banter with Sherman

"Yes," I replied "You can yet see a pretty woman some distance."

He smiled. "Oh, she is as good as she is lovely. I've known her since a child. She was raised in Louisville, Ky. A pure lovely girl."

He was plainly dressed in citizens costume.

Today I saw him sitting on the floor of the Senate listening to Sen. Logan speak against reopening the Fitz Jno Porter case.[15] He sat in Blaines seat or next it & by Hamlin & occasionally whispered to Conkling.

During the debate when Hill of Ga. asked Logan some questions, Conkling & Carpenter prompted Logan in whispers & the trio put Mr. Hill to some disadvantage as the record will show. Mr. Hill had not studied the case, & when questions were put to him he replied rather evasively & sometimes with a degree of confusion & in all probability will have to make a speech in order to retrieve himself.

Sen. Hill on the Porter case

Mrs. Felton of Ga. has been very courteous to my wife, who is with me & today called to accompany us to Riggs House to see some crayon portraits of Mrs. Langtry the English beauty & several others by Duncan of New York. After seeing the pictures, Mrs F. sent our cards to Mrs. "Sunset" Cox & we found her a plain, but interesting lady of 45, & evidently was willing for the newspapers to believe that she sometimes might possibly write speeches for the fiery orator of the House. It was untrue, of course, but yet they would assert it &c. She had not been here much this winter & they ought to hold her responsible &c.

Mrs. Tuggle's association with Rebecca L. Felton

---

[15] Fitz-John Porter, a general of the Union Army, was charged in 1862 with disobedience during the second battle of Bull Run. Porter was found guilty, and this verdict was the cause of much controversy until twenty-three years later when a bill was passed restoring Porter to the army with the rank of colonel.

She & Mrs. Felton condoled with each other on the burdens of a Congressman's wife, who acted as a clk for her statesman & send out books, *pub. docs &c* & wrote so many letters to constituents.

I'm reading "The History of Our Own Times" by Justin McCarthy & find it very fine indeed, full of instruction & written in a racy, interesting style.

Congressional inefficiency

My Congressional business seems to be doing well, but it is difficult to attend to regular business before such a *politico-business* assembly, which must save the country once a year & legislate for 40,000000 of sovereigns every one of whom can petition for the redress of grievances. It will grow worse every year & the fellow who comes here in the year 1980 will have a lovely time awaiting his turn in the legislative mill, which now grinds slowly if not xceedingly fine.

Intellectual degeneration in Congress

Both bodies seem to be degenerating in scholarship, in knowledge of the political history & science of government as shown in the debates. Little time is here allowed for study & most of the members come here not well-versed in laws & lawmaking & kindred subjects. The debates compare unfavorably with those of 30, 40 & 50 yrs ago & instead of progressing to a higher knowledge of governmental science, constant reference is had to the sages of the past for both facts & theories.

No aspirations to ancestral planes

Should it be so? The fathers availed themselves of what had gone before & advanced to a higher plane, & why should not the Statesmen of 1880 do the same? They are the fathers of the statesmen of the centuries to come.

I do not mean crude innovation, revolution, or mere change, but something deeper & nobler—a profound fidelity to all that is true & good of the fathers, but not a blind worship of ancestry. Certainly ignorance of the past is wholly inexcusable for legislators who should deal intelligently with the problems of the present & contribute their share to the future.

Mch 4, 1880.

For the special enjoyment of posterity I give the following gossip.

The papers one day this week stated that Jessie Raymond had sued Sen. B. H. Hill[16] for $10,000.00 for seduction in 1877, that a child resulted &c.

The next day the same paper contained a card from Jessie Raymond stating that she had no claim on B H Hill & that he was not her seducer.

Seduction or blackmail?

Rumor told many tales of similar female amusements on the part of Mr. Hill. Why the sudden change? One day she sues & swears to her claim & the next day states that the suit was without her knowledge & consent & that she has no claim. A female lawyer filed the suit, & today she was out in an interview stating that Jessie Raymond employed her to sue B H Hill, & that B H Hill Jr. & James Banks, the private secretary of Mr. Hill, had called at her office recently about said suit. Mrs. Belva A. Lockwood is the lawyer's name, & she sued in the Supreme Court of the District of Columbia.

Of course the Senators friends say that it is a case of "Blackmail." His enemies say that he is guilty & has paid the woman to sign the paper.

Sam Cleghorn, a door keeper in H. R., says that Howard Williams admitted to him that perhaps Jim Banks had bought RR tickets for the woman to return home on. I heard Jim say that he was in Jessie's room when the paper was written. I was in the room of the Comtee on Apptms of H. R. this morning & there were present J. H. Blount of Ga., Hyster [Hiester] Clymes of Penn., McMahon of Ohio, Adkins of Tenn., & Singleton of Miss—The Hill [The top half of the next leaf, Tuggle's no. 38, is missing. The verso side of the remaining portion of leaf 38 is blank, save for one word—"them." The recto side is given below.]

Washington gossip

"Well, if [obliterated] charged with su[ch an?] offense, I shall lie out of it & stick to it to the end."

---

[16] Senator Benjamin H. Hill (Democrat, Georgia), member of the United States Senate from 1877 to 1882.

"But Ben. Hill tells such incredible lies," said Blount.

Such is fame. Such is Washington life behind the scenes in Mch 1880.

Mch 10, 1880.

De Lesseps, Eads, and plans for Panama Canal

Yesterday I heard M. De Lesseps, the famous French Engineer who built the Suez Canal, explain to a Comtee of the House the canal project across the isthmus of Panama.

De Lesseps is a fine looking old man, about 75 yrs old—white hair, cut short, gray mustache, dark hazel eyes & very restless, stout for a Frenchman, well shaped head, forehead slightly receding & resembles LaFayette's pictures when the profile is presented.

He spoke with animation, gesticulated freely with both hands & used the French language, while Mr. Appleton interpreted when he finished. Capt. J. B. Eads, of "Jetty" fame, spoke of a project to convey ships over an immense RR, of 12 rails, about the usual distance apart, wheels every three feet under the car, a cradle on the car to hold the ship, which would be drawn from the water by two engines & transported across the land, at about 12 miles p hour. He said the cost of the RR would be about 1/4 of the cost of the canal, & the project was entirely practicable, that the Khediver engineer, an Englishman when asked by Capt. Eads, "Is it practicable?" answered, "Of course it is. See my report on the RR to carry steamboats around the cataracts of the Nile."

Capt J B Eads is a slender, medium size man, bald-head, well shaped, & dresses very plainly.

When he began he said, "Count De Lesseps has complimented me. He only knows me from what he has heard of my work. I know him & have seen his great works & can return the compliment with ten-fold force."

The Count smiled, bowed & extended his hand—& they took a shake.

Capt. Eads & Count De Lesseps both used maps [&] drawings to illustrate their remarks.

Was stopped today (9th Mch) by Mrs. Dr. Mary Walker & had an amusing scene. She mistook me for Sen. Farley—of California—& wished me to make amends for some great outrage of the Press on her womanly feelings by having her appointed physician of the City Police at 100$. salary!

I've been mistaken for Bliss of N. Y. in HR, for Sen. Blaine, & for Farley.

Apl 8, 1880. Washington, D.C.

Have been very busy working on the claims I represent & have my business in very good shape. In the Senate yesterday—a sub-comtee authorized me to write their report covering 350,000$. The Creek Orphan claim.

There is a manifest disposition to defer, delay & prevent money bills from passing. The dominant party wishes to show the country that it is economical. Would a man be called *economical* who refused to pay his acknowledged debts?

Yet the session of Congress which precedes an election for members, or for President, is always a bad time to present claims against the Govmt. After the election they say "Well, we promised to be economical." Such poor little fellows imagine they are statesmen. For political purposes they will vote millions foolishly away, when they would not pay a cent on an acknowledged debt.

My wife left Mch 22nd for Ga. Tis a lonely life to a man who spends his evenings in his room. But books? Yes, these unchanging friends are with me. I've just finished Wilhelm Meister. Can not say that I particularly like it. Many fine sayings—but marred by its free love notions. The world is doubtless honestly pictured, but such a picture is not very attractive, nor elevating, nor would many boys be much benefitted by such an apprenticeship. Ideal, to show the "harmonious culture of his moral being." *Immoral* being, perhaps. These may be old fashioned views based on Jewish traditions &c, but practically, human society is perfectly dependent on such old fashioned

Mistaken identity

More delays on Creek Orphan claim

Statesmen, indeed!

Old fashioned views

notions, & such pictures of ideal beauty & such harmonious culture of moral being would people penitentiaries here & perdition hereafter. Goëthe was a grand man, but he did not elevate the standard of morals by his life. If Shakespeare was his beau ideal of an author, then he did not follow him, for while Shakespeare holds the mirror up to Nature, he does not approve & endorse his Knaves, his Lotharios, nor does he call vices, virtues.

Tuggle's literary pastime

When my wife left, I was lonely & tried reading novels for killing time, or ennui. Jane Eyre delighted me—strong characters strongly delineated—I felt no desire to skip. Often I skip fearfully & sometimes read the first chapter, then the last, & sip here & there. Not so with Jane. She was a friend—a companion & her society was desirable at all times & under all circumstances. My attention was completely absorbed. Villette failed to win my attention & by no means equals Jane Eyre.

One was the work of adversity. She wrote for fame. The other was the work of prosperity. She wrote for what? I do not know, but the divine afflatus is not there.

The Egoist by Geo. Meredith—I skipped nearly all of it. "Henry Esmond" by Thackeray failed to interest me. Eöthen by Kinglake, mostly skipping.

Then I would take some solid food—"American Almanac for 1880" by Spofford, the walking encyclopedia of the national library, an epitome of the world, facts & figures, which if our statesmen would study as a school book they might be benefitted.

Congressional reading habits

By the way, the records of the library do not show much reading by members of Congress. More by Northern men, perhaps, than southern. Those who read the most are said to be Garfield, Hoar, Thurman, Edmunds, Conkling.

Members really have little time for reading outside of newspapers, correspondence & necessary matters pending before Congress.

The country would save by allowing a clk for each

member. Then the local affairs of his district would be attended to, & he would have time to study the affairs of the nation. The debates show vast ignorance of even the matters under discussion.

Congressional clerks

Another improvement would, perhaps, be the removal of the desks from both houses & allow only chairs. The English parliament have done well without desks, & they serve to accumulate objects which distract attention from pending business.

Many read & write most of the time.

I'm trying to read Carlyle's "Frederick the Great." His broken style, Herculean force, eccentric darts here, there & everywhere, these are pleasing as a recreation, but may become tiresome. Not tired yet, however.

Carlyle

He certainly is a giant.

The outlook is not very favorable for the passage of laws this session paying debts of the United States, & I shall not feel badly disappointed if my bills fall by the way. Yet I'm hopeful as to one, or two.

Politically the outlook is mixed. The Democrats are divided & a house divided against itself can not stand. Suppose the house has not been quite finished? The candidates & their friends on both sides are plotting & scheming to pull the head man back & each is scrambling to the front. The usual devices are resorted to, declinations by the modest, announcements by the bold, puffing & blowing in hotels, in papers— persuasive suggestions of filthy lucre, or the lively xpectation of favors to come. Spoils at present & in future— So the pot begins to boil & bubble.

Election year intrigue & chaos

Hell-broth? Perhaps, the Prince of the Power of the Air does not neglect such opportunities.

Opportunity is fate sometimes.

Of course, events are being shaped, & no man can tell what the exact result will be. Availability, He is the coming man. Luck is a fraud & pluck is a hero. Don't be too sure.

Luck & pluck—
like genius & work

Luck & pluck in worldly wisdom generally go hand in hand—like genius & work.

Chicago's man will draw Cincinnati's man.[17] The Democrats will try to trump the Republican card. See him & go one better.

The Devil must be laughing in his sleeve as he is suggesting to platform patriots xactly how to shape their sentences, & mystify the people so they will imagine wondrous differences between my platform & your platform. Me um & tu um. Orthodox & heterodox, my dox & your dox.

Factions or
parties

The votes every day in Congress make it difficult to see what distinct governmental policies separate men into parties. Finance, tariff, everything is mixed.

The fight is really preparing in the unwillingness of the North to see the South shape the legislation of the United States. The Northern people think they have made a mistake, in allowing the South to return to the Union so soon, & in giving the negroes suffrage.

A balance of
power in Negro
suffrage

They are tormented daily at the sight of southern men holding the balance of power by means of negro suffrage & are reading the "Fools Errand by one of the fools,"[18] & looking at the census of 1880 to change the seat of national power from the South to the West.

The South by uniting on material interests can protect herself, no matter who is the Executive Chair.

Political trading

We could have traded with Mr Hayes one year ago on fair terms & had a President of our own, made out of the result of the Electoral fraud[19] & a family quarrel based on Hayes Southern policy.

The corporations, the money power really makes the nominations, & the man at Chicago who wins must say to this Sovereign, "I would like to live in the White House if you please." The same truth applies

[17] Chicago and Cincinnati, the respective sites of the Republican and Democratic national conventions in 1880. Garfield was nominated at Chicago, Hancock at Cincinnati.

[18] Albion Winegar Tourgée, *A Fool's Errand* (New York: Fords, Howard, & Hulbert, 1879).

[19] The Hayes-Tilden election fraud, in which Tilden was deprived of the presidency through a switch in Louisiana's electoral vote. See note 6.

to Cincinnati, & he will be the lucky man who is the favorite of that potent sovereign on June 21th & June 22nd.

Money makes the mare go. & the horse, be he light or dark, will soon follow.

Apl 9, 1880.

Called to see Hon. A. H. Stephens yesterday. He was sick in bed. He requested me to take his carriage & visit Genl. F. A. Walker, Supdt of Census, & see the chances of obtaining a position after July next for a Mr. Howard Smith of Macon Ga.

A call on Alexander Stephens

Genl Walker returned his compliments & stated that he could not absolutely promise, but thought he could make the appointment beyond any reasonable doubt, as he would have about 700 clks to appoint &c.

On returning I said, "Well, I thought I'd get you to tell me who would be the next Presdt, but you are sick."

He evidently wished me to remain & as Dr. Walsh left us alone, he said, "So you want to know who'll be Presdt?"

Stephens prognosticates the nominations

"Yes."

"Well, see the N. Y. Herald reporter. He called here yesterday & I told him that I never changed my opinion & he could see my views xpressed one year ago & just copy them."

"Who will be nominated at Cincinnati?"

"It looks like Tilden will get it, or he will dictate the man."

Suggests Tilden for Democrats

"What are the chances of the Democrats winning the victory?"

"Oh, I lost all hope during the xtra session. With a good platform we could have elected a President. It makes me sad to think of it. You remember my platform I put out. On that we could have swept the country."

"How about Morrison?"

"He's no account, not worth a damn!" I looked at the old shriveled statesman lying like Richelieu on his dying bed, apparently from physical indications, & was surprised at his vigor. "Nothing in him."

"How about the other side?"

"Blaine & Sherman seem to have the inside track just now, but I think Grant perhaps [will] get it. He never says a foolish thing. The Democrats seem to think Grant will be easily beaten. I don't think so."

Grant for the Republicans

We were talking of Conventions past before Dr. Walsh left & Mr. Stephens said "I remember just before Benton died he sent for me & George W. Jones. He asked me to superintend his condensed debates, speeches &c. I promised him I would."

Tells of condemnation for the nominating convention

"To Jones he said, 'I wish you to vindicate my memory. I never went into a bawdy house. I never entered a gambling saloon, & I never was a delegate to a nominating convention. I despised & avoided these three things & in the order I've named them. A lot of worthless, irresponsible fellows who couldn't buy a decent suit of clothes & have to borrow money to get there,—they select the candidate.' "

He continued, "As to the 2/3rds rule. It did well in slavery times, but I've always opposed it. At Cincinnati under it of course Tilden can control the result, as he could manage 1/3."

"Can Tilden reconcile Kelly? I know Kelly. I correspond with him. He is a honest upright man & Tilden can not buy him off— I told Watterson of the Louisville Courier-Journal that he was mistaken about Kelly's strength last year. W said K— wouldn't poll 25000. I said 75000. He had about 80000. Kelly ran in order to defeat Tilden as a candidate for President, & he will not yield."

Grant's unfortunate appointments

Dr. Walsh said, "As to Grant, his great mistake was in selecting his friends."

"Well, what could he do? When good men stand aloof, bad men come forward. If the best men of the country had come to Grant he would have made a good President."

May 21, 1880.

Went to Ga. 15 Apl & returned to W[ashington] —& reached here Apl 29th.

I had written the report for the sub-com. Indian Affairs Senate, before I left, & on my return, I found that no progress had been made, but delay had been caused by the Com. calling on the Secty of Interior for information & advice.

Delay on sub-committee report

This looked unfavorable. I went to the clk (Cox) in Indian office & there was the letter unanswered.

After a weeks work I obtained an answer referring to past letters & recommending that the Orphan claim be paid in money & not invested in bonds, & again another recommendation that the item be inserted on an appropriation bill. This last suggestion was of value.

The Com. adopted the report, granting all I asked, principal $251,055.97 & interest on $176,755.97 from Apl. 6, 1872 at 5 prct interest, & the sub-com. was instructed to endeavor to pass the bill separately & also to put it on the Sundry Civil Apptn bill when it reached the Senate.

Creek Orphan bill reported favorably in committee

Today (May 21) this bill has been reported in the House.

Col. Jno. L. Tufts Agt. of Indian Terty is here, & offers to aid me. I requested that he speak to Sen. Allison & also Sen. Davis (W. V.) Ch. Com. Appts.

Matters look very favorable, & if the Comtee can put it on the Sundry Civil, it will go through.

This is my only chance for this session.

Sen. Jno. B. Gordon[20] surprised the country on 19th last by resigning his seat in U. S. Senate, alleging that his private affairs demanded his attention. I infer from what he tells me that the Louisville & Nashville RR Co. has offered him a position as confidential attorney, or agt, at a salary of $15,000 pr. an.

Sen. Gordon of Georgia resigns

Somewhat strange, & certainly unusual. H. W. Grady[21] seems to be at the bottom of the affair & has

[20] John B. Gordon was extremely influential in Georgia politics. He not only served brilliantly in the Confederate Army, attaining the rank of lieutenant general, but also as governor of the state and as a United States senator from Georgia.

[21] Henry Woodfin Grady, the noted southern journalist.

Henry W. Grady
a fickle bright
fellow

been acting as the go-between for Gordon & Victor Newcome, the Presdt of the L. & N. RR Co. Grady is a fickle bright fellow, & it is strange that Gordon should follow such an ignis fatuus in so solemn & important a movement.

Tis said that there was some understanding between Gordon & Ex Gov. J. E. Brown, who has been appointed by Cov. Colquitt as the successor of Gordon.

A political
trade-off

Some insinuate that it is a political trade & that Brown secured the pecuniary position for G. & in consideration stepped into his shoes.

Gov. Colquitt has thus made a bold move, which has excited comment all over Ga. Some say he has made a great blunder & others will think to contrary.

Brown will sustain himself & make a good impression in the Senate. Gordon has injured himself politically & people will say he bartered his high station for money, & cooperated in putting a man over Ga. who was xceedingly distasteful.

Yet, when the case is summed up, the result for Ga. will be good. Individuals may suffer but the State will be benefitted.

Hill disappointed
in Kellogg affair

Mr. Hill has been sadly disappointed in his Kellogg report, as it is evident that Kellogg will not be unseated—[22] & in the debate Hampton & Butler of S.C. have been very severe on Mr. Hill—about his not being in the Confederate army & his allusions to there having been an understanding between K— & Butler's friends that both should be admitted &c.

[22] William P. Kellogg was elected Republican governor of Louisiana in 1872. The Democrats claimed fraud and set up their own governor and legislature. In the ensuing struggle President Grant supported the Republican Kellogg regime. Gubernatorial elections were held again in 1876, and again the returns were contested. Under the Electoral Count Bill of 1877 the Republican returns were accepted, S. B. Packard was elected governor, and Rutherford B. Hayes received the Louisiana electoral votes. Under the Packard regime Kellogg was chosen United States senator and was seated by a vote of 30 to 28; he was not unseated. See Senate Reps., No. 388, 46th Cong., 2nd. Sess., Vol. IV.

Before he made his speech—a few days—I was in Mr. H's comtee room, & he referred to the Louisiana Returning Bd., & the Electoral Commission as having been frauds &c.

I smiled. I had heard Mr H. in 1877 defend the Electoral bill as an act of great statesmanship & that it saved the country from war &c—I had always opposed it & wrote several letters against it.

Mr H— said "Well, I voted for the bill, but I must confess that the vote satisfies me that I was not fit to be a Senator. I had just come, was a new member, & Edmunds put the job up on us." *Hill's self-deprecation*

He made a tremendous effort, but it fell flat here, made some enemies, & Hampton, Pendleton, Butler spoke against Hill's report.

Bayard, Thurman, Gordon, Lamar, Ransom & others are said to oppose H's report.

Money. The love of it. What will not men do for it?

In Gordon's comtee room today he was xplaining to Gen. Bradley Johnson why he resigned. "I intend to make money & to save it." *Gordon's reason for resignation*

Mrs Gordon laughed "The idea of John's saving money—!"

"Well, give me a year. I intend to be very prudent, & after I pay some little obligations—no great amount—I shall invest my money in bonds & real estate &c."

He then gave a glowing, a la Grady acct of Newcome's[23] speculations in RR, & that N. was going to Europe, & he—G—would act as his atty., & agt in his absence.

That is Gordon steps from his lofty pedestal as U. S. Senator & plays tail to Newcome's kite—an unscrupulous young speculator—who has lately nearly ruined some young men of Atlanta.

It may result well, but I can not put much confidence in the schemes of Grady & Newcome. *Little confidence in Grady*

[23] Victor Newcome, president of the Louisville & Nashville Railroad.

How much better for Gordon to have adjusted his debts, lived cheaply & retained his lofty position—representing as no other living man can do—the South militant perfectly quiet, reconciled, & loyal in the highest sense.

Still, Gordon is the best Judge, perhaps, & yet I fear his struggles with debts have made him act precipitately & to his own permanent injury.

His hasty resignation indicates to my mind that his influence, acquired as a senator, is needed & needed immediately, here in Washington & his real Services are to be rendered not far from Washington.

———

The Presidential game is rapidly being closed. Grant carried Illinois today & thus secures the nomination at Chicago on June 2nd, if he does not happen to [have] some unforeseen accident, & Tilden is moving quietly on Cincinnati.[24]

Should this be the result, the election will be close & hotly contested—Grant will present a strange contrast if put on a bloody shirt platform after his liberal speeches regarding the loyalty of the South from the time he landed at San Francisco.

Dreams of a Grant-Gordon ticket

It would be a grand movement for the whole country to make a real reconciliation over Grant & Gordon —one & only one ticket!

But the place hunters would never submit!

The people are willing but those who depend on strife for a livelihood, will keep up strife to the end of the Chapter.

———

Feb. 1, 1881.

Nearly one year has passed since I made the foregoing memoranda, & here I am still dancing attendance on Congress, watching & waiting for my Indian & Ga cases to be acted on.

Orphan bill still delayed in committee

On June 5, 1880 the Senate passed my Creek Orphan bill, just as the comtee reported it. In an

[24] Tuggle was a poor prophet on both counts: Garfield and Hancock were the nominees.

hour, by my personal efforts & aid, the bill was carried to the House, was reached in a few moments, & would have passed easily, but Warner of Ohio, objected & moved its reference to the Indian Com. of the House, & today, the bill stands just there, as the House adjourned on June 5, '80, while a motion for reference was pending.

The Indian Com. of the House instructed Mr. Gunter to ask the passage of the Senate bill when it should be reached, but day after day has passed & no opportunity has been found to catch the Speaker's eye, or to be in order to move to go to the Speaker's table with any hope of success.

How near & how far a bill can be from becoming a law, this case illustrates most forcibly. It has passed the Senate, it has been favorably reported on, informally, by the Indian House Com. & a member has been instructed to ask its passage, but suppose it were reached tomorrow, & a member were to move its reference to a com.—it would fail, simply because of the fact that, even should the Com. make a favorable report thereon on day after tomorrow, the report would be placed on the Calendar according to its date, & there are already ten times more reports on the Calendar than will be acted on during the remaining thirty days of the 46th Congress.

Only one stumbling block

"Let patience have her perfect work."—Reader, you can never fully know the force of this precept till you have watched a bill pending in Congress for ten months, every day xpecting that lightning might strike your bill.

The snow falling today reminds me that this winter has been the severest within my recollection. Here in Washington the snow which fell the week before Christmas is still on the ground on the north side of houses. The thermometer has been as low as 12 degrees below zero. Last May & June it was as high as 100 in the shade.

Rough Washington weather

In Ga—the lowest degree reached was 4–6 below zero—during Christmas week.

*Dispute on
electoral vote
counting*

The Presidential election resulted in another lease of power for the Republican party & the Senate is this week discussing the plan of counting the votes of the electors. For 90 yrs—the words of the Constitution "he (the vice-President, or the presiding officer of the Senate) shall open the certificates & the votes shall then be counted," have been examined & re-examined & still the question remains undecided as to who ought to count the votes. The fathers evidently thought that any ten yr old boy would be competent to *count* the votes & they did not regard the task as worthy of any great consideration, but in less than a century, *counting* becomes the most important factor in American politics. "Let me do the counting & I care not who does the voting" is the watchword.

The resolution of Sept. 17, 1787, which was sent out with the Constn to the states, showed that in the opinion of the framers of the Constitution the President of the Senate was the proper officer to "receive the certificates, open & *count* the votes"—but as soon as conflicting party interests made the counting important—differences of opinion were common—& as circumstances required, the parties of the hour would change their relative positions on the subject. Today in the House the Democrats oppose the right under the Constitution to count the votes, while the Republicans zealously defend the power of said officer to discharge this great function.

Edmunds & Conkling in 1877 stood with the Democrats on the subject, but today Mr. E. seems inclined to change his views.

The truth is, that the Constitution leaves the matter in doubt & no amt of discussion can remove the doubt & especially as opinion & precedent are divided on the subject. The only effective remedy is to amend the Constitution & change the plan of choosing a President in conformity with the evident wishes of the people, to wit—let the people vote directly for President. The present plan has been in substance completely ignored & public opinion makes the Con-

*Suggests direct
election by the
people*

stitution wholly inoperative in so far as leaving the selection of a chief Magistrate to the electors.

Time has not changed my opinion regarding Gordon's resignation of his Senatorial dignity in order to accept a place under the L&N RR Co. The people of Ga. suspected his motives, made cruel charges against him & after the most bitter personal campaign ever known in this generation, Colquitt was elected & Gordon vindicated. But how fearful the cost? Enemies created, friends alienated & boon companions saying when asked, "What is G— doing for a livelihood now?"

"Dont ask. We all have agreed to stop talking about it. Some mystery which we can not solve."

Why? Because the public does not believe that a RR Corporation would give $15,000 per an. to any lawyer for the services which G— renders. "Then, why does the RR Co. pay him this sum? What has he done, or is he doing to give value recd for his compensation? If, indeed, he renders no sufficient services there is not something wrong somewhere?"

Such queries can not result in good to a public man, whose integrity must be above suspicion. Not that a public man can not in spite of suspicion maintain his place—but he does it at a sacrifice.

Besides all this G's condition, or tenure of office, may be altered any day. Since he accepted his place, Newcome, who gave him the position, has resigned, & Greene is now the Presdt. I met Gordon in Jany '81 at Willard's & asked him if the public rumor was correct that he had lost his place on acct of Newcome's resignation.

"Oh, no. I did not care to answer the insinuation. When N. resigned, I went to New York & asked Mr G. about it, & he told me that I would continue & that Newcome's contract would be confirmed. But, I could get as good an offer else where if I should lose this place, so it is of no great consequence."

Colquitt elected, Gordon vindicated

Public doubt over Gordon's position

This caused me [to] believe that G— had felt uneasy when Newcome resigned & that even now he was preparing his mind for any event.

I venture the prediction that in less than 2 yrs Gordon will not be the attorney of the Louisville & Nashville R.R. Co.

Tuggle's respect for Gordon

He is a great, magnanimous fellow, full of human sympathy, but he has made a sad mistake. He could have represented the South during his life in any position within his gift, & voluntarily put himself in a position where this is almost impossible, without a humiliating acknowledgement of his error of judgment.

Expectations for Joe Brown

Old Joe Brown assumes the role of the apostle of a New South—loyalty to the flag & an *appropriation!*

His career in the Senate will be a success. He knows human nature thoroughly & will try very few experiments, & such only as will give him credit for good motives, whether successful or not, in obtaining what he asks for on the surface.

I was in the room of a member elect of H. R., 47th Congress, in Jany '81, a Mr. George of Oregon, a Republican—Ex-Senator Hipple-Mitchell came in. Mitchell is a tall handsome man, with dark eyes, open brow & a very interesting talker. He had been very unfortunate in his youth—married—left his wife—changed his name from Hipple, to Mitchell, & now has two families, one in America & one in Europe, & is the atty of the Pacific RR Co. at a salary of $10,000 pr. an.

Hayes accused of habitual lying

The conversation turned on Hayes & Mitchell said, "The New York Sun expressed my sentiments the other day when it spoke of him as Hayes the Liar. I know Hayes thoroughly & he is a deliberate & habitual liar. When Hayes came here to W— just before his inauguration in Mch 1877 I was in the Senate, & I know he made Blaine an enemy by lying to him. Hayes offered a cabinet position to Eugene Hale of Maine, & when Hale declined, Blaine supposing that the honor had been intended for Maine, offered

Frye for the place. Mr. Hayes told him he would favorably consider the matter. It turned out that Hayes had arranged his entire cabinet before he left Ohio, & was lying to Blaine. The same thing occurred in substance with Conkling. I know, of my own knowledge, that the Pacific states decided to apply for a cabinet place & that I was chosen as the spokesman of the delegation. I went to see Mr. Hayes & told him the object of our visit. He sat near me & put his hand familiarly on my knee & looked me squarely in the eye & told me he was delighted at the interview & would certainly favorably consider the application. He was lying all the time. Why didn't he tell the truth & say that he had decided the matter & not lie to us in such a way. He can't help it—he is by nature a liar.

The old story. Not a President, nor a Governor has ever escaped similar charges to some extent.

Every applicant construes the language of courtesy into a quasi promise of bestowal—& when the lucky fellow is named, the illstarred host—at once pronounce the unfortunate umpire as a liar.

"Col. Tuggle you got me into a scrape yesterday," said Sen. J. E. Brown recently to me in his private office, 108 Metropolitan Hotel.

"Well, I bet you got out of it gracefully, as you always have" replied I.

He smiled—"I went to Sen. Cockrell of Mo. & spoke to him as you asked me, of the Ga. claim pending before his com., & he snapped me up & said 'Why does he keep sending men after me? I told him that I would have the Ga case taken up at the first chance & Hill has been after me & now you come.' Well, I explained it the best I could & urged him to have it attended to."

Tuggle as a persevering lobbyist

"I'm greatly obliged Senator, & regret that I have caused the Senator from Mo any annoyance, but the Ga. claim was referred to his comtee in Jany 1880, & he can not be accused of undue haste in considering it —& besides, there is only one way of getting anything done here & that is on the doctrine of final perseverance. The dose is disagreeable to statesmen but it must be given."

I went to the comtee room of Claims in Senate, waited an hour & for my pains was informed by the clk that the comtee had deferred action out of respect for Sen. Hereford, of W. Va—who had made the report for the sub-comtee & had been called home suddenly on acct. of illness of his wife— Hereford had told Cockrell that he was called home & delivered the report & papers to C— & requested him to make the report.

Claims bill deferred again

I met Sen. C— just as the comtee adjourned & he gave me the lifeless ends of his ecumenical fingers & said "It was postponed till Hereford returns."

"Suppose he does not return?" meekly suggested I.

"Oh, he'll return if his wife doesn't die & if he does not, then something must be done."

Pro-cisely.

I dropped in Sen. B. H. Hill's comtee room to report my luck in the Ga. case & he said "No, Tuggle, there's no use. They'll find one excuse, & then another. They do not intend you shall get that money this session. Should they report favorably, old Edmunds will bounce it as soon as it gets in the Senate."

Hill suggests the case is futile

Mr. Hill had just failed to get Kellogg's case up, & when I asked about it he said "Tis sad. The country can never be safe under such doctrines. I venture the prediction that if we lose the Senate, there will never be another Democratic Senate in my day, or in yours. Why? Because if the Senate can decide which is the true legislature of a state, when two bodies claim to be, then we are gone. They will do in South Carolina, Fla., & Louisiana[25] just what Kellogg did. The Republicans who get elected to the Legislature will meet, organize, & declare the Republican candidates who were beaten by Democrats, to be entitled to the seats on account of bulldozing,[26] then elect U. S. Senators

Far-reaching effects of Kellogg case

[25] These were the three states which submitted two sets of election returns in the election of 1876. See note 6.

[26] Voter coercion, usually involving Negroes. Under Louisiana law all votes of a district, not merely the fradulent ones, could be thrown out on indication of fraud.

&c, & the Senate of the United States being Republican will seat those who have been thus elected, & in this way perpetuate themselves in power. So in Fla. & S. C. & maybe, in other Southern States. The right doctrine is that Louisiana alone can decide which of two rival bodies is her real Legislature & when she decides for herself, she decides for the Senate & for the world, & yet, 8 men in the Senate go with the Republicans for retaining Kellogg in his seat. Two men have ruined our party."

"Hampton & Bayard?" asked I, supposing he meant them.

"No, Thurman & Bayard. Poor Hampton made some stupid blunders & did all he could, but Thurman & Bayard ruined our party. And yet these confounded newspaper fellows say I did it. You know, I have nothing to do with them—low down creatures most of them are—& Kellogg puts them up to it, in my opinion."

Hill claims maligning by newspapers

"Mr. Hill," said I, laughingly, "You ought to take these newspaper fellows in hand; the circumstances would justify you."

"Mr. Stephens, what do you think of Tourgee's 'Fools Errand'?"

Tuggle queries Stephens about A Fool's Errand

"Why, the book contains some true pictures of Southern life. Of course, it is a partial view & by a Northern man, but he paints a true picture so far as he goes. Some of the characters are well drawn."

"I hear that Dr. Harrison is writing an answer to it" (Dr. H— had read me many pages of his manuscript).

"He had better let it alone—that is, an acknowledged reply, professing to controvert the book." Sending Alec his negro servant after the book, Mr. Stephens read me the scenes describing the war-like Southern Col. & the old Ga. cracker, with great relish.

I borrowed the book, & found it strongly written, & a Carpet baggers version, or perversion of the South during the days of "Reconstruction."

The book condemns & justly the abandonment of Southern Republicans by Northern Republicans & thinks the only mistake, or the main one, was in not keeping the Southern States under military rule until all disloyalty was crushed, ceased, & correct ideas prevailed. How long?

Tuggle relishes a Northern error

It is rich to hear the deep toned sigh of the North over the blunder of negro suffrage. Instead of weakening the power of the whites of the South it strengthened them & now the great question with the North is, how can we remedy our mistake?

No matter how they may shape their platforms & policies—when they get together, by themselves—Republican politicians will for years plot & scheme to decrease the power of the Southern whites. The 47th Congress will begin the inquiry, as to how many members of the House, & perhaps, of the Senate, are here by fraud, intimidation, bulldozing, & they will keep up this agitation for years. If they succeed in reducing Southern representation—all right, & if not, then, none the less, will the laudable effort serve to keep party passions alive.

Agitation on Southern representation

Negro suffrage in the South

"Free ballot & an honest count" will be the cry. If negroes do not vote, they are intimidated & ought not to be represented. If they vote Democratic tickets, they are deceived &c. In order to protect the negro in his right to vote, they will take from him the right to vote at all, if necessary.

"Having given the negro the ballot, we will protect him in a free ballot."

All right, let the South run the same schedule in the North & inquire how many men, white men, are bulldozed by employers, at factories, &c. How many white men are deprived of the right of voting in Mass, Rhode Island, &c!

Fortunately for the South, one phase of the disease will be a mania for educating the negro, on the idea that whenever he becomes an intelligent voter he will cease to be a Democratic voter!

In any event the South can afford to try the experiment. Let the negro be educated & yet the Southern whites can hold their own against the world—or if not, they deserve to go down.

I'm reading a new book by Henry George, "Progress & Poverty" in which he asserts that the remedy for poverty is the abolition of private ownership in land—the vesting of the fee simple in the State & his plan is gradually to impose all taxes on land so that eventually all rent would go to the State. Like all nostrums which pretend to cure all diseases it is a fraud. Undoubtedly there is much truth in his book, but the millenium will not come, even, were his doctrines to prevail. While human nature remains the same, want & misery will remain in the world. "The poor ye have always with you."

Henry George's Progress and Poverty: *a fraud*

The Indians can use George's book as an argument against dividing their lands & allotting them in severalty, that, the most advanced thinkers advocate holding realty in common as the panacea for all the ills society is heir to.

The right of *local*—self govmt—is as near a panacea for all social diseases as the wisdom of man has yet asserted—for this preserves the power of treating each locality according to its own symptoms. What would cure one locality would kill another.

Self-government: nearly a panacea

Feb. 3, 1881.

Senate Com. on claims reported my Ga. case favorably yesterday for $22,567.42.

I wrote the report for Sen. F. Hereford.

Is it possible to pass it? Yes, but not probable. The only way is to pass the Senate & to pass it from the Speaker's table in the H. R.—a hard thing to do.

Senate reports claims favorably

Met Col. Robert G. Ingersoll, the famous free thinker & asked him "Col when do you preach again?"

"Oh—I do not preach anymore. What's the use of fighting a dead man? I killed the Church when I demonstrated that no untrammeled intellect could be orthodox. Whenever I meet a man who is thor-

Robert G. Ingersoll: an undue pride in his intellect

oughly orthodox, I know he does not know a d—n thing."

Poor fellow. In the pride of his intellect he pities his fellow creatures who feel the need of some support above & beyond the power of man.

---

*The dead
statesmen*

In the Senate yesterday I witnessed a meeting between Sen. Bailey of Tenn, who has just returned from an unsuccessful campaign before his State Legislature, & Senator Thurman & they evidently were joking each other about being *dead* Senators. Then Senator Hereford who sits in front of Sen. Thurman came up to & shook hands with Sen. Bailey & then one more dead Senator was added—then Sen. Randolph. Sen. Kernan & Sen. McDonald, & thus a group of dead statesmen were gathered around the great man from Ohio.

What a contrast between Thurman & Hereford! Mediocrity & superlative intellectual force.

A resolution regarding the counting of the electoral votes next week was under discussion. Edmunds offered an amendment inviting the H. R. to come to the Senate Chamber, that being always the place where the custodian of the certificates would be found, to wit, the Vice-Presdt.

Ingalls of Kansas stated a secret connected with the counting of electoral votes in 1877. He was one of the tellers & there was a rumor that as the certificates were being carried from the Senate Chamber to the House, certain parties intended to capture them by violence. Perhaps it was only a rumor but steps were taken to prevent such an occurrence.

The resolution was passed—about in the language used in 1837.

---

*Challenge to
counting system
for electoral votes*

Heard in the Senate today a fine speech by Conkling on a resolution denying the power of the President of the Senate to count the electoral votes. Conkling agreed to the resolution & was answering White [Whyte] of Md., who had argued in favor of the power of the President of the Senate—& among other authorities cited Kent.[27]

Conkling took issue with him & insisted that stress ought to be laid on the words "*In the absence of all legislative provision*," (I presume the President of the Senate can count the votes &c) & argued that this clearly showed that Kent thought the Constitution vested in the legislature (Cong.) the power to provide for the count, & hence it could not be vested by the Constn in the President of the Senate.

Edmunds took the position that neither Congress nor the President of the Senate could count the votes, in the sense of deciding all questions, & that the Constitution did not vest the power in any one nor in all three of the parties, President of Senate, the Senate, & House.

George Edmunds of Vermont

Feb. 4, '81.

Yesterday I called at Mr. Stephens room. "How are you today?" and I squeezed his little feeble hand.

Another visit with Stephens

"Oh, oh," he groaned & jerked his hand away.

"What's the matter?"

"A felon on my finger." I apologized & asked how he was.

"Been snowed up for several days."

A clk was busy writing & I saw that he was making a reply for Fitzsimmons, Marshal, U. S. for Ga., against whom certain parties had made charges. F. had been made U. S. marshal by Mr. Hayes at Mr. S's suggestion.

Today I called again & found him still hard at work on the same paper with two clks. He is full of sympathy. I asked him if he could not go to the House tomorrow & help me with my Creek Orphan bill, by moving to go to business on the Speaker's table. He consented, if he was able.

[27] James Kent (1763–1847), noted American jurist. Kent served as master in chancery for the City of New York, as professor of law at Columbia College, and as judge of the Supreme Court of New York. See *Congressional Record*, Feb. 3, 1881.

The story
of an ex-slave

Dr. Wills was asking Mr. S. about Harry Stephens, colored, who has recently died in Ga. at Mr. S's home. I asked him how old was Harry.

"About 49—or 50. He was very true to me and I trusted him without limit. He had about $1000.00 at the close of the war & when he died he left about $15,000.00 worth of property. I don't know how it will turn out. I never knew a more trustworthy man, black, or white. His loss to me is irreparable. He has been my major domo since the war & everything I had was in his hands. He died worth more than I am. I chose to spend my money & Harry saved his. He had a remarkable judgment on mules & many farmers paid Harry's expenses to Atlanta in order to get him to buy mules for them. He owned two plantations when he died & was bargaining with me for another when he died. I offered it to him for 1500$ in two payments. It was worth $2000. I sent him a deed some time ago, but he was too sick to attend to any business when it reached him. He was always ready to serve me, in heat, & in cold & his place cannot be supplied." The old man's eyes were full of tears while he spoke.

Tuggle dines
with Stephens

He has evinced a kind interest in my business & tomorrow invites me to dine with him.

Sen. B. H. Hill said to me yesterday, "Blaine smiled & nodded his head to me when I said the lion & the lamb would lie down together, & of course he would be the lion & you know I'm so lamblike, so lamblike," & he laughed his peculiar laugh for half a minute.

"Yes," said I, "the lamb would keep very close to the edge of the bed."

"Well, Blaine is very popular with us Democrats & we will all be glad to see him become Garfield's Secty of State."

"Just to get rid of him in the Senate?"

"Oh, no. He will make a good secretary & we all think him entitled to the position. I told him recently that our quarrels were all in the past & I think we can get along pretty well in future."

"I'm greatly bothered about how to vote on re-tiring Gen. Grant, or putting him on the retired list," said the Senator to me.

"Why, vote for it. It's no new thing & many hard things will be said of us if we fight the bill," said I.

He looked surprised & was evidently pleased. "Well, I'm inclined to do it. A Senator said to me, 'You Southerners will miss a great opportunity if you do not vote for Grant's bill. Every little Cross wind politician will curse you in the North & say,' "Yes, d—n 'em. They won't pay Grant a cent, & now we will cram him down their d—n throats." '

"I really think it would be a great accomplishment to retire Grant from politics & this may do it," [Hill continued].

Grant does not deserve a pension, perhaps, but the South can afford to be magnanimous to her conqueror, & she cannot afford to be misconstrued. The principle is recognized every day in pensioning ex-soldiers. Really, it threatens to be a serious financial trouble in future, & the annual xpenditures for pensions will soon be more than the total disbursements of the Govnt prior to 1861.

The new census has been a sad surprise to the North. They thought it would certainly show a decrease at least, relatively, but on the contrary, the census shows the South entitled to a slight increase in Congress, & the North—New England especially—to be decreasing. With wisdom on the part of our representatives, the South can wield the balance of power, & ensure fair & equal treatment, no matter who fills the Presidential chair.

Our interests are peculiar, & neither party in the North sympathizes with us on many material questions, & we should so manage as to feel free to act independently when our best interests are involved. We can cooperate on national issues & yet retain some degree of freedom as to home affairs.

Feb. 5, '81.

Dined with Hon. A H Stephens at his rooms at National Hotel & there were present, Senators, Wade Hampton, B. H. Hill, members of House, Phil. Cook, & Mr. O'Connor of S. C. Dr Wills, Dr Hubbell, J. R. Randall, poet & editor, Col. Fitzsimmons, U. S. Marshal of Ga—& myself—at Mr. S's right. Sen. Hampton sat by me.

Somewhat remarkable—a V. Presdt of Confederacy, an Ex. senator of same, Hill, & two generals of the army—all now members of Congress.

The dinner consisted of raw oysters, soup, fish, beef, mutton chops—cheese, celery, salad, potatoes, pastry of several kinds, Jelly, fruits, nuts, & various wines. I & Senator Hill did not drink—rest did.

The conversation was on a variety of topics— mainly political. Guesses were made as to the future of the Senate, Hampton saying that Mahone would vote on the organization of the Senate with the Democrats, & some that David Davis would vote one way, & some another.

Mr. Hill suggested that perhaps the Vice President might decide if there should be a tie. Hampton thought that the V. P. could not vote for officers of the Senate, but Mr. Hill thought it was a question admitting of doubt.

Hampton thought Blaine, Alison [Allison] & Robt Lincoln would be in Garfield's cabinet.

Reference was made to the recent senatorial elections in Tennessee & Mr Randall asserted that there was no doubt that Maynard had bought two Democrats, but that Jackson being related to both of them, they voted for him & deserted Maynard.

Hampton said "Maynard reminds me of a blacksnake with a viper's head. He turned off a poor woman since he returned from Tenn, in fact he's making a clean sweep of all Democratic appointees since his defeat, & I got so mad while talking with him that I left & went to headquarters & told Mr. Hayes 'One of yr chiefs is playing the devil up here,'

& he said he would put a stop to it at once. He turned off Miss Cunningham, Mr. Stephens."

Said Mr. Hill, "I venture the prediction that Blaine will pursue a liberal, conservative policy. He is frank, & will let you tell him of his faults & will admit them."

"Yes"—said Hampton "I told him the other day, 'Blaine, you ought not to have made such an insinuation against me the other day.' 'No,'—he replied 'that's so.'"

"Is he a lawyer, Mr. Hill?"

"No—no part of one."

"Why I thought from his Geneva award speech that he was a pretty good lawyer."

"No, that speech showed that he was no lawyer" said Hill. "Had he been a lawyer he would have seen the advantage he had over Thurman, Conkling & Edmunds & could have crushed them, for he was right—on the side of the sheep owners & others, & against the Insurance Companies."

Hill & Hampton have been cool towards each other since their speeches on Kellogg's case last spring, & on my way to Mr. Stephen's room I overtook Mr. Hill. Said I, "Where are you going in this direction so late?"

"To Stephens'—to dinner."

"So am I, but I thought you & Hampton were not very congenial & he is to be there."

"Oh—well—we speak. I do not think much of his political judgment, however."

At the table while discussing party management, Mr. Hill said, "We are all Democrats here, but I do think our party has more votes & less sense than any party ever had. We are an aggregation of inharmonious fractions—the northern part will not follow a southern leader & they fail under their own leadership. We are too cowardly. Look at the Senate; we have several Democrats who are always willing to help the Republicans in an emergency."

Hampton was sitting next to me & whispered to

Discussion of
James Blaine

Hampton and
Hill at odds

Fitzsimmons, "He means me. I will reply to him."

"Oh no, General, he does not."

Hampton was feeling his wine, & sitting directly opposite to Hill, who had exchanged seats with him, as he, Hampton, did not wish to sit near the fire. He was not pacified, & soon remarked, "I think that the Democrats would recover sooner if they could slough off all their doubtful members, all who [do] not believe in true Democracy."

Evidently he was referring to Hill, who had written a letter after Garfield's election, intimating that both parties ought to disband.

[The upper three-fourths of the next leaf, Tuggle's number 84, is missing.]

Roscoe Conkling of New York

Mr. Hill said, "I've been here six winters, have dined out a great many times, & have never met Conkling yet at a dinner."

Mr. Stephens said, "I can say more than that. I have never seen him to know him in my life."

After talking of the gloomy prospect of Democrats, Mr. Stephens said, "With good issues, common sense & patriotism we can win yet, & I propose

A toast to democracy

a toast to "Democracy—true Democracy. May it be crowned with success."

"Yes, & soon" said Hampton.

"Immediately, if not sooner" added Stephens.

"Well, I can drink that toast" replied Hill, & touched his glass to his lips, without drinking.

After cigars were lit, Hampton asked Stephens what were good issues.

Good issues to split the Republicans

"Repeal the internal-*infernal* revenue tax—odious to the people, revise the tariff—the west is really with us for free trade, re-monetize silver by restoring its full purchasing power, refund our bonds at low interest & on long time—these are some of the issues with which we could split the Republican party in 60 days after Garfield is inaugurated."

"Do you mean to retain the silver dollar at 412½ grains?" asked Hampton.

"Yes. It is founded on the experience of 500 yrs, 25⅛ grains of gold to a dollar, & 212½ [412¼] grains of silver, & that is right, but the bond holders want gold as the only standard."

"But cannot we compromise with those who wish 485 grains of silver, say at 430 grains?" asked Hampton.

"No. It will only add to our debt. We must remove the burden from the toiling masses. We are now just in the condition of France before her revolution in 1792. The nobles paid no taxes & refused to pay any. Vanderbilt pays less tax on his 100 millions than my colored tenant Bob, who has an income of $120.00."

Tax loopholes for wealthy

"I tell you—it will not always so continue. The working people will rise some day & armies can not put them down. We need wisdom, courage, patriotism, ideas, for they rule the world—good newspapers, or batteries as we called them in 1848, when seven (7) men of us determined to elect Taylor, & we did it."

Then he told of Toombs going to New York & making the first Taylor speech by the aid of *Isaiah Rynders*.

"But we cannot succeed without becoming aggressive, & we cannot become aggressive with[out] courage, & what courage have we shown in the last six years, & how many days have passed without truckling to Republicans?"

"They will not follow Southern men, & their chosen leaders have ruined us. Two men have done it. When I came here—in Senate—four years ago I was young in politics & green—very. I did not know where the 'Electoral Commission bill came from.' I know now. Thurman is completely under the influence of Edmunds. Thurman is greater than Edmunds, but not so well informed. Edmunds is technically a better lawyer & more unscrupulous. Thurman can do nothing without consulting Edmunds, & Bayard he always runs off to consult some liberal Republican correspondent. He has had an idea that he could be

Two ruined the Democratic party

President if he could conciliate the liberal, conservative element. These two men have ruined the Democrats by their leadership."

"I hardly think so. A few years ago we had only seven Democratic senators, & even in next Senate we will have 37. We have had both houses, & in last election Hancock had 6000 more votes than Garfield. With good issues & fidelity to them *through* the *campaign,* our cause is not hopeless."

A politician's advice to young reporter

"The Press came up"—said Hill—"Randall, I told a young fellow the other day, who came to me for advice, telling me that he had just come here as a newspaper correspondent—'My young friend, there are three rules which will ensure success.

1. Put in your letters as much as possible that is not true. 2. Put in as little as possible which is true. 3. Respect neither age, sex, position, nor condition.'"

"Nor previous condition!" suggested Hampton. "All the papers wish is a sensation, not the truth."

"Well," responded Randall, "I've met with some success on the opposite plan."

"It is a strange fact," said Hampton, "that a fellow, whose judgment on any practical question no body in the world would regard in the least, can by taking up a pen & calling himself 'we'—become a wise statesman & give valuable advice on the gravest matters of State."

Opinions on Sen. B. K. Bruce of Mississippi

Opinions were xpressed on Sen. Bruce, the only colored member of Congress.

Mr. Hill thought he behaved very well, but was only fit for a head waiter in a hotel.

Hampton thought B— had more sense than Mr. Hill gave him credit for.

"Well, he knows no more of the Constitution than a jaybird does of music," replied Hill.

"Well, a jay-bird sings pretty well, you know" laughed Hampton.

"How about Don Cameron?" someone asked.

"Why, he knows nearly as much about the Constitution as Bruce," said Mr. Hill.

"Well, he's a clever fellow anyway, & will always

sign any paper for us to get a poor fellow a place, &
frequently helps us out," added Hampton.

Feb. 7, '81.

Mr. Stephens said this morning in answer to my
question "Can the V. Presdt vote for Secty of Senate if there should be a tie?"

"Well, I've not examined the question. I remember in Jany 1865 in secret session of the Confederate
Senate, when I as V. P. was presiding, I had occasion
to decide on the power of the V. Presdt. The Con-
script law was under discussion & the Senate was
equally divided. I rose & stated that there being a tie,
it was my duty to vote & decide the question, & proceeded to give my reasons for the vote I should cast.
A debate sprang up, & finally a senator from N. C.
stated that he would change his vote & break the tie.
I decided that he was too late. The Senate reversed
my decision. I called Hunter of Va. & told him to be
present next morning as I should immediately resign, as the Senate had virtually voted a want of confidence. I did not attend next morning, but the Senate
passed resolutions asserting that it did not intend
any want of respect & asked me to come in & address
the body. I did so, & they reconsidered the votes. I
cited Dallas' vote on the tariff bill, I remember, when
he was V. President." *Stephens' vote to break tie in C.S.A. Senate*

"Will you go up today?"

"Yes, I'm expected to make some remarks on Collamer[28] whose statue was unveiled last week in statu-
ary hall. I knew him well. We sat side by side in the
House. I told him one day, 1848, that Clay could
never be elected, & taking out an envelope I took a
pencil & said, 'I'll give you the result if Clay should
be nominated. Vermont & New Hampshire = 12. If
Taylor is nominated the following states will be certain for him, & then I made a list including N. C. &
Ga.' Collamer said, 'Why, you do not give Ky. to
Clay.' 'No, he can't carry Ky.' Howell Cobb came
up & looked over the envelope & laughed & said, *Stephens comments on Clay and Taylor*

[28] Jacob Collamer (1792–1865), Vermont was United
States congressman, 1843–1849, and senator, 1855–1865.

'You've got Ga down for Taylor.' 'Yes & he'll carry Ga.' 'Well, I'll bet you the best suit of clothes which Brown (a Washington tailor) can make that Cass will carry Ga. by 15000 votes.' 'All right.'

"Church of N. C. took a similar bet for N. C. [Stephens continued].

"After the election, it turned out that Taylor carried every state, & no other, which I guessed. I kept that envelope till the war, but it was lost during the last raid.

"I knew the power of an issue. It is the same yet."

Tuggle away from Washington

[As noted in the introduction to this chapter, Tuggle spent part of the nine-month interval between the preceding and the next entry on a return trip to the Territory. While there he took down in rough draft the "last batch" of Indian myths which he began "writing out" in December with the intention of submitting them to Scribner's.]

Dec. 4 & 5, '81.

Again at Washington, willing to suggest a method of distributing the surplus revenue. At Mr. Stephen's rooms, the same in National where Clay died—& there the old man sits in his baby chair, his eyes as lustrous as ever, & his mind as clear, taking an interest in everything & in everybody. A sore on the left cheek bone is troubling him as the doctors hint that it may be cancerous.

Stephens' lucidity and attitude

"What a fate. Cancer to carry off two great Georgians, Hill & Stephens?" He smiled placidly.

"What of Avery's book?"[29]

"I'm reading it now. It's very readable. Joe Brown is the hero."

Stephens, the oracle

He chatted away & told again the story of reconstruction, his talk with Lincoln at Hampton Roads —&c.

"What of Guiteau.[30] I believe they'll return him crazy," said I.

[29] I. W. Avery, *The History of the State of Georgia from 1850 to 1881* (New York: Brown and Derby).

[30] Charles J. Guiteau, President James A. Garfield's assassin.

"Well, tis hard to find a perfectly balanced mind. Every body's crazy—they only differ in degree."

"What of Arthur's admtn?"

"He is a Republican—a stalwart, & will run it on that line, but I believe he will execute the laws in a business way."

"Will he not be under Grant's influence?"

"If he is, it will be well. You know I believe in Grant. I never knew him to say a foolish word, or do an unwise act. He was quick to decide & did as he promised. Johnson said he lied, but others said it was Johnson. I remember John J. Crittenden's daughter—Mrs. Coleman of Baltimore came to me with a long petition signed by Senators &c asking for her son the position of Secty of the Legation to Spain. I told her to throw the paper away & go to see Gen. Grant.

" 'I don't know him.'

" 'Send in yr card—he'll see you & report to me.'

"She came back & told me that Grant saw her, & when she told her mission, asked can he talk French? Yes. Spanish? Yes. German? Yes.

" 'Well' said Grant, 'the place is now filled, but in May I shall promote Mr. Fish, & yr son shall be appointed.'

" 'Yes, & he'll do it. Now, send to Balt. for yr. son & let him escort you to Mrs. Grant's levee tomorrow night, introduce him to Grant & say nothing more.'

"She did so, & when May came, Coleman got his commission."

"If Arthur will follow Grant, he will do well" [I said].

"Yes, but the South need expect no favors."

"No, no offices."

"I do not mean that. I mean that she will be given the cold shoulder in every way. Grant has not forgotten the South's treatment of his candidacy for the 3rd term."

"Well, how could he? They did not respond to his almost open overtures."

Admiration for Grant

Grant's honesty

A Grant &
Stephens ticket?

Again I was reminded of my former suspicion that Stephens dreamed that *Grant & Stephens* might have been the ticket in 1880.

"How's yr. book?"

"My history of the United States? Nearly completed, if I can find a publisher."

"You'll not fail to do that."

Georgia's
cotton claim

The Gov. of Ga. asked me to investigate the Cotton Claim of the state. In 1872 H. V. Johnson, Wires & Co. made a contract with Gov. J. M. Smith to recover the proceeds of certain cotton &c. Eight years afterwards—1880—Johnson wrote to Gov. Colquitt that Congress had never been in a favorable temper to pass a special bill, & that he—J—was willing to have his power of atty revoked, & T. M. Norwood substituted in his stead. In 1878—perhaps—Dr. J. B. Hambleton, formerly of Atlanta Ga.—but then & now of Washington D. C. applied to Gov. C.—for power to represent the state, & was endorsed by the Ga. delegation. Before negotiations were completed the first contract by Gov. S[mith], with H. V. J[ohnson], W[ires] & Co., was discovered, & Hambleton's inchoate powers were suspended.

H[ambleton] had sold an interest to Norwood & Schley for 1000$, & now Schley writes to Gov. Colquitt for power to represent the state in order to save his money &c.

Hambleton called on me at my room at Metropolitan, & after a long & entertaining talk, I recd very little information as to the basis of the claim, & he evidently possesses no evidence beyond hearsay. He claims that a man pretended to have certain valuable paper, & he got the 1000$. from Norwood to buy them, & paid the man 600$ & had never seen him since, nor recd a paper.

His first information was derived from Gasway B. Lamar, while he was here prosecuting his cotton claim before the Court of Claims. According to H.—Lamar bribed one of the Judges—Drake to render judgment for 500 & then gave Ben Butler 25,000$ to bribe Atty Gen. Williams to dismiss the appeal to Supreme Ct. & then died in 6 weeks after getting his money.

Even granting that Ga. had 3000 bls seized by Sherman in 1865 at Savannah, the chances are all against a recovery. A Republican congress will be very slow to pay Ga. for such a claim—& indeed, my fear is that another agitation of Ga's claims against the U.S. will resurrect the suspended "Direct Tax." Sherman & Edmunds will think it eminently just that Ga. should be allowed to pay this tax, as most of the states have done—South Carolina—since the war. Georgia asked for the privilege of assuming it in 1866, & was refused.

Dec. 6.

Ran over in Library McIntosh's Origin of Am. Indians—(Tartars), Swanton's Myths of New World, Bancrofts Native Races of Pacific States (Myths) Legends of Hiawatha (Schoolcraft)—& Tales of Indians by Barbara Somebody—all to see if my Creek fables were in print, & found nothing like them.

Checks library for published myths

Met Mr. B. H. Hill & felt extremely sorry to see that he is sensitivity conscious of his imperfect utterance resulting from the surgical operation for cancer under his tongue. The whole floor of his mouth & about 1/4 of his tongue were removed. He is fat, & to a stranger doubtless looks well, but to one who knew him intimately there is a sad change in his lower face & his fine enunciation is gone & I fear forever. Still he can be understood readily.

Sen. Hill's operation

There was a stampede of bills to get in for reference in Senate yesterday. No especial advantage to be gained, as the comtees are not yet appointed. I followed suit & started my Creek Orphan bill today via Sen. Slater of Oregon—& had the papers taken from the Senate files & referred with the bill to Indian Comtee of Senate, Dawes of Mass—probable chairman.

Strolled in Senate just as they met, & was in while

the Chaplain prayed. I did not intend to violate the rule, & was merely caught by accident.

Said to Sen. Joe Brown, "The Gov. of Ga asks me to examine the cotton claim of Ga. I told him I wouldn't give a nickel for it."

"No, I wouldn't invest 5cts in it, on a speculation" replied the Senator.

Tuggle asked to check Delaware claims

The Delewares asked me to investigate their pending claims & to take charge of them, & accordingly today I found,

1st. That there was due the Delewares under treaty of July 4, 1866—art. 14—the sum of $14,740.00 for 23 sections of land, called "Half breed Kaw lands."

Comr of Indian Affairs reported favorably on it Feb. 1, 1878. Bills HR 1194, 1st 46th Congress, & HR 1171, 1st 45th—covered the claim—

2. The timber claim was reported against by the Comr. June 6, '78, as the Delewares had recd $30,000 in full settlmt under art. 14, treaty 1866.

3. Right of way claim for lands taken by Leavenworth Pawnee, & Western RR Co., whose franchise was afterwards bought by the Union Pacific, & its by the Kansas Pacific—was ascertained by the agents of the Indian Dept. to be $28,959.40. The RR Co. refused to pay, & the Secty turned the case over to the Dept. of Justice, with suggestion to sue the RR Co. in name of U. S. as Trustee for Delewares. See Dept. of Justice as to result & present status.

4. Stock claim taken by whites since treaty of 1854. This was provided for in treaty of 1866, & in 1867 the Dept. acted on it by appointing a Special agent, who reported the claim at $26,284. See also H. Ex. Doc. 108, 2nd Session 41st Congress. Secty of Interior recommended Congress to pay this claim. H.R. bill 1172, Jany 23, 1878 covered this claim & was reported favorably on by Indian Comr. June 7, 1878.

5. The Leavenworth Reservation claim was carried to the Supreme Court & was decided adversely in 2 Wallace, 525, the Court holding that the Delewares had no title to the land in dispute.

Wrote to Charles Journeycake, ex-chief of the Delewares, at Lightning Creek, Indian Terty, also to John T. Smith,[31] Coody's Bluff, C. N. [Cherokee Nation] Indian Terty, & to Maj. Vore,[32] on the Deleware claims, & consented to represent them.

I am contemplating an arrangement with a Stalwart Republican to aid me in my business.

Correspondence with Delaware chiefs

Sent Deleware Charlie, a full blood—a Harper's Weekly—with Giteau's picture & the trial &c. He lives in Western Cherokee Nation, but I sent it care of John T. Smith, Coody's Bluff.

Called to see Sen. B. H. Hill at his residence 918. 17th St, on Farragut Square. He met me in hall, & with a cordial grip said, "Do you know Thornton?"

Amusing visit to Sen. Hill's Home

Thinking he meant the English Minister I replied, "Why, no."

"What, don't [know] Marcellus Thornton?"

"Lord, yes."

"Come in."

In the parlor I found Mrs. Hill, M. E. T. (of Ga) a hair harried, cranky creature, half democrat—half Republican & all fool, the laughing stock of the boys, & there sat his new wife, a North Carolina widow, very motherly, very fat, with seal-skin sock, red muff, red ribbon, red *face*, & I simply melted. The evening was warm & I had carried my overcoat on my arm, & the grate glowed & Mrs. Thornton, if not too polite, would have been rendered into leaf-lard, but there she sat & felt proud of Marcellus who, bolt upright à la militaire, sat with gloved hands a la Arthur.

"Do you like society Mrs. Hill?" whimpered Mrs. Fatty Thornton, (75000$ in weight).

"Well, I sometimes enjoy it. You know we've been here over 7 years" & the quiet gentle woman sat patiently & listened to distilled nonsense.

They soon left, after telling that Col. Thornton had purchased the Post Appeal of Atlanta Ga. & would conduct the evening journal &c.

Mr. Hill gallantly escorted them to the door, & I

[31] John T. Smith, a former chief of the Cherokee Nation.
[32] See note 10.

heard him groan in disgust as he closed the door & as he entered the parlor said, "The fools are not all dead yet," & so we proceeded to dissect the society insects, & nothing was left but a few wings after the performance ended.

Mr. Hill asked about many people & things at LaGrange & took a kind interest in the people among whom he first struggled to wealth & fame.

Pathos of disappointed ambitions

The key note was sounded to his inner life when he after telling me he had divided out his property among his children & had nothing left for himself, "Oh, yes, you have your head," & then with a deep sigh he said, "My life is behind me."

Poor, disappointed ambition. He had ascended the latter nearly to the topmost round, had obtained the *places* he wished, but the other things, the spirit, the zest of enjoyment, was not there—& his latest physical affliction cut him to the heart.

"Ben. will talk so, though Dr. Gross tells him he is permanently cured," his true wife said as she glanced in sympathy at him as he sat with down cast eyes.

"Ah, well. If I could live my life over I'd stick to law, practice my profession."

He talks very *indistinctly* & is sensitive, & watches his listener closely for indications of observation of his misfortune.

Gordon's and Colquitt's success

He asked me about Gordon & Colquitt's reported good fortune[33] & I told him I knew nothing, only I heard they were paying their debts.

"Buddie (Ben Hill Jr.) says the Gov. received $100,000.00."

"Oh, you do not know, & you ought not to state what you do not know," impatiently interrupted the Senator. "I think" said he "they recd a good sum in

[33] General John B. Gordon and Governor A. H. Colquitt, with Gordon's two brothers, acquired the almost-defunct Georgia Western Railroad and organized the Georgia Pacific Railroad. The Gordon-Colquitt system was taken up by the Richmond and Danville railroad syndicate. The various roads involved in the two syndicates were worth $75,000,000. The union of the Georgia Pacific with the powerful Richmond and Danville enabled Gordon and Colquitt to realize a speedy return on the original investment.

cash & also stock in the enterprise, & that while the Richmond & Danville RR Co, & their partners in New York are the real owners of the Ga-Pacific, there will [be] a construction Co. to build the RR at two prices & this ring will try to sell bonds enough to pay for the work & make a big thing besides. Everything depends on selling the bonds."

Dec. 8, '81.

Heard the Giteau trial about an hour & a half & left believing him crazy, for the most perfect actor could not play such a part. As to whether his unsoundness xcludes a perception of right & wrong, I cannot say. I rather think his view is that it was wrong & illegal to kill Garfield, but he was justified by inspiration. His preparation for escape from the mob, his confession of sorrow for the pain inflicted, his statement yesterday while I listened that the Giteau's were high toned folks & did not do anything wrong xcept in Abram's getting drunk & when it was suggested "till this case," he assented "Yes, till this case" —all show perception between right & wrong in this case.

Tuggle attends Guiteau trial

My belief is that he will never be hung, for if not insane, he must hang as a *Stalwart*—[34] and many people would find this disagreeable—& will argue, "better for American institutions to find him crazy, better for *us*," &c.

Went to hear Dr T. DeWitt Talmage lecture on "Big Blunders," & was not impressed with his greatness, xcept his mouth, & his acting, but I enjoyed the lecture xceedingly. Another man might say the same things & receive little applause. His manner excels his matter in many points, & the audience go to hear & applaud Talmage & not the lecture.

T. DeWitt Talmage

[34] The "Stalwarts" were uncompromisingly partisan Republicans led by a clique in the Senate under the direction of Senator Roscoe Conkling. Garfield challenged the Stalwarts' command of the Republican Party. Tuggle misjudged the tenor of public reaction, however, for the assassination led to a popular demand for the proscription of the New York Stalwarts, and Guiteau was hanged.

"What a pity for such a man to play the buffoon & pander to a vitiated taste instead of elevating the public standard of popular lectures," said Sen. B H Hill, who was coming down the gallery stairs with Mrs. H. as I came out, with my host Hon Mr. George M. C. from Oregon.

I called to see George, & he invited me to hear the lecture. I met George last winter & he seems to enjoy my extravagant & humorous criticisms of men & measures, for instance he kept in a titter all the evening at my description of Talmage's mouth being like "a slit made in a side of bacon by a butchers knife." Not original with me. I had heard Clay's mouth so described.

Formed the two Deleware bills, one for 9,000$ & the other for 26,000$ & will start them at once.

Creek delegates to Washington

Porter, the Creek Delegate came yesterday & is at 1224 F St. with his wife & 2 children, & pays 80$ for board & lodging on 4th floor.

Coachman[35] & his wife & baby (8 mths) came today & I & Porter found him a small room & parlor at 507, 11th St NW., at 30$ & his board at 40$.

Tuggle aids in Seminole claim

I also prepared a letter to the Indian Dept. on the Seminole land matter 175,000$[36] asking an estimate of appropriation be sent to Congress.

This evening went to visit Navy Yard with Hon. Hugh Buchanan M. C. 4th Ga Dist—a new member.

The question of the hour is "Who is Arthur's man?" Who has most influence with him? Such a man is much sought—& I am also on the stool of inquiry.

---

[35] Ward Coachman, principal chief of the Creek Nation in 1876–1879, served as a member of the Creek National Council and as Creek delegate to Washington.

[36] When the Seminoles were removed to Indian territory, many settled on Creek lands because of an error in the government survey of the Creek-Seminole boundary. Rather than move, the Seminoles bought 175,000 acres of land from the Creeks at one dollar per acre. This purchase occurred because of government error, and the Seminole claim was for reimbursement.

Creek Indian words defined by Porter (in my room Metropolitan).

    Elkahatchee (Cr in Ala)
    Ilka-hutchee
    Ilka = death
    hutchee = creek
    hōtchee = figured

    Chartee = Red
    hutchee = creek, river
    Chartō = Rock
    hōtchee = figured
    Chartō-hotchee-hutchee "Chattahoochee
      river"

    Kialigee—a Creek town, or part of tribe & one
      of the tribes of the Creek Nation.
    Hatchechubbe (Ala)
    Hutchee = Creek, or river
    Chuppah = half way, or part of the way.
    Part of the Kialigee town, which settled up on
      the creek.

    Opelika = bottom place
    Loocha = terrapin
    Poka—collected, or gather
      Terrapin—roost!

    Wetumpka
    We = water
    tumpka = sound of falling water, imitation of
      the sound.

    Talladega
    Tulwa = town (tribe)
    artekee = border

    Notasulga
    Notee = teeth
    Sulka = many

    Wehadkee
    Wewa = water
    hartka = white

Ala bama = name of one of the tribes of the Creek Nation.

December 9, '81.

The Creek
Orphan Claim

Filed new contracts, in duplicate, with Porter & Coachman, as to Creek Orphan fund & the general business, & also made a private agreement as to the Seminole land matter that we would fix the Commissions of the $175,000 after the services were rendered.

Called with *P&C* on Comr. H. Price, & filed a petition for an estimate to be forwarded to H. R. in Seminole matter & he (Price) promised to do so.

Also called on A. Bell, Asst. Secty Interior.

Dec. 10, '81.

The Delaware
claim

Called at Dept. Justice, & found that in 1874 March 26 Hon. C. Delano wrote to Atty Genl. Williams about the Deleware right of way claim. It was refd by Dept Justice, June 20th 1878, to Dist. Atty. Topeka, Kansas, or rather he was written to for information. George R. Peck, Topeka Kansas, was Dist. Atty in 1878. No response was on file from the Dist. Atty up to date.

The Chf. Clk. Sam Muliken, wrote in my presence to Hon. J. R. Hallowall, Dist. Atty. Topeka Kansas, as to present status of the case. The amt due at the Delewares at the date of settlement was $28,959.40. Interest ought to be added.

Delawares vs.
the railroad

Called on Asst. Sect. Bell & asked if Dept. would sanction a reasonable compromise between Delewares & the RR Co.

Ascertain who represents the Kansas Pacific Co. here, & if the case can be settled.

Gave memoranda of several points to Richardson, reporter Atlanta Constitution, for use as interview—complimenting Blount for starting star—routes investigation in Jany 1880. Gov. Brown—Stephens & Hill. Also giving correct etymology of Chattahoochee river—& touching Indian land tenure—in commonalty. *Ireland* vs. *Indian* Terty (Severalty vs. Commonalty).

Went to 146 Ebbitt House & agreed to divide fee

in Deleware right of way claim with Ex. Sen. Mitchell of Oregon. I think he can render aid in the Depts & perhaps has some influence at the White House, as he stood by Arthur in his fight with Hayes & Sherman over the N. Y. custom house in 1879. He is a handsome, clever, chatty fellow, & runs with the Stalwarts of the Stalwarts.

Dec. 12, '81.

Filed a request with Indian Comr.

1. to send to Speaker of House an estimate of Apptns for the stock claim due Delewares, $26,402.

2. Copy paper filed by Inspector Pollock recommending Creek Orphan fund be paid.

3. Also poked up the Seminole land estimate.

Porter & Coachman were with me & P. had an animated talk with Comr. Price about $5000 which Cong. apptd to "rebuild Tallahassee Mission School." The money has been spent on a new house 30 miles from old one, & Comr. P insisted that the law meant to "rebuild the old house in same place," & the 1st Comp. Treasury had so decided. But the money has been spent! & both Indians & Presbyterians agree that it was well spent in a better locality.

Went with Porter & got his little son, Willie, 7 yrs old, in Franklin Square public School, 1st grade.

Gave Ga. papers to Sen. Brown to have filed with Ga. bill in Senate to be refd to Com. on Claims. He says *Greene* wrote to him to introduce the bill!!

Asst. Secty Interior Bell, told me to go ahead & see what Kansas Pacific RR Co. would propose to pay the Delewares in right of way claim, & the Dept. would consider the matter. Could not bind the Dept. to any settlement. Must see the offer first. They owe $28,959 & ought to pay it, &c &c.

Scribner & Co. answer me saying they will look over the manuscript, but can not greatly encourage me &c.

Fading hopes for publication of Indian myths

Am writing out the last batch of fables gathered in summer, 1881, & shall forward to Scribner & Co.

My baby threatens to die *a-borning!* Too many babies, I suppose, in the world already.

Governor's race in Georgia, 1882

Spent an hour in J. H Blount's room, 142 Metropolitan. He is evidently looking with fair hope to the governorship of Ga in 1882. Thinks Colquitt wishes to come to Senate; that Ben. Hill will lose strength by personal contact with the people in Ga, that his health is so robust, & his articulation so bad from his cancer-operation on his tongue & lower mouth that sympathy will be lessened. Was very anxious to know my views on the question of candidates. I told him there would be a scramble—many candidates but whoever had the assistance of Gordon, Colquitt & Brown would be nominated. "Then there is no man who can get it. I mean these three will not actively support any one man. Brown will be thinking of his own return to Senate, Colquitt wants to come to Senate & Gordon if he does not run himself will not be for any one else, as he wishes to keep out of politics."

Brown's private Secty, Maddox told me today that Blount was his man for Govr., & perhaps "As is the man so is his Master."

Blount thought Bacon was weak, but would go in the convention with a fair delegation, but that Brown, C, & G would never let him succeed.

From these things I judge there is a tacit understanding to favor Blount.

He says Colquitt asked him last summer if he (B) wanted it—& he virtually said he did.

I gave him a chance to explain how the Creek-Seminole land item was lost in the Comtee of Conference in Mch. 1881, but he did not xplain.

B. thinks Crawford, Walsh, Bacon, Jim Brown & Underwood will be in the race.

I told him his chances were as good as any, but that Gordon could get it if he wanted it.[37]

[37] Alexander H. Stephens was elected governor in 1882, Alfred H. Colquitt was elected senator, Senator Joseph Brown was reelected to the Senate in 1884, and John B. Gordon was elected governor of Georgia in 1886.

B. says he wishes to be left off Comtee on apptns, & go on Comtee Ways & Means. Very likely he wished to avoid all the responsibility possible for fear of issues in future.

Dec. 13, '81.

Called at library & asked Spoffard who was a competent critic to look over my Indian sketches. He refd me to Maj. Powell, at Smithsonian & on visiting him he said he would xamine it for me—during the next two weeks.

Tuggle seeks reviewer for his manuscript

Got copy Creek Orphan bill & gave to Mr. Deering to introduce in house.

Same in Ga. bill for Buchanan.[38]

Creek Orphan bill was refd by Senate Comtee Indian Affairs to Sen. Slater & as he reported it favorably last Congress, I am hopeful to get an early report.

Been writing out my Indian myths & stories, so as to leave with Maj. Powell, when I go home for holidays.

Blount tells me that a *prominent* member of the Indian Com. of House sent word to the Conference Com. on Sundry civil during the last night of the session that the Seminole land payment was an *outrage*, & ought not be paid! Who could it have been? S . . . . s![39] Possibly.

Jany 11, 1882.

Been home, remained during Christmas, & reached Washington Friday, Jany 6th.

Have been very busy indeed. Was employed Friday night by the Choctaws & Chickasaws to protest against Sen. bill 60, alleging that Choctaw council

Tuggle lobbies for Choctaws and Chickasaws

[38] Georgia's Indian expense claim.

[39] Tuggle refers to Alfred M. Scales, the only member of the Committee on Indian Affairs whose name began with an "S."

passed a bill granting right of way to St. Louis & San Francisco RR Co. on Nov. 9th 1881.

Wrote during Saturday till Midnight that night, rose at 1:40 AM. Monday morning & by 8 o'clock had both protests ready. At 9 A.M. had interview with Secty Interior Kirkwood, then at 11 AM. had interview with Presdt Arthur, accompanied in both cases by Speaker B. F. Smallwood, of Choctaw House R— also by Isham Walker, journalist [Choctaw H. R.], J. P. Folsom, member [Choctaw H. R.], D. O. Fisher, Choctaw & B F Overton, delegate of Chickasaws. Succeeded in both cases & by 12 N. Monday, 9th Jany I had the protest sent by message by Presdt U. S. to Senate.[40] The bill had been reported to Senate favorably before Christmas. Choctaws say the bill never passed the House, the Chickasaws say they were not consulted & have an equal joint interest with Choctaws.

(Gov) Sen. J E Brown of Ga.—on sub comtee on RR's in Senate—reported the bill.

Today 11th Jany ascertained that same bill was before House Comtee on Indian Affairs, arranged a hearing at 10 1/2, & by 11 o'clock had the Indians driven at a John speed down Penn. Av. & got them to Comtee room & had the hearing all over by 12 o'clock.

Haskell (Ch.) & Deering, Sub-comtee, were evidently favorable to the bill [Senate bill 60], but the majority of the Comtee seemed to be disposed to side with Indians.

This evening I arranged for a possible hearing before Atty. Genl Brewster on my Deleware right of way

Interview with Pres. Arthur

Continues lobby for Indians

Considers governmental appointment

[40] The bill in question was one which would grant right of way through Indian land to the St. Louis & San Francisco Railroad. The bill was passed (although its passage was disputed) by the Choctaw legislature and sent to the United States Congress for ratification. The Chickasaws protested the bill because they held a joint interest in the land involved, and they had not been consulted. Certain Choctaws also protested that the bill was never legally passed by the Choctaw legislature. However, the bill was passed by Congress, August 2, 1882; therefore Tuggle's protest was not successful. See U. S. *Statutes at Large*, xxii, 181; House Reps., 47th Cong., 1st Sess., No. 934.

claim & have almost decided to try a new plan, that is, accept an apptmt as Special Asst. U. S. Atty for Deleware case, then confer with Union Pacific RR Co., get an adjustmt if possible, & if not, then have a suit ordered.

8 yrs. ago a suit was ordered, the atty Peck at Topeka was *persuaded* by RR Co, & no suit was begun.

Quixotic, isn't it? A Rebel—a Democrat now, to contemplate holding a position under Arthur's administration, of any form!

Shall try it in morning, if after sleeping on it, I approve it.

Henry Hodges, a northern man, married at LaG. a southern woman. He came to W— during Grant's 1st term, & is still in office of Atty Gen'l. He advised me to get letters from Stephens, Hill & Brown & be at Atty Genl's office by 9 A.M., & he thought he could help me. He is & has been for 15 yrs a Republican. He was my pedagogue a while.

Mr. A. H. Stephens gave me [a letter without delay] for I went from Atty Genl's office at 3 P.M. & by 4 PM I had the letter as follows;

Recommendation to the attorney general

"Natnl Hotel
WDC, Jany 11, '82

Hon Benj H. Brewster
    Atty Genl U. S.
        W D.C.

Dear Sir:
    I understand that Hon. W. O. Tuggle of Ga, who is the Atty for the Deleware Indians, has some matters connected with their interests to submit to yr. consideration.

I respectfully bespeak for him yr kind attention & favorable consideration. I know Mr. Tuggle well. He is a gentleman of high character, of great probity, of unsurpassed industry & unsullied integrity. He is a lawyer of distinction in our State & has held several high & honorable positions in the State. Was a member of our last Constitutional Convention in 1877, which formed the present Constitution of the State & in this body he distinguished himself.

Mr. Tuggle has never failed in any enterprise he ever undertook. His argument before the 1st Compt. of the Treasry in April 1879 upon the subject of 'Direct Taxes' is I think one of the ablest upon that subject to be found in American Jurisprudence.

This led to a compilation by him on Direct Taxes, which was published by the Govmt.

Yrs. truly

Alexander H. Stephens"

(This was added)

"Mr. Tuggle is entitled to the highest consideration.

B H Hill

Joseph E Brown"

Pretty good endorsement from such men. Worth more to my posterity than the money I may win.

I am at 910 F St N.W. I am in one bed room, Sen. J. H. Slater of Oregon in an adjoining one, & we share a parlor, fronting on F st.—25$ each pr. mth. I take my meals at Metropolitan at 35$ pr. mth.

Hill's indignance at Felton's letter

Had an interview with Mr. Hill. He felt indignant at Dr Felton's letter just out. Mr. Stephens regarded Mr. H's recent article calling the new movement by Ind. Demos. & Republicans "an infamous attempt to Africanize the State, &c" as very imprudent.

Was in Sen. J. E. Brown's room at 6 P.M. at Metropolitan. He said in reply to my referring to a rumor that he would lead the new movement in Ga—

"I shall vote the regular Democratic ticket for Gov. of Ga, & for Presidential candidates in 1884. Nonsense to talk of new parties. Dr Felton can not do much on such a line."

Brown takes position on specie

Then referred to his intentions to make a speech on the silver question &c in a short time & try to crystalize some issues for the party. That he had been silent so far, being a new senator &c. I told him that the people looked to his common sense to get them out of a rut & I hoped he would accept the gauntlet thrown down by Arthur in his message on Silver Certificates, Silver, & other questions, & get up some planks for the platform of a live party fighting for the interests of the people against wrongful corporations &c. Arthur's message is all on side of Capital, make fight on that line. "True strength lies in Right" said Prince Metternich, & if Democrats are to keep their own & gain from other side, they ought to stand for the Right, & not toady to *Might*.

[Tuggle's entries in the first notebook stop at this point, p. 120, but they continue without noticeable interruption in the middle of p. 18 of his second notebook. Having drawn a line across the page just below his account of why the possum has no hair on his tail, Tuggle resumed his Washington Journal entries as follows:]

Been very busy with my Indian matters. Write out about

  1   Chickasaw Protests
  2   Choctaw   ″
  3   Creek business—Powell &c
  4   Deleware ″ , Atty Genl. &c
  5   Seeds, agriculture &c

Jany 15, '82.

Gov. A. H. Colquitt came yesterday with his wife. His daughter Hattie is here at Mrs. Arther's school— I did not know till 3 PM of their presence. Went to their room 170 Metropolitan & soon had Mrs. C & her daughter at City Hall. Just missed Giteau, then to Capitol, library &c, then to White House—& after dinner to National Theater to see Robson & Crane in "Sharps & Flats." The Governor went to theatre with us. He goes to N. Y. on some RR business private.

Gov. Colquitt and family in Washington

Jany 15th, 1882.

I dined with Hon. A. H. Stephens. There were 10 at the table, in his rooms at the National Hotel arranged as follows

Dinner party at Alexander Stephens'

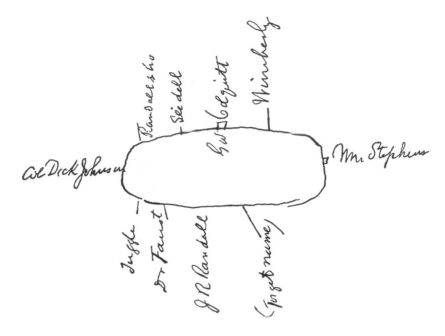

There were many courses, several kinds of wine & whiskey, though none drank excessively, indeed only a few sipped a little wine. It was a Georgia dinner, by a Georgian, & Georgia tales were told & a 'Possum graced the table.

Dinner party conversation

Col Dick Johnson, now living at Baltimore, but is an old Georgian, writes "Dukesberry Tales" in Georgia Cracker dialect for Harper's Magazine.[41] Mr. J R Randall wrote "Maryland, My Maryland" a popular Southern ballad during the War & now is editor of the Chronicle & Constitutionalist Augusta Ga.

Abortion in New England

He told some fine stories, referred to growing practice of foeticide in New England & the North, to its practice in France, & contributed his full share to amuse the crowd. ["Foeticide" apparently means abortion.]

Black bishop with Southern sentiments

Gov. Colquitt related how Bishop Holsey, a colored man in Methodist Church & who was once a slave of Col. Dick Johnson, made the most impres-

[41] Richard Malcolm Johnston, author of *Dukesborough Tales* (1879).

sive speech at the London ecumenical council in 1881, by surprising the council in advocating Southern sentiments, stating that the negroes became civilized as slaves, by contact with their owners, were taught the Bible by their mistresses &c.

He also related an incident where he at Atlanta, handed a glass of water to a strange colored preacher who asked for it in a crowd. The fellow was amazed & wouldn't drink it, & referred publicly to David's pouring out the water obtained from the well of Bethlehem &c.

Mr. Stephens told many anecdotes, among them in response to a reference about President Arthur's having sent him a bouquet on the 11th Jany thinking that his birthday, whereas the 11th February was the right day—his 70th.

Pres. Arthur's faux pas

"Yes, I wrote him that he was a *little previous.* It reminds me of my speech for Mrs Madison. She was here copying in one of the Depts, & was the first lady ever employed by the Govmt. Some friends selected me to press & advocate a resolution to relieve her by buying Madison's papers. I made a highfalutin speech & the resolution passed. I stopped at her house, on my way to Crittenden's, where I & Toombs were living, to tell her the news, but she had heard it & met me with both hands extended & cordially thanked me. 'But' said she, 'you were mistaken in my age. You said I was 82. I am only 80!' I've never liked to mention a lady's age since. When I got home, I told Mrs. Crittenden of it.

Dolly Madison and Alexander Stephens

"Well, she is 82, anyhow [Stephens continued]. I left them to settle it."

When reference was made to the fact that Mr. S. had read his obituary "Yes, I made Dick Johnson there read it to me, & it was pretty good. by the way Governor Colquitt you sent in a special message to the Ga Legislature on my death, did you not?"

"I prepared it & a telegram came just as I was to send it in, & corrected the rumor of your death," said Gov. Colquitt.

Col. Dick Johnson said, "The town council at

Crawfordville cut down some magnificent oaks in the cemetery, where many old citizens, & many Baptists were buried. Mr. Stephens was very sorry & told Toombs about it."

"Well, Alec—I don't know but they were right to cut them down. It may be best to let the sunshine in on those old Baptists & dry a little of the water out."

Colquitt wants Stephens as next governor

Governor Colquitt said to me after the dinner was over as we walked along the Avenue, "Tuggle—when the time comes—I think Stephens is the man to run for Governor. The Independents look to him & he can kill the new movement. What do you think of it?"

"Splendid. It would be a fitting close for the career of the Great Commoner, & there would be a lot of sweet revenges to somebody I know to many somebody's in Ga. for too readily believing stories on a Governor of Ga in 1879."

He laughed.

"How is Brown on it," I asked.

"He'll be all right."

So here's a new scheme, & if the old man can pull through & scare death off a little longer, he may be Governor of Ga yet.

I wrote a kind letter about him to LaGrange Reporter, telling about his dinner, his fine health & mental condition &c—in order to pave the way.

Jany 16.

Col. N. J. Hammond asked me at the breakfast table what I thought of A. H. Stephens for Gov. & afterwards told me that Gov. Colquitt mentioned it to him.

I sit at a table with Hammond & Buchanan.

Interactions with attorney general's office

A slight hitch in the Deleware Case before Atty Genl. Mr. Chase yesterday asked its delay till he came back from New York, but Dutton & Hodges told me it would turn out all right they thought. I offered to withdraw my letter, but they said no.

Rec'd the following letter directed to Atty Genl Brewster, from Gov. A. G. Porter present governor of Indiana.

E. Dept. Indianapolis
Jany 14, 1882

Sir:
When I was Comptroller of the Treasy W O Tuggle Esq of Georgia made an argument before me, in a very important matter which evinced a high order of ability. I was very much impressed with the fairness, of Mr. Tuggle, as well as with his learning & intellectual face.
I am with great respect

Yours very truly
A. G. Porter

Hon. Benj Harris Brewster
U. S. Atty Genl

*Tuggle and
Gov. Porter
of Indiana*

This from a man whom I quarreled with & told to his face that men had offered to bribe him for me! during my Ga case in April, or Mch 1879. Of course, I apologized & we grew to be friends.

Jany 18, '82.
Yesterday morning I & Porter called at office of President Arthur's private Secty—, Phillips to see why the Creek-Seminole estimate for 175000 was delayed.
"Couldn't find the papers—looked all over Presdts room."
"Mr. Kirkwood says he gave it to the Presdt. Very well, will ask him when he comes to Cabinet meeting today."
When I went to Atty Genls', Mr. Hodges told me that Mr. Chase had withdrawn his objections. Mr. Dutton asked me to call again at 3 1/2 PM. (Then 10 AM) Called at 3 1/2 P.M. Mr. Dutton saw Mr. Brewster & returned to me & said "Mr B says he prefers that or the Dept Interior has immediate

*More delays
on claims*

charge as trustee of Indians that he, Secty Intr, should first suggest &c." I at once went to Dept Intr. Office hours close at 2 PM. It was then 3.50—but the guard passed me. I saw Asst. Secty Bell. He said Mr. Mc-Cammon would decide the matter. I went to McCam-mon & he agreed to recommend me as Special Asst U. S. Atty for the Deleware case—& to act at once, so I come to get papers tomorrow.

Recommended as special assistant U.S. attorney

Got papers in Creek Orphan case from Senator Walker & delivered them to Mr. Deering, of House Indian Comtee. I called his attention to the fact that this was a *private* claim & I hoped he would put it on the private calendar so it could be reached soon. He xamined the rules & agreed with me. He says he will report soon & likely make the Senate report.

Went with Choctaws & Chickasaws to Senate, & thence to Printing Office, got my protests for them, & went through the building & showed them the wonders of printing & electrotyping.

Politics and the claims

Had Ga case in Senate refd to Sub comtee on Claims. Sen. Hoar— They had decided to send it to Mr. George of Miss. but I preferred a Republican, for should he report it, it will pass & George's report being a Southerner & Democrat would do me no good.

Called on Gen. Armstrong & Gov. Brockmeyer at Ebbett. Found A. out. Brockmeyer has a keen analytical mind. Knows much of ancient forms of government, a fine judge of human nature &c. He was at Creek Council last Oct. in behalf of the M. K & T. RR—& is here in same interests it is said.

Met Armstrong on side walk as I came out.

Meets minister from Hawaiian Kingdom

On my return to my room 910 F St NW. I found George, Mr. C. of Oregon, & Mr. Carter, Minister from Sandwich Islands, Hawaian Kingdom, in our room, talking to Sen Slater on the abrogation of the reciprocity treaty made in 1875. It seems Sen Hill of Ga has introduced a resolution to abrogate, or give notice to that effect.

Sugar is admitted free of duty & Mr. Hill is fighting a monopoly on that line, I xpect.

Carter told how he man[a]ged Lord Darby in London who was offended because he made this treaty with U. S. also his diplomacy with Bismark, through his wife & daughters, after 4 months endeavor &c.

He was born in the Islands, but his parents were English.

The population is 60,000—(30,000 natives, dark (not negroes), 15,000 Chinese, & rest white).

The Govmt is a Constal Monarchy.

Maj. J. W. Powell, Head of Bureau of Ethnology suggests that (1) I make a book of myths of Creek Nation, (2) Publish Black Beaver separate, as magazine article—(3) Use the sketches separately. I am inclined to adopt his suggestions. *Publication advice from Maj. Powell*

Jany 22, 1882.

Went to N. Y. on Thursday night, Jany 19th. On Friday met Mr. Sidney Dillon, Presdt Union Pacific & talked on the Deleware right of way claim. Gov. Colquitt & Gen. Gordon accompanied me & introduced me in very complimentary terms.

We arrived at no conclusion, but I left the paper & he told me he would write to his lawyer—Wilson, of Shellaberger & Wilson, W D. C. & we could arrange it.

I met the Gov & Genl G. at 16th Wall St. They are very anxious to lease, or obtain farm & grazing privileges in Indian Terty. I told them I did not think it practicable.

I was invited to dine at W. E. Dodge's, 225 Madison Av. on Friday evening, & on Saturday night attended a reception at Mr Dodge's tendered Gov. Colquitt, who was Mr. D's guest.

I met Jay Gould, C. P. Huntingdon, Talmage, Peter Cooper & many other celebrities—Whitelaw Reid was there. *Meets celebrities at the Dodge reception*

Short speeches were made by Govr St Johns, of Kansas, by Gov. C. of Ga, Gen. Gordon, Gov. Jerrill

& Presdt Hitchkok, on peace & good will between North & South. About 200 guests were att.

I put on a swallow tail, low vest, tie to match, &c. First time since I was married in 1866, 16 yrs ago!

Gov. C. wrote letters to a few leading importers & called their attention to me as a lawyer.

Jany 27.

A professional reputation

My Choctaw & Chickasaw case is developing into a very important one. I am before a House, or Senate Comtee every few days, conducting the investigation into the method of pushing the RR bill before the Choctaw Council. I am content with the outlook just now—& am making some reputation by my management.

Senator Hoar's courtesy

Saw Sen. Hoar, in marble room yesterday & he was very polite, carried me to his comtee room & instructed his clk to deliver the Ga papers to me &c &c.

I am up writing now at 4 1/2 A.M. & have fallen into a habit of this sort within the last few weeks, owing to a press of business & the activity of my mind I retired at 8 P.M. & hence had sleep enough at 4 A.M.—8 yrs.

I read to Mr. A. H. Stephens my letter in LaG. Reporter about his dinner on 15th inst. & also an editorial which was written at my suggestion.

The old man was affected almost to tears. He has been very kind to me & I was glad to cheer him by instigating such an editorial.

Unusual compliments

Queer compliments I get occasionally. Sen. J. H. Slater of Oregon, with whom I am rooming, said to me the other day "Well, Tuggle, I believe I'll resign & go into a partnership with you."

Mr. Colquitt said to me yesterday as I told him good bye on the sleeping car "Remember to find some work for my old man to do. You know his time is soon out."

This for a Governor, & a man who was in Congress when I was wearing frocks!

Gov. Brown replied to a lawyer who insinuated that my clients, the Choctaws had "*recited* their lessons well," "No, I know Tuggle. He would not teach them anything wrong"—

Sen. Brown reported the bill favorably before Christmas & is still apparently favorable to the passage of the bill.

Jany 28, 1882.

A change occurred in my Choctaw case. The St Louis & S. F Co. sold out to Gould & Co. & my Indians left for home last night against my advice, but under the advice of Gov. Brochmeyer an agt of Gould. It seems he brought them here.

Complications on the claims

In the xamination before the Senate Comtee I employed a stenographer & when the Comtee was informed of it, a resolution was adopted that the Comtee would pay the stenographer or call on the official reporter Mr. Murphy. Some questions were asked by Sen. J. E. Brown about Brockmeyer, if the Choctaws knew him, if he was not supplying them with money &c.

This frightened B— so Porter tells me; & hence his sudden departure.

The cream of the joke is that Sen. Brown left for Ga Friday morning at 7 A.M. & B. left at 7 P.M. Friday, not knowing that Brown had gone to stay some 2 weeks!

The wicked flee when no man pursueth.

Philosophizing

The Choctaws left without paying me for my services but said they would do so after they reached home.

"All the world's a stage & men & women are merely players" I whispered to Porter as we sat & watched Tananshek at Ford's play Deborah—referring to the Choctaw case. I must write out the details in full some day—from time I was employed, Friday the 6th Jany to the sudden departure Jany 27th 1882. Some of its features are remarkable—& will prove historical.

March 22, 1882.

Almost 2 months since I wrote a line in my journal. Many things have happened.

Some success
in Indian cases

1. In the Choctaw case, the Senate Comtee abandoned all idea of ratifying the alleged act of the Choctaw Council, & presented an original bill for a Charter & recognized the Chickasaw Nation as joint owner of the proposed route. So both of my points were carried.

2. The Choctaws have agreed to pay me 1000$, & more if they carry the elections this year. The Chickasaws agreed to pay also 1000$. Each has paid 1/2—that is 500$ each—cash.

Orphan claims
reported favorably

3. The Creek Orphan claim was reported favorably in both Houses. Was called in Senate under the Anthony rule which permits unobjected bills to be considered in the morning hour & Sen. Sherman objected. He first said the Creeks had enough, then that the bill was wrong because the lands brought $108,000 in 1832 & more than that had been paid! The accumulations of the fund have been 1/2 million; actual interest on real investment. Again he told Sen. Brown of Ga that the 74 300$ in State bonds ought not to be paid because the Presidt could not buy any U. S. bonds as the law required, because there were no bonds out!

There were at least 75 millions out when the bonds were purchased.

Porter says letters from Creek Nation suggest that Sherman has a relative who wishes to be bought!

His wife visits,
becomes ill

3. My wife came to Washington to see me on Feb 6. She was well & happy, or I surely was for two weeks but then she was taken ill & now as I write after 5 weeks she lies here in my room, 112 Metropolitan Hotel, very weak & it will require 10 days before she can sit up. We will go home, at least. I'll carry her, as soon as she can bear the journey.

I had first the allopathic doctors & am now trying homeopathy. Dr Pope & Dr Stevens, & we both are pleased by the change.

Business and
pleasure reading

4. I have been reading a good deal lately. 1st I read Auerbach's novels to my wife, "On the Heights" & "Villa on the Rhine." He writes in a splendid manner & hardly a page was read from which I did

not feel tempted to stop, & copy a few sentences for memorizing.

Then my business required reading on ancient laws of property, & I have just finished "The Ancient City" (Wonderful book) by Coulanger, "Primitive Property" by Laveleye, & Sir Henry Maine's lectures on "Village Communities." Wonderful books. "Our Indian Wards" by George W. Monypeny, who acted as couns[el] in negotiating most of the treaties from 1854 to 1866. I met him here recently.

5. The Delewares came in to see me & Jonney cake entered into a contracts with me for his people, to look after 3 pending cases, amtg to about 75 to 80,000$, & also looking after the "General Distribution" of the trust fund, $874,000. They own this sum, besides their rights by purchase as Cherokee citizens.

Attorney for four Indian nations

So I'm the atty of the Creeks, the Chickasaws, the Delewares, & part of the Choctaws.

Was employed this week by 13 Southern RR Co's to pass a bill readjusting their accts with U. S. by which 25 prct is to be returned. Contingent fees about $25,000. What a nice time I'd have if all my ships would come home."

Of fees and ships

1st Creek Orphan's fee	$25,000.
2 RR's	25,000.
3. Creek-Seminole at least	
5 pct 175,000	8,750.
4 Deleware, present cases	5,000.
Expected—General Fund—	
say	25,000.
	$88,750.
Ga case	3,000
Cash cases	2,500
	$94,250

But, when?

Never, with all of them, but most probably a few will pass during the 47th Congress.

May 22, 1882.

Again two months have passed.

Wife's illness persists

1. My wife remained very feeble from xcessive uterine hemorhages till Mch 30th when I carried her on a bed to Ga, taking a sleeper & making no change from W. to LaG. I left LaG. & went to Venita, Cherokee Nation, Indian Terty, remained at Lightning Creek two days with the Delawares, arranged my business & reached Washington on Apl 10th.

Injured in fall

2. Had a severe fall on rock pavement, bruised my left leg, hip & arm, injured my lungs & coughed blood for some days & not recuperating promptly I went to Ga on Apl 27th & have just returned Saturday night, 20th inst.

Porter met me & informed me that Creek Orphan bill was still untouched on Senate & House Calendar, but the Seminole land item of 175,000$ was on the "General Deficiency bill, Apptn" & would certainly pass, without some unforeseen accident.

Wife recuperates

3. Found my wife, Apl 29th still in bed, but she recuperated while I was at home so that she could be up most of the day, could ride & walk in house & out to the garden.

Party factions: the New Movement

4. As I came by Atlanta the Chairman of State Democratic Come, Hon. L. A. Trammell, boarded the train & came as far as Dalton. He told me of the private talk in the Comtee room about Mr. Stephens (A H). The "New Movement party" in Ga through a Comtee of 9 men put out Mr. S. as their candidate, their standard bearer, to fight the regular organized Democratic party, & it is commonly believed that the "New Movement" is an administration party & in alliance with the Republican party. Some time ago a few prominent Democrats (Gov. Colquitt & others) put out Mr. Stephens name in a quiet way as the candidate of the Organized, regular Democratic party. The issue now is, will Mr. Stephens allow the use of his name as head of this New Movement in their fight on the organized Democrats?

Trammell asked me to see Mr. S. on my arrival & yesterday I had a full free talk with Mr. Stephens at his rooms at the National Hotel & left him satisfied that he would soon put all doubts at rest by a plain declaration that he will be a candidate only in the event of his nomination by the regular Democratic organization.

Stephens decides for the regular Democrats

After telling him the news he said, "I suppose they want me to say I am a Jeffersonian Democrat?"

"No. They know you are a Jeffersonian Democrat, but the trouble now is that Marcellus E. Thornton & others in the New Movement are telling the people of Ga that they consulted you & that you are in perfect sympathy with them in their fight on the regular organization & that you consented to be their leader in the fight & they now put out your name as their candidate & dare the reg[ul]ar party not to nominate you & Speer's telegram from Washington on the day of the meeting of the New Movement Comtcc in Atlanta Ga saying you would not reject their endorsement or recommendation gave color to these statements. In other words, while the people wish to vote for you to be Governor they first wish to know how you stand on this "New Movement" & whether you are in sympathy with it & have authorized your name to be used as the candidate for Govr on that line, in opposition & antagonism to the Organized Democracy."

"Surely no body can think I authorized Thornton to make any such statements. I did not, & Mr. Speer was not authorized by me to send his telegram.

Stephens denies New Movement connection

"I am not a candidate, not even an aspirant, & will only be a candidate if the organized Democracy put me out as their candidate.

"I have always thought that when any party evils xisted that it was best to correct them within the party, & not to go outside & fight the regular organization. Such organization is absolutely necessary to success & my record, with a few xceptions, has been on that line, even when grave questions of war were involved."

Tuggle speaks
for Stephens

"Well, I told some friends that I could dictate your reply to the New Party."

"What was your idea?"

"I said, Mr. Stephens will make a respectful reply, for I thought they would write to you that they had put you out as their candidate, & not merely state the fact to the "People of Ga." I said he will say about this:

" 'Sirs: Your communication recd & resply considered. As an xpression of confidence & of yr. willingness to vote for me for Govr of Ga. please accept my sincere thanks.

'I am not a candidate & will not be unless the Democratic party of Ga should deem proper to nominate me for that office, in which event, if my health permits, I should regard it as such an xpression of the people's will, that I should not decline.

'Should I be elected Govr of Ga, I shall try so to discharge the duties of the office that I shall be regarded as the Governor of the whole people irrespective of party affiliations. Respy Yrs.' "

"Well," he laughed "you came near hitting the nail on the head, for I should have said about that."

After a long talk I left him saying "Gov. Colquitt is here, would you like to see him. He asked me to inquire if you were well enough, had sufficiently recovered from yr late fall on the Capitol steps, to see him."

"Oh, yes, tell him to come over."

Stephens states
his position

Later in the day, the Govr saw him & again in the afternoon with Sen. J. E. Brown & the result was that Mr. Stephens consented to write a letter very soon plainly stating his position.

It is very important to Ga politics to get him squarely committed to the regular organization, for it will kill the "New Movement" & prevent trouble in the Legislature & in the Congressional races this fall.

Felton & Speer are hoping to be elected to Congress by Mr. Stephens' influence & some of the counties in Ga might be lost if Mr. Stephens should remain in doubt, or cast in his fortunes with the "New Party." Hammond & Clements agreed with Colquitt to help fix Stephens & get him to write a statement of his position &c.

May 29, 1882.

The Ga pot begins to boil & Felton & Co are waxing cool on Stephens, while the friends of other candidates are waxing hot. Albert Lamar writes bitterly in Telegraph & Messenger. He is for A. O. Bacon.

Felton cools on Stephens

Felton now comes out in a Card & copies a letter from Mr. S. dated May 18, saying "You did admirably at Atlanta!" &c & Mr. Stephens now admits that Speer read the telegram to him & while he said "I can give you no authority to send it from me, still it speaks the truth. I will not reject an endorsement from the Independents."

I told Mr. S. he had better write a detailed explanation of the occurrences & give them to Constn at once & he said he would & asked me to send the Reporter Richardson to him.

The Creek Orphan bill was debated Thursday & Friday last in Senate & will come up again today & be passed, from all indications. Nothing was said against it of any weight, though Sen. John Sherman made two speeches on the subject & said all he could against its passage. Sens. Dawes, Slater, Brown & Allison are managing it & certainly no better heads can be found.

Orphan bill passage likely

Went to Mt Vernon Saturday with Sen. Brown & family. Mrs. B, Mrs. Conally & her two children, Mary & Joe (Sen. B's daughter) & Miss Sallie. The day was pleasant & all enjoyed the trip.

A visit to Mount Vernon

June 1, '82.

Still on the "ragged edge" as my Creek Orphan bill is yet being discussed. Sherman is trying to defeat it by postponement, & by wearing out the patience of those not interested. The votes yesterday were all favorable & the probability is that the bill, amended, will pass today.

I am reading Kennedy's life of William Wirt, & enjoy it exceedingly, so full of human nature, talent & worth. The copy I am reading belongs to Mr. Stephens & was presented to him by Wirt's daughter "Elizabeth Wirt Goldsborough" in April 1881.

June 8, '82.

Creek orphan bill passes

1. My business has progressed. The Creek Orphan bill passed the Senate last week, & my chances are fair to insert in one of the Apptn bills, either Deficiency or Sundry civil.

2. The Seminole land item passed the Comtee of Whole House yesterday & my friends regard it as safe.

3. My Ga case was saved, perhaps, by Sen Brown, my good genius lately, on last Tuesday, before War Claims Com. of House. At last. I regarded it as dead before he appeared in the Com. room & now I hope to get a favorable report Friday, June 9, tomorrow.

Stephens confides in Tuggle

4. Last night Mr. Stephens asked me to remain in his room till the guests left about 9 Oclock, his usual retiring hour. He & I were alone & he said "I've been thinking since Sunday last (this was Wednesday) of telling you something. I see that Lamar says I am playing a double game & that if elected Govr, I will be a candidate for Senator. I know your intimate relations with Colquitt, & I want to say to you, & you may tell him, that nothing is more foreign to my intentions & desires, & I shall not be in his way. He came to me first with the suggestion of my being Govr & while I have in the past wanted to go or been willing to go to the Senate, I now feel that I can discharge the duties of Govr while he, being on his feet, can discharge the duties of a Senator."

"Yes," said I, "I knew yr sentiments & have already written to Gov. Colquitt that you would not antagonize him for the Senate."

Spiritual trial passes, son joins church

5. A great trial to me has just passed. Albert, my oldest child, joined the Methodist Church without

notifying me of his intentions, & without consulting me. I had written him an urgent letter on his duty to join the Church, but did not dream of such precipitate action. First, I doubted his preparation & instruction. Second, I felt hurt at his taking such an important step without advising with me. Third, it conflicted with my cherished plan for all my family, if possible, to worship in the same church.

His mother is a Methodist. My own parents were Methodists & of course, I do not feel that he can not be a good Christian in that Church, but it is painful to have divisions in a family in church relationship & I was constantly hoping that my wife could unite with the Baptist Church, as she told me years ago she was ready to do so.

God's will be done & thanks to Him for my noble boy's conversion.

6. Wirt's life is as readable as a romance, so simple, unaffected, human, elevating, & purifying. A boy to the boys of his School days to the last & keenly alive to all the joys of friendship & friendly communion.

Tuggle's opinion on biography of William Wirt

What charming letters! At last a mans private letters constitute the best index to his true character & a biography which simply weaves the letters into a connected story of life, is the most faithful portrait of the man. Few can stand the test.

7. Maj. J. W. Powell, Chief of the Bureau of Ethnology, has at last come to my opinion that if a publisher can be found for my "Indian Sketches Myths &c" who will illustrate amply, it is best to publish them as they are, & then continue the researches this summer & fall in the Indian Terty & perfect (1) a collection of all the myths of the Creek Nation, in a systematic form & (2) an account of the ancient form of government, laws &c of the Creek Nation.

Further plans for publishing myths & sketches

On this idea, I have yielded to a request by J. C. Derby, agt of Houghton Mifflin & Co. New York, & have forwarded the Ms. this week for inspection & if it suits them, will agree to publication. Maj P strongly endorsed me & the Ms & said it would repay publication &c.

In coming out of the Senate basement wing of the Capitol the other day, I passed Sen. J E Brown & Judge J W H Underwood of Rome Ga. I bowed & passed them. They stopped & Sen B. called to me, "Hello, Tuggle. What are you cutting us for. What have we done to merit such treatment?"

"Why nothing. I thought you & Underwood were talking about making him Congressman-at-large from Ga & didn't wish to stop yr secrets," said I, walking back & shaking hands. "Cut you, no—I've just written my wife that you are my good genius—& have helped all my money bills."

"What of the Ga case?"

"I think you saved it. Robertson of La. tells me it is all right. They didn't get a vote but will do so at next meeting. My only fear is no quorum of the Comtee, as you know tis hard to secure that so late in a session."

Fondness for Senator Brown

Wonderful man—Joe Brown the embodiment of common sense—that most uncommon of all sense— the equilibrium resulting from a well-balanced mind. The result of development of all good mental faculties. If he will guarantee to live 10 yrs. I will take a contract to seat him in the White House.

Brown & Underwood had just come from Presdt Arthur & had secured a coveted office for U—on the Tariff Comsn—Merely for the asking.

June 9, '82.

Mr. Stephens is getting anxious about the Ga. campaign. Today Judge H. K. McCay of Ga entered his room while I was there & said to him

"You left out one word in yr. letter. You ought to have said you would submit to a *fair* Convention of Democrats."

"No, I was right. Such a position would split the party."

Tuggle assures Stephens of election

After McCay left having expressed fear that Bacon, Lamar & others would pack the convention against Stephens, the old man said, "Is it possible?"

"No, you will get 3/4 of the Convention."

"Well Tuggle you must write confidentially to Colquitt & tell him I am his candidate and he must not let me be beat."

"You need not fear. There is only one thing can prevent yr. being Gov. of Ga & that is dying. You will be nominated & elected."

Grady's name was mentioned as Congressman at large & both Stephens & McCay spoke favorably of G. McCay said, "We all like Grady, but I really think journalism is his forte."

Mr. S. said, "He'd make as good a member as Waterson of the Louisville Courier-Journal."

June 12, '82.

Yesterday, Sunday, I went to S. S & Church & then called on Mr. Stephens, finding him answering letters.

A politician on theology

"Ah" said I, "if you had become a Presbyterian preacher, you would have preached such a sermon as I heard today."

"What was that?"

"Why a good sermon on a common evil. He preached on the text 'Remember the Sabbath day to keep it holy.' "

He laughed, "Well, I would have been a preacher if it had not been required of me to subscribe to all the doctrines of the Presbyterian Church, & I couldn't honestly do it."

"What one couldn't you believe 'Calvinism'[?] I believed, or rather I think I believe what is meant, that God knew all things & controls all things."

"Yes, but it seems to me that something was included more than that, which asserted that God selected some to be damned—I couldn't believe that, & therefore I didn't subscribe the doctrines & didn't become a preacher. I joined the Presbyterian Church —for they didn't require a member to subscribe like a preacher—& I xpect to die a Presbyterian. I think all the Protestant Churches about alike—their main idea being to lead a good life."

Metropolitan Hotel
Washington D. C.
Dec. 8, 1882.

Stephens and
Colquitt elected

Time has wrought its work. Stevens is Gov. of Ga, was elected by 62000 majority, & Colquitt was elected Senator from Mch 1883; & Pope Barrow beat Ben Hill Jr. for the short term.

Gov. or Sen. Brown gave last July $50000.00 to Ga University on the condition that the Legislature would invest it in 7 pr ct bonds, & the legislature has just refused to accept the donation on the terms specified.

Brown's bequest
to University of
Georgia rejected

Sen. Brown feels mortified & so told me yesterday. "Well, I shall see if some state will not accept the trust, & I now contemplate offering it to So Ca, my native State."

In a long talk with Mrs. Brown I ascertained that she hoped he would not send it out of Ga. & I encouraged her idea, by suggesting that he wait awhile & not decide the matter while laboring under the mortification of defeat, & again not to permit a few politicians to prevent his aiding poor young men in Ga to obtain an education, & that he could soon see that the people of Ga would not endorse the action of the Legislature.

Conditions on
Brown's bequest
questioned

Strange world! Gen. Phil Cook told me at the dinner table (He is Member of Congress from Ga). "Brown went to Ga in July to help Stevens & he never intended that money to be accepted, hence he hampered the donation with so many conditions that he knew it never would be accepted. Besides it is unconstitutional for the Legislature to tax the people to pay interest on bonds to help the University."

In the Ga Legislature the reasons assigned were various, but the principal were

      1st It was unconstitutional

      2d 7 prct was too high,

      3d The Browns reserved the right of visitation.

It is understood that Hammond drew the bill accepting the donation. He is a Trustee of the State University & a fine lawyer.

My orphan bill passed in Aug. 1882, & I rec'd my compensation, not 10 prct as the contract called for, but 8 prct, making $27,112.00.

*Creek orphan
bill passes*

Now comes one Latrobe of Baltimore, & says he rendered services & ought to be paid & in an interview with Secty Interior Teller today I find him inclined to pay him something & the fund is held up on account of this claim. He promised me in presence of Sen. Slater of Oregon, that he would decide it in a "day, or two."

An eventful three years, the last have been to me, & now the Ga members are much more cordial than when I came. Success softens mens hearts, if not their heads—& money adds to a mans opinions.

*Success breeds
cordiality*

Men come from distant states to consult me, because I have been successful for Ga & for the Creek Indians.

'Tis the only test of virtue the world employs, & perhaps, the safest for said world, but oh, how torturing to the ambitious unsuccessful, yet meritorious struggler!

God has wonderfully blessed me this year. He has given me success in money matters. I have won an enviable reputation as a successful claim agent & attorney. I have gathered some rare myths among the Creeks. My wife has been restored to health. My oldest child has professed Christianity, and oh, how can I enumerate the thousands of benefits He has bestowed on me! I love & adore Him all the more & pray for strength to stand prosperity & to use wisely what he entrusts to my stewardship.

*Tuggle's faith
and humility*

12 1/2 Oclock, Friday night, Dec. 8, 1882.

I have just left Sen. Colquitts room. He arrived at 10 Oclock, had an interview with Sen. Brown & suggested that he give his 50000$ to Mercer & Emory, 1/2 to each, provided they accept his donation on the terms offered to the Legislature. I have been trying to prevent a decision for two days adverse to young men in Ga, & Brown seemed to take Colquitt's suggestion

*Brown's bequest
sought for
Emory & Mercer*

very kindly. After we left Brown's room, I went to Colquitt's room & we talked an hour & agreed to try to carry out the plan. He wants the Colleges to buy 7 prct bonds & pay the premiums themselves, so that Browns 50000$ will not be reduced. I agreed to be responsible for Mercer's part. May God bless the effort & give us success, if consistent with his Holy will.

Dec. 10, 1882.

Yesterday Sen. Colquitt had another talk with Sen. Brown & the result was that Brown consented to consider the proposition to give 1/2 to Mercer & 1/2 to Oxford & today I telegraphed the Trustees of Mercer, through Rev. A. J. Battle, Macon, Ga to authorize me to act for Mercer.

Sen. Lamar appears strange with his hair shingled close as he has always worn it long. He went into a barber shop in St Louis to be shaved & the barber asked to trim his hair & while the Senator was in a reverie his hair was shorn & his long locks were raped. He is very sad over his wife's condition—her mind lost, & he said to me "Your wife was the very last person to receive her ministrations."

Sen. Brown's war arrest

Tonight I have been in Sen. Brown's parlor with Hammond, Clements, Mrs. Boteler of Va—Mrs. Brown, Miss Sallie & Sen. Brown. He told me of his arrest after the war & his imprisonment. The officer told him he must leave in 30 minutes & to bring his private correspondence. "Then I can not leave in 30 minutes & get it." After they had gone, Julius his 10 yr. old son & Mrs. Brown destroyed all his private correspondence which he would now like to keep.

"If you wish evidence of my treason you need not look into my private correspondence. Examine the public records"—said he to the officer.

I told him of my increased admiration of the Constitution from reading Bancroft's History of its formation, & my surprise at Washington's influence in all the States during the discussion on its adoption & mentioned the remarkable letter he sent to all the Governors, when he resigned his commission & its statesmanlike suggestions & profound legal wisdom.

"Yes," said he. "The first time I ever saw Washington's own signature was to that letter among the archives of Ga at Milledgeville when I was Governor."

I am learning to love Sen. Brown & his family the more I see their quiet old fashioned ways & his good nature, & I believe him more amiable than he gets credit for. He fights back promptly but when the fight is over, he cherishes no malice.

Deep admiration for Sen. Brown

Dec. 19, 82.

Made a new contract with Creek Delegates, G. W. Grayson & L. C. Perryman about a balance of 157,754 acres, due them under 3d Art. treaty June 14, 1866, at 10 prct, & xpect to associate Ex Gov. S. J. Crawford, of Kansas with me.

I went before Judge Andrew Wylie, Judge of District Supreme Court & who is now trying Ex Sen. S. W. Dorsey, & Asst P.M.G. Thos J. Brady et al for robbing the Govmt under the forms of law—to sign my Creek Indian contract. Was introduced to Judge Wylie by Mr. Wilson of Wilson, & Shellabarger attys, & found him very obliging, indeed.

I presented to Sen. J. E. Brown as a Christmas present a beautiful little boat 2 ft long, made of beach bark & embroidered in gay colors & patterns by an Ottawa Indian girl, named "Oga bah-ji-ji-yak-me" (or Margaret Bird) & I wrote on the bottom of the boat.

Christmas gift to Sen. Brown

> "There was a boy, both brave & true
>   He plowed a bull & paddled his canoe.
>   That boy's a man, a friend of Fate
>   He's paddling still—the Ship of State
>
> "From State to Nation, on he rows,
>   His skill increasing as he goes
>   List! I'll whisper (be still as a mouse)
>
> "His boat may land at a big White House
>   By Creek Orphan
>   to
>   Sen. J. E. Brown
>   Dec. 25 1882"

I read it to Mrs. Brown & it tickled her a good deal.

I'm not sanguine about Brown's giving anything to Mercer. It seems that he's been importuned on this subject till he's *sore*.

APPENDIX A:
CONTENT AND SCOPE OF THE TUGGLE COLLECTION

H AD WILLIAM O. TUGGLE not died at the early age of forty-four, it seems likely that he would eventually have seen his collection of Indian myths through the press, and quite possibly published other works based on his extensive knowledge and observations of life in the Indian Territory. But, too ill to continue the laborious task of revising his materials, he apparently delegated the publishing responsibility to J. W. Powell, first director of the Bureau of Ethnology of the Smithsonian, whom he instructed on February 28, 1883, to "do whatever you deem best with the creek myth and I'll be content."[1] Instead of publishing the collection of myths, however, Powell returned it, presumably for further editing, and nothing further was done about the manuscript until after Tuggle's death, although Powell later indicated that even in its unfinished state the collection showed that Tuggle "possessed both the interest and the ability to produce a work which would have proved a credit to himself and a lasting contribution to anthropology."[2] At the suggestion of Tuggle's old friend, G. W. Grayson,[3] Mrs. Tuggle again tried to interest Powell in publishing her late husband's collection and was instructed by him to forward the manuscript once more to the Smith-

[1] BAE MSS 566, Smithsonian Institution, Washington, D.C. Tuggle later said: "I do not see how I can work any more on the Creek myths, these you can feel free to publish them in their present form" (ibid).

[2] BAE MSS 566.

[3] Grayson, a veteran of the Second Creek Volunteers, served as treasurer of the Nation, secretary of the International Council of the tribes, member of the House of Warriors, and delegate many times to Washington. See Carolyn Thomas Foreman, "Jeremiah Curtin in the Indian Territory," *The Oklahoma, Chronicles of Oklahoma,* xxvi (Autumn 1948), 341.

sonian.[4] She did so on April 17, 1886.[5] Nine months later Mrs. Tuggle inquired, somewhat impatiently, concerning the disposition of the manuscript; and a month after that she was informed by Powell that "in its present form [it] was too fragmentary to publish."[6] Five days later (February 17, 1887) Mrs. Tuggle requested the immediate return of the manuscript; whereupon the Smithsonian assigned H. W. Henshaw to reexamine it.

Precisely what happened to the collection during the next two weeks would be interesting to know, since a memorandum from Henshaw to Powell indicates that "a copy [had] been made of such portions . . . as were deemed desirable to retain,"[7] while a second admonitory memorandum, in another handwriting, reminds Powell: "Don't mention copy."[8] Smithsonian records show that the original manuscript collection was returned to Mrs. Tuggle on March 3, 1887. And at that point in its history it dropped out of sight, becoming for all scholarly purposes an unsolved mystery until its rediscovery in April 1960 by Dorothy Hatfield.

After 1887 various conjectures were made regarding the whereabouts of the original Tuggle collection, along with sporadic efforts to locate it. In 1900 J. R. Mooney, who had examined twelve years before what he apparently thought to be the original collection,[9] and who quoted parts of a few of Tuggle's Creek stories[10] for comparative purposes in his own Cherokee Indian collection,[11] suggested that the Tuggle collection was located in the Wisconsin Historical Society.[12] Some years later J. R. Swanton, also mistakenly assuming that he had consulted the original Tuggle materials in gathering the forty-six stories from the Tuggle collection which he reprinted in his *Myths and Tales of the Southeastern*

[4] BAE MSS 566.

[5] Ibid.

[6] Ibid., February 12, 1887.

[7] Ibid., March 3, 1887.

[8] This note was in the handwriting of James C. Pilling, chief clerk of BAE (ibid., n.d.).

[9] Mooney is known to have examined the Smithsonian copies of the Tuggle material on July 2, 1888 (see BAE MSS 566). Since the original Tuggle manuscript had been returned to Mrs. Tuggle more than a year earlier, it seems probable that Mooney did not see it, but worked from copies instead. For further details supporting this view, see Hatfield, pp. 34–36.

[10] The stories quoted were: Article 19, pt. 2, pp. 430, 432, 435, 436, 447, 449, 450, 452, 455, 473, 476, and 504 (BAE 566).

[11] James R. Mooney, "Myths of the Cherokee," *19th Annual Report to the Bureau of American Ethnology*, ed. J. W. Powell.

[12] BAE MSS 566.

Indians, stated that "the original [Creek myths] . . . are preserved among the documents in the Bureau of American Ethnology."[13] The assumptions of both men were later proved to be incorrect. Mooney's error was finally exposed in 1932 when the Smithsonian, having sent an inquiry to the Wisconsin Historical Society, learned that the manuscript was not and never had been there.[14] The same year Swanton's mistaken belief that he had been working from Tuggle's original manuscript while gathering materials for his own book during the years 1908 to 1914 was disproved in a letter from the bureau, regretfully acknowledging that the Tuggle manuscript housed in its archives was only a copy and that the office had "no way of knowing whether it has a copy of the entire manuscript or not."[15]

Repeated efforts to find the original manuscript in the 1930s having failed, the mystery surrounding its location created little further scholarly interest, and Tuggle's significance gradually disappeared. In 1956, however, a study undertaken by William Sturtevant, who collated Swanton's published collection of Indian myths with the two manuscript copies housed in the Smithsonian,[16] apparently stimulated renewed efforts from the Bureau of Ethnology to locate the original Tuggle manuscript. On January 10, 1957, a letter from the bureau addressed to Muriel Wright, editor of the *Chronicles of Oklahoma,* indicated that the bureau was "currently trying to locate the manuscript of the myths" and would appreciate "any information on Tuggle and . . . the identity of his informants."[17] To this inquiry Miss Wright replied:

> We have no record of such manuscript in the collection of The Oklahoma Historical Society. However, we do have original letters . . . relating to the appointment of W. O. Tuggle as attorney for the Creek Nation. . . . A letter (#36 439) in the Archives . . . shows that W. O. Tuggle was attorney

[13] John R. Swanton, *Myths and Tales of the Southeastern Indians,* Bureau of American Ethnology Bulletin 88 (Washington, D. C.: United States Printing Office, 1929), p. 1.

[14] BAE MSS 566 (letter from Margaret C. Blaker).

[15] Ibid (letter from J. W. B. Hewett to Dr. M. W. Stirling, August 5, 1932)

[16] Study comparison of 566A and 566B, BAE MSS 566, Smithsonian Institution, Washington, D. C., 1956. In attempting to determine which of the two copies of the Tuggle manuscript Swanton had used, Mr. Sturtevant made a careful comparison of Swanton's stories with both of the Smithsonian copies. He noted several discrepancies between the two copies, gave the complete list of Tuggle stories copied, and concluded: "Almost the entire contents of this [BAE 566A copy] have been published by J. R. Swanton. The tales are sometimes given slightly different titles by him, and there are occasional minor verbal changes; but it is evident that J. R. S. used this manuscript [566A] rather than 566B." Ibid.

[17] BAE MSS 566 (letter from Margaret C. Blaker, archives assistant of the Bureau of American Ethnology, to Muriel H. Wright).

for the Home Mission Board, Southern Baptist Convention (1883). An original letter (#29917) written by Tuggle on March 12, 1884, has printed letterhead: 'W. O. Tuggle, Attorney-at-Law—La Grange, Georgia.' In our brief and hurried search for reply to your request, we find no mention of W. O. Tuggle in the back files of old newspapers . . . we shall be glad if any of the above give a clue in your search." [18]

As late as 1957, therefore, search for the original Tuggle materials, as well as for a glimmer of information about him, remained at a standstill.

Two years later the key leading to solution of the Tuggle mystery finally appeared, when a study of Celia B. Taylor, completed at Auburn University and entitled "Cherokee and Creek Folklore Elements in the Uncle Remus Stories," [19] noted certain interesting relationships between Tuggle's myths and Joel Chandler Harris's tales,[20] but also emphasized primarily the values inherent in Tuggle's original collection, if it could be found. Although Mrs. Taylor's interest had centered chiefly on the work of Mooney and Swanton, rather than Tuggle, she called specific attention to the fact that Harris had used and commented favorably upon Tuggle's manuscript. Accordingly her observation that the "Indian story-tellers and the collectors, such as Mooney and Tuggle, offer rich biographical raw material hitherto neglected" [21] provided the incentive to undertake a renewed and intensive search for the Tuggle materials. This quest was rewarded beyond all expectations when, in April and May of 1960, the entire Tuggle collection was discovered in the possession of three different members of the Tuggle family.[22]

In their present state the original Tuggle materials are thus assembled in three separate collections, owned respectively by Mrs. Sara Tuggle Douglass, daughter of W. O. Tuggle; Mrs. Steffan Thomas, daughter of

[18] Letter to Margaret C. Blaker from Muriel H. Wright, dated January 30, 1957. A copy of this letter was sent by Miss Wright to Dorothy B. Hatfield, March 4, 1960.

[19] Unpublished master's thesis, Auburn University, 1959.

[20] "There is no question that Harris was familiar with the Creek stories and aware of their similarities to his. Mrs. Tuggle stated in one letter that 'Mr. Joel Chandler Harris . . . borrowed the manuscript from [her] husband to read.' In his Introduction to Nights with Uncle Remus, Harris outlined six Creek stories [In Songs and Sayings, nos. 2, 4, 6, 7, 8, and in Nights, nos. 35, 48, 58] collected by 'Mr. Tuggle of Georgia, who has recently made an exhaustive study of the folklore of the Creek Indians.' . . . Linear comparisons of the stories in question reveal that Harris's stories follow, almost to the letter, his outlines of Tuggle's stories." Ibid., p. 16.

[21] Ibid., p. 80.

[22] Details of the process of discovery, of interviews granted by members of the Tuggle family, and of the study made of the Tuggle materials with their permission may be found in Hatfield, pp. 42–45. Full credit for the discovery of the Tuggle materials belongs exclusively to Dorothy B. Hatfield.

Mrs. Douglass; and Mrs. Elizabeth W. Bethea, first cousin of Mrs. Thomas. Of the three Mrs. Bethea's collection is by far the most impressive, since it contains in addition to the original manuscript copies by the Smithsonian in 1887 numerous other manuscript items of comparable value, of which no copies heretofore existed. A bare listing of the items in the first two collections must suffice here, so that sufficient space can be given to a more detailed descriptive analysis of the third. The Douglass collection contains the following items:

1. The W. O. Tuggle family Bible. In it are recorded the names of W. O. Tuggle's parents, date of his birth and marriage, and the names and birth dates of eight children, plus the death dates of seven of them.

2. A scrap album (7½″ by 5¾″) dated 1879 and containing many newspaper clippings relative to Tuggle's varied activities. Among these are some of the articles written by him for Georgia newspapers from the Indian Territory.

3. Three chapters of a handwritten manuscript entitled "Recollections of an Escape from a Northern Prison by an Unreconstructed Reble." The episode is recorded on lined paper (7¾″ by 12½″), each sheet of which bears a small circular embossed emblem with the word "Congress" in the top arc, a picture of the Capitol and the words "Irving Mill" in the lower arc of the circle. The manuscript shows signs of wear and water damage but is, for the most part, legible.

4. Two daguerreotype photos of W. O. Tuggle and his wife.

5. An Indian pipe and a bow, relics brought by Tuggle from the Territory.

The Thomas collection is smaller and would be of interest chiefly to a biographer concerned with Tuggle's legal affairs. It contains the following:

1. An unorganized quantity of newspaper clippings similar to Item 2 above.

2. A large assortment of legal papers pertaining to Tuggle's transactions as a LaGrange attorney.

3. A seventeen-page manuscript, handwritten on blue lined legal paper (8½″ by 13″), the contents of which pertain to a legal compilation which may also be the text of a speech.

Although these two collections are of minor concern to the folklorist, having been located first they pointed the way toward the discovery of the much more significant collection owned by Mrs. Bethea. A fascinating sidelight on the history of this material, so urgently sought for in recent decades and so nearly lost irreparably when the cyclone of 1918 destroyed the Tuggle home in LaGrange, is the rescue of the scattered manuscripts by Mrs. Bethea's mother, the late Mrs. Orrie Cox Hinton Tuggle Williamson, who passed them on to her daughter. Carefully preserved by the latter since 1938, the extant collection contains the following assortment of source materials, on which the present volume is based:

1. One notepad diary with covers missing (approximately 1½" thick and measuring 6½" by 4") completely filled with entries and observations written on both sides of unlined paper. Many entries in pencil but all fairly legible. (This is the Indian Diary.)

2. One journal containing lined and columned pages (9" by 5¾"). On the front leather cover in Tuggle's handwriting: "W. O. Tuggle Mem— While in Indian Terty, 1881 and Journal in 1882." Though the covers are badly damaged, the entries are clear. As Tuggle's title implies, this notebook contains two kinds of material. The first seventeen and one-half sheets are devoted to the first eight Indian myths presented in Chapter III; as is stated in the headnote to that chapter, Tuggle heard four of these in September of 1881 in the Territory, and he was told the others in mid-January of 1882 while in Washington. The remainder of this notebook continues the Washington Journal, beginning with the entry for January 15, 1882. The material embodied here thus covers the period from September 3, 1881, through December 19, 1882, but the record is continuous only from January 13 through December 19 of 1882.

3. One leather-bound diary containing lined pages (7" by 4⅝") and covering the period from January 21, 1880, to January 11, 1882. Inscribed on the front cover in Tuggle's handwriting: "W. O. Tuggle LaGrange, Georgia Jany 1880." Primarily this diary records Tuggle's activities in Washington, with numerous references to his work on his manuscripts and his efforts to have them published. Its condition on the whole is fair; its entries, clear. (This is the first three-quarters of the Washington Journal.)

4. One notepad of the same dimensions as the Indian Diary containing 161 sheets of entries running from February 15 to April 20, 1879, when Tuggle was in Washington. This is a miscellaneous collection of notes about pending legislation in the U.S. Senate, comments about Tuggle's own efforts on behalf of Georgia in a tax case with the federal government, extensive citations from tax law, quotations from various classical writers and many other sources, brief descriptions of senators, and so forth. This document lacks continuity and a definable mode; its only interest is biographical in that it reveals the breadth of Tuggle's interests.

5. The manuscript, consisting of about 350 pages, a substantial part of which was copied at the Smithsonian in 1887. For purposes of discussion here, the contents may be subdivided as follows:

A. THE ORIGINAL TALES COPIED BY THE SMITHSONIAN.

The extant material for this part of Tuggle's manuscript is unfortunately quite small by comparison with its original scope. Only the last eight myths in Chapter III remain from the many which Tuggle originally recorded, and in addition to these myths there are four pages of Indian baby songs and fourteen pages of medicine songs which Tuggle painstakingly transcribed in rough phonetic form. The editors have decided not to include these songs in this book.

B. THE OBSERVATIONS IN THE TERRITORY.[23]

The extant material for this part of Tuggle's manuscript runs to approximately 150 pages. A large proportion of these scenes and narratives are included in Chapter II of this book; the remaining "sketches and observations" may be briefly listed in the order of Tuggle's chapter numbers: "An Indian Sermon" (Chapter 5, 2 pages), "My Mule, Prairie Trails, Wewoka" (Chapter 8, 14 pages), "Mule Riding, An Indian Town, A Church, Prof. Doughty, Mrs. Smith, Her Daughter, Abuskey, Sofkey," (Chapter 11, 8 pages), "Indian Doctors" (Chapter 32, 6 pages), and "Among the Mammouth Bones" (Chapter 34, 4 pages). These narratives are more fragmentary and less finished than those we have chosen to present in Chapter II, and the diary versions of them in Chapter I are nearly as detailed.

C. THE EXTANT CHAPTERS OF THE BLACK BEAVER STORY.

Much the same might be said of another book he intended to publish based on his Black Beaver manuscript, the third significant piece in the Bethea collection, which Tuggle acknowledged having received in manuscript form from Major I. G. Vore. It is difficult to estimate now just how long this original manuscript was and whether it was written in as finished a style as can be seen in some of its extant portions, since only a little more than half of the original has been preserved—a total of 179 handwritten sheets—and the surviving sheets are in a fragmented and disorganized state, many of them mutilated and barely legible. However, since Tuggle himself recorded in his diary that he had submitted it to Harpers for publication and that it would make a book of about 350 pages, it seems likely that a complete manuscript of at least that length had already been written. This assumption is further confirmed by the fact that the extant Black Beaver manuscript presents the same orderly arrangement and chapter divisions as shown in the other manuscripts, and that as many as forty-two chapters of the story are accounted for. There is, moreover, another clue to the

[23] Mrs. Tuggle in her letters to Powell had written that she was sending some pages from another manuscript of observations in the Territory. According to a note "no copies of observations" (BAE MSS 566 folder), these observations, though sent to the bureau, were significantly not copied in MSS 566.

plan of organization which Tuggle was apparently working out for
the Black Beaver story. On a single surviving sheet, numbered 318, he
listed the numbers and titles of six chapters as follows:

Chapter 22. Comanches, Killing an ox for his horns, a Strange buffalo
—Distributing tools, Going to Mexico, Robbing bees, Nueces,
Panthers.

Chapter 23. Rio Grande, Kiowas, Blanket for a horse, Hide-the-bullet
—Wild bull—Bears, Kickapoos, Catching a thief—San Antonio—
Prof John Audubon—Enlisting.

Chapter 24. Mexican War. In the rear. Mustered out, Twenty deer in
a day—Bears, Trading, Germans, Ransoming captives, Norther,
Finding money.

Chapter 25. Across the plains, Stealing, My brother officer killed,
Mules freeze, Indians idea of an engine & telegraphs.

Chapter 26. Horse race, Wild Indians, Burying the tomahawk, Guide,
Quarrel, A good shot, Indian prophet. Cutting off a murderer's
head—Guide to soldiers, Loses his property, Delegate to Washington, Busts, Last days, His death. Last words.

Chapter 27. Civilized & wild Indians at a fair. Scenes, [Talks?] by
Indians, Result, The fate of Indians.

All but the last of these are concerned with the adventures of Black
Beaver, and two of them—Chapters 23 and 24—survive almost in
toto. Unfortunately only some parts of Chapter 25 remain; while
Chapter 26, recording the death and last words of Captain Beaver, is
missing altogether. Since Chapter 27, however, apparently deals with
some of Tuggle's own experiences as told in his sketch of the Muscogee
Fair, it seems possible that he intended to round off his Black Beaver
story with a summarizing conclusion drawn from his own observations
and contacts in the Territory, perhaps a conclusion designed to draw
comparisons and contrasts between the primitive conditions of the
savage tribes whom Beaver and his associates came in contact with in
the 1840s and those of the semicivilized Indians whom Tuggle himself
came to know in the late 1870s and 1880s.

Besides the chapters listed above, the extant manuscript includes
numerous other chapters and parts of chapters from the Black Beaver
story. Two of these—Chapters 3 and 15—can be pieced together from
scattered sheets of the manuscript, but much of the material evidently
came between them and Chapter 23 is either partially or entirely
missing. Moreover, the problem of ordering it consecutively is further
complicated by several other factors: the Black Beaver manuscript
appears in two different handwritings, one of which is almost certainly
Major Vore's; some of the episodes are repeated in slightly different

versions; and some of the chapter headings are numbered with both arabic and roman numerals which do not agree (for example, the figure "3" in Chapter 3 is scratched through and the figure XLII appears beside it). Finally there is a quite noticeable difference between the sentence structure and rhythms of the Black Beaver narrative as a whole and those of Tuggle's sketches, enough difference to suggest that in reorganizing or rewriting the narrative he was leaning rather heavily on the style of another writer, presumably Major Vore.

Despite these difficulties and uncertainties, however, it can be seen from what remains of the Black Beaver story that Tuggle both recognized and planned to exploit fully its rich potentialities. For the surviving portions of the narrative *are* rich in both characterization and suspenseful action, as well as in specific details. Covering a span of roughly two decades from the mid-1830s to the 1850s, they reveal in the dominant figure of Captain Beaver himself a heroic, almost mythical yet warmly human character, whose service as a guide carried him into remote fastnesses of the virgin West from the regions of the Yellowstone and North Platte to those of the Brasos and Rio Grande, and whose close association with such prominent white men as Jack Hays, the Texas Ranger; James Bridger; and particularly John James Audubon resulted in many colorful experiences which add further depth and meaning to the always dramatic story of western expansionism. One example is that of Audubon's employment of Black Beaver to shoot animals and birds for him to paint and his portrait of Beaver himself in full regalia. Another has to do with Beaver's refusal to explain to a fellow Indian chief (Buffalo Hump) how the telegraph functions because he couldn't believe in it himself: serving as a paid interpreter for Captain Marcy whose mission was to placate the Comanche tribe by promising to bring the benefits of the railroad into their territory, Beaver could readily translate these into the imagery of an iron horse that fed on wood and water because he had seen it. But, he said: "I do not believe your telegraph tale. I cannot tell anything I do not believe. If I tell him, he will not believe me & every time he sees me he will say, 'There goes that Indian that tells lies' " (sheet 346).

Since, however, the surviving portions of these chapters are too incoherent to justify inclusion in a volume which otherwise presents a fairly consistent and representative sampling of Tuggle's writing in its several states of development, we have decided to omit the Black Beaver chapters, although further consideration of the value of these materials may warrant their publication later.

APPENDIX B:

SWANTON'S VERSION OF THE TUGGLE MYTHS

As WE HAVE PREVIOUSLY NOTED, John R. Swanton consulted the Smithsonian Institution's copy of the Tuggle collection in the preparation of his book *Myths and Tales of the Southeastern Indians,* which was published in 1929. Swanton at that time assumed that he was working directly from Tuggle's own manuscript, although later it became apparent that his source had been one (or both) of the Smithsonian copies, BAE MSS 566 A and BAE MSS 566 B. In his book Swanton included a total of ninety-one myths under the general heading of CREEK STORIES, which he numbered consecutively beginning on page 2 and ending on page 86. Of this total Swanton attributed forty-six myths to W. O. Tuggle by clearly indicating in a parenthetical reference centered below the number and title of the myth that it had been taken from Tuggle's collection. Occasionally he employed footnotes to explain terms found in the myths or to comment upon variations between one version and another of the same myth, and these are retained in the present edition.

The forty-six myths taken from Tuggle's collection are here reprinted verbatim in the order in which Swanton arranged them and with the numbering which he assigned to them. His grouping of Creek Stories begins with a myth from the Tuggle collection entitled "How Day and Night were Divided"; and the last one attributed to Tuggle is number 91, entitled "The Monkey Girl." Swanton, it should be added, was a fairly careful scholar; yet a comparison between his printed text and the myths in the still extant portions of the original Tuggle manuscript discloses that he made numerous slight changes in Tuggle's wording, possibly as a result of his having worked with the Smithsonian copy but more likely because he wished to correct what he considered lapses in Tuggle's grammar and syntax.

1. HOW DAY AND NIGHT WERE DIVIDED

THE ANIMALS held a meeting and No-koos-see (Nokosi), the Bear, presided.

The question was, how to divide day and night.

Some desired the day to last all the time; others wished it all night. After much talk, Chew-thlock-chew (Tciłoktco), the ground squirrel, said:

"I see that Woot-Kew (Wotko), the Coon, has rings on his tail divided equally, first a dark color then a light color. I think day and night ought to be divided like the rings on Woot-Kew's tail."

The animals were surprised at the wisdom of Chew-thlock-chew. They adopted his plan and divided day and night like the rings on Woot-Kew's tail, succeeding each other in regular order.

No-koos-see from envy scratched the back of Chew-thlock-chew and thus caused the stripes on the back of all his descendants, the ground squirrels.

8. THE ORPHAN AND THE ORIGIN OF CORN*

AN OLD WOMAN lived alone. She walked along a certain path until it became hard and smooth. At one place a log lay across the trail. One day as she stepped over this log she saw a drop of blood in her track. Stooping down, she carefully scraped up the dirt around the blood and carried it home. She put the blood and dirt in a jar. She looked in the jar occasionally and discovered that the blood clot was growing. After several months she saw that it was beginning to look like a human being. In 10 months it was developed into a boy. She took him out of the jar and dressed him.

The boy grew. She made him a bow and arrows and told him to go and kill birds. He went and killed birds.

When he grew older she said, "Go and kill squirrels." He went and

* Third Version.

killed squirrels. Again she said, "Go and kill deer." He went and killed deer.

One day on his return from hunting she gave him new food to eat. The boy wondered where she had obtained this delightful food. He asked her, but she refused to tell him.

One day she warned him not to go beyond the mountain which could be seen from their house.

He thought there must be something strange beyond the mountain. He went there. He beheld a lovely sight in the valley beyond the mountain.

When he returned home he sat by himself and looked lonesome.

The old woman said: "You have been beyond the mountain. I will make you a garment and let you go. Go to the woods and bring me a singing bird."

He brought the singing bird. She made him a flute and taught him how to play on it. Then she made him a headdress and put it on his head. He played on the flute and the singing bird flew on the headdress singing to the music of the flute.

She said: "When you go beyond the mountain you will come to a stream, and the first house beyond the stream is the home of three women. The woman who cooks something for you will become your wife. Marry her, and when you come back to see me all will be changed. You will not see me; you will see something growing where my house stood. When you come again it will be ripe. Build a rock house and gather it. Come when you need something to eat and take your food out of the rock house."

He went across the mountain. He crossed the stream, stopped at the first house and saw three women. One of them offered him food which she had cooked. She became his wife. He lived with her people. He saw that the people were suffering for food. He said: "Follow me to the stream." They followed him. He took some pieces of an old log and threw them into the stream. He played on his flute and the bird sang.

Soon the fish came to the surface of the water and the people shot them with arrows and had a great feast.

Chufee (Rabbit) saw the young man lay aside his flute and headdress and stole them and ran away.

The people pursued him and found him trying to play on the flute, but he made no music. Because it refused to sing he struck at the singing bird and injured its feathers.

Chufee thought he could win a wife if he could only make music. He failed. The people took from him the headdress, with the singing bird, and gave it back to the young man.

One day the youth and his wife went to his old home. Behold, all was changed. The house was gone. Where it had stood were some tall green stalks. The old woman was not there.

Again he and his wife returned. The stalks were dry and the grain was hard. He built a rock house and gathered the grain and put into the house.

Again he returned and found all the birds gathered around the house. They were trying to tear the house down.

The Owl said: "Let me knock it down." He flew at the house and struck it with his head. He made himself humpshouldered by the blow. He could not knock it down.

The Eagle said: "Let me knock it down." He sailed at the house, but flew over it. The Hawk said: "I can knock it down." He flew at the house. He knocked it down. The blow drove his neck in and ever since he has had a short neck.

The birds all came and ate up the grain. The man saw some crows flying and fighting in the air. They let some grains fall. He took them and carried them to his new home. He planted the grains and from them sprang corn.

9. THE ONLY SON AND RABBIT

A widow had an only son, whom she cautioned never to pass beyond the mountains, which were in sight of her home. "My boy, never pass the mountains, never go beyond," was her constant warning.

One day while hunting he reached the top of the mountains and on looking into the valley beneath he saw a lovely city, surrounded by green meadows, lakes, and groves. He was tempted to visit so lovely a spot and yielded. He saw scenes of beauty and fair maidens.

When he returned home in the evening he sat by himself and looked lonesome and his mother saw from his manner that something unusual had occurred.

"My son, you have passed beyond the mountains." "I have, mother; I had beautiful visions."

"Ah," sighed his mother, "that is why I warned you. All who see the lovely city are never contented elsewhere. I knew home would lose its attractions when you wandered over the mountains. Since it must be so I will do all I can for you."

The next day she made for her son a wonderful costume. She sent him to the forest to catch all manner of singing birds. She made for him also a flute. When all of her preparations were completed, she arrayed her son in the new costume and arranged for him a peculiar headdress, on which sat the singing birds.

"Now try your flute," she said, and at the first sound of the flute the birds began to sing, keeping time to the music of their master.

"Go, my son, to the beautiful city beyond the mountains. When within the city, ask for the council of the king and as you enter the council ground play on your flute, while your singing birds accompany you."

He passed the mountain and as he approached the city he began to play, while the birds sang. The crowd which gathered and watched the stranger with the wonderful birds told him where the king dwelt. He entered the council, playing on his flute, while his birds sang.

A seat of honor was offered the musical stranger and all were enraptured with his music. Ere he had been there long, no honor was too great for him and everyone strove to do him some kindness. Soon it was rumored that the daughter of the king was to be given as a bride to the young stranger.

One day he invited the king and his council to go with him to a river near the city. On reaching the stream he quickly cast aside his costume, plunged into the water and dived under and crossed the river four times, when all the fish came to the surface and were killed with arrows and a great feast was enjoyed.

The Rabbit, envious of the wonderful stranger, had followed the crowd and while all were intent on killing the fish, he stole the costume of the musical youth and ran away to the woods. On coming out of the river the garments could not be found. No one knew what had become of them.

The next day when the council was assembled, behold the Rabbit strutted in, puffing and blowing with all his might at the flute and, as the birds would not utter a note, he hit at them and said: "Why don't you sing?" He was dressed in the costume of the stranger and before he could be seized he said: "Well, come with me to the river and let us enjoy another feast."

Away he ran and the council followed him. In he jumped, casting the costume and flute on the ground, and though he crossed four times under the water not a fish appeared.

As his head came above the water they all cried:

It is the lying Rabbit.
It is the lying Rabbit.
Seize him, seize him.

He was tried by the council and chased from the council ground as an envious and rascally deceiver.

The king's daughter was married to the wonderful stranger and, as their hands joined, the singing birds flapped their wings and sang with wild melody.

13. MAN-EATER AND THE LITTLE GIRL

ONCE THERE was a beautiful girl who lived with her brothers on the bank of a river. Her youngest brother was named Kut-che-he-lo-chee (probably Katcilutci, Little Panther-foot).

The Lion, Istepahpah (Man-eater), came near their house in a boat and landed. He asked the little girl to enter the boat, but she refused. He told her he had some young lions in his boat and begged her to come and see them. She consented and entered his boat. Then Istepahpah pushed his boat from shore and carried her away to his home. On reaching home Istepahpah put her in his wife's charge. The next day as he was starting off on a hunt he said to the girl: "Take some acorns and wash them in the stream. I love acorns. And make soup of them with my meat. Wash them before my return." After Istepahpah went away his wife said to the little girl: "I am sorry he brought you here. He treats me cruelly and he will treat you the same way. When he fails to obtain any game, he eats a piece of my flesh with his acorns. He will punish you in the same way. I wish you to escape."

She called Kotee (Koti), the water frog, from the stream and asked him if he would take the girl's place and wash the acorns. Kotee said he would. She instructed him to answer Istepahpah, when he asked if the acorns were washed, "No."

She then helped the girl to climb over the house and told her to run to her brothers' house.

When Istepahpah returned he called out to the girl, "Have you washed my acorns?" Kotee answered, "No."

Again Istepahpah asked, "Have you washed my acorns?" Kotee replied, "No."

Istepahpah, not understanding this, went down to the water and Kotee, hearing him approach, jumped into the stream.

Istepahpah, thinking it was the girl, plunged in after, but he could see her nowhere. He said in gentle tones: "Little girl, why do you run away from me?"

After searching in vain he came from the stream and went to his house.

Istepahpah possessed a Motarkah, a wheel, which could find anything which was lost. He threw Motarkah from him and it ran a short way and returned. He tried several directions, but Motarkah came back to him.

At last he threw Motarkah down in his yard. It went over the house and started off in a straight course, following the trail of the girl. Istepahpah followed Motarkah, for he knew the girl had gone that way.

Soon they came in sight of the little girl, who was running and singing. "I wonder if I can reach my brothers' house before they catch me. I wonder if I can reach my brothers' house before they catch me."

While Kut-che-he-lo-chee was playing he thought he heard his lost sister's voice in the distance. He said to his brothers, "I hear my sister's voice."

Kut-che-he-lo-chee insisted that he had heard her singing in distress.

Nearer she came, pursued by Motarkah and Istepahpah, and again she sang as she ran: "I wonder if I can reach my brothers' house before they can catch me. I wonder if I can reach my brothers' house before they catch me."

Kut-che-he-lo-chee was now convinced that he heard his sister's voice. He called his brothers and persuaded them to go with him. They went and now heard their sister crying in distress: "I wonder if I can reach my brothers' house before they catch me. I wonder if I can reach my brothers' house before they catch me."

They said to Kut-che-he-le-chee: "You can stay here. You are too young to help us. Remain behind."

But Kut-che-he-lo-chee would go with them. They now saw their sister pursued by Motarkah and Istepahpah. As they came nearer the brothers shot arrows at Motarkah, but could not stop it. Their sister passed them and ran to the house. Motarkah followed. Kut-che-he-lo-chee ran to Motarkah and struck it with the little wooden paddle he used in parching his food and Motarkah rolled to one side and stopped. Istepahpah still came on. The brothers shot at him but could not kill him. Then Kut-che-he-lo-chee ran to Istepahpah and struck him on the head with his little wooden paddle and killed him. His brothers said Kut-che-he-lo-chee was the bravest of all and had saved their sister's life.

15. HOW THE ALLIGATOR'S NOSE WAS BROKEN

"In the old days," said Fixco, the Seminole, "all the animals determined upon a big ball play. The four-footed animals, with the Alligator for their chief, challenged the fowls, with the Eagle at their head, for a game. Sides were chosen, the poles put up, the ground measured off, and the medicine men conjured the balls.

"The day came and they all met on the ground. The animals ran around their poles, all painted and dressed up, while the birds flew and screamed around their poles.

"At last the ball was tossed into the air and the game began. The Alligator caught the ball as it came down and, grasping it in his teeth, ran toward the poles. The birds in vain attempted to snatch it from him and at last gave it up in utter despair. The Eagle, however, soared aloft and circled in the air till almost out of sight, and then like an arrow he swooped to the earth and struck the Alligator on the nose and broke it. The Alligator's wife had run along with her old man and was shouting at the top of her voice: 'Look at the little striped alligator's daddy, just look at him,' while all the animals shouted in triumph.

"But when the Eagle struck the Alligator all was changed. The Alligator's teeth opened on the ball and the Turkey poked his head in among the teeth, pulled it out, and ran to the poles of the birds and threw the ball between them.

"The fowls won the game and ever since that time the Alligator has had a sunken place on his nose where the Eagle broke it."

16. STORY OF THE BAT

The birds challenged the four-footed animals to a great ball play. It was agreed that all creatures which had teeth should be on one side and all those which had feathers should go on the other side with the birds.

The day was fixed and all the arrangements were made; the ground prepared, the poles erected, and the balls conjured by the medicine men.

When the animals came, all that had teeth went on one side and the birds on the other. At last the Bat came. He went with the animals having teeth, but they said:

"No, you have wings, you must go with the birds."

He went to the birds and they said: "No, you have teeth, you must go with the animals." So they drove him away, saying: "You are so little you could do no good."

He went to the animals and begged that they would permit him to play with them. They finally said, "You are too small to help us, but as you have teeth we will let you remain on our side."

The play began and it soon appeared that birds were winning, as they could catch the ball in the air, where the four-footed animals could not reach it. The Crane was the best player. The animals were in despair, as none of them could fly. The little Bat now flew into the air and caught the ball as the Crane was flapping slowly along. Again and again the Bat caught the ball, and he won the game for the four-footed animals.

They agreed that though he was so small he should always be classed with the animals having teeth.

28. THE KING OF THE TIE-SNAKES

A CHIEF sent his son on a message to another chief, and delivered to him a vessel as the emblem of his authority.

The son stopped to play with some boys who were throwing stones into the water. The chief's son threw his vessel upon the water and it sank. He was frightened. He was afraid to go to the neighboring chief without the vessel, and he did not like to return home and tell his father of the loss. He jumped into the stream and, reaching the spot where the vessel had sunk, he dived into the water. His playmates waited a long time for him, but he did not reappear. They returned and reported his death.

When the chief's son was beneath the surface of the stream the Tie-snakes seized him and bore him to a cave and said to him: "Ascend yonder platform." He looked and saw seated on the platform the king of the Tie-snakes. The platform was a mass of living Tie-snakes. He approached the platform and lifted his foot to ascend, but the platform ascended as he lifted his foot. Again he tried, with the same result. The third time he tried in vain. The Tie-snakes said, "Ascend."

He lifted his foot the fourth time and succeeded in ascending the platform and the king invited him to sit by his side. Then the king said to him:

"See yonder feather; it is yours," pointing to a plume in the corner of the cave. He approached the plume and extended his hand to seize it, but it eluded his grasp. Three times he made the attempt and three times it escaped him. On the fourth attempt he obtained it.

"Yonder tomahawk is yours," said the Tie-snake's king.

He went to the place where the tomahawk was sticking and reached out his hand to take it, but in vain. It rose of itself every time he raised his hand. He tried four times and on the fourth trial it remained still and he succeeded in taking it.

The king said: "You can return to your father after three days. When he asks where you have been, reply: 'I know what I know,' but on no account tell him what you do know. When he needs my aid walk toward the east and bow three times to the rising sun and I will be there to help him."

After three days the Tie-snake carried him to the spot where he had dived into the stream, lifted him to the surface of the water, and placed the lost vessel in his hand. He swam to the bank and returned to his father, who was mourning him as dead. His father rejoiced over his son's wonderful restoration.

He informed his father of the Tie-snake king and his message of proffered aid. Not long afterwards his father was attacked by his enemies. He said to his son: "You understand what the king of the Tie-snakes said. Go and seek his aid."

The son put the plume on his head, took the tomahawk, went toward the east, and bowed three times before the rising sun.

The king of the Tie-snakes stood before him.

"What do you wish?" he said.

"My father needs your aid."

"Go and tell him not to fear. They will attack him, but they shall not harm him or his people. In the morning all will be well."

The son returned to his father and delivered the message of the king of the Tie-snakes.

The enemy came and attacked his town, but no one was harmed. Night came. In the morning they beheld their enemies each held fast in the folds of a tie-snake, and so all were captured and the chief made peace with his foes.

29. THE STORY OF THE TURKEY

THE SEMINOLES have a story about the Turkey, who was once the king of the birds and flew high in the air like the eagle. He would swoop down on the council ground and bear away a man. Then people devised a plan to catch him. Four men were to roll four big balls along the ball ground, so as to attract his attention as he circled in the air above them, and four swift warriors were to watch the Turkey as he came down and seize him. The Turkey was seen flying in the clouds over the council ground and at last down he swooped, having the scalp of his last victim hanging at his breast. All of the warriors were afraid to touch him, but an old dog seized him by the leg and they then killed him.

Ever since then the turkeys have been afraid of man, but more alarmed at dogs. The turkey gobbler still wears the scalp lock at his breast as a trophy of his former valor.

31. THE MONSTER TURTLE*

THE PEOPLE were on the warpath. They wished to select a place at which to fight. They saw a large rock and decided to fight standing on that.

An old warrior said: "It is no rock. An evil spirit has blinded your eyes. That is the Big Terrapin," but the warriors called him a coward and told him to go back and sit with the women.

They ascended the rock, but soon it began to move. They became alarmed and tried to descend, but found that their feet were fastened.

The Big Terrapin crawled into the sea and drowned the warriors.

The old warrior returned and told of the fate of his comrades, but no one believed him. He said, "Come and see the trail of the Big Terrapin leading into the sea."

They followed him and traced the trail to the sea. Then they sent for the medicine man, who made medicine and began to blow and sing.

Soon the frogs came out of the sea. He made the medicine stronger, and, while he was blowing, the little terrapins came out of the sea. He

* Second Version.

made the medicine still stronger, and as he blew and sang a great noise was heard in the sea and out came the Big Terrapin.

They built a pen of logs, caught him, and burned him up.

32. THE BIG ROCK MAN

THE PEOPLE were engaged in a war. Whenever they were on the point of winning the victory the Big Rock Man came to the rescue of their enemies and saved them from defeat.

They called a council to devise measures to conquer the Big Rock Man, but in vain. They could not hurt him. Their arrows bounded from his body.

Then they consulted the Wise Rabbit.

"Shoot him in the ear," said the Wise Rabbit.

In the next fight they aimed their arrows at his ear and one struck him in the ear and killed him.

34. THE FAWN, THE WOLVES, AND THE TERRAPIN

AN INDIAN WOMAN told how the Terrapin's eyes became red.

A beautiful Fawn met a Wolf one day who asked how he came to have such pretty spots all over his body. "I got under a riddle (sieve) and they put fire over it, and that made the pretty spots."

"Will you show me how I can do that?" asked the Wolf. The Fawn consented. Then the Wolf obtained a large riddle, and lay down under it and the Fawn built a fire and burned him to death. After the flesh had decayed, the Fawn took the bones of the back and made a necklace of them. One day the Fawn met a pack of Wolves, who said to him: "Where did you get that necklace?" but he refused to tell.

"What is the song we hear you singing as you gallop over the prairie?" asked they. "If you will stand here till I get to the top of yonder hill I will sing it for you."

Ya-ha ya-ha	Wolf, Wolf
Ef-oo-ne-tul	bones only
Chesarsook, chesarsook	rattle, rattle

Chesarsook	rattle.
Kah-ke-tul	The ravens only
Methl-methl	fluttered, fluttered.
Soolee-tul	The buzzard only
Methl-methl	fluttered, fluttered.
Charnur-tul	The flies only
Sum-sum	buzzed, buzzed.
Choon-tah-tul	The worms only
Witter-took	wiggled
Witter-took	wiggled
Witter-took*	wiggled.

When the wolves heard this song they howled in anger and said: "We missed our mate. He is dead and those are his bones. Let us kill his murderer."

They started for the Fawn, who, seeing them, sped away for life, the bones rattling as he ran. He came to a basket maker and begged him to place him under a basket, but he refused. Then the Fawn came to a man who was getting bark to cover his house. "Oh, hide me from the Wolves," he begged, but the man would not. He ran on and came to a Terrapin who was making a spoon. "Tell me where to hide from the Wolves," said the Fawn. "No," replied the Terrapin, "I must not take sides." However, the Fawn saw a stream just ahead and on reaching it he jumped up and lodged in the fork of a tree and could not extricate himself.

The Wolves passed the man who was making baskets and the man who was getting bark to cover his house and came to the Terrapin, who told them the way the Fawn had gone.

When the Wolves reached the stream they could trace the Fawn no farther. They looked in the water and there saw him. They tried to go into the water to catch the Fawn but failed. In sorrow they began to howl. As they raised their heads in howling they saw the Fawn in the tree. They held a council to see how they could get the Fawn out of the tree. One Wolf said: "I know a man who can shoot him out"; so he sent for the man. Then he went to the Terrapin and brought him, and the Terrapin said he could kill him. He began to shoot arrows at the Fawn. He shot every arrow away and missed the Fawn. Afterwards while walking around the tree the Terrapin found one of his old arrows sticking in the ground near an old log. "This was one of my best arrows," said he. So he shot at the Fawn with this old arrow and killed him.

---

* *Yaha*, wolf; *ifoni*, bone; *tálki*, only (another informant used *tis*, instead of *tálki*); *tcásásakita*, to rattle; *kake*, raven; *miłmił*, flutter; *suli*, buzzard; *tcana*, common fly; *sám*, to buzz; *tcunta*, worm; *witáták*, wiggled.

Then the Wolves took the body and divided it into pieces. "We must pay the man for shooting him," one said, so they offered the Terrapin a piece of one leg. But he had some complaint in his leg and the medicine man had told him not to eat the leg of any animal. He whined out: "I can not eat leg; it will make my leg hurt, and I shall die."

When they offered him a shoulder he whined out: "I can not eat shoulder; it will pain my shoulder, and I shall die."

"He does not want any," they said, and went away carrying all of the Fawn.

After they had gone the Terrapin looked around and saw that there was blood on the leaves, so he gathered the bloody leaves into a big bundle saying: "I'll carry them home." He reached his house, threw down the bundle, and said to his wife: "There, cook it for the children." Then she unrolled the bundle but saw nothing. "Where is it?" she asked. "Way inside," replied he, so she separated the leaves, but finding only the blood, she threw it into his face. He called to the children to bring him some water, but as they were slow, he crawled around with his eyes closed and found the lye and washed his face in that. Some of this got in his eyes and made them red, and ever since terrapins have had red eyes.

35. HOW THE TERRAPIN'S BACK CAME TO BE IN CHECKS

A WOMAN was beating sofki in a mortar out in her yard when she heard someone calling to her and making fun of her. She stopped and looked around, but saw no one. She began beating the corn again, and again heard the voice ridiculing her. She stopped and searched but in vain. Again she heard the voice, which seemed to come from under the wooden mortar, so she lifted the mortar and there found a Terrapin. As he was the guilty one, she took the pestle and beat him on the back until she broke his shell into little pieces and left him as dead. After she left, the Terrapin began to sing in a faint voice:

Char-tee-lee-lee (tcatilili)	I come together.
Char-tee-lee-lee	I come together.
Char-tee-lee-lee	I come together.
Char-tee-lee-lee	I come together.

The pieces came together as he sang, but his back always looked scarred, and terrapins have ever since then had checkered backs.

36. HOW THE TERRAPIN'S BACK CAME TO BE IN CHECKS*

A TERRAPIN went hunting and met a woman. She accused him of having slandered her. He denied it, but when they passed a hollow tree into which he thought he could crawl, he said: "Yes; I did it; I am the man."

He tried to crawl into the tree but his shot bag got caught and he stuck fast. The woman caught him and beat his back to pieces.

By and by the ants came and he said:

I will give you my blood,
I will give you my fat,
If you will help me mend my back.

They consented and brought him some tar with which he mended his shell, but it was always in checks, and he never afterwards had any fat, nor any blood.

37. WHY THE OPOSSUM HAS NO HAIR ON HIS TAIL

WHEN there was a great flood all the animals were put in the ark, except the male opossum. A female opossum climbed up on the side of the ark and when the waters rose, her tail hung down into the water. When the waters subsided it was found that all the hair on her tail had come off and ever since then the opossum's tail has been without hair.

All of the male opossums were drowned, so this female went off alone feeling ashamed, and coiled herself up as if dead. Her nose was near her side, and after breathing a long time in this position little opossums appeared in her pouch, and thus the young opossums have been born ever since.

* Second Version.

38. WHY THE OPOSSUM HAS NO HAIR ON HIS TAIL*

THE RACCOON met the Opposum, and the Opossum said: "How did you make such pretty rings on your tail?"

The Raccoon replied: "I wrapped bark around my tail and stuck it into the fire."

Then the Opossum got some bark, wrapped it around his tail, which then had hair on it, and built a fire. He stuck his tail into the fire and burned all of the hair off and ever since then opossums have had no hair on their tails.

39. THE RACE BETWEEN THE CRANE AND THE HUMMING BIRD

A HUMMING BIRD challenged a Crane to a race. The Crane consented and selected the course from the spot on the stream where they then were to a spring at its head.

When the word was given the Humming Bird flew swiftly up the stream but soon lost sight of the water and found himself in the woods. Then he returned to the stream and decided to fly over the water, always keeping in sight of it.

The Crane knew the course of the stream and when the Humming Bird arrived at the spring he found that his rival had been there for some time.

42. RABBIT GETS MAN-EATER OVER TO THE OTHER SIDE OF THE OCEAN †

THE RABBIT was traveling from west to east and met the Lion going from east to west. The Rabbit was very fond of the ladies and felt jealous of the Lion and wanted to get rid of him.

* Second Version.
† Third Version.

"What," said he to the Lion, "Do you eat as you travel?"

"I eat a variety of things," said the Lion, "I eat everything as I go. What do you eat?"

"Oh, I eat a variety too, just like you. Suppose we travel together." They turned and went along in company. "We will camp tonight," said the Rabbit as they journeyed along, "at a creek called 'Throwing-hot-ashes-on-one.'" As night came they reached the creek. A fire was made and they sat and talked for some time. When they grew sleepy the Rabbit said:

"What sort of noise do you make when you sleep?" The Lion imitated a coarse heavy snore, and asked the same question of the Rabbit. "Oh, I just say n-o-ch, n-o-ch, n-o-ch" (the first syllable of the Muskogee word meaning "sleep").

Each took one side of the fire and the Lion soon heard the Rabbit saying n-o-ch, n-o-ch (sounding "nutz, nutz"). He thought the Rabbit was asleep and before long he fell asleep and began to snore loudly.

Meanwhile the Rabbit peeped at him constantly and finally jumped up. He threw some cold ashes all over himself. Then, taking a broad piece of bark, he threw a mass of hot ashes and coals on the Lion, who rose with a roar, exclaiming: "What's the matter?"

"Oh, I told you this creek was called 'Throwing-hot-ashes-on-one.' Look at me. Let's jump across the creek," and away he jumped across the stream, followed by the Lion. "Now back again," and across they went again. "Now again," and the Lion jumped again, but the Rabbit stood on the west bank. Suddenly the banks separated and the stream widened into an ocean. The Lion wandered along the bank, trying to cross. At last he met a Crane and said to him:

"How can I cross to the other bank?" "Just climb on my back and I will stick my bill in the other bank so that you can walk over," replied the Crane. The Lion jumped on the Crane's back, but when he walked out on his neck the Crane cried out in pain:

"Oh, you are breaking my neck." After several similar attempts the Lion returned to the eastern bank and never was able to cross the big water to the western side. So the Rabbit got rid of his rival.

44. RABBIT STEALS FIRE

ALL THE PEOPLE came together and said: "How shall we obtain fire?"

It was agreed that Rabbit should try to obtain fire for the people.

He went across the great water to the east. He was received gladly, and a great dance was arranged. Then Rabbit entered the dancing circle, gaily dressed, and wearing a peculiar cap on his head into which he had stuck four sticks of rosin.

As the people danced they approached nearer and nearer the sacred fire in the center of the circle. The Rabbit also danced nearer and nearer the fire. The dancers began to bow to the sacred fire, lower and lower. Rabbit also bowed to the fire, lower and lower. Suddenly, as he bowed very low, the sticks of rosin caught fire and his head was a blaze of flame.

The people were amazed at the impious stranger who had dared to touch the sacred fire. They ran at him in anger, and away ran Rabbit, the people pursuing him. He ran to the great water and plunged in, while the people stopped on the shore.

Rabbit swam across the great water, with the flames blazing from his cap. He returned to his people, who thus obtained fire from the east.

45. RABBIT TRIES A GAME OF SCRATCH WITH WILDCAT

THE RABBIT was hopping down a trail one day when he saw a track in the sand. He looked at it and said:

"That animal has no claws like these," and he then held up one of his forefeet and looked with admiration at his claws.

Soon he overtook the Wildcat, who was sitting in the trail. "Sure enough," he said, "he has no claws. He is the animal that made the tracks. I will have a little fun out of him."

"Let's play scratch," said he to the Wildcat. The Wildcat smiled and said, "Very well." "I will have the first scratch," insisted the Rabbit. "All right." So the Rabbit hopped close to the Wildcat and gave his hardest scratch and then looked at his claws, expecting to see them full of hair, but not a single hair did he scratch out.

"Well, he has no claws and can't hurt me," thought the Rabbit, and he called to the Wildcat, "Now's your time."

The Wildcat reached out one of his forefeet and gave a quick grab at the Rabbit's back and jerked the skin from his body.

(Others say he jerked his tail off.)

47. RABBIT GETS A TURKEY FOR WILDCAT*

A RABBIT was overtaken by a Wildcat, who threatened to kill and eat him. The Rabbit said: "Do not kill me; I will bring you a turkey." The Wildcat consented to let Rabbit try, so he ran into the woods to find the turkey, first telling the Wildcat to lie down and pretend he was dead.

Rabbit soon found some Turkeys and told them the Wildcat was dead and proposed that they all go and dance and sing around his body. The Turkeys agreed and went with Rabbit and when they saw the Wildcat's body stretched on the ground and his mouth and eyes looking white as if he were flyblown (for Rabbit had rubbed rotten wood on the edges of his eye and mouth) they were satisfied that he was really dead.

Rabbit took his place at the head of the Wildcat and began to beat his drum and to sing while the Turkeys danced around him.

After the song and dance had continued a while they heard Rabbit sing:

"Jump up and catch the red leg, Jump up and catch the red leg."

"Why, he is dead and can not jump," they said, but they objected, so he promised not to say that any more.

So Chaffee [Tcufi] sang and drummed away and the Turkeys again danced around their enemy's body; but soon Chaffee sang in a low tone:

"Jump up and catch the biggest, Jump up and catch the biggest."

The Turkeys stopped their dance, but too late, for the Wildcat jumped up and caught the biggest gobbler. Rabbit ran away to the woods and the Turkeys pursued him, threatening to kill him for his trickery. They chased him round and round the trees till at last one of the Turkeys bit at his long tail and bit it off, and ever since that time all rabbits have had short tails.

* Second Version.

48. RACCOON GETS A DEER FOR PANTHER

A PANTHER met a Raccoon and was about to eat him, when the Raccoon said: "I am a little fellow. Do not kill me. It would not do you any good to eat me. Let me find a way for both of us to get plenty to eat."

The Panther agreed, and the Raccoon said; "You make out you are dead. Lie down and stretch out. I will get some rotten wood and stuff it into your eyes, mouth and nose, to look like flyblows. Then I will tell the Deer that you are dead, and get a crowd of them to come and dance around your body. I will sit at your head and beat the drum and sing, and when a big buck comes near I will touch you and you can jump up and cut his throat so that both of us will have plenty to eat."

The Panther lay down and the Raccoon stretched him out and putting the rotten wood into his eyes, nose, and mouth, ran off to tell the Deer of the Panther's death. He met an old Deer and said: "The Panther is dead; come and see him."

But she was very shy, and replied: "If he is dead, let him stay dead."

Soon the Raccoon met a Fawn and told of the Panther's death, and the Fawn came near the Panther's body, looked, and then ran to tell the Deer that their enemy was dead.

A crowd soon gathered, and the Raccoon took his seat at the Panther's head and proposed a dance. He beat his drum and sang a song:

Ching a ching
Ching a ching
Ching a ching, ching.

Then the Deer danced around the dead Panther. By and by a fat buck danced near, and the Raccoon touched the Panther, who jumped up and killed the buck.

51. RABBIT ENGINEERS A TUG OF WAR BETWEEN TWO TIE-SNAKES*

ONE DAY a Rabbit saw a Tie-snake in a pool of water and proposed a trial of strength, which the Snake, to honor the little fellow, accepted. The Rabbit ran over the hill to another pool of water and made a similar arrangement with another Tie-snake, fixing the same time for the trial to begin. He obtained a long vine and put an end in each pool and gave the signal. Then the Snakes pulled against each other until they were amazed at the Rabbit's strength, and each fell on the same device to find out how the Rabbit was pulling so hard, which was to crawl out of the pool slowly, pulling all the while and gradually ascend the hill, where the Rabbit had agreed to stand. So they shortened the vine and crawled to the top of the hill, where, behold! the Snakes saw each other and no Rabbit at all, for he had concealed himself as he saw them coming up. After talking it over, the Snakes agreed that the Rabbit should not be allowed to drink any more water and accordingly the decree went forth to all the Tie-snakes, who are kings of the water, that the Rabbit should drink no more on account of his deception.

Day after day, as the Rabbit went to drink, the Tie-snakes ordered him away. Finally he adopted this plan to fool them. He found the skin of a fawn and putting it on approached a pool of water and began bleating like a young fawn in distress. A Tie-snake hearing the cry, crawled out and asked why he cried.

"Because the Rabbit says I can never drink any more water, for all the Tie-snakes have so ordered," said the pretended fawn.

"It is one of his lies," said the Snake, "it is only the Rabbit who was ordered to drink no more. Such a pretty little creature as you are can always get all the water he wishes."

So the Rabbit went to the pool and drank his fill.

* Third Version.

52. RABBIT ENGINEERS A TUG OF WAR BETWEEN TIE-SNAKE AND MAN-EATER

RABBIT saw a Tie-snake in the water and challenged him to a trial of strength. The Tie-snake laughed at him, but consented.

The Rabbit said: "I will bring a vine, and when you feel me jerk you pull."

Afterwards Rabbit went over the hill and met Istepahpah, the Man-eater (the Lion), and proposed to pull against him, and Istepahpah consented. Rabbit fixed the same time for the Tie-snake and Istepahpah; and when that time arrived he got the vine and put one end in the water and running over the hill gave the other end to Istepahpah, saying, "When you feel me jerk, then pull."

Presently he went up on top of the hill and jerked the vine. The Tie snake began to pull and Istepahpah, feeling the jerk, also pulled. Each was surprised and pulled harder and harder.

Rabbit enjoyed his deception and watched his victims pull until both were tired, and astonished at the strength of such a small animal.

(This same story is related of the sea cow and the elephant.)

55. RABBIT FOOLS ALLIGATOR*

THE ALLIGATOR was sunning himself on a log when the Rabbit said to him: "Mr. Alligator, did you ever see the devil?" "No, Mr. Rabbit, but I am not afraid to see him," replied the Alligator.

"Well, I saw the devil, and he said you were afraid to look at him," said the Rabbit. "I'm not afraid of him, and you tell him so," bravely responded the Alligator.

"Are you willing to crawl up the hill tomorrow and let me show you the devil?" asked the Rabbit. "Yes, I am willing," said the Alligator. The Rabbit spoke up and said, "Now Mr. Alligator, when you see smoke rising don't be afraid, the devil will be just starting out."

"You need not be so particular about me. I am not afraid," said he.

* Second Version.

"Now when you see birds flying and deer running past you, don't get scared." "I shall not get scared." "When you hear fire crackling close to you and the grass burning all around you, don't get scared. The devil will come along and you can get a good look at him," and with this advice the Rabbit left.

The next day he returned and told Alligator to crawl out and lie in the high grass and wait until the devil came. So out crawled the Alligator and took his position in the grass as directed by the Rabbit.

When he saw the Alligator so far from the water the Rabbit laughed to himself. He ran across the prairie till he reached a burning stump, got a chunk of fire, and returned to a spot near his confiding friend, where he kindled the grass and soon had the pleasure of seeing a blaze all around the Alligator. Then, running to a sandy place where there was no grass, he sat down to see the fun. He had not long to wait, for when the smoke rose in clouds and the birds flew by, and the animals ran for life over the prairie, the Alligator cried out: "Oh, Mr. Rabbit, what's that?" The Rabbit answered: "Oh, you lie still; that's nothing but the devil starting out." Soon the fire began to crackle and roar, and the flames swept over the prairie, and the Alligator called: "Oh, Mr. Rabbit, what's that?" "Oh, that's the devil's breath. Don't be scared. You will see him directly." The Rabbit rolled over in the sand and kicked his heels in the air. The fire came nearer and nearer and began to burn the grass all around the Alligator, and under him, till he rolled and twisted in pain. "Don't be scared, Mr. Alligator. Just lie still a little longer and the devil will be right there and you can get a good look at him," cried out the Rabbit, as he saw the movements of the Alligator. But the latter could stand it no longer and started down the hill to the water through the burning grass, snapping his teeth and rolling over in pain, while the Rabbit laughed and jumped in delight, saying, "Wait, Mr. Alligator, don't be in such a hurry. You are not afraid of the devil." But the Alligator tumbled into the water to cool his roasted skin, and wondered how the Rabbit could stand such awful scenes.

56. TERRAPIN RACES

RABBIT said to Terrapin, "Let us have a race." "All right," replied Terrapin, "Let me get ready for it and let us race across a ridge." "I can beat you," said the Rabbit. "I can beat you," said the Terrapin, and both boasted of what they could do. Terrapin said that he would have a little white feather in his head by which he could be recognized.

When he went away to get ready, Terrapin stationed another Terrapin halfway up the hill, a second at the top, and a third in the valley beyond, while he himself went to the starting place. Immediately after they began racing Terrapin pulled the feather out of his head and turned aside into the bushes. Rabbit, however, saw the Terrapin halfway up the hill and kept on. This Terrapin disappeared in the same way and then Rabbit saw the Terrapin at the top. But when he saw at the top of the hill the Terrapin he supposed he was racing he gave it up and ran off into the bushes.

57. TERRAPIN RACES*

THE DEER and the Ground Terrapin ran a race. The Terrapin stationed a second Terrapin at the beginning of the course, and two more at intervals along the course, while he himself sat at the end. Each time the Deer called out to know if Terrapin was there a Terrapin answered, and so with the one at the end.

58. TERRAPIN RACES

A TERRAPIN dared a Deer to run a race. On the appointed day they met and agreed to race over four hills. The Terrapin wore a white feather in his cap. Then he went off and found three other Terrapins and stationed them on the tops of other hills, one on each hill.

When the word was given the Deer ran swiftly down the first hill and up the second hill. Just as he was ascending the second hill he saw the white feather of the second Terrapin disappearing over the second hill. He ran faster but could not see the Terrapin, as he threw away his feather just before the Deer reached him. Deer ran down the second hill and as he ascended the third hill he saw Terrapin disappear over the crest of the third hill. Then the Deer ran from the track and gave up the race.

* Second Version.
† Third Version.

59. TERRAPIN RACES*

THE TERRAPIN proposed to the Wolf a race, and he scornfully accepted. The race was to begin at the top of one hill and to extend to a fourth hill. That night the Terrapin summoned all his kinfolk to help him and they were to take their stations all along the route, each to wear a white feather on his head.

The time came, the word was given, and when the Wolf reached the top of the second hill he saw a Terrapin ahead of him running down the hill, the white feather waving in the grass. He soon passed him, but, on reaching the third hill, there was the Terrapin still crawling ahead. He ran himself out of breath, but, on reaching the last hilltop, to his mortification there sat a Terrapin at the stake, his plume waving in triumph.

60. TERRAPIN RACES†

ONE DAY the Deer was lying in the grass chewing his cud, when a Terrapin crawled near. The Deer looked at him moving slowly along, and said: "Why, brother Terrapin, you crawl as though you are sick. Why don't you go faster?"

"Oh, brother Deer, I like to go this way. I can run fast, and I can beat you running," replied the Terrapin. The Deer laughed. "When do you want to try it?" he asked. "Any time. How will tomorrow suit you?" responded the Terrapin.

So it was agreed that they should have the race the following day. They selected the ground and chose the Rabbit as judge. The Terrapin went to see all his friends that evening and told them that the honor of the family was at stake and appealed to them to aid in maintaining it. All having said they would, he continued, "Now here is my plan. I will meet the Deer to-morrow on the ground we picked out, and tell him I prefer to run through the grass and let him run along the trail. Well, this is the way we can beat him. I will start off at the word through the grass and you will be stationed in the grass along the way, and when you hear the Deer run-

* Fourth Version
† Fifth Version.

ning on the trail, you can run a little way and stop. If the Deer calls out, 'Oh, brother Terrapin, where are you?' you can tell him 'Here I am crawling along in the grass,' and the last one can crawl up to where the Rabbit will be sitting, when he hears the Deer coming, and claim the race." They all agreed that this was a fine plan, except the Terrapin who was assigned to the last station, and he said the Deer would know he was not the same Terrapin and would suspect some trick. So the first and the last Terrapin exchanged places, the last being cautioned to hide in the grass near the starting place so that the Deer could not see him plainly. They separated and the Terrapins all took their places along the race course.

The next day the Deer galloped over the prairie and, reaching the starting point, called out: "Oh, brother Terrapin, where are you?" "Here I am," answered the Terrapin hiding in the grass. "Well, are you ready?" asked the Deer. "Yes," said the Terrapin, and at the word the Deer leaped forward. Hearing no sound in the grass after going some distance, he called out, "Where are you, brother Terrapin?" One of the Terrapins answered, "Here I am down in the grass crawling along."

The Deer was surprised, so he ran faster and called out, "Oh, brother Terrapin, where are you?" Another Terrapin answered, "Here I am, just a-crawling through the grass." So the Deer ran with all his might and did not stop till he reached the Rabbit. But just as he thought he had won the race, he saw the Terrapin crawl up to the end of the course. The Rabbit decided that the Terrapin had won.

61. THE BUNGLING HOST

THE BEAR invited the Rabbit to dinner. When he came the Bear called his wife and said: "Have peas for dinner. The Rabbit loves peas." "But there is no grease with which to cook them," said the Bear's wife.

"Oh," said the Bear, "that's no trouble. Bring me a knife." She brought the knife and the Bear took it and split between his toes, while the Rabbit looked on in wonder. "No grease between my toes," said the Bear. "Well, I know where there is some." So he cut a gash in his side and out ran the grease. His wife took it and cooked the peas, they had a fine dinner and vowed always to be good friends.

The Rabbit invited the Bear to take dinner with him the next day.

"Where do you live?" asked the Bear. Pointing to an old sedgegrass field, the Rabbit replied, "Way over yonder in that big white house."

The Bear started the next morning and sought in vain for the big white house, but while wandering in the sedge came near stepping on his new friend who was sleeping in his bed.

"What's that! What are you tramping over me for?" cried the Rabbit as he was awakened by the footsteps of the Bear.

"Oh, I am trying to find your big white house." Laughing at the joke, the Rabbit invited the Bear to be seated, and said he would have dinner ordered. He called his wife and told her to have peas for dinner. "But there is no grease." "That's a small matter. Bring me a knife," proudly exclaimed the Rabbit. When his wife came with the knife, he held up one of his forefeet and split between his toes. "What, no grease? Then I know where I can find it," and he gave a thrust into his side. But the blood gushed out, and he fell to earth with a scream. The Bear cried, "You little fool, your side is not like mine," and lifting his friend all covered with blood, he put him on his bed. "Send for the doctor, Doctor Turkey Buzzard," said the Bear to the Rabbit's wife, who was weeping bitterly, while the little Rabbits gathered around in tears. "Run for the doctor," she said to one of the little Rabbits, and away he ran at the top of his speed.

Then Dr. Buzzard came in haste and said, "What a sad sight; he must be kept quiet. Carry him to the top of his house and put him in a room where no one can come except his doctor, and in four days you may enter and see him." His orders were obeyed. But soon the Rabbit was heard screaming in agony. Running to the room, the door of which was closed, the wife asked, "Oh, what's the matter?" "Nothing," said the Buzzard, "I'm merely dressing his wound." Again the screams were heard, but fainter, and the Rabbit's wife asked, "What makes him scream so?" "Go away. I'm sewing up the cut in his side." No more screams were heard. After four days the Rabbit's wife opened the door and there lay a few bones and a pile of hair. The Buzzard had eaten the Rabbit.

62. HOW RABBIT WON HIS WIFE'S SISTER FOR HIS SECOND WIFE

RABBIT was lying down with his head in his wife's lap and she was gently rubbing it. Presently her sister, who lived with them, a beautiful girl, rose and said, "I must go after the water," and went out.

Then Rabbit jumped up and said to his wife, "I must go and attend to my business." He ran across the stream and hid in some low bushes.

Then the girl came to the stream and began to get water. Rabbit in a disguised voice asked her from his concealment:

"Is Par-soak-ly-ah (Pasikola, his own name) at home?"

"Yes," she replied, looking in the direction of the voice, but not seeing the Rabbit.

"Tell Par-soak-ly-ah that all the people have agreed to undertake a big bear hunt, and they have sent me to tell him to be sure to come. He must go ahead and select a camp and build a fire. No man is to carry his wife, but every man must take his wife's sister."

The girl ran to the house, and Rabbit ran around a different way, and, when the girl came in, he was lying with his head in his wife's lap.

The girl related what she had heard, except the point about every man carrying his wife's sister. Then Rabbit waited a while and said, "Is that all?" She then told it all. Rabbit's wife said:

"I will stay at home. You must go, my sister, on the bear hunt. Both of you must go." Then Rabbit's wife made all things ready for them, and Rabbit and the girl went to the appointed place, reaching it just before the sun went down.

Rabbit built a fire and swept the ground. He expressed great wonder that the other hunters did not come.

"I am disappointed," said he, and running to a log, he jumped on it, and looked in every direction to see if the hunters could be seen.

The sun went down and Rabbit complained bitterly that the hunters had not come.

As it grew dark he said, "Let us go to sleep. You make your bed on that side of the fire and I will make mine on this side."

He had selected a place for the girl where there was an anthill, and when she lay down she could not sleep. She tossed and scratched but could not sleep. Then Rabbit began his wooing, and succeeded in winning his second bride.

63. TURKEY, TURTLE, AND RATTLESNAKE

ONCE UPON A TIME the beasts, birds, and reptiles held a council to devise means of destroying their enemy, Man. It was decided that he must die. The Rattlesnake, being the most poisonous, was chosen to kill him; the Turtle was selected to bite off his scalp lock; while the Turkey was to run away with it. In accordance with this arrangement the three repaired to the cabin of Man during the night and while he was asleep. The Rattlesnake coiled himself up near the door, so that he could strike Man as he came out, the Turtle took a position round the corner of the house, and the Turkey stationed himself behind it.

When morning came Man awoke and stepped out. The Rattlesnake heard him coming and when he was sufficiently near struck his fangs deep into his leg. Man fell down and died. Then the Turtle crawled up to his head and after much labor bit off the scalplock, and the Turkey seized it and ran off with it. In his race he accidentally swallowed the scalplock, and ever since a scalplock has grown from the breast of the Turkey in honor of that event.

66. THE TASKS OF RABBIT*

RABBIT was discontented. He went to Esarketummessee (Hisakita imisi), the Life Controller, and said:

"I am unhappy. The other animals are better provided than I am for offense. When I am attacked I can only run."

Esarketummessee said: "Go and bring yonder Rattlesnake to me." The Snake was coiled and ready to strike. The Rabbit approached him and said:

"Esarketummessee has ordered me to take your measure, and, if you will get out of your coil, I will see how long you are."

The Rattlesnake felt flattered at this and stretched himself at full length. But Rabbit had provided a stick and a string, and quickly tying the stick to the snake near his head and tail he took him and ran away to Esarketummesee

"Well done," said he. "Now, go and bring yonder swarm of Gnats which you see flying in the air."

Rabbit ran to the place and sat near the swarm and while the king of the Gnats was playing ball with his young men Rabbit said to him, "You have a large band, and Esarketummessee has sent me to count them. If you will enter this bag I will count as they go in." Rabbit saw that they all followed their king, as the bees follow their queen.

The king felt flattered at this and entered Rabbit's bag, all his young men following him, whereupon Rabbit tied the bag and ran away to Esarketummesee, where he threw it down. Then Esarketummesee said to Rabbit, "See what you have done by using the faculties I gave you.

* Third Version.

Go and use the powers I have bestowed upon you and you will fulfill the destiny I designed for you."

67. WHY THE RABBIT STEALS

IN THE BEGINNING all the animals held a meeting and agreed that each should select a tree the fruit of which should belong to the descendants of the chooser. The first choice fell to the Rabbit, who went down to a river and ran slowly up the bank looking first at one tree and then at another. At last he stopped under a sycamore tree and, seeing the large balls hanging from its limbs, he chose the sycamore. All the other animals picked out such trees and fruits as they liked, the Raccoon taking muscadines and the Opossum persimmons, till all the different fruits were taken. Then the Rabbit, becoming hungry, ran down to his big tree and hunted on the ground for some of the fine balls, but none were on the ground. He looked up into the tree and there were hundreds on the limbs. Thinking some would fall in a little while, he sat under the tree and waited. Night came and he hopped away home hungry. Next day he came back and looked again on the ground. None of the balls had yet fallen. He sat under the sycamore all that day and again had to go to bed hungry. The third day he came to his tree and his body was thin and his eyes were big, and they got bigger looking while he longed for the balls to fall to the ground. His body got thinner and his eyes bigger and all his descendants have been like him. He waited till he nearly perished, and at last he decided to go around at night and steal from the other animals, as there were no more trees from which he could select. In this way the Rabbit learned to steal for a living and he has always kept up the habit.

68. WHY THE OPOSSUM LOOKS ASHAMED

ONE TIME an Opossum got very hungry. He went about the world hunting something to eat. At last he looked up into a tree and saw some big balls hanging low down on the limbs. They looked so fine that he danced around the tree for joy.

After his dance he jumped up and caught one of the balls and mashed it in his mouth. It was very bitter, for it was an oak ball. He felt so bad that he crawled away, lay down, and made out that he was dead. Whenever anyone comes where he is, he remembers his mistake and feels ashamed of having been so badly deceived.

70. HOW RABBIT GOT THE WIDOW'S DAUGHTER*

ONCE THERE was a widow who had a very beautiful daughter. She had many lovers but still remained single.

The Rabbit, an old bachelor, lived near by and fell in love with the widow's daughter. He thought he stood no chance, as he was so small and insignificant, especially as he knew more likely beaus had been rejected, but he determined to see what cunning could accomplish. So with this end in view he made a new blowgun of a cane, and, seizing his opportunity, he slipped up to the chimney of the widow's house, made a hole in the back of the chimney near the ground, penetrating the fireplace on the inner side, and then inserted his blowgun in this opening. The night after he had completed his device he ran up and put his ear to the other end of the blowgun and listened to what the widow and her daughter were saying.

"My daughter, why do you not marry? I am getting old and you ought not to reject all your lovers."

"But mother, none of them suits me."

"You are too particular, my daughter."

Soon he heard the widow tell her daughter to run to the spring for water. Then he ran through the weeds to the spring and lay concealed near by in the grass.

The pretty girl came singing down the trail and, while she was getting the water, the Rabbit sang out in a low, deep, monotonous tone: "Hok-te mar-pe hum-ke ehe-sekart elun, elun, elun-n-n-n."† (The girl who remains single will die, die, die.)

She was alarmed, and looked in vain to see who spoke the awful words. She drew a long breath and soon in a quick frightened manner began dipping up the water again. Forthwith the Rabbit slipped through the grass to the other side of the spring and sang out in the same voice: "Hok-te mar-pe hum-ke ehe-sekart, elun, elun, elun."

* Second Version.

† *Hokti*, woman; *maniti*, young; *hamki*, one; *ilisikat*, without a husband; *ilan*, shall die.

In alarm the pretty girl ran to the house and cried to her mother: "Oh, mother there was an awful noise at the spring and I could see nobody."

"What was it, and what did it say?" she asked. The Rabbit was at his blowgun listening.

"It said in a low deep voice, 'Hok-te mar-pe hum-ke ehe-sekart elun, elun, elun!'"

"I told you so," exclaimed her mother.

"And then I heard it on the other side of the spring, and I ran here."

"Yes, I told you to marry and you wouldn't do so."

Suddenly the Rabbit sang through the blowgun in the fireplace: "Hok-te mar-pe hum-ke ehe-sekart, elun, elun, elun."

"That is it."

"Oh, I hear it," the widow screamed in terror; "you will die. You must marry and shall marry the very first one who asks."

"Yes, yes, I will," said the daughter.

Rabbit had carried his point and so away he ran in glee to his home and summoned his aunt, saying to her:

"I wish to marry the widow's daughter and you must go at once and make the offer of my hand."

The old lady went to the widow's home and no sooner had she entered than the widow told her of the strange occurrence. When the story was finished the widow added:

"I have told my daughter that girls ought to marry and I am determined she shall accept the first offer."

"I have come to propose my nephew, the Rabbit," said the visitor.

The widow hesitated. The silence was broken by a sound from the ashes in the fireplace: "Hok-te mar-pe hum-ke ehe-sekart elun, elun, elun."

"Yes, he shall have her. Take her, take her for the Rabbit's bride," the widow cried.

So they were married, and thus the Rabbit won the widow's beautiful daughter.

74. RABBIT RIDES WOLF*

The Rabbit wanted to get a wife and the Wolf was courting at the same house.

The Wolf being finer looking made the better impression, so Rabbit one day said to the ladies:

* Third Version.

"The Wolf is my riding horse."

They did not believe him, so he told them he would prove it by riding him there the next day.

Then Rabbit went to the Wolf's house and said to him: "Let us go courting to-morrow."

The Wolf agreed and Rabbit told him to call for him the next day so that they could go together. But when the Wolf called at the Rabbit's house Rabbit pretended he was too sick to go. He said: "I can not walk, but if you will carry me on your back I will go." The Wolf consented to carry him on his back, so Rabbit got up and they started. As they were ascending a hill the Rabbit fell off and complained that he was still sick and that he could not stay on unless the Wolf consented to let him put on spurs. The Wolf agreed and Rabbit put on spurs to steady him as he sat on the Wolf's back.

As they went along Rabbit said:

"Suppose you make out you are my horse. You know a horse always gets the most to eat and has the best time. Wherever we stop I promise to bring out your dinner first, before I eat."

The Wolf agreed and they went on in a friendly way.

When they got in sight of the house of the ladies, who were looking for them, Rabbit said:

"Now, we must make a good appearance as we go up near the ladies and you must caper and dance gaily."

The Wolf said he would do so, and, as they approached the ladies, Rabbit stuck his spurs into the Wolf's side and up he dashed in fine style. Then Rabbit fastened his horse to a post, walked up to the ladies and said:

"You see I told you the truth. There is my horse."

They were pleased at this and so he won his bride.

75. THE TAR BABY

A MAN missed peas from his garden and, after vain efforts to catch the thief, he made a tar-person and put it in the garden near the peas.

A Rabbit had been coming every night for the peas and the tar-person was quickly discovered by him. Stopping near, he said: "Who's that? What's your name?" and, receiving no reply, he hopped close to the figure and said: "If you don't speak I will hit you." He struck the tar-person and his paw stuck. Again he asked, "Why don't you speak? Let go of my foot or I will hit you harder," but the second paw stuck as he hit him again. "I have got another foot, stronger than these, and I'll hit you still harder," and the third time he hit the tar-person. "I have got one more foot and I will have to kill you if you don't let go of my feet." He kicked with the last foot and that stuck fast. The Rabbit then struck with his head and it stuck.

Next morning the man came into his garden and, when the Rabbit saw him, he called out "Oh, I have caught the thief who's been stealing your peas. Here he is."

"Yes, I see the thief," replied the man, "and I intend to kill him." Seizing the Rabbit he pulled him away from the tar-person and carried him to a stake near a pigpen. There he securely fastened the Rabbit, saying:

"I will go to the house and get some boiling water and scald you."

As soon as the man had left a Wolf came along and, seeing the Rabbit tied, asked him what it meant.

"Oh, this man wanted me to eat up all these pigs in the pen and because I could not do so he tied me here."

"I can eat them for him," said Wolf, "let me take your place." "All right," responded the Rabbit, so the Wolf untied him and took his place at the stake and was in turn tied by the Rabbit, who ran away and crawled into a hollow tree. When the man returned and saw the Wolf, "So," he said, "you are at your old tricks and have changed yourself so as to look like a wolf. Well, I will scald you anyway." He poured the boiling water on the Wolf, who howled in pain and finally broke the string and ran off. Then he sat at the foot of the very tree in which the Rabbit was concealed and as he licked his scalded hide the Rabbit reached down and stuck a splinter into him. Jumping up, the Wolf exclaimed, "I wish the ants would stop biting me and adding to my afflictions!"

76. RABBIT DECEIVES THE OTHER ANIMALS

THE RABBIT was under arrest and, when brought before the assembled council of all the other animals, he said to them:

"I have a great message to deliver to all of you. God has appeared to me and he has told me that he intends to destroy the world, because you animals are so wicked. The only way for you to escape is to choose me to rule over you to guide you aright. God will destroy the world in a short time if you do not act better."

The animals greeted his speech with laughter. "You are such a great liar," said they, "that we know this is another trick."

"Well, all you have to do is wait and see," replied the Rabbit, with a solemn look.

"We are not afraid of your lies."

The following night, after the council had separated, the Rabbit sought out the king of the Partridges and said to him:

"I have a plan by which you can save me from this trouble and I can be of great service to you. If you will help me I will see that you and your subjects shall have the privilege of roving over the whole world and eating where you will instead of being restricted to one kind of food, as you now are."

"What can I do?" asked the king of the Partridges.

"This. Go and gather all the Partridges into one immense flock and tomorrow, when the council meets, station your subjects to the south of the council ground and, at a certain signal from me, let every Partridge fly into the air and flutter with all his might, and make as much noise as possible."

The king of the Partridges consented.

"On the second day," continued the Rabbit, "carry your subjects to the east of the council ground and act likewise when you see me stand before the council and give the signal. On the third day go to the north, and on the fourth day be in the west, but remember to keep out of sight all the time, and on each day make a louder noise than on the preceding day. Do this and the world shall be your feeding ground."

Then they separated.

The council assembled again and summoned the Rabbit, who came smiling and bowing and said: "I love all of you, and am sorry to know that your wickedness is leading you to destruction. God will not permit such wicked animals to live. Today, I fear, you will hear a warning in the south. If you do not heed it and turn an innocent brother loose, then, tomorrow, the warning will become louder in the east. On the third day the sound of coming down will be heard in the north and, if you still persist in your persecution, a terrible rumbling in the west will precede the world's destruction, and then, on the fifth day, the world will be destroyed."

For this the animals jeered at him and cried, "Oh, what a lie. Tell us another."

Then the Rabbit turned to the south and gave the agreed signal when a strange low, rumbling sound came from that direction.

The animals looked at one another and whispered, "What is that?"

"God's warning," replied the Rabbit.

Some said: "Let's let him go. He may be innocent." Others said, "It's one of his tricks. He is a cunning little rascal."

The second day came, and the Rabbit said, "You are doomed. Today another warning will come from the east." He gave the signal and there was a louder thundering than on the previous day.

Some of the animals became alarmed at this and said, "Perhaps he's speaking the truth this time. Maybe the world will be destroyed."

"It is one of his tricks," said others. "But how can he make such a noise? He is here and the noise is yonder."

The council separated without a decision. On the third day the Rabbit appeared with a solemn air and, when called on, said:

"You still refuse to do me justice. The warning will come to-day from the north." Hardly had he spoken, when there came a tremendous roar, shaking the air and ground, and the animals trembled in terror.

"Let him go, let him go," shouted many to their leaders.

It was decided to wait one day more and if no trick could be discovered the Rabbit should be let go.

On the fourth day the animals came slowly to the council ground and cast fearful looks to the west. The Rabbit, amid profound silence, was led out.

"Alas," said he, "what a fate—all the animals to be destroyed when one act of justice could save them," and suddenly from the west came such a fluttering, buzzing, quivering, shaking roar that all the animals cried aloud:

"Let him go, let him go. He is right. The world will be destroyed."

So they let him go, and away he hopped to the king of the Partridges. "The world is yours," said he, "Go where you will and eat your fill."

Ever since then partridges have roved over the whole world, whereas they had no such privilege before that time.

77. RABBIT ESCAPES FROM THE BOX

THE RABBIT had so often deceived mankind that a council was held to try him and, being found guilty, he was condemned to death by drowning. A box was made and he was put into it, carried to the banks of a stream and left there for a while. A little child came to the box during the absence of the people and, discovering the Rabbit, asked him what he was doing here.

"Oh, I am listening to the sweetest music in the world," said he. "Let me get in there too," begged the child. So the Rabbit told the child how to open the box, and once out and the child fastened in, away he ran to the forest. When the people returned they lifted the box and threw it into the stream and said: "There, we will never be troubled by the Rabbit again." The next busk came, when every criminal is free to return, and hardly had the dancing ground been swept clean when in jumped the Rabbit, all dressed in red, and danced with the pretty girls, while all the people stood amazed.

Did we not drown him?" they said. "We put him in a box and threw him into the water, yet here he is." Being asked how he came back the Rabbit replied: "I am glad you threw me into the water. I did not die, I went to a beautiful country, where there were thousands of pretty girls who begged me to stay, and I am now sorry I came away from them." The young warriors crowded around him and did not tire of hearing of such a lovely land. They begged him to show them the way, and he selected those whom he most envied and told them to prepare boxes in which they could be placed. When all were ready their friends carried them to the stream and the Rabbit ordered them thrown in. Again the busk rolled around and anxious friends awaited the return of the young warriors, but they did not come. At last the boxes were found on an island and in the boxes were the bodies of the ill-fated young men. A little box was also found containing the bones of the child. Then it was known that the Rabbit had deceived them again. On being questioned he said:

"I told you I was the only one who had ever returned from that beautiful country. I warned the warriors, but they would have me show them the way, and no one can be blamed except themselves."

78. RABBIT'S IMPOSITION IS DETECTED

THERE were three pretty girls who lived near a spring. Every day they went to this spring for water. The Rabbit fell in love with them and frequently came to visit them. One day the news came that one of the fair maidens was missing. The alarm was given, but search was made in vain. She could nowhere be found and never came back. It was suspected that the Rabbit had made away with her. Not many mornings afterwards another sister was lost. The same mystery surrounded her fate. She was seen going to the spring but was seen no more. The hand of the third sister was offered as a reward for the discovery of the fate of the two beautiful girls and for the killing of the monster who had destroyed them. Many entered the contest and among them the suspected Rabbit. A warrior watched the spring day after day, and at last saw an enormous serpent crawl forth, as if watching for his prey. He slew the monster, cut off his head, and bore it away as a trophy of victory. But the Rabbit had also seen the monster serpent and after the warrior had departed with the head, he took up the body of the snake and, dragging it to the council ground, exclaimed:

"See the monster! I killed him. I claim the bride."

Everybody congratulated the Rabbit, and the beautiful girl, arrayed in rich costumes, was brought forth. But just as the Rabbit approached to take her hand the warrior stepped within the circle and said:

"Behold, the monster's head. I cut it off after slaying him, and I left his body at the spring. I claim the beautiful bride."

She was given to the brave warrior, and the Rabbit was made to drag about the dead and putrid body of the snake and was also chased away as a tricky rascal, who made his way in the world by deception. "Go and live with the dead snake," they said. "You are corrupt like him."

79. THE FLIGHT TO THE TREE

ONCE THERE was a little boy who lived with his grandmother. He grew up to be very fond of hunting and had three dogs named "Simursitty," "Jeudawson," and "Ben-boten."* His name was "Tookme." He killed many bison and that caused them to hold a council at which two bison agreed to turn themselves into pretty girls and attempt to destroy Tookme. They went one evening to his grandmother's house and, though they made themselves very agreeable, the old lady did not fancy them and warned her grandson against them. The dogs growled at them whenever they came near. As night came on the bison begged Tookme to chain his dogs, for fear they might bite them during the night. He consented and chained them, for they said they could not sleep if the dogs were loose. Tookme was pleased with the girls, but his grandmother insisted that something was wrong. The next morning the girls said they

---

* The names of the dogs in this story may be corruptions, and it has been suggested that they ought to be Pin-Poyer (pin poya), "the turkey destroyer," Cho-arsur (tce asa), "the deer runner," and Nuss-arsur (yanas asa), the buffalo runner."—Tuggle. This seems far-fetched. [Swanton.]

must return to their home and asked Tookme to go with them. "No," said his grandmother, "he can not go." But finally it was agreed that he should go a part of the way to a certain prairie. When they came to this prairie, a herd of bison was feeding there. Suddenly the girls changed to bison, at whose signal the herd surrounded Tookme. In alarm he stuck one of his arrows in the ground, when, behold, it turned into a cotton-wood tree; and Tookme quickly ascended it out of reach of the angry bison. They began to punch at the tree with their horns and continued doing so until it fell. Then Tookme stuck another arrow in the ground and another cottonwood tree shot up in the air, into the branches of which he jumped as the first one was falling. This he repeated until his arrows were all gone, when he threw down his bow and a tall sycamore sprang up. While he was in the sycamore he began to call his dogs:

> Simursitty, come,
> Jeudawson, come,
> Ben-boten, come,
> Come to Tookme,
> Come to Tookme.

The Bison mocked him, saying: "Tookme," "Tookme."

His grandmother was asleep, but the howling of the dogs awakened her, and running to them she saw them trying to break their chains and then she heard the voice of her grandson in the distance:

> Simursitty, come,
> Jeudawson, come,
> Ben-boten, come,
> Come to Tookme,
> Come to Tookme.

She knew he was in danger, so she broke the chains and away flew the faithful dogs. They frightened the bison away and rescued their master.

80. COW AND DOG ARE DISCONTENTED

"I AM UNHAPPY," said the Cow to her Maker, "because I see the sow is more fruitful than I am. Pray make me more fruitful."

God told her to go to a certain fine garden full of vegetables, stay there all night and return the next morning.

She went into the garden, but instead of sleeping she fed on the vegetables all night and destroyed the beautiful garden, and when she went to God in the morning he said to her: "See what destruction you have caused in one night. Were I to grant your request, the world could not furnish food for your progeny. Go and be contented."

The Dog came to God and said: "I am required to fight all kinds of animals, but I am not provided with horns like the cow, or tusks like the hog. I have only short teeth. Make my teeth long."

Then God said: "Go to yonder pile of skins and pass the night; come again in the morning."

The Dog went. During the night he rose and injured the edges of all the skins by gnawing them.

When he came on the morrow his Maker said to him, "Behold what your short teeth have done in one night. Were I to make them longer, great destruction would result."

84. THE ORDERING OF FIELD WORK

AWAY BACK in the first times God lived on the earth with men and he so arranged it that their hoes, plows, and all other tools worked without being guided. All a man had to do was to tell the hoe or plow where he wanted work done and it was done by the tool itself.

One day God was passing a field where some young men were at work clearing the ground. He asked them:

"What will you plant?" Said they, in derision, "Rocks."

When they returned to the field the next morning it was covered with enormous rocks, so then they could plant nothing.

Another time God passed a house of mourning where a man was lying dead in his coffin. He asked: "Why do you mourn?"

"Our friend is dead," sighed they. "He is not dead," said He, and straightway the dead arose.

Some other young men thought they would deceive their Maker. They put one of their number in a coffin and forthwith began to cry aloud. God asked them: "Why do you cry?"

"Because our friend is dead," they said in pretended sadness.

"If he is dead, he is dead," said He, and when the box was opened, lo, their friend was dead.

Some wicked women passed a field where the hoes and plows were at work and said, "See what a foolish way to work."

"Since you are not contented with my plan, henceforth do the work yourselves," said He, and ever since the women have worked the fields.

90. THE CREATION OF THE EARTH*

IN THE BEGINNING the waters covered everything. It was said "Who will make the land appear?"

Lock-chew, the Crawfish, said: "I will make the land appear."

So he went down to the bottom of the water and began to stir up the mud with his tail and hands. He then brought up the mud to a certain place and piled it up.

The owners of the land at the bottom of the water said:

"Who is disturbing our land?" They kept watch and discovered the Crawfish. Then they came near him, but he suddenly stirred the mud with his tail so that they could not see him.

"Lock-chew continued his work. He carried mud and piled it up until at last he held up his hands in the air, and so the land appeared above the water.

The land was soft. It was said: "Who will spread out the land, and make it dry and hard?" Some said: "Ah-yok, the Hawk, should spread out the soft land and make it dry." Others said "Yah-tee, the Buzzard, has larger wings; he can spread out the land and make it dry and hard."

Yah-tee undertook to spread out and dry the earth. He flew above the earth and spread out his long wings over it. He sailed over the earth; he spread it out. After a long while he grew tired of holding out his wings. He began to flap them, and thus he caused the hills and valleys because the dirt was still soft.

"Who will make the light?" it was said. It was very dark.

Yohah, the Star, said, "I will make the light."

It was so agreed. The Star shone forth. It was light only near him.

"Who will make more light?" it was said.

Shar-pah, the Moon, said: "I will make more light." Shar-pah made more light, but it was still dark.

T-cho, the Sun, said: "You are my children, I am your mother, I will make the light. I will shine for you."

She went to the east. Suddenly light spread all over the earth. As she passed over the earth a drop of blood fell from her to the ground, and from

* These names are in the Yuchi language.

this blood and earth sprang the first people, the children of the Sun, the Uchees.

The people wished to find their medicine. A great monster serpent destroyed the people. They cut his head from his body. The next day the body and head were together. They again slew the monster. His head again grew to his body.

Then they cut off his head and placed it on top of a tree, so that the body could not reach it. The next morning the tree was dead and the head was united to the body. They again severed it and put it upon another tree. In the morning the tree was dead and the head and body were reunited.

The people continued to try all the trees in the forest. At last they placed the head over the Tar, the cedar tree, and in the morning the head was dead. The cedar was alive, but covered with blood, which had trickled down from the head.

Thus the Great Medicine was found.

Fire was made by boring with a stick into a hard weed.

The people selected a second family. Each member of this family had engraved on his door a picture of the sun.

In the beginning all the animals could talk, and but one language was used. All were at peace. The deer lived in a cave, watched over by a keeper and the people were hungry. He selected a deer and killed it. But finally the deer were set free and roved over the entire earth.

All animals were set free from man, and names were given to them, so that they could be known.

91. THE MONKEY GIRL*

AN OLD WOMAN lived with her grandson, who was a great hunter. They had a field of corn which the raccoons and monkeys destroyed, and though the young man killed a great many of them, the destruction went on. One day two pretty girls came to see the old lady. She did not like them, but the grandson fell in love with one of them and married her. When he went out to hunt he would ask his wife to watch the corn for him, and every day she went to the field. Strange to say, the corn disappeared faster while she was watching than at other times. Then the youth's grandmother told him to follow his wife and watch her closely

* An African Story.

when she went to the field. He did do and saw her turn into a monkey
and sing a song as follows:

Dungo, dungo
Dar-mar-lee
Co-dingo
Dungo, dungo
Dar-mar-lee
Co-dingo
Dungo, dingo
Co-dingo dingo
Dar-mar-lee
Co-dingo.

While she was singing the monkeys came in troops and destroyed the
corn. The youth returned to his grandmother and told her what he had
seen, whereupon she told him to take his fiddle and play the tune and
sing the song, and when his wife returned to sing it to her.

Oh her return he said to her, "I know a fine song; listen," and he began
her song:

Dungo, dungo
Dar-mar-lee
Co-dingo.

Then she cried, raved, and twisted until she turned into a monkey and
ran away.

APPENDIX C:

BIOGRAPHICAL INDEX

The following names are mentioned in Tuggle's Indian Diary and Washington Journal.

ALLISON, William Boyd (1829–1908). Congressman from Iowa (1863–1871). U.S. senator (1872–1908). Allison was one of the most influential Republican senators in the latter part of the nineteenth century.

ANDERSON, Mary (1859–1940). Starred in *Evadne* with some apprehension, but the play was a success. In 1890 she retired from the stage and soon married M. Antonio Navarro.

ARMSTRONG, Frank C. (1835–1909). After service with the Confederate army at the end of the Civil War, Armstrong served as a U.S. Indian inspector and later as an assistant commissioner of Indian affairs.

ARTHUR, Chester Alan (1830–1886). President of the United States (1881–1885). Arthur had been a member of Roscoe Conkling's political machine in New York state as collector for the port of New York. Arthur was removed by Pres. R. B. Hayes. Conkling's Stalwart faction of the Republican party was pacified in 1880 by having Arthur chosen to run for vice-president with James A. Garfield. Arthur became president after Garfield's assassination. As president he deserted the spoilsmen Stalwarts by supporting civil service reform.

AUDUBON, John James (1785–1851). Famed Haitian-born artist whose love of nature caused him to prepare a volume of colored plates called *The Birds of America* (1827–1838) and an accompanying text, *Ornithological Biography* (1831–1839). In collaboration with John Bachman,

325

Audubon produced *The Viviparous Quadrupeds of North America* in two volumes (1842–1845) and a three-volume text (1846–1854).

AVERY, Isaac Wheeler (1837–1897). Served as a colonel in the Confederate army and was severely wounded during the war. During Reconstruction Avery was active in Georgia politics and journalism. He was editor in chief of the *Atlanta Constitution* for a time. In 1881 he wrote his *History of the State of Georgia from 1850 to 1881.*

BACON, Augustus Octavius (1839–1914). Democratic U.S. senator from Georgia (1895–1914). Bacon lacked but one vote in the 1883 Georgia Democratic convention to receive the nomination for the governorship.

BAILEY, James Edmund (1822–1885). U.S. senator from Tennessee (1877–1881). Bailey, a Democrat, had been appointed to his seat to fill a vacancy.

BANCROFT, George (1800–1891). Most renowned American historian of the nineteenth century. All of his writings are marked by a pronounced patriotism.

BANCROFT, Hubert Howe (1832–1918). Publisher and writer. *Native Races* took eighteen years to prepare (1871–1889) and was published over the period of 1875 to 1890. Bancroft owned a publishing house in San Francisco.

BARNES, George Thomas (1833–1901). Lawyer and Democratic congressman from Georgia (1885–1891). In 1880 Barnes was a member of the National Democratic Executive Committee.

BARROW, Middleton Pope (1839–1903). A Democrat. Elected by the Georgia legislature (1882–1883) to fill the unexpired term of Sen. B. H. Hill.

BAYARD, Thomas Francis (1828–1898). U.S. senator from New York (1869–1885). Secretary of state in Cleveland's cabinet in 1885, Bayard was a candidate for the Democratic nomination in 1880 and 1884. His considerable support came from his advocacy of civil service reform and of a sound currency. He opposed the issuance of greenbacks as currency and favored only "a currency of value"—the gold and silver coin directed by the Constitution.

BECK, James Burnie (1822–1890). Democratic U.S. senator from Kentucky (1877–1890).

BENTON, Thomas Hart (1782–1858). Democratic U.S. senator from Missouri (1821–1850). Congressman (1850–1856). Benton died of cancer in 1858 just after his house with all of his papers burned.

BLAINE, James Gillespie (1830–1893). Member of the House of Representatives from Maine (1863–1876). Speaker of the House (1869–1876). U.S. senator (1876–1881). Blaine led the Half-Breed faction of the Republican party. This group favored civil service reform and conciliation of the South. Blaine was the popular "plumed knight" of the party and tried for the presidential nomination in 1876 and in 1880. Each time he had to bear the burden of the Mulligan Letters which purported to link Blaine with a railroad fraud and scandal. The 1880 ticket was a compromise between Blaine and Conkling. James A. Garfield, a friend of Blaine's, got the presidential nomination while Stalwart Chester Arthur became the vice-presidential nominee. Garfield appointed Blaine secretary of state, but Blaine resigned in 1881 after Garfield's assassination. Blaine won his party's nomination in 1884 but lost the presidency to Grover Cleveland.

BLOUNT, James Henderson (1837–1903). Democratic member of the House of Representatives from Georgia (1873–1893). Blount was chairman of the Committee on Post Office and Post Roads and the Committee on Foreign affairs. He is remembered chiefly as President Cleveland's special commissioner to Hawaii, whose report largely determined the policy against annexation.

BOTELIER, Helen Macomb Stockton. Wife (m. 1836) of Alexander Robinson Botelier (1815–1892), assistant attorney in the U.S. Department of Justice.

BOUTWELL, George Sewall (1818–1905). Republican politician from Massachusetts. Boutwell helped organize the party in Massachusetts. As a member of Congress (1863–1869) he led in the impeachment proceedings against President Johnson. Boutwell served as Grant's secretary of the treasury (1869–1877).

BREWSTER, Benjamin Harris (1816–1888). President Arthur's attorney general of the United States (1881–1885). Brewster is best remembered for his prosecution of the Star Route frauds.

BRIDGER, James (1804–1881). Most famous of the "mountain men," trappers and traders of the Rocky Mountains between 1822 and 1845. The Virginia-born trailblazer and explorer discovered the Great Salt Lake, acted as a guide for the Bonneville explorations, and surveyed the Bozeman Trail. His success was greatly aided by his knowledge of Indian languages.

BROKMEYER, Henry C. (1828–1906). Attorney for the Gould railroads in the 1880s. An expert hunter, Brokmeyer was called the "Great White Father" by the Creek Indians.

BROWN, Joseph Emerson (1821–1894). Civil War governor of Georgia. After the war Brown switched to the Republican party and was appointed chief justice of the Georgia Supreme Court (1868–1870). In 1870 Brown retired to become president of the Western and Atlantic Railroad Company. In 1871 he switched back to the Democratic party. Governor Colquitt appointed Brown to the U.S. Senate where he served from 1880 until 1891. Brown was a member of the Gordon-Colquitt-Brown triumvirate which ruled Georgia. Brown was the least liked of that group because of his seemingly opportunistic Republican affiliations during Reconstruction.

BRUCE, Blanche K. (1841–1898). Republican U.S. senator from Mississippi (1875–1881). He was raised as a slave and was tutored by his master's son. At the beginning of the Civil War Bruce claimed his freedom. He later attended Oberlin College, Oberlin, Ohio. Bruce served creditably in the Senate and concentrated mostly on issues concerning election frauds, southern disorders, and civil rights.

BUCHANAN, Hugh (1823–1890). Democratic congressman from Georgia (1881–1885).

BUTLER, Benjamin Franklin (1818–1893). Union soldier, congressman, and governor of Massachusetts. Butler commanded the forces which occupied New Orleans (1862–1863). Butler served in Congress (1867–1875) and took the lead in the impeachment proceedings against President Johnson.

BUTLER, Matthew Galbraith (1836–1909). Democratic U.S. senator from South Carolina (1877–1895). Butler was also involved in a disputed election in 1876 whereby a rival South Carolina legislature dominated by the Republicans sent D. T. Corbin to the U.S. Senate. The Senate decided to seat Butler through the secret influence of Senator Cameron of

Pennsylvania, who was repaying a debt of kindness that had been rendered by Butler's uncle to Cameron's father.

CARPENTER, Matthew Hale (1824–1881). Republican U.S. senator from Wisconsin (1869–1875, 1879–1881). Carpenter was a Stalwart supporter of Grant and Conkling.

CARSON, Christopher (Kit) (1809–1868). Trapper, guide, Indian agent, and scout. During the Civil War he fought for the Union in the Southwest. In Texas in 1864 with a force of four hundred men he attacked three to five thousand Kiowas and Comanches but was compelled to withdraw.

CARTER, Henry Alpheus Pierce (1837–1891). Carter worked diligently to protect Hawaiian sugar producers as minister from Hawaii (1883–1891).

CASS, Lewis (1782–1866). Secured the Democratic nomination for the presidency in 1848 but lost the election.

CATLIN, George (1796–1872). Artist and author. From 1829 to 1838 Catlin painted some six hundred portraits of distinguished Indians.

CHANDLER, William Eaton (1835–1917). U.S. senator from New Hampshire (1887–1901). Secretary of the navy (1882–1885). Chandler was secretary of the Republican National Committee and active in the 1868, 1872, 1876, and 1880 presidential campaigns. He refused to concede victory to Tilden in the disputed election of 1876 and was counsel for the Florida electors favorable to Hayes before the Electoral Commission. In 1880 Chandler led the Blaine faction against Grant for the nomination. Chandler eventually supported Garfield and was nominated for solicitor general in 1881. The Senate refused to confirm him.

CHEPETA. Wife of Ute chief Ouray. Chepeta married Ouray in 1859 and survived his death (1880) by thirty years.

CLAY, Henry (1777–1852). Henry Clay served the United States well as congressman and senator from Kentucky and as secretary of state under Pres. John Quincy Adams. Clay was known as the "Great Compromiser" because of his major roles in the Missouri Compromise, the Compromise of 1833, and the Compromise of 1850. Clay ran for the presidency as a Whig on numerous occasions but failed ever to win.

CLEMENTS, Judson Claudius (1846–1917). Democratic congressman from Georgia (1881–1891).

CLYMER, Hiester (1827–1884). Democratic congressman from Pennsylvania (1873–1881).

COBB, Howell (1815–1868). Democratic congressman from Georgia (1843–1857). Secretary of the treasury under Pres. James Buchanan (1857–1861). Confederate general in the Civil War.

COCKRELL, Francis Marion (1834–1915). Confederate soldier and Democratic U.S. senator from Missouri (1875–1905).

COKE, Richard (1829–1897). Democratic governor of Texas (1874–1876) and U.S. senator (1876–1895). As governor of Texas Coke was not known to be sympathetic toward Indians.

COLLAMER, Jacob (1791–1865). Republican U.S. senator from Vermont (1856–1865). In 1861, Collamer introduced the bill which granted President Lincoln his war-making powers in dealing with the rebellion.

COLQUITT, Alfred Holt (1824–1894). Democratic Governor of Georgia (1877–1883). In 1880 John B. Gordon resigned from the U.S. Senate. Colquitt appointed ex-Gov. Joseph E. Brown to finish out Gordon's term. Brown was generally detested by Georgians at this time, and the cry of bargain and corruption was raised. Supposedly Gordon resigned in return for a promise of the presidency of the state-owned Western and Atlantic Railroad, then under the control of Brown. Brown would then support Colquitt in return for being named senator. This triumvirate ruled the state. Colquitt was appointed in 1883 to fill the unexpired term of Sen. B. H. Hill, who died in office. Colquitt remained in the Senate until his death in 1894.

COLQUITT, Walter Terry (1799–1855). Colquitt served in the United States House of Representatives (1839–1842) and the United States Senate (1842–1848). He was also a Methodist preacher and an impressive speaker. His son was Alfred H. Colquitt.

CONKLING, Roscoe (1829–1888). U.S. senator from New York (1867–1881). Conkling led the Stalwart faction of the Republican party. He disliked President Hayes because Hayes had appointed William Evarts as secretary of state. Conkling hated his fellow New Yorker Evarts because of his defense of President Johnson during the impeachment proceedings. Furthermore Conkling regarded New York as his private preserve and felt that any appointments of New Yorkers should have his approval. Conkling resigned from the Senate in 1881 over the issue of his control of New York patronage.

COOK, Philip (1817–1894). Lawyer, Confederate soldier, and Democratic congressman (1873–1883).

COOPER, Peter (1791–1883). Philanthropist. Cooper built Cooper Union (or Cooper Institute) in New York City to advance science and art.

COX, Samuel Sullivan (1824–1889). Democratic congressman from Ohio (1857–1889). Cox earned the nickname "Sunset" after he had written a particularly glowing account of a sunset while serving as editor of the *Ohio Statesman*. His wife was the former Julia A. Buckingham and reportedly the couple was inseparable.

CRANE, William Henry (1845–1928). Acting partner of Stuart Robson (1877–1889). Crane's career included at least two motion pictures made before his death in 1928.

CRAWFORD, Martin Jenkins (1820–1883). Associate justice of the Georgia Supreme Court (1880–1883).

CRAWFORD, Samuel Johnson (1835–1913). Governor of Kansas (1865–1868). Crawford spent the last half-century of his life in Washington as claim agent for his state.

CRITTENDEN, John Jordan (1787–1863). U.S. senator from Kentucky (1817–1819, 1835–1840). Attorney general in the administration of Pres. William Henry Harrison (1841). Crittenden returned to the U.S. Senate and served from 1842 to 1848 and 1855 to 1861. Before the outbreak of the Civil War Crittenden tried to prevent the breakup of the Union by bringing forth a compromise, but his propositions failed.

CUNNINGHAM, Ann Pamela (1816–1875). Best remembered for her successful efforts to preserve Mount Vernon, George Washington's home, for posterity.

CUSTER, George Armstrong (1839–1876). Custer was a brash commander of Union Cavalry during the Civil War. In 1876 he and his entire command were massacred at the Little Big Horn.

DALLAS, George Mifflin (1792–1864). Democratic vice-president of the United States (1845–1849) under Pres. James K. Polk. Dallas broke the tie over the Walker tariff in 1846 by voting for the bill.

DAVIS, David (1815–1886). Justice of the Supreme Court of the United States (1862–1877). U.S. senator from Illinois (1877–1883). Davis had roots in both the Democratic and Republican parties. Democrats in the Senate were upset when he left the bench to enter the Senate. They had supported the Electoral Commission Bill because they felt Davis would be the Court's fifth member on the fifteen member Electoral Commission to decide the disputed votes in the Hayes-Tilden election. Davis was re-placed on the commission by a Republican who voted for Hayes, thus insuring his victory.

DAVIS, Henry Gassaway (1823–1916). U.S. senator from West Virginia (1871–1883). Davis, a Republican, retired from the Senate in order to devote his attention to his numerous railroad interests.

DAWES, Henry Laurens (1816–1903). U.S. senator from Massachusetts (1875–1892). Dawes's most enduring work was accomplished as chair-man of the Committee on Indian Affairs. He was the author of the Dawes Act of 1887 which conferred citizenship upon the Indians and made land grants available to them.

DEERING, Nathaniel Cobb (1827–1887). Republican congressman from Iowa (1877–1883).

DELANO, Columbus (1809–1896). Republican congressman from Ohio (1845–1847, 1865–1869). From 1870 until 1875 Delano served as Presi-dent Grant's secretary of the interior. During his tenure charges of fraud in the Bureau of Indian Affairs became public.

DE SOTO, Hernando (1500–1542). Spanish explorer who discovered the Mississippi River. He was buried in the river.

DILLON, Sidney (1812–1892). President of the Union Pacific Rail-road (1874–1884, 1890–1892).

DODGE, William Earl (1805–1883). Wealthy wholesale goods mer-chant and philanthropist. President of the National Temperance Society (1865–1883).

DORSEY, Stephen Wallace (1842–1916). Republican U.S. senator from Ohio (1873–1879). As a senator Dorsey introduced several bills and reso-lutions concerning the Post Office. Later he and T. W. Brady, second assistant postmaster general, were indicted in the Star Route frauds for conspiring to defraud the government of nearly one-half million dollars. His first trial ended with a hung jury, and he was acquitted in the second.

DRAKE, Charles Daniel (1811–1892). President Grant appointed Drake chief justice of the U.S. Court of Claims (1870–1885).

EADS, James Buchanan (1820–1887). Eads was a gifted inventor and engineer. He built armored gunboats during the Civil War. In 1874 Eads proposed to Congress a way to open one of the mouths of the Mississippi River into the gulf and keep it open. His plan was attacked as ridiculous by army engineers. Eads succeeded however by constructing a system of jetties so arranged that the river deposited its sediments where he wanted them. Eads's counterproposal to Ferdinand de Lesseps's canal was a railroad across Mexico. A bill embodying his suggestion passed the House but failed in the Senate.

EDMUNDS, George Franklin (1828–1919). Republican U.S. senator from Vermont (1866–1891). Edmunds proposed the act whereby the Electoral Commission was established to oversee the counting of the votes for president and vice-president in the disputed Hayes-Tilden election of 1876.

FARLEY, James Thompson (1829–1886). Democratic U.S. senator from California (1879–1885).

FELTON, Rebecca Latimer (1835–1930). Writer, Democratic U.S. senator (1922), and wife of William H. Felton. She was appointed to the Senate by Georgia Gov. Thomas W. Hardwick to fill the seat left vacant at the death of Thomas E. Watson. She has the distinction of being the first woman to occupy a seat in the U.S. Senate. Mrs. Felton castigated many Georgians in her well-known book *My Memoirs of Georgia Politics* (1911).

FELTON, William Harrell (1823–1909). Physician and politician. Felton became a Democrat after the Civil War but ran successfully for Congress as an independent in 1874. He served in Congress from 1875 to 1881. He led an independent movement in Georgia politics. In January 1882 Dr. Felton wrote to Georgia's U.S. Senator Hill vowing to fight the Bourbon Democrats in Georgia to the death. To accomplish this end Felton claimed "for every man, white and colored, the right to vote a free ticket and to have that vote counted."

FILLMORE, Millard (1800–1874). Thirteenth president of the United States (1850–1853).

FISH, Hamilton (1808–1893). Secretary of state in President Grant's administration (1869–1877).

FISK, Clinton Bowen (1828–1890). Fought in Arkansas and Missouri as a general with the Missouri volunteers. Fisk worked with the Freedmen's Bureau after the war and founded Fisk University for Negroes in 1867. In 1874 Fisk was appointed by President Grant as president of the Board of Indian Commissioners (1874–1890). Fisk voted Republican until 1884 when he supported the Prohibition party.

FRYE, William Pierce (1831–1911). Frye was a political protégé of Senator Blaine of Maine and succeeded Blaine in the U.S. Senate in 1881.

GARFIELD, James Abram (1831–1881). Union soldier, congressman from Ohio, and Republican president of the United States (1881). Garfield was the compromise candidate in 1880, but the convention did succeed in antagonizing the Conkling Stalwarts who retaliated by electing Chester Arthur as the vice-presidential nominee. Garfield was shot by Charles Guiteau on July 2, 1881, and died in September. Guiteau was a disappointed office seeker and a self-proclaimed Stalwart.

GEORGE, Henry (1839–1897). Published *Progress and Poverty* in 1879 in which he urged a "Single Tax" on the unearned increment on land as a means of financing the government and relieving economic distress. In 1886 he ran for mayor of New York City and came in second.

GOLDSBOROUGH, Elizabeth Wirt. Wife (m. 1833) of naval officer Louis Malesherbes Goldsborough (1805–1877).

GORDON, John Brown (1832–1904). U.S. senator from Georgia (1873–1880). Gordon was a member of the triumvirate which included Joseph E. Brown and Alfred H. Colquitt. The three men rotated offices and ruled Georgia and the Georgia Democratic party during the 1880s and 1890s. Gordon was governor from 1886 to 1890, and he reentered the Senate in 1891 and served until 1897.

GOULD, Jay (1836–1892). Railroad financier. Gould owned one-half of all the railroad mileage in the Southwest.

GRADY, Henry Woodfin (1850–1889). Editor of the *Atlanta Constitution* (1879–1889). Grady was the South's most eloquent spokesman for the New South, a term which he popularized.

GRANT, Ulysses Simpson (1822–1885). General of the armies and president of the United States (1869–1877). Hamilton Fish served ably as Grant's secretary of state, but other "friends" of the president used Grant's friendship to turn his administration into one of the most scandalous ever. Grant's successor in 1877, R. B. Hayes, got rid of many of the spoilsmen Stalwarts who had enjoyed the protection of President Grant. His friends urged him to try for a third term in 1880, but the Republican convention at Chicago went for James A. Garfield. In retirement Grant had to live on the income from a two-hundred-fifty-thousand-dollar fund raised by his friends. He went bankrupt in the brokerage business and died of cancer just after completing his memoirs.

GROSS, Samuel David (1805–1884). Gross was one of the greatest surgeons of his time and one of the founders of the American Medical Association.

GUITEAU, Charles Julius (1840–1882). Hanged in 1882 for the assassination of Pres. James A. Garfield, Guiteau, who claimed to be a Stalwart, tried to secure an office in the federal government but was rebuffed. He shot Garfield because he was incensed at the president's civil service stand. With Garfield out of the way, Arthur, a Stalwart, would become president.

GUNTER, T. M. (1826–1898). Democratic congressman from Arkansas (1873–1881).

HALE, Eugene (1836–1918). Republican congressman from Maine 1869–1879). Hale turned down cabinet positions on two occasions. He declined the post of postmaster general in 1874 under Grant, and he refused to serve as Hayes's secretary of the navy.

HALE, Sir Matthew (1609–1676). English judge who presided at the witchcraft trial of Amy Drury and Rose Callender.

HALL, John Iredell (1841–1913). Member of the Georgia House of Representatives (1879–1888).

HAMLIN, Hannibal (1809–1891). Vice-president of the United States during the Civil War (1861–1865) and Republican U.S. senator from Maine (1869–1881).

HAMMOND, Nathaniel Job (1833–1899). Graduated with honors from the University of Georgia in 1852. Served as solicitor general of the Atlanta Circuit during the Civil War. In 1879 he entered Congress as a Democrat and served from 1879 to 1887. For twenty-five years Hammond served on the board of trustees of the University of Georgia and championed the cause of that institution at a time when it was unpopular.

HAMPTON, Wade (1818–1902). Democratic U.S. senator from South Carolina (1878–1891). Hampton "redeemed" South Carolina for white supremacy with his election to the governorship in 1876.

HANCOCK, Winfield Scott (1824–1886). Presidential nominee of the Democratic party in 1880. Hancock had served with distinction as a Union general in the Civil War. His status as a military hero qualified him for the nomination. He was narrowly defeated by James A. Garfield.

HARRISON, William Pope (1830–1895). Clergyman of the Methodist Episcopal church, South. In 1877 Harrison served as chaplain to the House of Representatives. From 1878 until 1882 he pastored Mount Vernon Place Church in Washington. His last position was that of book editor for the general conference. Harrison was an excellent preacher and did much to popularize churchgoing.

HASKELL, Dudley Chase (1842–1883). Republican congressman from Kansas (1877–1883). Haskell worked for the establishment of Indian schools which he saw as the solution to the Indian problem.

HAYS, John Coffee (1817–1883). Known as "Texas Jack," he was an Indian fighter in the military service of the Republic of Texas who also served in the Mexican War. He advanced quickly in the military and won large repute because of his courage and success in battle.

HAYES, Rutherford Birchard (1822–1893). President of the United States (1877–1881). Hayes, Blaine, and Conkling were rivals for the Republican nomination in 1876. Hayes was nominated and received the support of Blaine's Half-Breed faction of the party in the campaign. The Half-Breeds were known to favor some civil service reform and conciliation of the South. Reformers like Carl Schurz were pleased by the Hayes nomination. In the election of 1876, neither Hayes nor Tilden received a majority of the electoral votes. Congress authorized the appointment of an Electoral Commission of fifteen members (five each from the Senate, House of Representatives, and Supreme Court). The electoral votes from the disputed states of Florida, South Carolina, and Louisiana were awarded to Hayes by partisan votes of eight Republicans to seven Democrats. Southern Democrats in Congress united with northern Republicans to approve the vote of the commission. Hayes was declared president, and after his inauguration removed federal troops from the South, thus ending Reconstruction. Hayes antagonized Conkling and his Stalwarts by removing Chester A. Arthur from his post as collector of the port of New

York. Hayes served only one term. He had antagonized too many party leaders to hope ever to secure his party's nomination again.

HEREFORD, Frank (1825–1891). Democratic U.S. senator from West Virginia (1877–1881).

HILL, Benjamin Harvey (1823–1882). U.S. senator from Georgia (1877–1882). Hill belonged at various times before the Civil War to the Constitutional Union party and the Know-Nothing party. He ran for governor against Joseph E. Brown in 1857 but was defeated. He opposed secession but participated in the Confederate government after secession. In Congress, he championed the South. He was the object of Dr. Felton's letter. Hill died of a cancer on the tongue in 1882.

HILL, Benjamin Harvey, Jr. (1849–1922). Son of Sen. B. H. Hill and solicitor general of the Atlanta circuit (1877–1885).

HOAR, George Frisbie (1826–1904). U.S. senator from Massachusetts (1877–1904). Hoar was a Republican member of the Electoral Commission which decided the Hayes-Tilden election.

HOLSEY, Lucius Henry (1842–1920). Bishop of the Colored Methodist Episcopal church (1872–1920). Bishop Holsey had been the slave of Georgia planter James Holsey, who was his father.

HUNTER, Robert Mercer Taliaferro (1809–1887). Secretary of state of the Confederacy (1861–1862) and Confederate senator (1862–1865). Hunter participated with Alexander H. Stephens in the Hampton Roads conference with Abraham Lincoln in 1865.

HUNTINGTON, Collis Potter (1821–1900). Builder of the Central Pacific and Southern Pacific railroads.

HUTCHINS, Stilson (1838–1912). Founder in 1877 of the *Washington Post*.

INGALLS, John James (1833–1900). Republican U.S. senator from Kansas (1873–1891).

INGERSOLL, Robert Green (1833–1899). Best known as the "great agnostic." As a lawyer he was noted for his skill in debate. As a lecturer he preached the doctrine of agnosticism. Ingersoll was the attorney for former Senator Dorsey and others charged in the Star Route scandal. Ingersoll succeeded in obtaining a verdict of acquittal.

JACKSON, Howell Edmunds (1832–1895). Democratic U.S. senator from Tennessee (1881–1886). Jackson had not been a candidate for the Senate seat, but he was nominated for it by a Republican member of the state legislature in order to end a deadlock in that body.

JANAUSCHEK, Franziska Magdalena Romance (1830–1904). Actress born in Bohemia but made America her home in 1880.

JOHNSON, Bradley Tyler (1829–1903). Confederate general during the Civil War. After the war Johnson served in the Virginia senate (1875–1879), and from 1879 to 1890 he practiced law in Baltimore.

JOHNSON, Herschel Vespasian (1812–1880). Johnson served as judge of the Middle Circuit (1873–1880). He had been Democratic governor of Georgia (1853–1857) and a Confederate senator (1862–1865). In 1866 he was elected to the U.S. Senate but was denied his seat.

JOHNSTON, Richard Malcolm (1822–1898). Johnston began writing because of the encouragement of Sidney Lanier. Johnston's *Dukesboro Tales* (1871) are rich in humor and local color.

JONES, George Wallace (1804–1896). Democratic U.S. senator from Iowa (1848–1860).

KELLEY, John (1821–1886). Kelley was instrumental in ousting the Tweed Ring from Tammany Hall (1871).

KELLOGG, William Pitt (1830–1918). Republican U.S. Senator from Louisiana (1868–1872, 1877–1883). Governor of Louisiana (1873–1877). Member of the House of Representatives (1883–1885).

KENDALL, Amos (1789–1869). Journalist and supporter of Andrew Jackson. Jackson appointed him fourth auditor of the treasury and later postmaster general. He was a member of Jackson's "kitchen cabinet" of influential advisors. In 1843 he earned a living as an agent for the collection of claims against the government. He would assist the Cherokee Indians in one of their successful claims.

KERNAN, Francis (1816–1892). Democratic U.S. senator from New York (1875–1881).

KIRKWOOD, Samuel Jordan (1813–1894). Secretary of the interior during Garfield's short administration and for only a few months thereafter (1881–1882).

LAMAR, Gazaway Bugg (1798–1874). Cotton merchant and blockade runner during the Civil War. When Sherman took Savannah, Lamar took the oath of allegiance to the United States in order to save his property. He retained Gen. Benjamin F. Butler to press his claims against the government.

LAMAR, Lucius Quintus Cincinnatus (1825–1893). Mississippi statesman, Democratic U.S. senator, and associate justice of the Supreme Court. Lamar served in the Senate (1877–1885). He favored the New South image. To demonstrate his belief in reconciliation between North and South Lamar eulogized Massachusetts Sen. Charles Sumner, a leader of radical Reconstruction policies in Congress.

LANGTRY, Lillie (1853–1929). British actress and celebrated beauty. She was one of the first society women ever to go on the stage, thereby creating quite a sensation.

LEE, John Doyle (1812–1877). Mormon elder, notorious for his part in the Mountain Meadows Massacre in 1857 whereby a regiment of federal troops were killed by a group of Mormons and Indians. Lee was tried twice and convicted the second time of first-degree murder. He was executed (1877) on the spot where the massacre had taken place nearly twenty years before.

LEFT HAND. Arapaho chief who survived the infamous Sand Creek massacre of Colonel Chivington in 1864.

LESSEPS, Ferdinand de (1805–1894). Builder of the Suez Canal (1869). De Lesseps tried unsuccessfully to win American support for a Panama canal. In 1889 de Lesseps's canal company went bankrupt.

LIEBER, Francis (1800–1872). German-born political scientist who migrated to the United States in 1827. Professor at Columbia University (1857–1872).

LINCOLN, Robert Todd (1843–1926). Eldest and only surviving child of Pres. Abraham Lincoln. He was appointed secretary of war by President Garfield in 1880.

LOCKWOOD, Belva Ann Bennett (1830–1917). Lawyer and suffragist. Lockwood was the first woman admitted to practice before the Supreme Court, and she specialized in claims against the government. She centered her life around the struggle for women's rights.

LOGAN, John Alexander (1826–1886). Union soldier and U.S. senator from Illinois (1871–1877, 1879–1886). Logan was a Stalwart Republican who associated himself with all matters of veteran relief.

LONE WOLF. Kiowa chieftain who battled the U.S. Cavalry in the vicinity of Fort Sill in the Indian Territory of Oklahoma. Lone Wolf surrendered in 1875 and died a few years later of malaria which he had contracted while a prisoner in Florida.

McCARTHY, Justin (1830–1912). Irish novelist and statesman. Mc-Carthy wrote *History of Our Own Times* (1877) just before entering Parliament in 1879.

McCAY, Henry Kent (1820–1886). Judge of the District Court of the United States for the Northern District of Georgia (1882–1886).

McDONALD, Joseph Ewing (1819–1891). Democratic U.S. senator from Indiana (1875–1881).

MAHONE, William (1826–1895). Railroad president, Confederate soldier, and U.S. senator from Virginia on the Readjuster ticket (1880–1889). Mahone organized an independent political movement in Virginia known as the Readjusters which favored a scaling down of the state's huge debt. In the Senate he sided with the northern Republicans and thereby was accused of being a traitor to the South and to the Democratic party.

MAYNARD, Horace (1814–1882). An unsuccessful Republican politician in Tennessee. He repaid his constituents by using the power of patronage granted to him as Hayes's postmaster general (1880–1881).

MEREDITH, George (1828–1909). English novelist and poet who claimed to have never written a word for the public yet became furious when his works failed to please the public.

MITCHELL, John Hipple (1835–1905). Republican U.S. senator from Oregon (1872–1878, 1885–1897). Mitchell had trouble throughout his career because of his Pennsylvania "past." He had married Sadie Hoon in Pennsylvania and had fathered her two children. In 1860 he went to Oregon and changed his name to Mitchell. There he married a Mattie Price and had six children by her.

MORGAN, John Hunt (1825–1864). Confederate raider during the Civil War. Morgan raided northern states and was captured in Ohio. He escaped from Ohio State Penitentiary in Columbus, Ohio, but was surprised and killed in 1864.

MORRISON, William Ralls (1824–1909). Congressman from Illinois (1873–1887) and chairman of the Interstate Commerce Commission (1892–1897). Morrison was mentioned on several occasions as a possible Democratic presidential nominee. He failed to obtain support because of his advocacy of bimetallism.

MURROW, Joseph Samuel (1835–1929). Missionary to the Indians. In 1872 he organized the Choctaw and Chickasaw Baptist Association. He began mission work among Indians largely through John McIntosh, the native Indian preacher.

NORWOOD, Thomas Manson (1830–1913). Democratic U.S. senator from Georgia (1871–1877). In 1880 Norwood ran for governor but was defeated by Alfred H. Colquitt.

O'CONNOR, Michael Patrick (1831–1881). Democratic congressman from South Carolina (1879–1881).

OURAY (1833–1880). Head chief of the Utes (1863–1880). Ouray discouraged violence, but he always defended the interests of his people.

PECK, George Record (1843–1923). U.S. attorney for the District of Kansas (1874–1879). Peck's most notable achievement in this office was the winning of the Osage Ceded Land Case.

PENDLETON, George Hunt (1825–1889). Democratic U.S. senator from Ohio (1879–1885). Pendleton is best remembered for lending his name to the civil service reform act in 1883.

PENN, William (1644–1718). Founder of Pennsylvania (1681) and Quaker divine. Penn's finest achievement was in the area of Indian affairs. Several treaties between Penn and the Indians have been idealized under the one heading of Penn's Treaty made under an elm tree at Shackamaxon. The treaty was kept with great fidelity by both sides as long as Penn lived. His heirs, however, did not keep faith and violated the treaty.

PERSONS, Henry (1834–1910). One-term Democratic congressman from Georgia (1879–1881).

PICKETT, Albert James (1810–1858). Historian. Pickett's chief work was his *History of Alabama and Incidentally of Georgia and Mississippi from the Earliest Period* (1851).

PORTER, Albert Gallatin (1824–1897). Governor of Indiana (1881–1885).

PORTER, Fitz-John (1822–1901). Union army general in the Civil War. During the Second Battle of Bull Run in the summer of 1862, Porter commanded a corps in General Pope's new Army of Virginia. Pope engaged Stonewall Jackson's troops at Bull Run. Pope hoped to crush Jackson before he could join Lee's forces. Porter's corps was to attack Jackson on August 29, cutting him off from Longstreet and thus insuring Jackson's defeat. Porter did not attack until August 30, when it was too late. Porter was cashiered in 1863 after his court-martial for his failure in this maneuver. His case was reopened in 1879, and in 1886 he won vindication.

POWELL, John Wesley (1834–1902). Director of the new Bureau of Ethnology (1879–1902) in the Smithsonian Institution. Powell had charge of all anthropological investigations.

PRATT, Parley Parker (1807–1857). Mormon apostle. Pratt was murdered for alienation of affections. Before the escapade which cost him his life, Pratt tried to give one of his wives to an Indian chief in exchange for ten horses.

PRICE, Hiram (1814–1901). Commissioner of Indian affairs (1881–1885).

RANDALL, James Ryder (1839–1908). Poet and journalist. Editor of the Augusta, Ga., *Constitutionalist*. Randall served as secretary to Rep. W. H. Fleming and later to Sen. Joseph E. Brown.

RANDOLPH, Theodore Fitz (1826–1883). Democratic U.S. senator from New Jersey (1875–1881).

RANSOM, Matt Whitaker (1826–1904). Democratic U.S. senator from North Carolina (1872–1895). Ransom was a leader in securing the Compromise of 1876 and 1877.

RED CLOUD (1822–1909). Chief of the Oglala Sioux. Red Cloud visited Washington in 1870 and opposed war in 1876. Before he left the warpath he had made a record of eighty individual feats of courage.

REID, Whitelaw (1837–1912). Editor of the *New York Tribune* (1869–1888).

RICHARDSON, Francis Henry (1855–1904). Washington correspondent of the *Atlanta Constitution* (1880–1887).

ROBERTSON, Ann Eliza Worcester. Wife of W. S. Robertson and daughter of the Rev. Samuel A. Worcester, a missionary to the Cherokees. Worcester is best remembered for the Supreme Court decision which bears his name—*Worcester* v. *Georgia* (1832). Chief Justice John Marshall ruled that the laws of Georgia did not apply to the Cherokee Nation.

ROBERTSON, Edward White (1823–1887). Democratic congressman from Louisiana (1877–1883).

ROBERTSON, William Schenck (1820–1881). Pioneer educator among the Indians. Robertson published a Creek language newspaper called *Our Monthly.* For years he was interested in the work of the Indian international fair held annually at Muskogee. In his later years he began the translation of the New Testament into the Creek language.

ROBSON, Stuart (1836–1903). Robson was an actor and comedian noted for his odd voice and quaint personality. In 1877 he began a long association with William H. Crane at the Park Theater in New York which lasted until 1889.

ROSS, William Potter (1820–1891). Cherokee Indian leader and nephew of John Ross, the great Cherokee chief. William Ross was the first editor (in 1844) of the *Cherokee Advocate.* Ross was active in the Okmulgee intertribal councils which were held from 1870 to 1878. On two occasions he served as principal chief of the Cherokees (1866–1867, 1873–1875).

ST. JOHN, John Pierce (1833–1916). Governor of Kansas (1879–1883). St. John believed in prohibition and favoritism for railroad corporations.

SAULSBURY, Eli (1817–1893). Democratic U.S. senator from Delaware (1871–1889). Saulsbury was a southern sympathizer and a firm believer in white supremacy.

SCALES, Alfred Moore (1827–1892). Democratic congressman from North Carolina (1857–1859, 1875–1884).

SCHOOLCRAFT, Henry Rowe (1793–1864). Explorer, ethnologist, and geologist. He made pioneering studies of the American Indian, producing voluminous works—among them *Historical and Statistical Information Respecting the History, Condition, and Prospects of the Indian Tribes of the United States* (1851–1857)—which had much influence on later writings about the Indians.

SCHURZ, Carl (1829–1906). Minister to Spain, Union soldier, senator from Missouri, and secretary of the interior (1877–1881). Schurz, a German immigrant, was a liberal Republican reformer. Above all else he worked for civil service reform. As secretary of the interior in Hayes's cabinet, Schurz was noted for his enlightened treatment of the Indians and the installation of the merit system in his department.

SHELLABARGER, Samuel (1817–1896). Republican congressman from Ohio (1861–1863, 1865–1869, 1871–1873). U.S. Civil Service Commission (1874–1875).

SHERMAN, John (1823–1900). U.S. senator from Ohio (1861–1877, 1881–1897) and brother of Gen. W. T. Sherman. Sherman tried unsuccessfully for the Republican presidential nomination in 1880, 1884, and 1888. Sherman lent his name to two important pieces of legislation during this period: antitrust law and silver purchase law (1890).

SHERMAN, William Tecumseh (1820–1971). Union general during the Civil War. After Grant's appointment as commanding general, Sherman assumed command of the West. He marched through Georgia to the sea at Savannah. His army lived off the land and brought "total war" to the citizens of the South. Sherman had many southern cities burned, including Atlanta. His march thoroughly demoralized the South. Sherman retired from active service in 1883 and refused to take part in presidential politics.

SINGLETON, Otho Robards (1814–1889). Democratic congressman from Mississippi (1853–1855, 1857–1861, 1875–1887).

SLATER, James H. (1826–1899). Democratic U.S. senator from Oregon (1879–1885).

SMITH, James Milton (1823–1890). Governor of Georgia (1872–1874). Railroad commissioner in Georgia (1879–1885).

SMITH, Joseph (1805–1844). Mormon prophet and founder of the Church of Jesus Christ of Latter-Day Saints (1830). He died a martyr in Illinois while campaigning for the presidency of the United States.

SPEER, Emory (1848–1918). Congressman from Georgia (1879–1883). Speer was first elected as an Independent Democrat but later switched to the Republican party.

SPOFFORD, Ainsworth Rand (1825–1908). Librarian in chief of the Library of Congress (1864–1897).

STEPHENS, Alexander Hamilton (1812–1883). Congressman from Georgia (1843–1859). Vice-president of the Confederacy (1861–1865). Elected to the U.S. Senate in 1866 but was excluded as a rebel. Rheumatism made him resort to a wheelchair or to crutches, but nevertheless he ran for the Senate in 1872 only to be defeated by John B. Gordon. He did win election to the House of Representatives in 1872. Stephens supported the Compromise of 1877 and resigned from congress in 1882. Elected governor of Georgia in 1882 Stephens died a few months after taking office. Stephens was a frail man who never weighed more than one hundred pounds. In 1856 Stephens challenged Benjamin H. Hill, later U.S. senator from Georgia, to a duel, but Hill declined.

SUMNER, Charles (1811–1874). U.S. senator from Massachusetts (1851–1874). He was elected by a coalition of the Democratic and Free-Soil parties for his first term, but he ran as a Republican in the later senatorial elections. Sumner opposed slavery and attacked the South on that particular issue throughout the 1850s. In the debate on the Kansas-Nebraska Act Sumner denounced Senator Butler of South Carolina; whereupon Preston Brooks, congressman from South Carolina and nephew of Senator Butler, beat him unconscious with a cane on the floor of the Senate. Sumner was unable to attend the Senate for three and one-half years. After the Civil War, Sumner championed Negro civil rights legislation and radical Reconstruction policies in the South. He died of a heart attack in 1874.

TALMAGE, Thomas DeWitt (1832–1902). Clergyman, editor, and lecturer. Talmage was such a popular speaker that a tabernacle had to be built to accommodate all the people who wished to hear him. He was noted for his sensational style of gestures, but was criticized for being a pulpit clown.

TAYLOR, Zachary (1784–1850). President of the United States (1849–1850). Taylor was a southern-born Whig, but his attitude toward the Wilmot Proviso, which prohibited the extension of slavery into the territories gained from the Mexican War, alienated his southern supporters. Taylor died from eating too much ice milk and cherries on a hot July 4 just before the Compromise of 1850.

TELLER, Henry Moore (1830–1914). President Arthur's secretary of the interior (1882–1885).

THURMAN, Allen Granberry (1813–1895). Democratic U.S. senator from Ohio (1867–1881). Thurman was a Democratic member of the Electoral Commission which decided the Hayes-Tilden election in 1877.

TILDEN, Samuel Jones (1814–1886). Governor of New York (1875–1877). Democratic presidential nominee in 1876. Tilden won the popular vote in 1876 against Hayes, but he lost in the electoral count due to the rulings of the Electoral Commission. Tilden was mentioned again for the nomination in 1880 and in 1884, but he refused to be considered due to his age and physical infirmities.

TOOMBS, Robert Augustus (1810–1885). Toombs served as a Whig congressman from Georgia (1844–1850). Toombs opposed Pres. Zachary Taylor's stand with the North over the Wilmot Proviso which would have prohibited slavery in the territory gained from the Mexican War. In his famous "Hamilcar Speech" in 1850, Toombs championed the South and threatened independence unless southerners were given their rights. During the Civil War, Toombs served as a general and as secretary of state in Davis's cabinet.

TOURGÉE, Albion Winegar (1838–1905). North Carolina carpetbagger and judge of the state superior court (1868–1874). He is known chiefly as the author of A *Fool's Errand* (1879) which is a novel of life in the South during Reconstruction.

TRAMMELL, Leander Newton (1830–1900). Chairman of the Georgia State Democratic Executive Committee (1881–1882). As chairman Trammell secured the abolition of the objectionable two-thirds rule.

UNDERWOOD, John William Henderson (1816–1888). Judge of the Superior Court of Georgia (1867–1869, 1873–1882).

VANDERBILT, Cornelius (1794–1877). Vanderbilt was a steamship and railroad promoter famous for originating the statement "the public be damned." At his death his fortune was well over one hundred million dollars.

WALKER, Francis Amasa (1840–1897). Superintendent of the census (1869–1870, 1879–1881). Walker reorganized the Bureau of Statistics along scientific lines and tried to free it from political influence. From 1871 til 1872 he served as commissioner of Indian affairs.

WALKER, James David (1830–1906). Democratic U.S. senator from Arkansas (1879–1885).

WALKER, Mary Edwards (1832–1919). Physician and women's rights advocate. Dr. Walker served in the Civil War as an assistant surgeon. She dressed in men's clothing throughout her career but wore her hair in curls so everyone would know that she was a woman. In 1897 she founded a colony for women called "Adamless Eden."

WARNER, Adoniram Judson (1834–1910). Congressman from Ohio (1879–1881, 1883–1887). Warner's favorite issue was the free coinage of silver.

WATTERSON, Henry (1840–1921). Editor of the Louisville, Ky., *Courier-Journal* (1868–1918). Watterson served briefly in the congress (1876–1877) and was Tilden's floor leader during the election crisis that ended with the election of Hayes.

WESLEY, John Benjamin (1703–1791). Theologian and founder of the Methodist church.

WHYTE, William Pinkney (1824–1908). Democratic U.S. senator from Maryland (1868–1869, 1875–1881).

WILLIAMS, George Henry (1820–1910). Attorney general of the United States during the administration of President Grant (1871–1875).

WILSON, James Falconer (1828–1895). Director of the Union Pacific Railroad (1874–1882). Republican U.S. senator from Iowa (1883–1895). Wilson was one of the original framers of the Interstate Commerce Act of 1887.

WIRT, William (1772–1834). Attorney general of the United States (1817–1829). In 1832 Wirt was an unwilling candidate for the presidency.

WOODFORD, Stewart Lyndon (1835–1913). Woodford was lieutenant governor of New York (1867–1869) and ran unsuccessfully for the governorship in 1870. He served in Congress from 1873 to 1874. In 1876 he nominated Roscoe Conkling for the presidency at the Republican convention. Woodford was federal district attorney for the Southern District of New York from 1877 to 1883.

WYLIE, Andrew (1814–1905). Justice of the District of Columbia Supreme Court (1863–1885). He presided at the Star Route fraud trial involving Dorsey and Brady.

YOUNG, Brigham (1801–1877). Young led the Mormon church after the death of Smith to Utah where he displayed his genius for colonization.

INDEX

The text of this book was set on the Linotype in 10 point Electra on a 12 point body. Electra was designed by William Addison Dwiggins and introduced in 1951 by Mergenthaler Linotype Company. The book was printed from the type on 60 lb. Warren's Olde Style Wove on a flatbed letterpress by Heritage Printers, Inc., Charlotte, N.C.

The signatures were Smyth sewn and cased in with Interlaken cloth over boards by Carolina Ruling and Binding Co., Charlotte, N.C.

The text of *Shem, Ham and Japheth* was established in the house.

E 78 I 5 T83

Tuggle, William
   Orrie, 1841-1884.

Shem, Ham & Japheth

DATE			

per ct. of whatever sum he may collect
or have collected & hereby authorize him to
retain ten (10 pr. ct. of whatever sum may
be recovered & we personally agree to
aid said W.O. Tuggle Esq in obtaining his
fee out of the sum collected on said Orphan
Claim - We authorize said W.O. Tuggle Esq
to take charge of the entire case & to take possession of all the papers connected there-
with at Washington City

In witness whereof we hereto set our hands
seals.

D. N. McIntosh
m. P. Porter
Israel G. Vore
Ward Coachman

Representing. Timothy Barnett's estate.

Attest
John McIntosh
Chief Justice
Supreme Court M.N.

Robt A Leslie
Private Secretary
Executive Office Muscogee Nation
Ockmulgee Ct. Oct 13. 1879. I hereby
Certify that I witnessed the above signatures &
that said parties do represent the Creek